INTERDISCIPLINARY RELATIONSHIPS
IN THE SOCIAL SCIENCES

Interdisciplinary
Relationships
in the
Social Sciences

edited by Muzafer Sherif and Carolyn W. Sherif

PENNSYLVANIA STATE UNIVERSITY

ALDINE PUBLISHING COMPANY / CHICAGO

CONTRIBUTORS

SIDNEY H. ARONSON, Chairman, Sociology Department, New York University, University Heights

DONALD T. CAMPBELL, Professor of Psychology, Northwestern University

DANIEL CALHOUN, Professor of History, University of California at Davis

RAYMOND E. CRIST, Research Professor of Geography, University of Florida

KARL DE SCHWEINITZ, JR., Professor of Economics, Northwestern University

FRANCIS P. DINNEEN, Associate Professor of Linguistics and Acting Dean, Institute of Languages and Linguistics, Georgetown University

ROBERT DUBIN, Research Professor of Sociology, University of Oregon

WILLIAM J. McGUIRE, Professor of Psychology, University of California, San Diego, and Editor, *Journal of Personality and Social Psychology*

ROBERT B. MacLEOD, Professor of Psychology, Cornell University

RAYMOND W. MACK, Professor and Chairman, Department of Sociology, Northwestern University, and Editor, *The American Sociologist*

MARVIN W. MIKESELL, Professor of Geography, University of Chicago

STANLEY MILGRAM, Professor of Social Psychology, Graduate Center, City University of New York

ARNOLD A. ROGOW, Graduate Professor of Political Science, City University of New York

KENNETH D. ROOSE, Dean, College of the Liberal Arts, Pennsylvania State University; now Vice President, American Council on Education, Washington, D. C.

JOHN PAUL SCOTT, Research Professor, Division of Graduate Studies, Bowling Green State University

CAROLYN W. SHERIF, Associate Professor of Psychology, Pennsylvania State University

MUZAFER SHERIF, Professor of Sociology and Director, Psychosocial Studies Program, Pennsylvania State University

HENRI TAJFEL, Professor of Social Psychology, University of Bristol

SILVAN S. TOMKINS, Professor of Psychology, Livingston College, Rutgers University

MURRAY L. WAX, Professor of Sociology and Anthropology, University of Kansas

PREFACE

Most of the chapters in this book are based on lectures given by their authors at the symposium (May 1967) on problems of interdisciplinary relationships in the social sciences that we organized as an integral part of the activities of the newly initiated Psychosocial Studies Program at The Pennsylvania State University. Both the symposium and this volume of chapters by distinguished social scientists are among our efforts toward building a self-image for the program, of which the intent was interdisciplinary from the outset.

The book that developed from the symposium is the seventh we have organized with the generous collaboration of interested colleagues who contributed chapters on persistent and strategic problems of social psychology. This seventh undertaking coincided with the need we felt for re-evaluation of the state of relationships among the social sciences as they affect interdisciplinary efforts, particularly in the face of recent setbacks to such efforts, as well as notable gains.

Each of the seven symposia coincided with the focus of our program of research and publication during a particular period. For example, the sixth symposium and the resulting volume (*Attitude, Ego-Involvement and Change*, 1967), our first at The Pennsylvania State University, followed a period of intensive concentration on problems of attitude and attitude change research, as exemplified in our book *Attitude and Attitude Change* (1965) and the monographic volume with Carl Hovland on *Social Judgment* (1961). The fifth volume in the symposium series on *Problems of Youth* (1965) was the outcome of preoccupation with research on conformity-deviation of adolescents, as exemplified in the book *Reference Groups* (1964). The fourth symposium volume, *Intergroup Relations and Leadership* (1962), was prompted by a period of research and writing on group and intergroup relations bounded by our *Groups in Harmony and Tension* (1953) and *Group Conflict and Cooperation: The Robbers Cave Experiment* (1961). The complete list of seven volumes resulting from symposia, the first five held at the University of Oklahoma, is included at the end of this preface.

Each of the seven volumes reflects persistent concerns with interdisciplinary relations in the social sciences on the part of social psychologists and other social scientists seriously tackling specific problem areas of human development and functioning, group identifications, group and intergroup relations. The reflection is not accidental, nor are the problems merely of academic concern. It is a reflection of our own personal educational backgrounds.

When the senior editor had his first course in social psychology at Harvard University, the text was F. H. Allport's *Social Psychology* (1924), as it was in many major departments of psychology at the time. The important contribution of that text—namely, its persistent effort to bring social psychology firmly into the camp of experimental science—made its shortcomings all the more difficult to assimilate. In view of his own experience in different cultures, this student in the course found a lack of perspective on cultural values, institutions, and ideologies as these affect the viewpoints and tastes of the human individual. The lack amounted, so it seemed, to ignoring sets of stimulus factors confronting the individual in any culture, thereby conducive to a social psychology that could not help being ethnocentric, even though unwittingly.

Armed with the instrumentalities for experimentation from graduate study at Harvard, it was a fresh breeze to find that some psychologists in the 1930's (like Otto Klineberg, influenced especially by the Boas school of anthropologists) had discovered that there is such a thing as culture, which can be different from one's own and which can produce variations in psychological reactions, as exemplified in problems of development to adulthood, in standards used for evaluation, and the individual's mode of selectivity. Thus, it was no accident that the expansion of Sherif's doctoral thesis at Columbia University on social factors in perception into the little book titled *The Psychology of Social Norms* (1936) contained laboratory experiments, many anthropological illustrations, and an opening chapter entitled "The Lack of Perspective of the Social Psychologist." It is perhaps more accidental that the co-editor found and read that book in the library at the University of Iowa as a graduate student formulating a problem for her thesis research.

Many years later, in planning the symposium that resulted in this volume, we were guided by three concerns:

1. The substantive problems of relationships among the social sciences as these pertain to theoretical formulation and research on problems that cross the lines of the traditional academic disciplines.

2. The present status of interdisciplinary efforts in the social sciences.

3. The administrative and institutional riddles posed by interdisciplinary efforts, whose answers can make or break even the most creative intellectual and cultural developments.

The reader will find these concerns reflected, in varying combinations, in the chapters of this book, written by authorities in their own disciplines who were invited to contribute to the volume precisely because their own experiences had led them to grapple with the complex problems of interdisciplinary relationships. Once invited to contribute, each author was free to formulate the problem and scope of his own paper and to present it in his own way, with minimum editorial interference. The high quality of the resulting chapters comes as no surprise to us, nor does the wide range of specific problems and their ramifications thus explored. Our greatest debt and the reader's is to the distinguished contributors of chapters to the book.

The chapters in Part I represent orientations to conceptual, theoretical, and research problems of interdisciplinary coordination from the perspectives of social psychology, sociology, and anthropology. Necessarily, the selection was somewhat arbitrary, for scarcely a chapter in the book neglects such problems. However, the five chapters in Part I represent the wider lens focused on the general need for orientation.

Part II contains six chapters dealing more explicitly with problem areas common to several disciplines—to social psychology, behavioral biology, political science, history, anthropology, and economics. Each is viewed from the perspective of an outstanding representative of one discipline as he has faced the interdisciplinary nature of his problem in actual formulation of theory and research.

Part III includes six chapters on the interfaces of a particular discipline—human geography, linguistics, political science, sociology, or history—with other disciplines. Notably, perhaps, it is geography with its apparently most concrete variables of land, water, and resources that seems most reflective of its multiple interfaces, as it increasingly brings their human use into its ken. However, neither linguistics, nor political science, nor sociology, nor history—as represented by the authors in Part III—is immune to the growing need to deal with problems and variables traditionally considered in the domain of another.

Part IV contains two chapters most clearly focused on the organizational riddles, though by no means neglecting the substantive problems. One was written by an economist turned enlightened administrator and the other by a social psychologist long concerned with the rationale of his work and with a keen eye for both organizational hurdles and potential strengths.

Substantive Problems. It has been our growing conviction that the substantive considerations that brought problems of interdisciplinary relations in social science to the foreground in an irreversible way will ultimately force continuing interdisciplinary efforts, no matter what ups and downs may be suffered from the imperialisms and self-contained ethnocentrisms of the various disciplines or from blind spots in administrative arrangements and judgment. The most obvious issue of substance is that the various social sciences do not deal with entirely discrete and separate domains. For example, there is a sociology of groups as functioning social units, and a psychology of groups in terms of their individual members. For decades, sociologists collected information on group life, and more recently psychologists have turned out abundant research on individual functioning within groups. Surely the two lines of research should be related if we are to have a rounded picture of the problem area. Surely the generalizations reached at the sociological level and the psychological level of analysis should not be contradictory. In fact, the question of whether or not they mesh constitutes one test of their validity.

It is impossible for a single person to know all the vast accumulation of findings, the research techniques, and the formulations on even a single problem area across the social sciences. There has to be a division of labor at the levels on which one masters the technical equipment, the concepts and wealth of information—all of which are becoming more and more specialized. Since no one can be a know-all, the substantive problem becomes one of learning and knowing where, what, and how to borrow from other disciplines. Such borrowing cannot be done intelligently simply by putting pieces together from the accumulated fund of knowledge from various disciplines. Such juxtapositions have resulted in an inconsistent, unassimilable hodgepodge that muddies the problem and brings despair to the graduate student.

Insightful borrowing among the disciplines is predicated on realizing at least two major requirements. In order that we not complicate these requirements unduly, we shall consider them for just two disciplines, psychology and sociology.

1. While not becoming a specialist in the other discipline, either the psychologist or sociologist has to be concerned with *what* developments in the other have been accumulating in problem areas that relate to his own research interests, so that he will know *where* to turn when he needs to borrow methods and information. Needless to say, this requirement presumes opportunities to become aware of developments in the other discipline through any or all means potentially available in educational settings (joint seminars, programs, conferences, and so on, as well as readily available literature).

2. When exploring, studying, or interacting with the other discipline, either the psychologist or sociologist must understand that he is unlikely to find a completely satisfactory solution to his own problems simply because the units of analysis in the two disciplines are different. The realization that the two disciplines typically operate at different levels of analysis, each with its appropriate unit (e.g., individual or group) is the thoroughfare for fruitful borrowing, on the one hand, and the only way to avoid futile wrangling over the respective prerogatives of the disciplines, on the other hand.

As we have emphasized in Chapter 1, if these two requirements are met, the methods and findings of two or more disciplines working on related problem areas can serve as a check on the validity of generalizations, to the advantage of each discipline involved.

Disappointments in the Present Status. In actual practice, interdisciplinary ventures have not always, or even typically, fulfilled the requirements above. They have not always provided a vantage point for a better view of one's own problems. They have not often produced rounded pictures of a problem area. Many have fallen far short of providing the advantages potentially inherent in mutual borrowing across the lines of disciplines for the benefit of all.

In a period during which interdisciplinary ventures have not been infrequent, the current picture of their products is rather bleak. The reasons are not difficult to decipher. In many interdisciplinary conferences and programs, the committed experts of each discipline talk *at* each other, rather than benefiting from one another's experience with appreciation that there are a few things that each can learn from others in related disciplines. Underlying this state of affairs there are, implicitly if not explicitly, disciplinary imperialisms with the tacit claim that each has the perspective, methods, and fund of information that, if not now, at least potentially will untangle the complexities of human problems when pursued far enough.

Interdisciplinary ventures become arenas for jockeying for position, symbols and instruments of power within one's own discipline. Both professional organizations and university departments promote such jockeying when they provide organizational benefits solely for activities within their bounds and insulate themselves—at times in the name of the best intentions, such as encouraging intensive study or raising standards. They, in turn, foster new generations of students with little opportunity or inclination to peek across disciplinary lines.

As a consequence, there have been recently several instances of university departments and programs, founded with interdisciplinary titles such as social psychology or social relations, that have returned to the security of the traditional departments. At times, the declaration of such failures is made in gleeful tones, as though they were natural, inevitable, and good. Even some in responsible positions in research foundations, agencies, and councils concerned with social science research have come to a cynical verdict that cross fertilization of the disciplines sooner or later ends in cross sterilization.

No one can deny that a bleak picture confronts interdisciplinary efforts in some quarters today. But it is worth going behind the surface to raise questions about its causes. None of those mentioned above makes failure inevitable, unless we look toward the people entrusted with actual conduct of interdisciplinary ventures. Were they experts who have shown any conviction, not to mention commitment, to the advantages to be gained from such efforts? Or were they experts or technicians with visibility who were brought to lend prestige to the effort, or who happened to be in the right place at the right time, or who were seeking an avenue for academic advancement or funds? Before reaching conclusions that interdisciplinary ventures are futile, it will be instructive to study objectively the backgrounds and work patterns of the participants before they were entrusted with the charge to make a go of interdisciplinary ventures. One of the established facts in experimental psychology is that the merits and shortcomings of any problem are perceived and judged *selectively*. The best ideas and plans in the world can be made into their caricatures, and their results a laughing stock, if entrusted to people dead set to disprove their worth and prompted by commitments to organizations inimical to them.

This bleak note should not, however, blind us to an undeniable fact. In actual practice, interdisciplinary borrowing has always occurred. For example, experimental psychology has been interdisciplinary from its origins, in that it borrowed avidly from physics, physiology, and mathematics. The necessity of borrowing from these disciplines was so compelling that it was not considered interdisciplinary. It was simply the thing to do, not a matter to be argued about. The natural and physical sciences borrow from one another increasingly. It is when borrowing involves the social sciences that interdisciplinary effort becomes a matter of controversy, beneath the dignity of a natural science.

In fact, interdisciplinary borrowing seems to follow an uncritical selectivity that is overawed in favor of models from disciplines more prestigeful than one's own, whether that is the physical sciences, as in the case of psychology, or psychology itself, as in the case of some social sciences. Such upward modeling would be acceptable if in fact it proved valid and fruitful. Unfortunately, it has not thus far been conducive to the breakthroughs anticipated in the social sciences, as evidenced by the soul-searching today about the worth and use of social science research, for example, in the four volumes prepared by the Staff for the Subcommittee on Research and Technical Programs of the Committee on Government Operations of the U. S. House of Representatives (1967).

Probably, cross-disciplinary ventures will continue to yield spotty or even bleak results until the actual reasons contributing to the failures as well as the successes are available to administrators. Of course, the traditions of administration, especially administrative "efficiency," make insight into these problems difficult. For one thing, it is thought more efficient to deal with personnel in various departments in a university or research organization through department heads or chairmen than to deal with the more complex arrangements required for interdisciplinary programs and research efforts. Similarly, the orthodox outlook on the use of facilities, space, and personnel in terms of the per-dollar-per-student idea—which may well be the only feasible criterion for shaping policies in high schools and undergraduate colleges where large numbers are involved—can effectively inhibit creative developments in interdisciplinary coordination. What is needed in most cases is the selection among the still small number of people dedicated to interdisciplinary ventures, and arrangements that permit sufficient time and opportunity for joint efforts without making supreme the physical aspects of the program or the contradictory demands from traditional departments. The great problem in interdisciplinary ventures is still the development of coordination among persons who can pull together, instead of being pulled asunder by schools or organizational pressures.

The Symposium on Problems of Interdisciplinary Relationships in the Social Sciences was made possible by the support of the College of the Liberal Arts and Kenneth D. Roose, then Dean of the College (now Vice President, American Council on Education), to whom we are also grateful for contributing a chapter to this volume that was originally delivered at the symposium dinner. Donald P. Kent, Head of the Department of Sociology, contributed substantially in the planning and execution of the Symposium. We are also grateful to Thomas F. Magner, Associate Dean of the College of Liberal Arts, for contributing substantive suggestions on the program and helping to implement them.

Several administrators gave generously of their time to address the symposium participants, and we regret only that their busy schedules prevented our including their views in this book. We gratefully acknowledge such contributions by Elburt F. Osborn, Vice President for Research; M. Nelson McGeary, Dean of the Graduate School; R. H. Heindel, Dean of Faculty, Capitol Campus; and Coleman Herpel, Director, Capitol Campus.

The following colleagues at Pennsylvania State University and other institutions served with insight and tact as chairmen at the various sessions:

Gordon F. DeJong, Associate Professor of Sociology
Helmut Golatz, Head and Professor of Labor Studies
A. Paul Hare, Professor of Sociology, Haverford College
Vytautas Kavolis, Professor of Sociology, Dickinson College
Donald P. Kent, Professor of Sociology
George Larimer, Assistant Professor of Sociology, Capitol Campus
Richard M. Lundy, Professor of Psychology
Thomas F. Magner, Professor of Slavic Languages
Stanley Milgram, Professor of Psychology, City University of New York
Dean Peabody, Professor of Psychology, Swarthmore College
Otto Sonder, Professor of Sociology, Lycoming College (Now Dean of Liberal Arts, Williamsport Community College)
George Theodorson, Professor of Sociology
David L. Westby, Assistant Professor of Sociology
John Withall, Professor of Education
George Wolf, Professor of History, Capitol Campus

In addition to serving as chairman, George Larimer was helpful during the entire symposium, making arrangements for the events of two days held at the Capitol Campus of the University. In addition, we are particularly grateful to George Wolf and Daniel Walden for making that part of the symposium a pleasant event for participants.

Many graduate students were involved in presentation of the symposium and assisted in the sometimes tedious details of preparing the book manuscript and reading proof. We particularly want to acknowledge the assistance of James Harper, Donald Granberg, Gian Sarup, Larry Rogers, James Glynn, Donald Schiermeister, and Michael Scott.

Editors of a book are always in debt to the person who attends to the tedious chores of preparing the manuscript. In this case, it should be noted that Mrs. Doris Sands not only retyped several chapters but shouldered the responsibility of making footnotes and references uniform and, for several chapters, did preliminary reading to assist the editors. Since each task was performed with her typical efficiency and cheerfulness, our acknowledgment is more than a compliment.

M. S.

C. S.

PREVIOUS SYMPOSIUM VOLUMES

Social Psychology at the Crossroads (J. H. Rohrer and M. Sherif, eds.) New York: Harper, 1951.

Group Relations at the Crossroads (M. Sherif and M. O. Wilson, eds.) New York: Harper, 1953; Harper Torchbooks, forthcoming.

Emerging Problems in Social Psychology (M. Sherif and M. O. Wilson, eds.) Lectures of the Third Social Psychology Conference, a publication of the Institute of Group Relations, University of Oklahoma, University Book Exchange, 1957.

Intergroup Relations and Leadership (M. Sherif, ed.) A publication of the Institute of Group Relations. New York: Wiley, 1962.

Problems of Youth: Transition to Adulthood in a Changing World (M. Sherif and Carolyn W. Sherif, eds.) A publication of the Institute of Group Relations. Chicago: Aldine Publishing Co., 1965.

Attitude, Ego-Involvement and Change (Carolyn W. Sherif and Muzafer Sherif, eds.) A publication of the Psychosocial Studies Program. New York: Wiley, 1967.

CONTENTS

xv

PART I
Exploring Orientations

1

INTERDISCIPLINARY COORDINATION AS A VALIDITY CHECK: RETROSPECT AND PROSPECTS

MUZAFER SHERIF AND CAROLYN W. SHERIF

The theme of this book is interdisciplinary relationships in the social sciences. The qualifying term—interdisciplinary—is fashionable these days. Talking about problems of interdisciplinary relationships is a mark of being one of the "in-crowd." In the current lingo, it is almost as prestigeful to use the term *interdisciplinary* as to speak of being *knowledgeable*. In fact, if we really want to show that we are not back numbers, we should characterize this book as a *dialogue* between *knowledgeable* colleagues seeking *viable* solutions to *interdisciplinary* problems. To use another fashionable term, we might even add that some of the participants are *behavioral scientists*.

However, interdisciplinary relationships today are a genuine concern beyond the fashions of academic chitchat. They are very much a part of the *Zeitgeist*, to use a term made fashionable among psychologists by E. G. Boring in his monumental *History of Experimental Psychology* (1950). The anthropologist A. I. Hallowell (1954, p. 173) traced the discontent with insulated academic disciplines back to the turn of the century. During the twenties, and especially the thirties, grant-awarding agencies sprang into being with the expressed aim of encouraging collaboration among the social sciences, as Clyde Kluckhohn and Henry Murray (1948) noted in their survey of interdisciplinary efforts (*cf.* Zetterberg, 1956).

Especially after World War II, interdisciplinary conferences, large-scale research projects, and interdisciplinary educational programs became commonplace, if not yet the rule. Today, agencies that award funds for research and training expect, almost as a matter of course, that some note will be taken of the need for "cross-fertilization" (which, incidentally, is still another fashionable phrase).

The most striking evidence of the interdisciplinary trend is its manifestation in professional and technical schools. Forty years ago—even twenty years ago—who could have imagined that some of the white-coated figures

3

in the antiseptic corridors and wards of medical schools would be, not medics, but sociologists, anthropologists, or even philosophers? Who could have thought that social psychologists and sociologists would be in business schools along with the professors of bookkeeping, business-letter writing, and marketing? How many engineers could have dreamed in their wildest fancy that their own professional organizations would put pressure on them to give greater exposure to the social sciences than what came through the traditional university-wide lecture series supported from student-activity fees? Who could have imagined then that engineering schools would have departments of management and courses on human relations?

These things have happened and they are happening. They reflect a trend in education and in research that is irreversible to the point of no return. We are living in a time of increasing interdisciplinary contact and concern, whether we like it or not.

To say that the trend is irreversible is not to say that all is milk and honey. On the contrary, the cup is bitter at times. We all know that many inter-disciplinary conferences consist of elbow-rubbing in congenial surroundings among colleagues from different disciplines who talk *at* each other, not with each other. We all know that interdisciplinary research projects sometimes cease to be interdisciplinary somewhere along the line after the research pro-posal is accepted, in spite of the fact that the initial proposal contained a list of distinguished collaborators or consultants from several disciplines because the grant-awarding agency *expected* it. We all know that social scientists in technical schools are sometimes merely tolerated because it is fashionable or financially necessary to have one or two on the roster. Such tolerance by formerly aloof professions is reminiscent of the days before desegregation of the schools, when some of the more progressive private schools imported a couple of minority children as visible evidence of their advanced thinking. We happen to know of such a case in a medical school (which has to remain nameless) where a Yale Ph.D. in sociology, who was interested in research and training of medical students, found that his office resembled a broom closet and that he was assigned to share it with another professor's assistant.

We are also aware of the continuing tendency within each academic dis-cipline to withdraw into the in-group confines of its own department and professional organizations. Some of these withdrawals represent ecological struggle that is not unique to academic life but is found in many larger organizations, and it reflects self-interest that has more to do with salaries and promotions than the intellectual or research problems of the discipline in question. Other withdrawals represent genuine concern that interdiscipli-nary programs and research will result in a discipline spreading itself too thin, to the neglect of the essentials in its own domain, thus preventing work in depth. And some of the withdrawals represent a distaste for the finishing-school type of interdisciplinary program which substitutes a mild assortment of social science courses for the former smattering of French, English poetry, and music appreciation that used to be considered appropriate for the cultured young lady.

Despite the bitter taste from such interdisciplinary experiences, we will be highly positive with regard to interdisciplinary efforts. Our thesis can be stated here at the outset in several steps, without embellishment at this point:

1. The trend toward interdisciplinary collaboration and coordination is irreversible to the point of no return.

2. Much of the discontent and many practical difficulties in interdisciplinary endeavors have arisen through failure to deal adequately with the central *substantive* issue, namely the core problem of why interdisciplinary efforts have come into existence and why they are a *necessity* for the development of each of the social sciences, and not a matter of individual preference. The nature of the central issue will be specified later.

3. An examination of the substantive problem at the core of interdisciplinary relationships will reveal that each discipline needs others in a fundamental and basic sense. We are not referring here at all to departmental prerogatives, programs, and their perils. We refer to the very basic issue of the *validity* of generalizations and theories. We propose that each discipline needs the findings from others as a check on the validity of its own generalizations. For example, formulations about intergroup relations, or leader-follower relations, or power relations cannot be one thing when taught in a department of psychology and another thing when taught in a sociology department, and still another in a political science department, if any one of the disciplines in question claims validity for its formulations.

4. When the substantive problem is examined, many current issues associated with interdisciplinary trends turn out to be minor issues—so many carts put in front of the horse. The carts can easily be pulled by hitching the horse to them properly. Such minor issues may seem very large, even insurmountable, *unless* the substantive issue is tackled at the outset. Issues referred to as minor are exemplified by such questions as the prerogatives of various university departments, or the number of courses to be taken in different departments during graduate training, or how to attain an understanding of one discipline and its techniques in depth while "broadening one's horizons" by studying other disciplines as well. Many such problems are reflected as acute issues for the administration of educational and research programs today and they are, therefore, sometimes called the "administrative problems" of interdisciplinary relationships. It is our thesis, on the contrary, that clarification of the substantive issues of relationships among the social sciences is the only way to move toward viable solutions through administrative means.

The rest of this discussion is addressed to specifying in more detail what is meant by the assertions just listed. Necessarily, it will reflect our own experiences, concerns, and work as social psychologists. Also, necessarily, it will be brief. Essentially the same points have been elaborated in some detail in our earlier writings (Sherif and Sherif, 1956, chap. 1; Sherif, 1959; Sherif, 1963, 1967, Part I; Sherif and Koslin, 1960). The titles of these works reflect our enduring concern with the substantive issues at hand. They may at least indicate that there are some fools convinced that interdisciplinary collaboration is a necessity.

WHY INTERDISCIPLINARY COLLABORATION IS A NECESSITY

One short route to the substantive core of interdisciplinary problems is to ask why the social sciences should be sought by professions that hitherto saw little need of them. Why, for example, should the once sacrosanct schools of medicine have any interest at all in the social sciences? The medical profession certainly has its own prestige, to the point that it is ridiculous to think that the social sciences could add to it. The medical profession is supported by the rapidly developing physical and biological sciences. Why social scientists? Why the behavioral science departments in many medical schools?

The answer is that the medical profession deals with man, and that even man's anatomy and physiology are not an insulated, self-contained subject matter for study. Most medical specialties today are highly technical, requiring mastery in depth of a great deal more theory and technique than most social sciences can offer their students. For example, the measurement and treatment of metabolic disorders is a highly technical affair these days. Yet when Dr. William Schottstaedt and his colleagues studied the detailed biochemical and physiological records of patients in a metabolic ward, they found that variations in these strictly physiological measures of metabolism were significantly related to the vicissitudes of interpersonal relationships among patients, with nurses and doctors, and with visitors (Schottstaedt *et al.*, 1958).

It is fairly easy to discover that these "interpersonal" relations were not all strictly personal problems: They involved nurses and doctors with definite roles in the hospital institution; they involved members of the patients' families from varying backgrounds and with different attitudes about the role of a sick person; they involved money and personal finances. If we start to inquire further why these particular patients were hospitalized for metabolic disorders, and not others, we would find ourselves immediately in problems requiring demographic study of different populations and in problems requiring an institutional analysis of admittance procedures and financing; and these might very well lead us to problems of the political and economic systems in which the institution functions. Certainly, the advent of Medicare for the aged should serve as a warning that medical practice is not insulated from problems of politics and economics.

This illustration was used only to highlight the core problem of interdisciplinary relationships. It shows us that man does not arrange his problems or divide them up neatly along lines laid down by academic disciplines. On the contrary, there is a great deal of overlap in the subject matter or topics considered by the social science disciplines. Which among the social sciences would care to abdicate altogether any reference to human motives, to language, to the family, to groups, to religious institutions, political or economic life? The different disciplines are studying and theorizing about many of the same problems and many closely related problems of the human condition.

Now it should be obvious that, even with the erratic advances that the social sciences have made as scientific endeavors, it is impossible for any one man to be a know-it-all. But it is not so obvious that a single discipline which buries itself in order to concentrate on its own problems, theories, techniques, and data collection to the exclusion of others will end up being a know-nothing. The self-insulation of a social science discipline is ostrich-like. It will not and cannot protect the bird from impending danger.

The impending danger to the disciplines concerned with man is the sacrifice of *validity* for its generalizations and theories. By validity we mean the ability of theoretical formulations to make accurate predictions and eventually to be translated into means for control of the phenomena in question. Very crudely, we mean by validity "being right."

Why is interdisciplinary coordination and collaboration required for the sake of validity? We shall illustrate the answer specifically in the case of social psychology later in this chapter. Here, let us refer back to the illustration of the metabolic ward. Some social scientists may object that this was an example of applied work. We chose such an example deliberately because in application the problem of validity has to be faced. Many social scientists are hesitant, often justifiably so, about premature attempts to apply their theories. Certainly a degree of humbleness is called for when we recall the fairly recent history of our disciplines as scientific ventures and the extremely uneven advance that has been made. However, this justifiable caution against jumping into action is no justification for evading the problem of validity. Within the confines of a single academic discipline, it is possible to avoid the validity criterion like the plague. As long as we have to deal only with our colleagues, we talk instead of *reliability* of measurement and *representativeness* of sampling techniques. We refine our tools and techniques for these purposes until we are in the gravest danger of being reliably and representatively *wrong*.

The best means available for checking the validity of findings and generalizations in social science today, before application is attempted, is to measure them against the findings and generalizations established on the same or related problems by another social science discipline. We shall illustrate this conclusion with specific reference to social psychology later in the chapter, but here let us state the core problem of interdisciplinary relationships from the point of view of any one of the social sciences.

The core problem of interdisciplinary relationship for a particular science is to determine what findings and what concepts it *has to borrow* and in what matters it *has to be in transaction* with other disciplines in order to stand firmly on its own feet, with all of the supporting evidence that it needs to insure the validity of its formulations. It will not gain this support by standing like an ostrich with its head ground into a fixed hole through the sheer force of orthodoxy. On the contrary, assessment of what it needs from others and with whom it needs to transact will provide ingredients for weaving its own fabric. It will provide a balanced view of its bearings relative to other disciplines.

After all, no scientific discipline is an island unto itself. It cannot develop firmly in isolation from others. Deliberate assessment by one discipline of what is needed from other disciplines and who it needs to transact with will provide a center of gravity for its *own* development that is conducive to probing its problems at any degree of intensiveness desired. In fact, intensive study of its own domain will gain both in depth and scope. Insulated from related disciplines and lacking firm bearings relative to them, intensive study within a discipline sooner or later starts to produce floundering expeditions into territories already explored by other disciplines, with the resulting exhibitions of ignorance that have been displayed in the past by psychologists who sociologized their own sociology of the family, or culture, or institutions, and by sociologists who psychologized their own brands of human motivation or perception. It should be clear that what is being advocated as the core problem of interdisciplinary relationship for a particular science is a far cry from hastily conceived notions of interdisciplinary study as a flashy veneer of the finishing school which aimed to turn out young ladies who could converse gracefully on diverse topics in a drawing room.

Considerable progress toward the sort of assessment needed in dealing with the core problem can be made if we also recognize that some of the social sciences are approaching the same or related problems at different *levels of analysis* (*cf.* Schneirla, 1951; Scott, 1958). These different levels of analysis are required by the particular units of analysis chosen as focal by the disciplines in question, and are associated with concepts appropriate to each. Crossing disciplinary lines that involve different levels of analysis poses even greater problems than crossing lines that represent merely historical and probably necessary division of labor. It involves greater problems because the processes underlying events at different levels of analysis cannot be presumed to be identical. For example, biological processes produce hunger, but they are totally inadequate as a basis for predicting whether or not widespread famine will or will not produce riots, social movements, or revolutions. Conversely, if we study food riots and movements associated with them, we find that some of the leaders are often among the less deprived and less hungry. Because we are more familiar with problems in crossing disciplines involving different levels of analysis, we shall devote the rest of this chapter to these problems, specifically to problems of interdisciplinary collaboration in social psychology.

INTERDISCIPLINARY RELATIONSHIP OF SOCIAL PSYCHOLOGY AND LEVELS OF ANALYSIS

Social psychology approaches many of the same problems and many related problems that are also topics in other social science disciplines. We might mention group interaction, leader-follower relations, political attitudes, intergroup relations, and collective interaction to make the point concrete. Historically, social psychology developed at about the same time within both psychology and sociology. In part, this twin development reflected a lack of concern on the part of most orthodox psychologists of the period with problems of behavior in its *social context*. In part, it reflected a conviction of influential social theorists that individual psychology and collective or social psychology would require completely different concepts and principles. For example, the French sociologist Durkheim regarded collective psychology as quite distinct from individual psychology because, in the words of George Simpson (1963) in introducing Durkheim's writings in a recent volume, "He could not foresee that one day we might be able to establish an individual psychology that would be inherently social" (p. 3).

Psychology of any kind takes the individual as its unit of analysis. Its basic data are the activities or behavior of the individual in relation to stimulus situations, either antecedent or current. In its earliest development as a scientific effort, psychology *was* interdisciplinary. It borrowed heavily from both the physiology and physics of its time in order to specify the sensory mechanisms, on the one hand, and the nature of the stimulus, on the other. It has long been considered essential in orthodox experimental psychology to do so. It even became such established practice that borrowing was not considered "interdisciplinary." The latter term connoted a lack of purity when it came to refer to relations with the *social* sciences. Although orthodox psychology has yet to solve its interdisciplinary relationships with the social sciences, it is clear that these relationships are immediately a central issue for social psychology. They arise as soon as anyone asks, as M. Sherif did many years ago, What Is the Stimulus Situation in Social Psychology? (Sherif, 1936, chap. 4).

When one attempts a comprehensive answer to this question, he finds that social stimuli must include other individuals and that they also include individuals in groups; they include other groups, social organizations, institutions, cultural objects, social norms, language systems, technological objects, and values. In short, they encompass the subject matter of social science disciplines such as sociology, anthropology, political science, and economics.

However, the social sciences do not and cannot proceed at the individual level of analysis. They are properly concerned with regularities, forms, processes, and their change at a different level of analysis. The sociocultural level of analysis takes as its units the human group, institutions, kinship systems, system of production and distribution, and cultural values. It is not imperative that the behavior of particular individuals involved in them be included in the analysis.

Herskovits (1949) emphasized this point in discussing the reality of culture:

There is a little doubt that culture *can* be studied without taking human beings into account. Most of the older ethnographies, descriptions of the ways of life of given peoples, are written solely in terms of institutions. Most diffusion studies—those which give the geographic spread of a given element in culture—are presented without any mention of the individuals who use the objects, or observe given customs. It would be difficult even for the most psychologically oriented student of human behavior to deny the value of such research. It is essential that the structure of a culture be understood, first of all, if the reasons why a people behave as they do are to be grasped; unless the structure of custom is taken fully into account, behavior will be meaningless (p. 21).

Now the question arises: What relationship does the study of the sociocultural level of analysis have with social psychology? Here, our answer must turn on how we are to conceive of social stimulus situations.

In the orthodox psychological tradition, with its concerns over sensory phenomena, the "stimulus" was typically conceived as a discrete item or dimension of the physical environment, for example as a patch of light, a tone, or a touch of given intensity. Following this tradition, the early learning psychologists specified very precisely the exact dimensions of their maze, their jumping platform or their puzzle box.

Through several generations of experimental work, it became evident that such specification of the stimulus as a discrete item or input is not sufficient. Psychologically, the significance of a particular stimulus was found to depend upon its relationships to other items surrounding it, as well as to the relevant past experience of the organism. For example, the work of Harry Helson (1964) on color vision showed very clearly that perception of color could, in his phrase, be made "anything we wanted" by varying the color of the background on which a patch appeared and the illumination. Even that creature sacred for many years in the psychological laboratory—the rat—was shown to perform differently in the same maze depending upon its location in the room relative to windows.

Now, what was the traditional practice in social psychology thirty years ago with respect to specifying the stimulus situation, and what is still practiced by many of our colleagues today? Today our colleagues are only starting to get down to specifying *what* it is that constitutes the stimulus situation in such a simple situation as a laboratory experiment that has been in front of their noses all along. There is a powerful and popular movement called "the social psychology of the psychological experiment." When the senior author of this chapter was a graduate student at Harvard in the early thirties, the textbook and teachers assumed that they knew what the social stimulus situation was and then simply took it for granted. The result was that some of their generalizations about, say, competition, about the family, about the effects of social situations were so completely out of line with his own experience in a different culture, namely Turkey, that the classroom experiences started him on this very exploration to specify the social stimulus situation. He was led to reading the works of anthropologists, sociologists, yes and historians too—not by the graduate training in that institution, but by the necessities of exploring this problem.

One thing was already well established at that time in the experimental laboratory: The individual's experience of and response to social stimuli— such as words, other individuals, or meaningful forms—was *immediate,* in the sense that it allowed no opportunity for differentiation and analysis of so many elements or cues conceived as discrete sensory inputs. Instead, the response was to patterned and meaningful events in their context.

Here, then is the reason that the social psychologist has to be concerned with social stimuli in terms of their patterned properties and form, even if he is to be a good psychologist and nothing else. And this necessity brings him to those social sciences whose problems have concerned the regularities of patterned actions, events, and objects in social life. It leads him to the social sciences that have studied the development, stabilization, and change of such regularities. In short, he becomes dependent upon sociology, anthropology, political science, or history, as the case may be. He becomes dependent upon their findings in order that he may properly specify the past history of the individual's social stimulation and the properties of situations and events that he faces in an immediate occasion. Certainly he does not thereby have to *become* a sociologist, political scientist, or anthropologist. In fact, to do so might defeat his purpose, for *what* he needs to borrow are ways of specifying *aspects* of social realities. The individual whose behavior he studies seldom, if ever, confronts the entire global reality of the social structures and cultures that social scientists study in their own right.

Many social psychologists are still prone to take the view that the social variables important to their study will inevitably be reflected in their research situation. Even if this were entirely true, it is not true that researchers who hold this view will detect the reflections of sociocultural variables in their miniature experiments, for they are not primed to look for them. They justify their lack of attention to the other social sciences that study such variables with the declaration that they are studying the *interaction of individuals,* which is the basic stuff of all social sciences. This view has led to literally tons of studies of "leadership" that have no bearing on leadership in real life, to grand psychological models of power relations that omit most of the major variables that make power the central problem in political science, and to a deluge of experimentation called "small group research" of which about 85 per cent is doomed to gather dust on library shelves, at least as far as anyone is concerned who is genuinely interested in group processes in real life.

At the basis of such neglect of other social science disciplines is a leftover from the cultural and philosophical heritage of the past that viewed the individual, on the one hand, and the group or society, on the other, as though they were completely independent entities. Of course if there were no individuals to interact, there would be no groups, no institutions, no values, no power relations, no leadership, and no culture. But what we can learn from the social science disciplines concerned with these topics is that groups, leader-follower relations, institutions, and social systems do have properties of their own. Once groups come into existence, their properties and values become significant aspects of the stimulus situation for individual members. The products of man's interaction with others are subject matters for study at their own level of analysis, which level is not psychological, but sociocultural. The patterned and meaningful properties discovered at that level of analysis are the properties that affect individual participants, even the very individuals who originated the interaction.

Of course, man creates social organization; but social organization, in turn, recasts man. Of course, men make machines; but machines, in turn, affect man. The individual is the proper unit of analysis for all psychology, whether social psychology or any other brand of psychology. But the products of his interaction with others become subject matters for study at their own level of analysis without any necessary reference to principles governing individual behavior. To insist that sociology, anthropology, economics, or political science must be based on social-psychological principles would lead to the absurd position of saying that everything is psychology—including physics and chemistry, since these sciences are also the works of men. In our opinion, the insistence that psychological principles are of no value to the social sciences is equally absurd: Cultures and institutions do change, and man's actions are certainly among the important sources of social change.

In the present context, however, our major concern is about the interdisciplinary problem from the viewpoint of social psychology. From this viewpoint, it becomes clear that social psychology has to borrow findings and concepts from the other social sciences for the fundamental purpose of specifying the nature of its stimulus situations. Furthermore, it should be obvious that this necessity imposes a certain *order or sequence* on research procedures: No experimentalist worth his salt would start a study of perception or learning without bothering to specify the nature of the stimulus situation. Similarly, no researcher on social psychological problems can afford to start his study without specifying the *social* stimulus situation. The interdisciplinary borrowing and interchange that must be done should be done *first, before the research starts,* not afterward.

Now, let's sum up some of the major points so far, so that we can use them as orientation to a few illustrations of the rewards of interdisciplinary efforts for social psychology, and indicate future prospects.

1. Social psychology and other social sciences are approaching the same or related problems at different levels of analysis, namely the psychological level (with the individual as its unit) and the sociocultural level (with social forms and systems as its units).

2. From the viewpoint of social psychology, the sociocultural level of analysis is the level required in order to specify the patterned properties of social stimulus situations. Therefore, for social psychology, borrowing from other disciplines is a necessity, not a choice. Far from spreading itself too thin through interdisciplinary efforts, social psychology itself will gain in proportion to its relevant interchange with other social sciences, as we shall attempt to show through illustration.

3. This conception of the relationships between social psychology and other social sciences imposes an order or sequence of study upon the research efforts of social psychology. This order, as we shall see, is also useful in selecting significant problems for research. But beyond this, the proposed order is necessary in all psychological research, namely that the researcher specify the nature of the stimulus situation *before* he undertakes to experiment. This order means, for social psychology, that borrowing from other disciplines must come first, before the research is executed, in order to specify the stimulus situation faced by the individuals studied.

4. Finally, interchange with the social science disciplines becomes crucial for social psychology as a check on the validity of its generalizations. This does not discount the importance of such a validity check for other disciplines, but serves to emphasize its peculiar significance for social psychology.

We will proceed by considering this last point first, namely how interdisciplinary checking can provide validity criteria for social psychology.

CROSS-DISCIPLINARY CHECKS ON VALIDITY

Very simply, the basis for using the concept of levels of analysis for checks on validity is the following: If a generalization reached at one level of analysis is valid, it is not contradicted by valid generalizations reached at another level of analysis. For example, sociologists have collected extensive data showing that interaction among members of a human group has properties that cannot be extrapolated from the individual characteristics or particular interpersonal encounters of unrelated individuals. If this is the case, a psychologist studying individual behavior in a group should find that participating individuals reveal attitudes and behaviors that are not typical of them when they are alone. In fact, this particular example is supported in both sociological and psychological literature.

On the other hand, suppose that a psychologist studying social interaction concludes that human social patterns are basically like the pecking order of domestic fowl or the dominance relations of subhuman primates, and erects a social-psychological theory of interpersonal relations on this basis. The comparative psychologist, Schneirla (1946), has pointed out that the capacities underlying social relations of fowls and humans are very different. The social scientist concerned with social systems and structure has ample data to show that human role relations do *not* fulfill the criteria used in animal behavior studies for the peck order. For example, human relations do not always or even typically meet the criterion of transitivity of dominance that is the basis for the peck order. Furthermore, they embody so many other dimensions other than dominance that the analogy can quickly be shown to be invalid.

As another example of the utility of cross-disciplinary checking on the validity of generalizations, consider the state of theorizing on memory before Sir Frederic Bartlett's classic work (1932). The prevailing theories proposed a fading neural trace, one based on Ebbinghaus' classic experimental model, proposing a simple decay function, and others, based on Gestalt psychology, proposing a fading toward Gute Gestalten. Observations in Africa and of Africans in England alerted Bartlett to the fact of *selectivity* in *what* is remembered and, even more profoundly, to the very little decay that occurred in remembering of material with high social and personal significance in the lives of the people studied. Turning then to the laboratory, he was able to show the same phenomena and to show further that the trend of forgetting was more in the direction of these meaningful social forms than of abstract stimulus properties alone (whether "good" or not).

The need for cross-disciplinary checking on the validity of psychological formulations is nowhere clearer than in the study of what is called by psychologists these days "verbal behavior." Fortunately the recent work of linguists is exerting a profound effect, even on psychologists with the most orthodox and insulated training, especially the younger ones. This impact is largely traceable to a review by the linguist Chomsky (1959) of the book *Verbal Behavior* by B. F. Skinner, in which that clever experimentalist with animals transferred his conceptions of animal learning directly to human social psychology. In exposing the verbal brilliance and the inadequacy of this attempt, Chomsky pointed directly to the need for interdisciplinary checking when he wrote "there is little point in speculating about the process of acquisition without much better understanding of what is acquired" (p. 55). This *what*, as he correctly pointed out, is not merely words or discrete verbal behaviors, but a system of grammar: ". . . we can predict that a direct attempt to account for actual behavior of speaker, listener, and learner, not based on a prior understanding of the structure of grammars, will achieve very limited success" (p. 57). Fortunately, a number of social psychologists, inspired in particular by G. A. Miller (1962) and the work of Roger Brown (1965), are today accepting this challenge, hopefully with the ultimate result that this most critical topic in social psychology will be brought into contact with the actualities of man's use and creation of linguistic forms.

BORROWING FROM OTHER SOCIAL SCIENCES AND THE SEQUENCE OF RESEARCH PROCEDURE

It should be obvious by now that the solution to the substantive problem of interdisciplinary relationships is not seen, in this chapter, as breeding a generation of supermen who know all about psychology and all about sociology and all about linguistics. Nor is it seen in a smattering of superficial acquaintance with this and that social science. It *is* seen in defining the bearings of one's discipline relative to others, of knowing when and who is needed, and in interchange directed toward borrowing from others what is needed for one's own discipline.

The procedure can perhaps be illustrated best through examples from our own program of research, since we know it best: Some of you may recall the experimental studies of social factors in perception by M. Sherif (1935) utilizing the autokinetic phenomenon in the laboratory. These experiments demonstrated the convergence of individual perceptions toward a common range or social norm, which subsequently affected the individual's perception when he faced the same situation alone. The experiments, which are frequently called "classic" now, utilized the laboratory and a visual stimulus that had long been known in experimental psychology. They could have utilized any one of a number of other ambiguous stimuli, as other experiments have shown subsequently. However, the conception of the experiments and the problem that they were designed to investigate did not develop from experimental psychology. Specifically, they were formulated from the author's contact with cultural anthropologists and sociologists, particularly of the Chicago school, who had already collected impressive data on the rise of norms distinctive to small groups in the interstitial areas of large cities, and from reading the work of the French sociologist Emile Durkheim, who kept insisting that new norms (*répresentations collective*) arise when people interact in ambiguous and fluid situations with more alternatives for behavior than those ordinarily available in the routine grooves of day-to-day existence. In formulating the problem and presenting it to psychologists, a large number of illustrations from anthropologists and sociologists were collected. For example, one of them was Malinowski's observations that the Trobriand Islanders see resemblance between father and sons, but not between the sons and daughters. Another was Malinowski's documentation of the exchange system called the Kula, with the observation that each participant fulfilled his obligations in the system without any one of them being able to explain how the entire system worked. These and other examples are now cited in many standard works and texts in social psychology—we should hope to the enrichment of the field, not to its dilution.

Similarly, consider the recent report by Segall, Campbell, and Herskovits (1966) on their research project into cultural differences in susceptibility to certain "classic" perceptual illusions, involving over 1800 subjects in fifteen different societies. The project reflects the sophisticated research skills of the psychologists (Campbell and Segall) in attempting to insure comparability of the research situation so that differences could be attributed to known differences in the subjects' environments. But it also reflects the knowledge of the anthropologist Herskovits and his colleagues of the actual variations in the ecology of the societies. It is to be doubted that the anthropologists in the project acquired the skill of the psychologists, or that the psychologists became anthropologists in the process. What did happen is that both psychology and anthropology benefited as disciplines from this research. According to the authors themselves, the project had its origins in a "running debate" between Melville Herskovits and Donald Campbell over the extent of cultural influences on perceptual tendencies. At least some of this debate occurred in a joint seminar, and we may well reflect how fortunate our disciplines are, respectively.

Its significance, it should be stressed, is not in demonstrating cultural differences in susceptibility to the illusions in question, for Rivers had commented on this at the turn of the century. Its significance does not even rest on the eventual validity of its rather tentative conclusions about similarities and differences in the perception of somewhat esoteric patterns. Its significance is that it seriously attempts to link definite sociocultural ecologies with differential susceptibilities to certain illusions. In other words, the project could not have been accomplished unless, first, the contrasts in social stimulus conditions had been established. There is a host of serious questions that can only be answered speculatively until more such attempts are made.

The payoff in delineating at least the major properties of the social stimulus situation, as studied by the social sciences at their own level, may be further illustrated through our work on group formation and intergroup relations (Sherif and Sherif, 1953; Sherif et al., 1961; Sherif, 1966). In a series of experiments in natural conditions, groups were formed among unacquainted individuals over a time period by presenting problem situations to them that had genuine motivational appeal and that required their coordination for solution. Here we had to face the problem of knowing whether or not we had a *group* in a collection of individuals. We turned to the empirical studies by sociologists in order to define criteria of "group-ness" that would be valid in real life as well as in experiments.

In sequence, the attitudes and behavior of individual members were studied as two groups, thus formed, came into contact. Their first contact was in a series of situations in which the achievement and success of one group necessarily meant failure and defeat for the other. Of course, and you may even say "naturally," intense conflict developed between the groups and their members. What was not so self-evident at the time was that individuals belonging to the two groups exhibited in striking, if rudimentary, form all of the nasty personal qualities, all of the prejudice and stereotyped views that traditional theorizing had been assigning either to innate biological tendencies or to products of extreme frustration in early childhood. (You may be sure that we took great pains to insure that we had very normal, healthy subjects without unusual deprivations in childhood.) By the additional stage of introducing a series of situations in which the same groups faced a superordinate goal, one which required that both groups pull together for its attainment, we succeeded in casting doubt that the aggressive tendencies displayed had been innate. At least, they were susceptible to change.

We cite these experiments to emphasize the same point again: The problem of the research and the specification of the procedures developed after years of studying and surveying the social science literature. Why was this effort put in before the experiments? First, to find out what criteria were essential before we could say that *groups* had formed—groups in the same sense that social scientists find them in real life. Second, to derive reasonable and testable hypotheses about the conditions in which intergroup hostility formed and in which such hostility, once formed, could change. We might add that we learned in the course of this research the extreme importance of history, even for such small groups over a few weeks. If an investigator had measured the attitudes and behavior of individuals during the height of intergroup conflict without any knowledge of what had gone before, he could only have concluded that he had stumbled upon a bunch of the most aggressive and nasty individuals he had ever seen.

PROSPECTS FOR CLOSING THE VALIDITY GAP

What are the prospects for closing the validity gap between research findings in social psychology and the actualities of life to which they are purported to pertain? We are, today, more hopeful than could have been possible even ten years ago. One reason is that more and more social scientists are becoming concerned to define their interdisciplinary relationships.

Another hopeful sign within social psychology and psychology in general is the research movement ordinarily called the "social psychology of the psychological experiment." We may note in passing, as others have, that its implications are by no means confined to experimentation or the laboratory, but pervade research on human subjects who are aware that their behavior is under investigation by a researcher. Earlier, we noted that this movement would not have been necessary had psychologists taken seriously their own findings on the importance of the social context of behavior, or had they taken seriously the evidence from other disciplines on the great impact of sociocultural variables. Now it is time to praise the emphasis on this movement, with the hope that it does not become just another parlor game for the profession. Certainly Stanley Milgram (1965) has shown that it is possible to utilize knowledge of the properties of an experimental situation for a significant investigation of several important variables affecting compliance to commands.

If the movement to explore the social psychology of research is to have lasting significance, it should apply the same logic to exploring the social psychology of other social situations, for example, of different neighborhoods, of different cultures, of different mass media, with the same intensity that it is now showing in studying the laboratory.

If psychology does move from the social psychology of the experiment to the social psychology of other social situations, it will necessarily have to turn to other social sciences that have been studying these situations—situations such as the family, the political group, the economic bargaining situation, the religious encounter, and so on. In doing so, social psychology will also have to find means to bring its techniques to bear in situations that cannot be transferred into the laboratory. In other words, greater progress is needed in integrating the benefits of field work and laboratory work.

The simultaneous and coordinated use of field and laboratory methods is another facet of our plea for interdisciplinary coordination. Since 1958, our research program has focused on bridging the gap between the laboratory and field, between experimental findings and the actualities of life, in a study of attitude and behavior of individuals as a function of their membership in small groups in different sociocultural settings (Sherif and Sherif, 1964). The individuals have been adolescents and the different settings have been urban neighborhoods in several large urban areas. From the very start, we had to face the problem of specifying the social stimulus conditions. We consulted and borrowed from sociologists, in particular those such as Shevky and Bell, and Walter Firey who had worked intensively to develop indicators of ecological and cultural characteristics of entire neighborhoods. We borrowed from other social scientists the survey technique to specify further the values or norms prevailing in the neighborhoods. We borrowed from sociologists a conception of what a group is. From our own previous work as social psychologists, we provided and further refined methods for assessing the attitudes and behaviors of individuals in their natural surroundings and without arousing their awareness that they were being studied.

In short, another hopeful sign that we see is the increasing and active effort to bridge the gap between laboratory and field research by a variety of means. Such attempts will, inevitably, bring the disciplines into closer interchange.

Finally, another prospect for the future is attention being paid by many social psychologists to consider the issue of the isomorphism between their experimental models and the actualities of the problems they purport to study. The political scientist, Sidney Verba, put this issue so well in his book on *Small Groups and Political Behavior* (1961) that we shall simply quote him.

> Abstract models have a certain elegance and appeal, but unless such models can be related at some point to reality they will have seriously limited value to social analysis. One of the major tasks of small group experimental research is that of connecting small group models more closely with actual social situations. If laboratory studies are to tell us about the behavior of "real" people, not laboratory people . . . the gap between the laboratory and the on-going social system must be bridged (p. 246).

Verba suggests that if the differences between the laboratory and actualities represent only a "constant error" always in the same direction, they can be accounted for easily in making predictions for real life. But, he continues, the better solution is in "the use of realistic settings, of long time spans so that groups can develop histories, and of problems that can engage the interest of the participants" (p. 247). In short, his plea is for research coordination between experimentalists and social scientists who study actualities at their own level.

Verba's final plea is for the experimentalist to select "significant social problems" for study, and he suggests that the best way to do so is to test hypotheses suggested by field research. Since this is precisely what our research program has been attempting to do for many years, we could not agree more. In fact, for social psychology, the brightest prospect for interdisciplinary collaboration is that, through interchange with their colleagues in social sciences working at the sociocultural level, their choice of problems may converge more and more toward those that are significant in the actualities of life. The payoff is far greater than we might think. For interchange with other disciplines will provide insight into what variables to include in the research design and will provide a basis for hypotheses that are both testable and fruitful for the disciplines in question.

REFERENCES

BARTLETT, F. C. 1932. *Remembering: a study in experimental and social psychology.* New York: Macmillan.

BORING, E. G. 1950. *A history of experimental psychology.* (2d ed.) New York: Appleton-Century Crofts.

BROWN, R. 1965. *Social psychology.* New York: Free Press of Glencoe.

CHOMSKY, N. 1959. Review of "Verbal behavior" by B. F. Skinner. *Language,* 35: 26–58.

HALLOWELL, A. I. 1954. *Culture and experience.* Philadelphia: University of Pennsylvania Press.

HERSKOVITS, M. J. 1949. *Man and his works.* New York: Alfred A. Knopf.

HELSON, H. 1964. Current trends and issues in adaptation level theory. *American Psychologist*, 19: 26–38.

KLUCKHOHN, C., and H. A. MURRAY (Eds.) 1948. *Personality in nature, society and culture*. New York: Alfred A. Knopf.

MILGRAM, S. 1965. Some conditions of obedience and disobedience to authority. In I. D. Steiner and M. Fishbein (Eds.), *Current studies in social psychology*. New York: Holt, Rinehart and Winston.

MILLER, G. A. 1962. Some psychological studies of grammar. *American Psychologist*, 17: 748–762.

SCHNEIRLA, T. C. 1946. Problems in the biopsychology of social organization. *Journal of Abnormal and Social Psychology*, 41: 385–402.

————. 1951. The "levels" concept in the study of social organization. In J. H. Rohrer and M. Sherif (Eds.), *Social psychology at the crossroads*. New York: Harper and Bros.

SCHOTTSTAEDT, W. W., RUTH H. PINSKY, D. MACKLER and S. WOLF. 1958. Sociologic, psychologic and metabolic observations on patients in the community of a metabolic ward. *American Journal of Medicine*, 25: 248–257.

SCOTT, J. P. 1958. *Aggression*. Chicago: University of Chicago Press.

SEGALL, M., D. CAMPBELL, and M. J. HERSKOVITS. 1966. *The influence of culture on visual perception*. Indianapolis: Bobbs-Merrill.

SHERIF, M. 1935. A study of some social factors in perception. *Archives of Psychology*, No. 187.

————. 1936. *The psychology of social norms*. New York: Harper (Harper Torchbooks, 1966).

————. 1959. Social psychology, anthropology and the "behavioral sciences." *Southwest Social Science Quarterly*, September, pp. 105–112.

————. 1963. Social psychology: problems and trends in interdisciplinary relationships. In S. Koch (Ed.), *Psychology: a study of a science*, Vol. 6 New York: McGraw-Hill.

————. 1966. *In common predicament. Social psychology of intergroup conflict and cooperation*. Boston: Houghton-Mifflin.

————. 1967. *Social interaction: Process and products,* Chicago: Aldine Publishing Co.

————. O. J. HARVEY, B. J. WHITE, W. R. HOOD, and CAROLYN W. SHERIF. 1961. *Intergroup conflict and cooperation. The Robbers Cave experiment*. Norman, Okla.: Institute of Group Relations.

————, and B. KOSLIN. 1960. The "institutional" vs. "behavioral" controversy in social science with special reference to political science. Norman, Okla.: Institute of Group Relations. (Mimeo.) Chap. 4 in Sherif, 1967.

————, and CAROLYN W. SHERIF. 1953. *Groups in harmony and tension*. New York: Harper and Bros.

————, ————. 1956. *An outline of social psychology*. (Rev. ed.) New York: Harper and Row.

————, ————. 1964. *Reference groups*. New York: Harper and Row.

SIMPSON, G. 1963. *Emile Durkheim*. New York: Thomas Y. Crowell Co.

VERBA, S. 1961. *Small groups and political behavior*. Princeton, N.J.: Princeton University Press.

ZETTERBERG, H. L. 1956. *Sociology in the United States*. Paris: Unesco.

2

THEORY-ORIENTED RESEARCH IN NATURAL SETTINGS: THE BEST OF BOTH WORLDS FOR SOCIAL PSYCHOLOGY

William J. McGuire

The main thesis I am defending here is that the time has come for reemphasizing a general methodological approach that has been neglected in social psychology during the past decade or two, namely, the conduct of basic research in natural settings. Such an approach would allow our continuing to do basic research; that is, we could continue to select our hypotheses for their aptness in testing, refining, and developing general theory (rather than for their usefulness in providing practical directives for action). But it would require our devising tests for these hypotheses, not so exclusively in laboratory settings as currently, but somewhat more often in natural field settings. Such a reorientation towards field settings would require us to train ourselves and our students to exercise creative ingenuity—now employed in contriving laboratory conditions that permit testing our hypothesis—to the detection and adaptation of naturally occurring situations that would provide a test of our hypothesis. These field tests would sometimes involve manipulational experiments in natural settings, but I am extending my permissiveness (or softheadedness) even to embrace nonmanipulational studies such as correlational research in the natural settings and even secondary analyses of precollected archival data.

The past twenty years has witnessed a progressively closer identification in the minds of the establishment (and of the students we train) of good social psychological research with laboratory manipulational research. In this apotheosis of the laboratory manipulational experiment as the paradigm for social psychological work, our field was probably emulating the preferred method of the older and more prestigeful fields of scientific psychology such as sensation, perception, and learning. The emulation was made more easy by the defection into social psychology of charismatic experimenters from these perceptual and learning areas, men such as Asch and Hovland. The pull to this paradigm was so strong that even the Lewinians (Festinger, Deutsch, Thibaut, Kelley, Schachter, etc.), despite their early sympathy for field tests, became almost exclusively devoted to the laboratory manipulational experiment.

It is hardly necessary for me to belabor the fact that the laboratory manipulational experiment is the "in" approach as regards contemporary social psychology. While some of us (Ring, 1967; McGuire, 1967) have suggested that it is too far and too exclusively "in," I do feel that all things considered this method is probably the most efficient one for the development of basic theory, which has been and will continue to be (and probably ought to be) the main purpose of social psychological research. I have myself used laboratory manipulational methods almost exclusively in my past research. Let me make clear then that I am neither urging nor predicting the abandonment of this method, nor even its subordination. It should probably continue to be the most efficient and powerful weapon in our social psychological research armamentarium.

What I am urging and predicting is that we correct the current, almost exclusive emphasis on this method by continuing the present level of laboratory manipulational work, but in addition upgrade in quantity and quality the use of natural field settings to test our basic, theoretically derived hypotheses. I am not suggesting that we abandon the physical science paradigm and stop acting like physicists. I am urging that occasionally we also start acting a bit like astronomers.

In the sections that follow, I shall first make a series of conceptual distinctions regarding social psychological research to clarify what it is that I am urging. Then I shall review some current forces that I think are making research in natural settings more attractive and some forces which are (unfortunately) making laboratory manipulational research somewhat less attractive. A final section will outline some recent methodological advances that make basic research in natural settings not only an attractive, but an increasingly feasible and powerful technique in social psychology.

SOME DISTINCTIONS REGARDING DISTINCTIONS IN RESEARCH

Two classical procedures purported to promote conceptual clarity are definition and distinction. I have never been enthusiastic about definitions, because they tend to petrify an area of study and remove from our consideration and approval lines of effort which lie outside the boundaries of our definition and which yet might have elucidated our inquiry had they not been so arbitrarily excluded. I regard distinctions with slightly more toleration. They can be enriching and creative. Where there had been one, after a distinction there are sometimes two. Admittedly, distinguishing can be carried to excess and obscure the main point beneath a flurry of distinctions that make no difference. There comes, no doubt, a time to weed out distinctions as well as a time to make them.

NEED FOR CLARIFYING DISTINCTIONS ABOUT METHOD

There is one situation where multiple distinctions can be not only confusing but even misleading. This occurs where in a conceptual area we make a series of distinctions on bases that are somewhat but not completely similar to one another, like the dimensions in an oblique-factor analytic solution. In such a situation, there is a tendency to confuse these partly correlated distinctions with one another. Or, to use a term that has been developed by our editor, Muzafer Sherif, "assimilation errors" tend to occur. There is, I fear, such a confusion among several partly correlated distinctions regarding the methods in the social sciences which I want to discuss here.

It would help to clarify my basic thesis if I start off by distinguishing among several distinctions that are made as regards social science methodology. I shall be exploring an area of common agreement among us, all of these being distinctions which we tend to make or at least accept, and most of us would probably also agree regarding the interrelations among these several distinctions which I shall lay out here. Nevertheless, it will be worth making these interrelations explicit at the outset to minimize the possibliity of initial misperceptions by providing, if I may use another theoretical construct of Muzafer Sherif, the correct "frame of reference." Because these various bases of distinction are rather similar and the terminology is rather irregular, there is some danger that the one which I am stressing might be misperceived.

CREATIVE VERSUS CRITICAL PHASES OF RESEARCH

The first distinction that I must make regarding method is that between the creative and the critical phases of scientific research. A full cycle of research involves the generation of hypotheses and the testing of these hypotheses. In the existential concrete case, these two processes tend to be intermingled somewhat: even while creatively generating hypotheses, we are critically censoring our more unusual thoughts; and the empirical testing of hypothesis often proves to be as heuristically provocative of creative insight as was the initial cogitation. Some practitioners in the area of creative thinking, such as the brainstorming advocates, have suggested that the two phases are too much intermingled in practice and that one must free the creative phase from any critical censoring, towards which end these brainstorming engineers employ group pressures and outlandish stage settings. But however indistinct the two processes are or ought to be in practice, they are conceptually distinct and the total research effort must involve both the creative aspect of hypothesis generation and the critical aspect of hypothesis testing.

BASIC VERSUS APPLIED RESEARCH

The next distinction relevant to my thesis is that between basic and applied research, which will be admitted by most of us as having some validity even if we feel uneasy regarding whether a line should be drawn between the two. Since this distinction is given various meanings, I should specify that I equate basic and applied research with theory-oriented and action-oriented research, respectively. In terms of our previous distinction, I regard the question of basic versus applied research as pertaining specifically to the first aspect of research, the creative, hypothesis-generating process. One is engaged in basic research to the extent that in his creative, hypothesis-generating phase he derives his predictions from some theoretical conceptualizations with the aim of clarifying, testing, and developing the theory. One is involved in applied research to the extent that he derives his predictions during this creative, hypothesis-generating phase from the practical need for making an informed decision in a natural situation requiring action. In either case, whether one is trying to formulate a prediction in order to clarify theory or to guide action, the researcher must exercise considerable creative ingenuity if his research is to provide valid new information.

LABORATORY VERSUS FIELD RESEARCH

Still another distinction calling for clarification is that between field and laboratory research. This distinction pertains to the critical, hypothesis-testing aspect of research. One is engaged in field research to the extent that he tests his hypothesis in natural settings, in the world he never made. One is engaged in laboratory research to the extent that he tests his hypothesis in artificial situations that he has contrived, aiming like Daedalus to be the skilled artificer forging conditions needed to test his prediction. There may be degrees of naturalness and artificiality, but my essential point is that the laboratory-field distinction pertains to the critical aspect of research and thus is in principle orthogonal to my earlier distinction between basic and applied research, which pertains to the creative aspect of research.

CORRELATION VERSUS MANIPULATIONAL RESEARCH

There is one further distinction having to do with the critical, hypothesis-testing aspect of research that needs mentioning here, that between correlational and manipulational research. By correlational research I refer to any hypothesis testing in which we do not ourselves manipulate the independent variable, but allow nature to do so. By manipulational research, I refer to the hypothesis-testing tactic of ourselves inducing the different levels of the independent variable; that is, we preselect a sample of people (or other units) and assign them at random (or by some matching procedure) to conditions producing the different levels of the independent variable. In principle, this distinction is quite different from the previous one dealing with testing hypotheses in natural settings and in the laboratory. Unfortunately, some behavioral scientists talk as if research in field settings necessarily involves the correlational tactic and as if research in the laboratory necessarily involves manipulation. While there may well be a tendency for these two dimensions to so correlate in practice, conceptually they are orthogonal, and manipulational research can be done in the field or laboratory. (There is a chapter devoted to this topic in the Festinger and Katz [1953] methods book and our editor, Muzafer Sherif [Sherif *et al.*, 1961; Sherif and Sherif, 1964], has done some of the classic examples of manipulational research in field settings.) Conversely, most of us laboratory-oriented social psychologists have at times done correlational hypothesis testing in the laboratory, particularly when testing interactions between situational and personality variables.

Experimentation

The term "experimental" tends to arise in the present context and is often used to refer specifically to laboratory research, or at least to manipulational research, whether in laboratory or field. It seems to me to be wiser to use the term in its etymologically correct sense of "to test" and grant that the researcher is engaged in experimentation so long as he is testing his hypotheses, whether in the laboratory or in the field, and whether by manipulation or correlational variation of his independent variable. Not only etymological correctness, but also charity requires that we broaden the application of "experimental" to make it conterminous with the second aspect of research, the critical, hypothesis-testing phase. Charity so ordains because the term "experimental" has come to be used almost ritualistically as an "OK" adjective in any social psychology enterprise. Thus the fine series of monographs that Leonard Berkowitz has been editing since 1964 is called *Advances in Experimental Social Psychology*. The new journal that John Thibaut has been editing impressively since 1965 is called the *Journal of Experimental Social Psychology*. The association that was formed in Europe around 1963 by the Lewinian-style continental social psychologists and their American cousins is called (if General DeGaulle will permit me a translation into Anglo-Saxon) "The European Society of Experimental Social Psychology." The American association founded in 1964 by the Edwardians (Hollander and Vinacke) is called "The Society of Experimental Social Psychology." (Incidentally, these association names illustrate how the old order passes. It used to be that those of us on this side of the Atlantic modestly employed the adjective to avoid nominal confusion. Thus, *The Times* meant *The Times* of London, while its Western counterpart we called with modest adjectival modification, *The New York Times*. Now, however, when social psychology societies are formed, the association without the adjective means, of course, the American one; while our colleagues across the sea modestly add "European" to the name of their society to provide the provincial distinction. O tempores, O mores—Sic transit gloria mundi.)

LA NOUVELLE VAGUE

Where does this discussion of multiple distinctions leave us? First of all, I want to make use of the distinction between the creative and the critical aspects of the scientific research. Second, I say that the distinction between basic and applied research (or, if you prefer, between theory-oriented and action-oriented research) is relevant to the creative phase of the research process. Third, I maintain that the distinction between field and laboratory research, or between correlational and manipulational research, pertains to the critical phase. Hence, I am insisting that, conceptually at least, the distinction between basic and applied research is orthogonal to that between field and laboratory research. Admittedly, in practice the two seem to be oblique to one another in that basic research is more likely to be conducted in the laboratory, while action-oriented research is more commonly done in field settings. But my point here is that this association is accidental rather than essential in that there is no reason why we cannot test action-oriented hypotheses in the laboratory or theoretically derived hypotheses in the field. Since I have certain prejudices in favor of theory-derived over action-oriented research, my discussion here will not deal with action-oriented research at all. I shall be dealing with the possibility of doing basic, theory-derived hypothesis testing in field situations. My essential message will be that this possibility has been rather neglected by us theory-oriented researchers and that the time is ripe for a correction of this neglect. I shall be devoting the major part of my discussion here to a review of the developments which make a greater emphasis on the use of natural settings in basic research both desirable and possible.

MY OWN PAST AND PRESENT METHODOLOGICAL PREJUDICES

It is easy enough to characterize my own past research in terms of the two basic distinctions above. As regards the creative phase of hypothesis derivation, I have characteristically formulated hypotheses for the purpose of theory development rather than to provide directives for practical action. As regards the critical phase, I have characteristically tested the hypotheses in laboratory rather than field situations. In the present discussion I am stubbornly adhering to my intuition that theory-oriented research is more valuable in the long run than action-oriented work. I have described my reasons for this preference in a talk given in 1961 (McGuire, 1965) and so do not feel obliged to recount them here. In my more audacious moments I would claim that basic research will prove of more practical usefulness than the same amount of effort put into applied research. As Lewin has said, there is nothing more practical than a good theory. This prejudice of mine is probably quite difficult to justify rationally, and it may prove incorrect historically. At any rate, it is my preferred mode of hypothesis generation and I do not propose to abandon it in this symposium. My guilt in adhering to this old prejudice in favor of basic research is partly assuaged by the knowledge that other papers in this volume will deal more positively with action research.

I am, on the other hand, ready to admit and even to urge that my own and the establishment's identification of good research with laboratory manipulational research has been excessive and has caused an unwise neglect of field and correlational research. There is, I would urge, need for both field and laboratory research. Enough of my old bias remains so that I still feel that, in general, laboratory manipulational research is usually the more efficient. But it seems to me that at this moment, field research and correlational research are being neglected to an extent that is inappropriate. Fortunately, the corrective for this situation seems already visible on the horizon. I shall turn now to a consideration of a number of influences that seem to me to be at work in redirecting our attention once again to the desirability and possibility of doing basic hypothesis-testing research, not only in the laboratory, but in natural settings to a greater extent than is currently fashionable.

We are maintaining that social psychological research is, and of course ought to be, tending towards a greater use of natural settings for hypothesis testing than is currently fashionable. My feeling is that there are both pushes and pulls inclining us in this direction, including forces pulling us into the field and forces pushing us from the laboratory. I shall take up the pulls and the pushes in turn.

FORCES MAKING FIELD TESTS MORE ATTRACTIVE

Intrinsic Factors

Factors both intrinsic and extrinsic to social psychology are pulling us towards field research. At this point we shall mention the intrinsic factors only in passing, since a later section will be devoted to spelling them out in more detail. They include recent progress in the area of experimental design, of data collection, and of analytic techniques which promise to make rigorous hypothesis testing in natural settings more feasible than has hitherto been the case. Progress in experimental design has included techniques for teasing out causal directions in correlational results, and in identifying the crucial variables in situations where there are too many unknowns for a precise solution. Progress in data collection includes such recent advances as the availability of social science data archives and the possibility of obtaining nationwide samples through caravan-type surveys. Advances in analysis include developments of descriptive and inferential statistics that allow applications of the traditional procedures to "dirty" data and the availability of relatively convenient methods of simulating social and cognitive processes through the use of the computer. Only in combination does this variety of advances make basic research in natural settings substantially more feasible, and yet individually they come from a wide range of social science disciplines. The possibilities which they jointly open become clearer to those of us in any one discipline only when we are made aware of interlocking advances in some of our sister disciplines. The necessity for a transdisciplinary cosmopolitanism, which is the theme of this symposium, becomes abundantly clear in the area with which my discussion deals. The occurrence of the great leap forward which I am projecting here assumes the end of disciplinary chauvinism and provincialism.

The extrinsic forces which are pulling us into making greater use of natural settings in hypothesis testing are of less interest to us and less under our control as professionals than are the intrinsic factors to which I shall return in a later section. Hence, I shall consider only briefly here these extrinsic factors before proceeding with the discussion. We have in mind three classes of extrinsic factors: first, the increasing political involvement of the academic community; second, the increasing concern among the political segment, especially the federal legislative and executive budgeteers regarding what dividends the increasing public expenditure on social science research might have for the public good; and finally, the problem of providing some psychic satisfaction to the exponentially increasing number of people who are engaged in social science research, a progressively decreasing number of whom will have the satisfaction of making fundamental contributions to theory. While none of these extrinsic considerations make it logically compelling that we opt for hypothesis testing in natural settings, each of them does seem to push us somewhat in that direction, as I shall try to develop in the paragraphs that follow.

THE INCREASING SOCIAL CONCERN OF RESEARCHERS

Ever since World War II, American scientists have shown an increasing sense of obligation to take a stand as scientists, or at least as individuals, on the burning social issues of the day. No doubt there are multiple causes for this growth of concern, including the scientists' increasing importance to the national economy and military posture, their increasing personal affluence and prestige, their growing feelings of guilt regarding the uses of their now important contributions, the entry of a greater proportion of the talented youth into their ranks, etc. In part also, the growing concern of scientists has been part of the more general feeling in this age of affluence that undesirable situations which formerly have been tolerated can no longer be countenanced, situations such as racial inequities, the sufferings of the poverty-stricken, the misery of the physically and mentally ill, the specter of war, etc. Also, the success of the scientists in contributing new devices (such as weaponry, communication systems, potent chemical products and byproducts, automation, etc.) that raise both dangers and opportunities for social progress has probably sensitized the scientist to the necessity that he speak out regarding the appropriate public response to these advances. It is our feeling that this increasing social concern on the part of the social scientists will incline them to be more sympathetic to testing their hypotheses in natural settings, since our theories will be made more relevant to existing social problems if they are developed and tested in a more realistic arena.

If this growing social concern is already visible on the part of the current generation of social science researchers, it is even more evident in the coming generation. The current activist college students who are likely to turn to the social sciences seem much more politically active than the silent generation from which the young researchers of today were recruited. I am not referring here to the dropout, apathetic, and alienated subpopulation that makes up the contemporary neuter generation but rather to the noisier (more troublesome though less troubling) protesting activists.

INCREASING PUBLIC CONCERN FOR SCIENTIFIC PAYOFF

So long as scientific research was a small-time operation with the experimenter required only to scrounge sufficient funds to buy a small electric motor and some aluminum scraps to build a memory drum and perhaps a few more dollars to have his final figures drawn by an engineering school draftsman, or to obtain envelopes and postage to do a local survey, the government and the other centers of power in our society had little influence in determining his line of research. Now, however, the social scientist has lost the anonymity of poverty and has learned to depend on large government grants for his considerably increased level of research. Federal government aid to the social sciences has been increasing steadily ever since World War II, at first through contracts from the Navy and Air Force and other military services and more recently through the NIH and the NSF. At the beginning of the present decade, support of social science research by the federal government had already reached $73 million; by 1966, this amount had increased 500 per cent to $380 million. This total still represents only about 2 per cent of the federal expenditures for research and development, but even so, a third of a billion dollars could not easily be made up out of the departmental petty cash if the federal source dried up. It is likely, then, that some response will be made to the growing concern in the executive and legislative branches of the federal government regarding what contributions the social sciences are making to the Great Society in return for this support. In May, 1967, the House Subcommittee chaired by Representative Henry S. Reuss released a four-volume report prepared by Dr. Harold Orlans (1967) of the Brookings Institution which reviewed the federal government's involvement in social science research. This report's conclusion that a great deal of social research was trivial and irrelevant and that, even where usable, went unused is merely the most recent and bulkiest of a series that have drawn the same conclusion.

Hopefully, we social scientists have led the examined life with sufficient self-consciousness so that we are unlikely to drop what we are doing in the face of criticism by the nonsocial scientist that we are engaging in trivia. Sophistication regarding scientific research has now developed to the point where even nonscientists appreciate that all research should not be evaluated in terms of its evident and immediate utility for solving some pressing human problem. Still, it seems unlikely that there will be no repercussions of the increasing concern of the economic gatekeepers that there be an occasional social payoff for an annual federal government investment in social sciences that has now reached a third of a billion dollars. I am suggesting that one response we might make with a minimum loss of essentials is to continue to do basic, theory-oriented research, but to carry out our tests of predictions somewhat more often in natural settings, rather than in contrived laboratory situations. I would count on the centripetal pressures towards basic research from the profession to be sufficient to keep us from being seduced by governmental economic enticements into action research. My best-of-both-worlds solution of testing basic theoretical derivations in natural settings would hopefully show the relevance to the real concerns of man of our seemingly trivial and jargon-laden theorizing. A more profound possible effect of such natural testing would be the development of theories in a somewhat more reality-oriented direction, since it would be necessary to find some relevant natural situations in which to test them.

Need To Find Gratification for the Greatly Increasing Number of Social Science Researchers

There has been a rapid growth in the number of active researchers in the social sciences, whether we take as our index the number of members of our scientific societies or the number of pages in our journals. The rough estimate is that the volume of research is increasing exponentially with a doubling rate of about ten to fifteen years. Licklider (1966) has pointed out that it is somewhat of an hyperbole to call this an information "explosion" when it takes ten to fifteen for expansion to double its volume, but whatever the appropriate word, we will agree that the number of researchers actively engaged in social sciences is continuing to increase at a rather impressive and even ominous rate.

It is my contention that in science the average and even the good research does not count for much. It is only the truly excellent work which contributes to the fundamental advances that makes science an accumulative area of inquiry. In my opinion, the total number of researchers grows more rapidly than the number of researchers doing the truly excellent work. The great majority of merely good researchers mark time in busy work and tidying up until the few make the next achievement of excellence that gives new direction to the routine work. But this rather depressing elitist situation obtains, I think, only with respect to developing basic theory. It is only when our gratification from social science work resides solely in its advancement of basic theory that frustration of the many will result as they perceive that they are adding very little to this fundamental progress. It is my expectation that we shall discover that there are additional utilities to our research besides the development of basic theory when we do more hypothesis testing in natural situations. In such settings, the outcome will have the double potential of advancing theory and of enhancing our understanding of and ability to control variables as they operate in specific natural situations. It seems to me that as regards the latter consideration, good (as well as excellent) research can contribute socially significant information and thus gratifications to the researcher.

If we are seeking positive motivation that will pull social sciences increasingly into field testing of their hypotheses, I would suggest the three sources just reviewed: the growing social consciousness of our researchers, the increasing worry about practical dividend by those who are paying the mounting bills for social science research, and the need to provide gratification for our ever-growing number of social science researchers. Given that there is such positive motivation, the question remains whether there is the response opportunity. Only when motivation combines with the response availability is the performance likely to occur. We shall point out in a later section that recent methodological advances do provide appropriate response possibilities. Before considering them, however, we shall review some more unfortunate motivations which I think will drive us towards an increasing use of natural settings for testing our theoretically derived hypotheses. We refer here to the negative motivation regarding laboratory manipulational experiments which derives from several growing concerns about problems associated with this type of testing.

FORCES MAKING LABORATORY MANIPULATIONAL RESEARCH LESS ATTRACTIVE

There seems to be growing concern in recent years regarding the extent to which the final solution of our social science problems can ever be achieved purely through laboratory manipulational research. Three worries in this connection can be listed, in decreasing order of importance, as follows: more and more artifacts have been brought to light in connection with laboratory research; concern has grown regarding the ethical problems involved in a great deal of social science manipulational research; and there seems to be a growing satiation with laboratory manipulational research, to the extent that the more stimulus-hungry researchers are looking elsewhere or are engaging in what has been called "fun and games" experimentation (Ring, 1967). We shall consider each of these worries in turn, though with a considerable lack of enthusiasm, since we would prefer that the current level of laboratory manipulational research be at least maintained while urging more positively that we increase our level of work in the neglected area of hypothesis testing in natural settings.

Artifact Problems in Manipulational Laboratory Research

Laboratory researchers, particularly in the social sciences, have always been at least preconsciously worried by the artificiality of their contrived situations. Yet it seems to me that currently these perennial worries have been accentuated by the convergence of several lines of research which have given empirical corroboration to anxieties about the generalizability of laboratory results, anxieties which had previously been only conjectural. The work by Orne (1962) on the "demand character" of the experimental situation and by Rosenberg (1965) on "evaluation apprehension" has raised the question of whether the crucial independent variable in the laboratory situation is the one that we had intended. Their work, and especially that of Rosenthal (1966) on the "experiment effect," has made the "social psychology of the psychology experiment" a field of study in itself. Our most elegant experimental designs have been called into question as possibly introducing artifacts. Thus, the use of the subject as his own control is suspected of washing out effects; and the use of before-after designs has aroused fears of pretest sensitization (Lana, 1968). Both of these refinements were intended to reduce error variance, but seem to have thrown out information with the noise and reduced the ungeneralizability of the results.

Our worries about sampling problems in laboratory experimentation have grown. We have always poked gentle fun at ourselves as being engaged in constructing the "psychology of the college sophomore" because of the narrow population from which we draw our samples. To this perennial worry has been added new concern about an even narrower self-selection bias due to the peculiarities of the volunteer subject (Rosenthal and Rosnow, 1968). We are also worried about the problem of the professional subject, that campus fixture who has seen experimenters come and go but who himself stays on forever and participates in all of them. Here we get into the problems of "debriefing" and the problem of how prior deception affects the success of subsequent experimental manipulations which have recently been investigated experimentally (Brock and Becker, 1966; Fillenbaum, 1966). There is also growing concern about violations of the secrecy pledge by early participants in the experiment which might make the results of the later-run subjects difficult to generalize (Aronson, 1966; Zemach and Rokeach, 1966; Wuebben, 1967). The main source of worry arises from our need for "naive" subjects, i.e., subjects who are not any more aware of the purposes of the experiment being conducted than are the persons in the natural situations to whose behavior we wish to generalize our results. Even more worrisome, therefore, is the possibility that even relatively naive subjects tend to be suspicious of the true purpose of certain experiments, and that this suspiciousness is systematically related to variables possibly related to our dependent variables (Stricker, Messick, and Jackson, 1967).

Still other artifactual worries arise in connection with the elegant measuring procedures used in laboratory research. Campbell and Fiske (1959) have pointed out that the achievement of symmetrical comparability among the instruments used to measure our several variables carries the danger of a methods artifact that can result in spurious positive relationships. If I may be permitted to sound a theme that has been played too often to be entertaining, we have also the problem of response sets and styles. There are the big biases, such as social desirability and acquiescence, and a host of less salient ones such as position preferences, erraticness, and even "faking bad" (Berg, 1966; DeSoto and Kuethe, 1959). Some students of the problem are more worried than others about response biases (Rorer, 1965; Rundquist, 1966), but the reasonable prescription would be to run scared on this issue. As regards the nicety of ourselves manipulating the independent variable in the laboratory instead of letting nature do the manipulating for us, as when we use the correlational design, McGuire (1965) and Sherif and Hovland (1961) have suggested that the laboratory-manipulated variable may be a different one from the identically named variable that is naturally manipulated in field settings. McGuire has also suggested that typically our hypothesis-formulation may assume the "field" meaning, and our hypothesis-testing, the laboratory manipulational meaning. Thus on several fronts we find suspicions arising that our laboratory manipulational experiments contain some refinements of elegance that have been carried to the excess where virtue becomes a vice.

Ethical Anxieties in Connection with Laboratory Experiments

Individual voices have been raised over the past several years regarding possible ethical problems in some laboratory manipulational research (Janis, 1965; Kelman, 1965, 1967; Smith, 1967; Weskoff, 1960). Currently, official recognition and institutional formalization has been given to the problem in the numerous committees formed by the federal government (Clark, 1967) and the several professional associations (Brayfield, 1967) to look into the ethical issues involved in behavioral research. Simply listing the kinds of issues that have arisen is terrifying enough to communicate the magnitude of the problem. Hence, I shall merely mention a variety of such issues without going into a detailed discussion of any of them. One problem is that of coerced and uninformed participation imposed on subjects. Another is the possible invasion of privacy in the testing involved in laboratory research (though, of course, the privacy problem might be raised even more urgently in connection with psychological testing outside the laboratory). The use of deception, which seems to be almost inevitable in most laboratory research, has been widely criticized. There is the possible betrayal of confidentiality in supplying the individual's identity or at least in revealing his demographic characteristic and its relation to some form of behavior so that a concept of confidence betrayal by category might be in order. Perhaps most serious is the use of noxious manipulations which tend to cause the subject physical or psychological distress of at least temporary nature and which in some cases might even have rather lasting effects.

The fact that laboratory-manipulations studies may give rise to these moral dilemmas does not mean that we should abandon such research. (Perhaps this goes without saying, but when the issue of morality is raised by some individuals and agencies it is well to be as explicit as possible.) Even the highest reverence for life, respect for human value, and concern for humanity does not protect one from being confronted by moral dilemmas and conflict situations where we must make choices with fear and trembling among alternatives, each of which arouses some moral anxiety. In these situations we shall have to live with our choice, continually reexamining it lest we be hardened by it into a more insensitive decision-making in the future. Those who feel that the potential ethical costs of their research outweigh the potential social dividends of that research so that they should perhaps give up their work are probably correct in so deciding. I would urge, however, that we wait until we are confronted by rather clearcut cases before we try to impose a like decision on a colleague who feels that his labors are worth their cost. Cessation of labor is not always the final ethical solution. When a friend came upon Wesley after he had just dragged himself from his death-bed to his desk to do one more bit of work and remonstrated with him, Wesley asked, "Would you have the Lord find me idle when He comes?" I have always suspected that Wesley dragged himself to his labors more out of joy than moral obligation. But perhaps there is some moral obligation to work and the decision to stop one's research (which seems to have been opted by some who advocate the higher morality) also constitutes a choice, and one that is not without its own moral problems. But if the growing moral anxieties about laboratory manipulational research is no clear indication that we should reduce (much less stop) such research, I suspect that such rising worries will and should make the social scientist more adventurous and enterprising in seeking alternative modes of hypothesis testing that arouse fewer qualms.

THE SATIATION PROBLEM WITH LABORATORY RESEARCH

It might seem like too great a predilection for paradox on my part, but I suspect that the very popularity of the laboratory manipulational experiment carries within itself the seeds of a strong reaction. Ring (1967) has recently argued that the predilection of the social psychological establishment for the laboratory manipulational experiment has repelled some of the better students who were initially attracted to the area and has diverted some of those who stayed into a "fun and games" approach. Mistaking the form for the substance, he maintains, many of us have adopted a gamesman approach to manipulational experimentation, getting pleasure from contriving an outrageous "happening" in the laboratory rather than from arriving at some substantive results that could be of use either to theory development or to social action problems.

My own feeling is that Ring is inflating an amusing sideshow into a major crime wave. It may be true that at the moment there seems to be a bit too much playfulness in laboratory experiments (and even that on occasions the playfulness is less excusably conjoined with some malicious pleasure taken from discomforting our subjects in some ingenious novel manner). But I feel that there is a serious intent behind most of this research and that the vast bulk of laboratory manipulational research remains, for better or worse, as dull as ever. If Ring should prove more correct than I now admit, then it would only strengthen the prognostication I am making here, namely, that the overwhelming establishment consensus regarding the paradigmatic value of the laboratory manipulational experiment will inevitably cause a reaction among the creative rebels in our field. I foresee that some of those bright young men who want new worlds to conquer, and who want to conquer them in their own way, will inevitably take on the champ and find alternatives to this establishment notion of what good research is. I think their rebelliousness will take positive form in redirecting their efforts into devising methods of testing hypotheses, not in the laboratory, but in the natural environment, and not by means of manipulation, but by correlational analysis, not by collecting data to test a priori hypotheses, but by post factum analyses of already accumulated data.

Lest I seem to prove too much, let me repeat once again that in my opinion the manipulational laboratory experiment is and probably ought to be the most commonly used method in basic research. But I am urging here simply that it probably will not, and probably should not, continue to be so exclusively the method used. We have in the preceding section tried to point out that there is sufficient motivation, both of a positive and (unfortunately) a negative nature, drawing us into increasing utilization of the natural environment and of correlational research for testing hypotheses derived from basic social psychological theory. For this motivation to eventuate in performance, it is necessary that to the drive be added a response capacity. The question remains, given the motive to do basic research in naturalistic settings, whether tools lie at hand adequate to let us act effectively on this motivation. In the section that follows, we shall review some recent trends which we feel do put in our hands new tools that make a foray into the natural world a promising enterprise.

RECENT ADVANCES THAT FACILITATE BASIC RESEARCH IN NATURAL SETTINGS

If the variety of forces just reviewed do make basic researchers more sympathetic to testing their hypotheses in natural settings and by correlational designs, the problem remains as to whether methodological techniques are available that would allow us to act effectively on this motivation. Traditionally natural settings have not been regarded as very hospitable to those seeking to test basic, theory-derived hypotheses, though the approach has not been competely neglected (French, 1953; Sherif et al., 1961; Sherif and Sherif, 1964). It seems to me, however, that during the past half dozen years a number of relevant advances have been made on the methodological front. These recent contributions have come from a number of disciplines, including anthropology, psychology, sociology, political science, geography, economics, etc. As a result of this diversity of origin, it does not seem to have been widely appreciated that this advance has occurred. I can myself claim only passing acquaintance with a number of these innovations, despite having made conscious effort to recognize and familiarize myself with them.

Here again the cost entailed by lack of interdisciplinary communication is illustrated by the present case where little effort seems to have been made to pull together these technical contributions into a composite program. Fortunately, I think that the lack of communication across disciplinary walls is being gradually rectified by the increasing frequency of symposia like the present one and the recent adventurous innovations in academic organization which are being attempted at various new universities and even at a few of the old established ones like Penn State. In my more realistic moments, I would predict that most of these adventurous innovations will fail, or at least regress to conventional disciplinary forms. But many such failures are the price one must be prepared to pay in the achievement of a successful innovation. It is estimated that in industrial settings, attempts at innovation are successful only once in seven to forty attempts (Schon, 1967). We must expect many explorers to set sail from the home ports before that one Italian navigator arrives in the new world. Indeed, in such innovation processes I do not think that it is quite appropriate to call "failures" those false starts which flop with a resounding thud. At the least, we should probably say of them what the Naiads said of Phaethon, namely, "They failed greatly, but greatly dared."

If I am correct in saying that these wide-ranging methodological advances have occurred, and that we have neglected so far to pull them together so as to indicate their contribution toward making research in natural settings feasible, then it might seem that my present discussion would better have concentrated on reviewing such advances rather than confining such a review to this last section of my discussion. However, it seemed to me that first it was necessary to provide what the mathematicians call the "motivation." To this end, I sought to clarify exactly what kind of research I felt was deserving of somewhat greater emphasis in the future, namely, basic research in natural settings, even if it involved correlational and post factum designs. Then it was necessary to point out that there are forces inclining us toward a sympathy for such an approach, so that if methodological advances are made, the opportunities they offer might be utilized. I felt that only if I did this preliminary spade work would my colleagues in social psychology take seriously this prognostication that we are about to see the testing of basic, theory-derived hypotheses move somewhat towards natural environments, nonmanipulational procedures, and secondary analyses.

With this groundwork completed, I shall review briefly some recent advances that seem to me to offer some promise. I shall review these advances under three highly interrelated headings: those having to do primarily with experimental design, those having to do with data collection, and those dealing with more efficient analyses of the results obtained in natural settings.

ADVANCES IN EXPERIMENTAL DESIGN

Achievements in experimental design relevant to the present discussion have to do either with the major problem arising when one tests one's hypotheses in natural settings (namely, the detection of the crucial factor among too many unknowns and uncontrollable variables) or with the major problem involved in correlational research (namely, teasing out causal direction among covariants none of which one can manipulate). These two problems tend to be interrelated, as shown in the analyses of Blaylock (1964). A number of fine minds have addressed themselves to these problems in the past few years, including political scientists like Simon (1957), Alker (1966a). MacRae and Meldrum (1960), Ando *et al.* (1953), Claunch (1965), Stokes (1965), etc.; sociologists like Blaylock, Coleman and Boudon (1965a, 1965b). etc.; industrial psychologists like Vroom, Pelz, etc.; measurement people, such as Guttman, Sheperd, Harris, etc.; econometricians like Tinbergen (1937). Valavanis (1959), Wold (1964), etc.; geographers and demographers such as Duncan (1961), Schnore (1961), etc., and also those people who have grown so much bigger than our disciplinary borders that it would be irreverent to classify them, such as Paul Lazarsfeld and Donald Campbell. (Where no references are given above, specific readings are cited later.) I have too much respect for my colleagues' grip on reality to want to pretend that I have grasped the full import of these recent advances. It seems to me that this progress deserves a symposium devoted exclusively to the presentation. evaluation, and interrelation of these lines of progress in teasing out the crucial variables and defining the direction of their causal impact. In the present discussion I shall do no more than name-drop and point vaguely in some directions where I intuit the action to lie.

One line of research deserving and receiving increased attention is the work on the cross-lagged panel correlation technique, especially in the hands of Campbell (1963; with Stanley, 1963; with Miller, Lubetsky and O'Connell, 1964; etc.) and his colleagues such as Rozelle (1965, 1966; with Campbell, 1966). While some of the latter work suggests that the technique is not as powerful in pin-pointing causal directions as had at first been hoped and although it seems to be rather sensitive to the unreliability variance that is often high in our natural measures, I feel that these difficulties should excite zest for solving difficult problems rather than despair in the face of adversity. A closely related example of this "path analysis" is that pursued by Pelz and his colleagues (Pelz, 1959; Pelz and Andrews, 1964). More distantly related procedures for teasing out the causal direction among relatively small sets of variables have been suggested by Coleman (1964). The problem has been put in broader perspective than this path analysis approach by Vroom (1966) and by Campbell and Stanley (1963) in their discussion of quasi-experimental designs. Dohrenwend (1966) has also attempted to deal with the causal problem, where sequential data were not available, by locating cases that would fill all the logically necessary cells. Perhaps the most indefatigable students of this problem who are casting the broadest net are Blaylock (1961, 1964, 1965, 1966) and Alker (1965, 1966a, 1966b).

It is my hope that these thinkers constitute an "invisible college" whose members are in reasonably close communication with one another and will generate in the near future economical depictions of the state of the art for the delectation of us outsiders. Since several interim reports have already been forthcoming and more are in prospect, I feel relieved of the obligation to serve as the self-appointed dean or public relations man for this invisible college by summarizing and evaluating their contributions in detail at this point. It suffices for my present purposes to point out that across the disciplinary spectrum from geography to psychology (or whatever poles you prefer for anchoring this spectrum), the perspicacious listener can hear the more-than-faint rumblings of approaching breakthrough. Any of you who, when you hear the word "breakthrough" reach for your gun, will perhaps excuse me the use of this word if I remind you that, to Rosenberg's frank and outrageous comment, "When I hear the word 'culture' I reach for my gun," Lionel Trilling has retorted, "When I hear the word 'gun' I reach for my culture."

ADVANCES IN THE COLLECTION OF NATURALISTIC DATA

Perhaps the greatest recent progress as regards opportunities for testing basic hypotheses in natural settings has to do with the increasing accessability to natural data on the social processes, including the amassing of data archives, the development of storage and retrieval systems for such data, the increasing accessibility to national samples, and recent developments in unobstrusive measures which can be used without disturbing the participants in their natural activities.

SOCIAL DATA ARCHIVES

The usefulness and possibility of social data archives probably derives in substantial part from the courage, ingenuity, and Herculean labors of the Yale anthropologists including Murdock, Ford, and the others, in setting up the Human Relations Area Files of cross-cultural data. More recently, the amassing of data archives has progressed on at least three different fronts. First, there are the archives in which are being deposited the results of public opinion surveys in the United States and abroad. Here we would have to mention as first in time the Roper Public Opinion Research Center at Williams College (Bisco, 1967). Currently, there are comparable centers at Berkeley, MIT, Harvard, Michigan, Chicago, Wisconsin, Illinois, UCLA, and North Carolina, among the American universities, and at such European locations as Cologne, Amsterdam, and London. Fortunately, since 1962 the Inter-University Consortium for Political Research, centered at the Institute for Social Research of the University of Michigan, has been operating to suppress some of the inefficient redundancy and rivalry that existed among these centers during the anarchical early years of the sixties. Increasingly this Consortium is regularizing the formats by which data are stored, organizing the areas of geographic responsibility of the several centers, and providing for the complete interchange of collections among them. As a result, most of the areas in the United States where researchers are concentrated have easy access to one of the seventy member institutions. Members are also distributed, though more sparsely, over Canada and Europe. Increasingly, the present generation of social scientists and their students will, we predict, become aware of this under-utilized resource and exercise their ingenuity in making good use of it to test their hypotheses.

A second type of archive which is growing in availability involves data other than opinions expressed on surveys. We have in mind here the various governmental, nongovernmental and academic treasure troves of demographic and factual information on the population. In the federal government, these are found typically in the Bureau of the Census and the Bureau of Labor Statistics (Bauer, 1966). The Council of Social Science Data Archives (Glaser and Bisco, 1967) surveyed these resources in the private sector and currently the NORC of the University of Chicago is, I believe, engaged in surveying the governmental resources of this nature. A movement was growing to centralize the federal government's data on individual citizens, which is now scattered over many agencies. This centralization was perhaps motivated by considerations of government efficiency, but it would have obvious utility for the social scientist as well. A reaction seems to have set in regarding this centralization of information on persons, since some observers have seen it as a potential threat to the political freedom of the individual. As a twentieth-century sophisticate myself, I feel as much as any man the desire for privacy and for the careful segmentation of who knows what about whom. Hence, I am not without sympathy for those who would discourage such convenient centralizing of data on individuals. Still, in my less romantic moments, I feel that this Luddite tactic of depending upon the continuance of inefficiency and disorganization to safeguard our privacy is probably doomed to failure. Perhaps in some way we could achieve the centralization of the data and safeguard the privacy of the individual by restrictions (even to the government itself) as regards access to and publication of information that would identify individuals. It behooves us to ally the cause of privacy and freedom with, rather than against, the forward thrust of history.

Progress in amassing factual information on individuals is also promised by a renewal of interest in life-history data. Psychologists particularly have been inclined to measure personality and to predict gross behavior from the person's self-reports about his feelings, attitudes, preferences, etc. Now there seems to be an increasing effort to substitute for such introspective self-reports concrete biographical data regarding the factual events in the person's life. Thus, for example, we would assess the individual's "independence" not only by asking him to respond to the item, "How much do you like to do things by yourself, rather than with the help of others?" but rather, "How old were you when you first had a driver's license?" The uses of the autobiography in psychological research have recently been reviewed by Annis (1967) and the Richardson Foundation has constituted itself as a repository for research on biographical inventories and life-history approaches to social phenomena (Lacklen, 1965).

A third area in which data archives are showing a pronounced advance includes the collection of data on grosser units than the individual person, particularly the nation state. Some of these political-data banks are group enterprises centered at universities, such as the MIT International Study, the Yale Political Data Program, or the Stanford Institute of Political Studies. Even more impressive as demonstrations of the possibilities are the archives assembled by one or two individuals to collect cross-national data bearing on a specific problem area in which they are interested, such as international conflict. We have in mind here such work as that by Richardson (1960) on the statistics of deadly quarrels, by Rummel (1966), Guetzkow, and Sawyer on the dimensionality of nations, and by Ivo and Rosalind Feierabend (1966) on international conflict. Some effort is also being expended by the Yale group and by the Consortium at Michigan for collecting data on subnational political units, though the latter is confined to one specific kind of data, namely, county-by-county election statistics for the United States from 1824 to the present. Some of this work has been conveniently brought together by Merritt and Rokkan (1966). The suggestion has also been made (Rokkan and Almond, 1965) that these data archives give more attention to amassing qualitative as well as quantitative data regarding political units, but I would give this opening to the right a rather low priority.

There is one area in which the compilation of data archives does not seem to have proceeded as rapidly as one would hope. This is the accumulation of data with an historical dimension. The U. S. election results from 1824 to the present being amassed at the University of Michigan is one of the rare exceptions. Most of the archives so far considered fail to collect successive time samples on the same individual units of study. The seriousness of this failure to accumulate historical series on the same units becomes clear if one remembers from our discussion of experimental design, above, that most of the techniques for detecting the causal direction among correlated variables require some kind of "path analysis" that assumed a time series. One hopes that this negligence will be corrected in the near future. The Feierabends' study does utilize a short-ranged historical dimension (starting with the entry of the League of Nations into recordkeeping). Several of us organized a symposium at the September, 1967 American Psychological Association Convention at Washington (Greenbaum, 1967) to discuss psychological contributions to the study of history which touched upon some related problems. Meanwhile, we can make do temporarily with some very ingenious case studies of historical processes of considerable interest in the social sciences, such as Foucault's (1965) or Ilza Veith's (1965) studies of the historical development of the concepts of mental illness or Ariès's (1962) study of the discovery of childhood in the declining century of the French monarchy.

It would not be too encouraging if these archival centers were merely accumulating footlockers full of data. In this day and age, one wants data stored in such form that it can be retrieved at one's fingertips, preferably already analyzed. Concomitant with the data amassing, there has been considerable progress in information storage and retrieval of a relevant type. Among the more advanced systems are the adaptation of the General Inquirer system (Stone et al., 1966) to the content analysis of social survey data and the comparable French system by Cros, Gardin, and Lévy (1964) called SYNTOL. Also deserving of mention in this connection are the MIT attempts to adapt the multiple-access computer facilities to the problem of retrieving and analyzing their survey data. As these developments continue, the new generation (which will supposedly have mastered the use of the computer by the time they complete junior high school) will not have to test their basic social science theories by means of hand-sorting thousands of paper slips. The availability of these retrieval systems will perhaps beguile the new generation into beginning the enterprise with the expectation that they can derive their answer by punching out a few data-control cards. They will find, of course, that they were misled in expecting to find a royal road, and that answers come only to those who ask the right questions. But the important thing is that they will have taken the first step, with which even the journey of a thousand leagues is supposed to begin.

Availability of Broader Samples

This somewhat extended discussion of data archives should not convey the impression that the new movement into the natural environment which I am urging and predicting involves only post factum, secondary analyses of already collected data. It involves also the collection of field data after the formulation of one's *a priori* hypotheses. With increasing frequency, however, it will involve collecting the data from a broader 'population than is represented by the local college-sophomore sample currently used in so many of our laboratory manipulational studies. Increasingly we will feel compelled to employ national and even transnational samples. Several advances, recently made or impending, promise to give us access to broader populations. One of these is the composite nationwide survey where the polling agencies combine into one survey the needs of several individual researchers. The NORC at Chicago and the ORC at Princeton are both organizing this "caravan" type of enterprise. It then becomes possible for several individual researchers, each of whom needs only five or ten minutes of questions put to the interviewees, to combine their items into a composite inventory which is then administered to a nationwide sample. In this way the big investment of locating the representative sample of interviewees is shared among the researchers, who then have to pay additionally only for that segment of the time which is devoted to the questions which they contributed to the inventory.

We must also broaden our concept of the nationwide survey along the lines suggested by Rossi and others, so that the interviewers would not merely put questions to the respondents but would also manipulate variables and create miniature experiments on the doorstep. We must also broaden our horizons to think of setting up a machinery that would facilitate cross-national research of the type exhibited by Segall, Campbell, and Herskovits (1966). This would involve organizing our American social scientists doing research in other cultural areas, as suggested by Campbell, so that they could be asked to conduct experiments or surveys for many researchers while doing their field work. Or it might involve establishing a mutually helpful network of social scientists in the various social areas so that they could carry out each other's research on a cross-national basis, as proposed at the recent Ibadan Conference (Smith, 1968) and whose implementation is beginning in the form of the newsletter being edited by Triandis (1967).

Unobtrusive Measures for Use in Field Situations

To conduct correlational and manipulational research in field settings, it is more important than in the laboratory to utilize measures of our independent, dependent, and control variables less reactive than paper-and-pencil questionnaires, requiring little overt cooperation from the subjects, and disturbing the ongoing processes as little as possible. Webb, Campbell, and their colleagues (1966) recently reviewed such nonreactive measures that have been or could be used in the social sciences. Many of these unobtrusive measures are quite ingenious and amusing. The finding of "traces" that allow the retrospective construction of events has often shown great ingenuity, such as McClelland's (1961) use of pottery remnants to chart the economic trends in Greece two or three millennia ago, or vase paintings to trace trends in Hellenic need achievement. Likewise demanding of ingenuity are prospective measures of behavior that will not disturb the individual being measured, such as Bechtel's (1967) study of the movement of visitors in museums.

Mere mention of such terms as "bugging" and "wiretapping" serves to remind us that use of these unobtrusive measures gives rise to some moral anxieties. We remarked earlier in this chapter that researchers are tending to look elsewhere than to laboratory manipulational studies because of certain moral qualms about such laboratory research. It is sobering to point out here that while testing in the natural settings provides relief to our moral sensibilities in some regards (e.g., in lessening the requirements for noxious manipulations) it is more worrisome in others, such as on this issue of the invasion of privacy. It seems that there will be no escaping the necessity for making decisions among alternatives, all of which involve ethical difficulties.

ADVANCES IN DATA ANALYSES

Several advances in techniques of data analysis also promise to facilitate utilization of natural environments for the testing of basic theoretical hypotheses. I am referring here not so much to the general recent progress in the area of mathematical analysis and statistical evaluation, but more especially to certain advances of particular importance in dealing with the problems inherent in utilizing field situations for hypothesis testing. In this discussion I can mention briefly only a half dozen of such advances, including content analysis, handling "dirty" data, computer simulation of social and prognative processes, mathematical models in social research, the multivariate analysis of qualitative data, handling the problems in measuring change, and dealing with complex units of sampling.

The problem of content analysis is, of course, a central one in the utilization of personal documents, responses to opinion surveys, recorded conversations, etc., such as tend to constitute the data relevant to the dependent (and even the independent) variables when we conduct our research in natural settings. Progress in this field was not terribly impressive in the decade after Berelson (1952) published his book on this topic. Much of it is found in the book edited by Pool (1959). More recently the field has shown signs of moving forward once again. Part of the impetus has come from developments we already considered, such as the use of computers in retrieving data from the archives of opinion-survey responses (Stone *et al.*, 1962; Cros, Gardin, and Lévy, 1964). The work by the Stanford group (North *et al.*, 1963; Moses *et al.*, 1967), on the analysis of international communication during crisis is another sign of renewed effort to solve some of the perennial problems of this area.

Several attacks have also been made on the problem of handling the "dirty" data that confronts one with more regularity in the field studies than in experimentation conducted in the laboratory. We have in mind here such problems as the disproportionate problem that arises when one must accept the differential availability of cases to fill his cells when doing work in the natural environment rather than being able to assign cases to cells as in laboratory manipulational experiments. The newer statistical texts (Winer, 1962) discuss in detail the adaptation of procedures like analysis of variance and covariance to the cases of disproportionate n's quite explicitly, whereas the earlier texts discuss them, if at all, only programmatically in footnotes. Likewise the problem of unequal intervals, which again arises more frequently in natural settings where one must intervene when the opportunity arises, rather than at predetermined regular times, now is less of an inconvenience than heretofore. Procedures for doing trend analysis with unequal n's and intervals, which previously required great effort and creative ingenuity on the part of the investigator when he tried to analyze his data, have now been laid out for us in cookbook fashion (Gaito and Turner, 1963; Gaito, 1965). The problem of noisy unreliability that confronts any social scientist who deals with the kinds of records one obtains in field research, such as observers' reports, autobiographies, etc., has also received some attention of late by the anthropologist Naroll (1962), who suggests procedures for extracting the information from such case-history materials.

Another methodological innovation for analyzing the multivariable data that we need to face when doing research in natural settings is the use of computer simulation techniques. We have in mind both the prognostic simulations of social processes, such as the election studies by Pool, Abelson, and Popkin (1964), and the process simulations, such as those by Gullahorn and Gullahorn (1963, 1965), of elementary social behavior, and the work by Abelson and Bernstein (1963) on community controversies. The application of simulation techniques using the computer in understanding social processes is conveniently reviewed by Abelson (1967, 1968).

Progress of a very noticeable and promising nature with broad implications for the social sciences, but having sufficient specific relevance to the problems of testing in natural settings to bear mention here, is the recent flourishing of the multivariate analysis area. Cattell (1967) has recently edited a handbook that reviews recent progress in this area. There have during the past several years been a number of ingenious applications of multivariate analysis to the archival data involving national units (Alker and Russett, 1965; Moses et al., 1967; Rummell, 1963). Of particular interest are the developments of multivariate analysis to deal with the qualitative, metricless data which frequently confronts one in field research. We have in mind here the procedures of Shepard (1962, 1963, 1964) and Kruskal (1964) that can start off with data consisting of no more than the rank ordering of pairs of stimulus objects with respect to similarity and can end up with a quantitative definition of the dimensions underlying those ordinal data. Similar procedures of multivariate analysis are being developed by Guttman (1967; in press) and Lingoes (in press). When I speak of multivariate analysis, I do so with the knowledge that though it is a big thing, there are those who do not love it. My feeling is that its misuse and overuse do not mitigate against its value when appropriately employed, as in field situations where we must deal with many simultaneous covariants. There have been some gropings forward on the problem of measuring change, which involves certain methodological and philosophical difficulties that arise even in laboratory situations. We have to deal with comparing changes from different baselines, or between pairs of groups that are different in absolute as well as relative scores. This problem confronts us with special urgency in field situations, where it is often impossible to control or equate the initial levels of our units. In laboratory situations which permit random assignment of subjects to conditions, it is usually possible to obtain at least equal initial levels as regards group means, so that we need worry only about different baselines of individuals within groups, as when we are estimating error variance. In field settings, the group means themselves frequently provide different baselines from which change must be measured. The scope of the problem and some possible solutions have been discussed by Bereiter, Horst, Cattell, and others in a book edited by Harris (1963). We should also mention at least in passing the area of sampling statistics, which has not to my mind witnessed any revolutionary advances in the past few years, but which does show some moderately interesting innovations, such as Kish's (1961) work in achieving homogeneity in areal units, which is relevant to research in natural settings utilizing political divisions rather than individual persons for our hypothesis testing.

CONCLUSION

Since we have traveled a rather circuitous route and paused along the way at several points, it would make for clarity if we here, in concluding our discussion, reviewed our main line of development. We elected at the outset to retain our "establishment" conviction that basic theory-oriented research will result in more useful contributions to social psychology in the long run than will action-oriented research. But we did argue that we social psychologists, while continuing to focus our main hypothesis-testing effort in laboratory manipulational experiments, should and will move out of the laboratory into the natural world more frequently than is now the custom when we undertake to test our theory-devised hypotheses. By so doing, we can hope that the research will not only contribute to the development of basic theory, but that it will also keep these theories from becoming Mandarin exercises—and might provide some immediate "fall-out" regarding directives for action. We reviewed a number of forces coming from within and from outside our academic community that are motivating a movement toward such hypothesis-testing in field settings. More important, perhaps, we have attempted to touch upon a number of methodological advances, contributed from over the whole range of the social sciences, that will make the doing of good basic research in natural settings not only desirable, but feasible as well. The exploitation of the possibilities inherent in these diverse advances will be facilitated by increasing cross-disciplinary communication. Volumes like the present one are a partial solution to the problem of providing this communication among specialists working on related problems but separated by conventional disciplinary walls.

REFERENCES

ABELSON, R. P. 1967. Mathematical models in social psychology. In L. Berkowitz (Ed.), *Advances in experimental social psychology.* Vol. 3. New York: Academic Press.

———. 1968. Simulation of social behavior. In G. Lindzey and E. Aronson (Eds.) *Handbook of social psychology.* (Rev. ed.) Reading, Mass.: Addison-Wesley.

———, and A. BERNSTEIN. 1963. A computer simulation model of community referendum controversies. *Public Opinion Quarterly,* 27: 93–122.

ALKER, H. R. 1965. *Mathematics and politics.* New York: Macmillan.

———. 1966a. Causal inference and political analysis. In J. M. Claunch (Ed.), *Mathematical application in political science II.* Dallas: Southern Methodist University.

———. 1966b. Comparison of aggregate political and social data: potentialities and problems. In S. Rokkan (Ed.), *Comparative social science research.* The Hague: Mouton.

———, and B. M. RUSSETT. 1965. *World politics in the general assembly.* New Haven: Yale University Press.

ANDO, A., F. M. FISHER and H. A. SIMON. 1963. *Essays on the structure of social science models.* Cambridge: MIT Press.

ANNIS, A. P. 1967. The autobiography: its uses and values in professional psychology. *Journal of Consulting Psychology.* 14: 9–17.

ARIÈS, P. 1962. *Centuries of childhood.* New York: Alfred A. Knopf.

ARONSON, E. 1966. Avoidance of intersubject communication. *Psychological Reports,* 19: 238.

BAUER, R. (Ed.), 1966. *Social indicators.* Cambridge: MIT Press.

BECHTEL, R. B. 1967. The study of man: human movement and architecture. *Trans-Action,* 4: 53–56.

BERG, I. A. (Ed.). 1966. *Response set in personality assessment.* Chicago: Aldine Publishing Company.

BERKOWITZ, L. B. (Ed.). 1967. *Advances in experimental social psychology.* Vol. 3. New York: Academic Press.

BERELSON, B. 1952. *Content analysis in communication research.* Glencoe, Ill.: Free Press.

BISCO, R. L. 1967. Social science data archives: progress and prospect. *Social Sciences Information,* 4: 39–74.

BLAYLOCK, H. M. 1961. Evaluating the relative importance of variables. *American Sociological Review,* 26: 866–74.

―――. 1964. *Causal inferences in nonexperimental research.* Chapel Hill: University of North Carolina Press.

―――. 1965. Theory building and the statistical concept of interaction. *American Sociological Review,* 30: 374–80.

―――. 1966. The identification problem and theory building: the case of status inconsistency. *American Sociological Review,* 31: 52–61.

BOUDON, R. 1965. Methodes d'analyse causale. *Revue Francaise de Sociologie,* 6: 24–43.

―――. 1965. A method of linear causal analysis: dependence analysis. *American Sociological Review,* 30: 365–74.

BRAYFIELD, A. H. (Ed.). 1967. Ethics in human research issues. *American Psychologist,* 22: 345–99.

BROCK, T. C., and L. A. BECKER. 1966. "Debriefing" and susceptibility to subsequent experimental manipulation. *Journal of Experimental Social Psychology,* 2: 314–23.

BUREAU OF APPLIED SOCIAL RESEARCH, Columbia University. 1965. *A directory of information resources in the U.S.* Washington, D.C.: National Referral Center for Science and Technology.

CAMPBELL, D. T. 1963. From description to experimentation: interpreting trends as quasi experiments. In C. W. Harris (Ed.), *Problems in measuring change.* Madison: University of Wisconsin Press.

―――, and D. W. FISKE. 1959. Convergent and discriminant validation by the multitrait-multimethod matrix. *Psychological Bulletin,* 56: 81–105.

―――, and J. C. STANLEY. 1963. Experimental and quasi-experimental designs for research on teaching. In N. L. Gage (Ed.), *Handbook of research on teaching.* Chicago: Rand McNally.

―――, N. MILLER, J. LUBETSKY, and E. J. O'CONNELL. 1964. Varieties of projection in trait attribution. *Psychological Monographs,* 78: No. 592.

CATTELL, R. B. (Ed.). 1967. *Handbook of multivariate psychology.* Chicago: Rand McNally.

CLARK, K. E. 1967. Privacy and behavioral research. *Science,* 155: 535–38.

CLAUNCH, J. M. (Ed.). 1965. *Mathematical applications in political science I.* Dallas: Southern Methodist University Press.

―――. 1966. *Mathematical applications in political science II.* Dallas: Southern Methodist University Press.

COLEMAN, J. 1964. *An introduction to mathematical sociology.* New York: Macmillan.

CROS, R. C., J. C. GARDIN, and F. LÉVY. 1964. L'automatisation des recherches documentaires: un modele general, le SYNTOL. Paris: Gauthier-Villars.

DE SOTO, C., and J. L. KUETHE. 1959. Set to claim undesirable symptoms in personality inventories. *Journal of Consulting Psychology,* 23: 496–500.

DOHRENWEND, B. P. 1966. Social status and psychological disorder: an issue of substance and an issue of method. *American Sociological Review,* 31: 14–34.

DUNCAN, O. D., A. CUZZART, and B. DUNCAN. 1961. *Statistical Geography.* New York: Free Press.

FEIERABEND, I. K., and R. L. FEIERABEND. 1966. Aggressive behavior within polities, 1948–1962: a cross-national study. *Journal of Conflict Resolution.* 10, 249–271.

FESTINGER, L., and D. KATZ. (Eds.). 1953. *Research methods in the behavioral sciences.* New York: Dryden.

FILLENBAUM, S. 1966. Prior deception and subsequent experimental performance: the "faithful" subject. *Journal of Personality and Social Psychology,* 4: 532–37.

FOUCAULT, M. 1965. *Madness and civilization.* New York: Pantheon.

FRENCH, J. R. P. 1963. Experiments in field settings. In L. Festinger and D. Katz (Eds.), *Research methods in the behavioral sciences.* New York: Dryden.

GAITO, J. 1965. Unequal intervals and unequal *n* in trend analysis. *Psychological Bulletin,* 63: 125–27.

―――, and E. TURNER. 1963. Error terms in trend analysis. *Psychological Bulletin,* 60: 464–74.

GLASER, W. A., and R. L. BISCO (Eds.). 1967. *Social science data archives in the United States.* New York: Columbia University, Bureau of Applied Social Research.

GREENBAUM, J. J. (Chm.). 1967. Symposium on psychological contributions to the study of history. *American Psychologist,* 22, 491.

GULLAHORN, J. T., and J. E. GULLAHORN. 1963. A computer model of elementary social behavior. In E. A. Feigenbaum and J. Feldman (Eds.), *Computers and thought.* New York: McGraw-Hill.

―――. 1965. Some computer application in social science. *American Sociological Review,* 30: 353–65.

GUTTMAN, L. 1967. Order analysis of correlation matrices. In R. B. Cattell (Ed.), *Handbook of multivariate experimental psychology.* Chicago: Rand McNally.

―――. (In Press) A general nonmetric technique for finding the smallest Euclidean space for a configuration of points. *Psychometrika.*

HARRIS, C. W. (Ed.). 1963. *Problems in measuring change.* Madison: University of Wisconsin Press.

JANIS, I. L. 1965. Professional roles, norms and ethics—a social psychological viewpoint. *Canadian Psychologist,* 6a: 143–54.

JOHNSTON, J. 1963. *Econometric methods.* New York: McGraw-Hill.

KELMAN, H. C. 1965. Manipulation of human behavior: an ethical dilemma for the social scientist. *Journal of Social Issues,* 21: 31–46.

―――. 1967. Human use of human subjects: the problem of deception in social psychological experiments. *Psychological Bulletin,* 67: 1–11.

KISH, L. 1961. A measurement of homogeneity in areal units, *Bulletin de L'Institut International de Statistique,* 31: 1–10.

KLEIN, L. R. 1962. *An introduction to econometrics.* Englewood Cliffs, N.J.: Prentice-Hall.

KRUSKAL, J. B. 1964. Multidimensional scaling by optimizing goodness of fit to nonmetric hypothesis. *Psychometrika,* 29: 1–27.

LACKLEN, R. J., (Ed.). Proceedings of 1965 Conference on use of life history data. Greensboro, N. C.: Richardson Foundation, 1965. (Mimeo.)

LANA, R. E. 1968. Pretest sensitization. In R. Rosenthal and R. Rosnow (Eds.), *Artifacts in social research.* New York: Academic Press.

LICKLIDER, J. C. R. 1966. A crux in scientific and technical communication. *American Psychologist,* 11: 1044–51.

LINDZEY, G., and E. ARONSON (Eds.). 1968. *Handbook of social psychology.* (2d ed.) Cambridge: Addison-Wesley.

LINGOES, J. C. (In press) An IBM 7090 program for Guttman-Lingoes smallest space analysis, I. *Behavioral Science.*

McCLELLAND, D. C. 1961. *The achieving society.* Princeton, N. J.: Van Nostrand.

McGUIRE, W. J. 1965. Discussion of W. N. Schoenfeld's paper. In O. Klineberg and R. Christie (Eds.), *Perspectives in social psychology.* New York: Holt, Rinehart and Winston.

———. 1967. Some impending reorientations in social psychology. *Journal of Experimental Social Psychology,* 3: 124–39.

———. 1968. Personality and susceptibility to social influence. In E. F. Borgatta and W. W. Lambert (Eds.), *Handbook of personality theory and research.* Chicago: Rand McNally.

MacRAE, D., and J. A. MELDRUM. 1960. Critical elections in Illinois: 1888–1958. *American Political Science Review,* 54: 669–83.

MERRIT, R. L., and S. ROKKAN (Eds.). 1966. *Comparing nations.* New Haven: Yale University Press.

MOSES, L. E., R. A. BOWDY, O. R. HOLSTI, J. B. KADANE, and J. S. MILSTEIN. 1967. Scaling data on inter-nation action. *Science,* 156: 1054–59.

NAROLL, R. 1962. *Data quality control.* New York: Free Press.

NORTH, R., O. R. HOLSTI, M. G. ZANINOVICH, and D. A. ZINNES. 1963. *Content analysis.* Evanston: Northwestern University Press.

ORLANS, H. (Ed.). 1967. *The use of social research in federal domestic programs.* 4 vols. House of Representatives, Subcommittee on Research and Technology Programs. Washington, D.C.: U.S. Government Printing Office.

ORNE, M. T. 1962. On the social psychology of the psychological experiment: with particular reference to demand characteristics and their implications. *American Psychologist,* 17: 776–83.

PELZ, D. C. 1959. Teasing causal connections out of "dynamic" correlations. Ann Arbor: University of Michigan, SRC.

———, and F. M. ANDREWS. 1964. Detecting causal priorities in panel study data. *American Sociological Review,* 29: 836–48.

POOL, I. de S., (Ed.). 1959. *Trends in content analysis.* Urbana: University of Illinois Press.

———, R. P. ABELSON, and POPKIN. 1964. *Candidates, issues and strategies.* Cambridge: MIT Press.

RICHARDSON, L. F. 1960. *Arms and insecurity.* Pittsburgh: Boxwood Press.

RING, K. 1967. Experimental social psychology: some sober questions about some frivolous values. *Journal of Experimental Social Psychology,* 3: 113–23.

ROKKAN, S., and G. A. ALMOND. 1965. International conference on comparative social science research, April 22–24, 1965. *Items,* 19: 29–31.

RORER, L. G. 1965. The great response-style myth. *Psychological Bulletin,* 63: 129–56.

ROSENBERG, M. J. 1965. When dissonance fails: on eliminating evaluation apprehension from attitude measurement. *Journal of Personality and Social Psychology,* 1: 28–42.

ROSENTHAL, R. 1966. *Experimenter effects in behavioral research.* New York: Appleton-Century-Crofts.

ROSENTHAL, R., and R. ROSNOW. 1968. *Artifacts in social research.* New York: Academic Press.

ROZELLE, R. M. 1965. An exploration of two quasi-experimental designs: the cross-lagged panel correlation and the multiple time series. Unpublished Master's thesis, Northwestern University.

————. 1966. Causal relations in attitude change as demonstrated through the cross-lagged panel correlation. Evanston: Northwestern University. (Mimeo.)

————, and D. T. CAMPBELL. 1966. More plausible rival hypotheses in the cross-lagged panel correlation technique. Houston: University of Houston. (Mimeo.)

RUMMEL, R. J. 1963. Dimensions of conflict behavior within and between nations. In General Systems, *Yearbook of the society for general systems research,* 8: 1–50.

————. 1966. The dimensionality of nations project. In R. L. Merritt and S. Rokkan (Eds.). *Comparing nations.* New Haven: Yale University Press.

RUNDQUIST, E. A. 1966. Item and response characteristics in attitude and personality measurement: a reaction to L. G. Rorer's "The great response-style myth." *Psychological Bulletin,* 66: 166–77.

SCHNORE, L. F. 1961. The statistical measurement of urbanization and economic development. *Land Economics,* 37: 229–45.

SCHON, D. A. 1967. *Technology and change.* New York: Delacorte Press.

SEGALL, M., D. CAMPBELL, and M. J. HERSKOVITS. 1966. *The influence of culture on visual perception.* Indianapolis: Bobbs-Merrill.

SHEPARD, R. N. 1962. The analysis of proximities: multidimensional scaling with an unknown distance function, I. *Psychometrika,* 27: 125–40. II. *Psychometrika,* 27: 219–46.

————. 1963. An analysis of proximities as a technique for the study of information processing in man. *Human Factors,* 5: 33–48.

————. 1964. Attention and the metric structure of the stimulus space. *Journal of Mathematical Psychology,* 1: 54–87.

SHERIF, M., and C. W. SHERIF. 1964. *Reference groups.* New York: Harper.

SHERIF, M., O. J. HARVEY, B. J. WHITE, W. R. HOOD, and C. W. SHERIF. 1961. *Intergroup conflict and cooperation: the Robbers Cave experiment.* Norman: University of Oklahoma Institute of Intergroup Relations.

SHERIF, M., and C. I. HOVLAND. 1961. *Social judgment.* New Haven, Conn.: Yale University Press.

SIMON, H. A. 1957. *Models of man.* New York: Wiley.

SMITH, M. B. 1967. Conflicting values affecting behavioral research with children, *American Psychologist,* 22: 377–82.

————. 1968. Conference report: international conference on social-psychological research in developing countries. Ibadan, Dec. 29, 1966–Jan. 5, 1967. *Journal of Personality and Social Psychology.* 8: 1–98.

STOKES, D. E. 1965. A variance components model of political effects. In J. M. Claunch '(Ed.), *Mathematical applications in political science I.* Dallas: Southern Methodist University Press.

STONE, P. J., R. F. BALES, Z. NAMENWORTH, and D. M. OGILVIE. 1962. The general inquirer: a computer system for content analysis and retrieval based on sentence as a unit of information. *Behavioral Science,* 7: 484–94.

————, D. C. DUNPHY, M. S. SMITH, and D. M. OGILVIE. 1966. *The general inquirer: a computer approach to content analysis.* Cambridge: MIT Press.

STRICKER, L. J., S. MESSICK, and D. N. JACKSON. 1967. Suspicion of deception: implications for conformity research. *Journal of Personality and Social Psychology,* 5: 379–89.

TINBERGEN, J. 1937. *Statistical testing of business cycle theories, II.* Geneva: League of Nations.

TRIANDIS, H. C. 1967. *Cross-Cultural Psychology Newsletter.* 1. Urbana: University of Illinois, Department of Psychology.

VALAVANIS, S. 1959. *Econometrics: an introduction to maximum likelihood methods.* New York: McGraw-Hill.

VEITH, I. 1965. *Hysteria: history of a disease.* Chicago: University of Chicago Press.

VROOM, V. H. 1966. A comparison of static and dynamic correlational methods in the study of organizations. *Organizational Behavior and Human Performance,* 1: 55–70.

WEBB, E. J., D. T. CAMPBELL, R. D. SCHWARTZ, and L. SECHREST. 1966. *Unobtrusive measures: nonreactive research in the social sciences.* Chicago: Rand McNally.

WESKOFF, M. 1960. Ethical standards and divided loyalties. *American Psychologist,* 15: 656–60.

WINER, B. J. 1962. *Statistical principles in experimental design.* New York: McGraw-Hill.

WOLD, H. 1964. *Econometric model building: essays on the causal chain approach.* Amsterdam: North Holland.

WUEBBEN, P. L. 1967. Honesty of subjects and birth order. *Journal of Personality and Social Psychology,* 5: 350–52.

ZEMACH, R., and M. ROKEACH. 1966. The pledge to secrecy: a method to assess violations. *American Psychologist,* 21: 612.

3

THEORETICAL AND SUBSTANTIVE BIASES IN SOCIOLOGICAL RESEARCH

RAYMOND W. MACK

Back when most of the people who are now faculty members in departments of sociology were graduate students in departments of sociology, the big news was methodological innovation and rigor. One of the role requirements associated with the status of graduate student is the obligation to feel contempt for one's predecessors, and we sighed or sneered, as befit our individual styles, for the poor souls who had tried to understand the gang without understanding sampling theory, or had groped toward insights about the ghetto or the professional thief without the aid of nonparametric statistics, or had tried to chart the course of the Polish peasant in Europe and America without the aid of scalograms. Nowadays, with computers able to run our analysis of variance with considerably more alacrity than we are often able to muster in meeting its assumptions, perhaps we should pause during one of the rounds of congratulations on our methodological sophistication and ask a few searching questions about our theory.

Acceptance of the value of objectivity in data-gathering and reporting is pretty much taken for granted by contemporary social scientists. Even the ethnomethodologists who deplore the raw empiricism of behavioristic social science are the first to support a Lundberg-like position on reliability: theirs is the suggestion that we need sound films as raw data for the analysis of social action.

But just as real as any bias in data gathering are those biases which are theoretical and substantive: pressures which influence the selection of a research problem, the formulation of a research design, and the interpretation of data. I want to address several of these biases:

1. Ethnocentrism, including the aggrandizement effect;
2. Tool bias, or problem selection on the basis of tool availability;
3. Fiduciary drift, or monetary magnetism in problem selection;
4. The debunking bias, or gee-whiz approach to social science;

5. Theory-shyness, or the false modesty cop-out; and

6. Theoretical inefficiency: labels and nonvariable frames of reference.

After brief comments on each of these theoretical or substantive biases, I shall close with a plea for comparative structural analysis, which seems to me one route helpful in avoiding most of these errors.

ETHNOCENTRISM

The lamentable fact is that the bulk of our principles, propositions, and laws in sociology are generalizations based upon observations and measurements made in Western, urban, industrial societies. We generalize about the human group, but we study the adult, middle-class, white, urban male. Some of what looks like ethnocentrism here may be simply the sin of studying what is most convenient. No matter, the consequences are the same: theories built upon data from samples of inadequate universes.

One need only examine the literature in such a limited institutional area as the family to see the extent to which our generalizations about all families are built on knowledge about middle-class families. If there is an area in American society about which social scientists know less than they know about the lower class, it is without doubt the upper class. It is perhaps the mixture of awe and horror with which we view the top stratum of our society that keeps us at such a distance from it and leads to some of our sillier generalizations about power elites. Social scientists look upon the upper class somewhat as John Birch Society members look upon communists: as a fantastic combination of evil intent and competence.

Ethnocentrism has led sociology to be about Western, industrial peoples, especially Americans, especially middle-class ones. Ethnocentrism is by no means limited to tribes, nation-states, and total societies. All sorts of groups have a higher opinion of themselves than of others, whether nations, street-corner gangs, religious denominations, universities, treaty alliances, or families. Caplow, in a study of 33 different types of organizations, found that raters overestimated the prestige of their own organization (as evaluated by others) eight times as often as they underrated it (1964). Research at two Strategic Air Command Air Force bases revealed that more than half the squadrons were ranked first in prestige by their own members, and that all squadrons ranked themselves higher than people in other squadrons ranked them (Mack, 1954). A study of 122 university departments showed that 51 per cent of the departments were rated by their own department chairmen as among the first five in the country; only 5 per cent even considered themselves below average (Caplow and McGee, 1962).

University of Chicago graduate students are likely to be better acquainted with the work of Keyfitz and Hauser than that of Campbell and Young; graduate students at Northwestern may be better read in Becker and Greer than in Janowitz and Rossi. In a multi-group discipline, however, departmental ethnocentrism is probably not terribly important. (I don't believe in a conspiracy theory of history.) The aggrandizement effect can have important consequences locally, however, especially if a department is heavily oriented toward a particular technique—which brings us to the second point.

TOOL BIAS

At a recent meeting of the American Sociological Association, an earnest graduate student whom I encountered at a publisher's soiree informed me that he was going to use analysis of covariance for his dissertation. This prompted a question from me, to which he replied that he had not decided yet what he would study. Such enthusiasm for tools as opposed to products reminds one of a little boy hard at work with hammer, nails, and wood, uncertain of what he is building.

Selecting a problem for social research on the basis of the availability of tools lets the sharpness of the tool determine what we shall build. This seems to me exactly backward: our theory should guide us to know what needs building, and lead us to select appropriate tools for the job. There are no inherently correct tools. Method is a matter of strategy, not of morals.

Tool bias accounts in part for the lack of historical perspective in contemporary sociology and for the absence of process analysis. Tool bias, in other words, is as serious a hindrance to the development of our discipline when the tools are theoretical as when they are technological. The structural bias in social science theory arises from convenience: it is easier to count our data at two points in time than to observe and explain how the differences in what we measure came about. Using cultural relativism as an example of the bias which can stem from commitment to a theoretical tool, Peter Worsley states the case nicely.

Little wonder, then, that the central process of our time, perhaps, in retrospect, one of the crucial thresholds in the evolution of human society—the crossing of the development-barrier—has not been, and could not be, meaningfully handled within such frameworks; nor that so many anthropologists, working as they do in societies where Development Plans, political parties, trade unions, cooperatives, cold and hot war, State intervention in peasant agriculture, massive labour migration, urban explosion, are part of the everyday experience of members of the very societies they are studying, nevertheless appear to be dealing with Platonic insulated micro-worlds where such things, apparently, never intrude.

The paucity, and relative poverty, of comparative studies which even touch upon problems of change from one type of society to another, is equally "built-in", since, for formalist universalism, all societies are temporally equal (the "ethnographic present"), and are never located in any developmental process or classified as cases of particular developmental types; and for holistic pluralism, even in its more sophisticated varieties, categories such as "state" or "stateless" are established, with little or no consideration given to defining the conditions for their emergence, persistence, or displacement. In other words, the typologies in what few comparative studies we possess are static and/or formal, rather than dynamic and processual (1966).

FIDUCIARY DRIFT

Not totally, I am happy to say, but to an extent, research emphases in social science tend to go where the money is. Because this is a somewhat embarrassing point, let us be brief about it.

The now enormous field of the sociology of medicine was virtually nonexistent until the magnetism of research funds drew scholars to turn their lamps that way.

This reverse Midas effect (i.e., all that turns to gold we touch) is of course related to our previous point about departmental ethnocentrism. The quality of their most productive scholars causes research money to flow to a department. The existence of the research money, in turn, helps some graduate students to decide what is their central theoretical interest, and to apprentice themselves to the moneyed scholars, who turn out more research, and receive more grants, and 'twas ever thus. This is not to argue that the apprentices are cruelly exploited. They often (and I suspect usually) receive good research training. But since most graduate students want the money, and most senior scholars want the best graduate students, the system does not encourage the most innovative degree candidates to gamble on their most far-out ideas.

While some scholars will insist on being exceptions to the fiduciary drift, graduate training programs in general socialize us to respond to such challenges as the war on poverty. As soon as Congress appropriated money enough to assure that we would not be poor, we began to study those who are.

THE DEBUNKING BIAS, OR GEE-WHIZ APPROACH

Social science in general, and sociology and anthropology in particular, have been built, in part, on a tradition of gathering data which show that what everyone believed was true is false, a tradition of questioning common sense. Such an approach has built-in rewards. It provides the practitioner automatically with one kind of intellectual superiority: he knows things most people don't know. For those of us who teach (and that's most of us), it has a certain charm as an attention-getting device. But debunking as an approach to problem-selection exacts a certain toll; it is hardly the most efficient approach to building a systematic body of theory.

Our traditional concern with fascinating data gives the content of the social sciences, and especially of sociology and anthropology, a certain journalistic, feature-story flavor. We have studies of dance musicians, janitors, medical students, and Wall Street lawyers, but we have little systematic data on the occupations in which most Americans work: semiskilled labor, and submanagement, subprofessional white collar jobs. Studies of the upwardly mobile far outnumber those of the stable or downwardly mobile; we have far more research on Who's Who listings than on delinquent credit listings. We know more about divorce than about stable marriage, and have more data on criminals than on law abiders.

This approach has an added disadvantage: it offers a seductive encouragement to select research topics congenial to our social, political, and economic biases, but to ignore related but personally unrewarding questions. Our body of knowledge on racial and ethnic stereotypes offers a reasonable example of the outcome. We have piles of studies documenting the falsity of some racial and ethnic stereotypes and probing the social and personal characteristics of people who believe them. I know of only one study, done by a sociologist at an action agency, which shows that, actually, Jews have more money than other people; he never published it.

What do we know about things we don't want to believe? Where are our studies of the white Southerner as an ethnic minority? Who measures the extent of prejudice and discrimination against white Southerners? How many studies have we of the relative efficiency of dictatorship and democracy, comparing and contrasting the two on a set of theoretically derived variables? In what social science textbook would you look for a discussion of the positive functions of fundamentalist Protestantism in American society? What work in criminology provides us with a thoughtful analysis of why the homicide rate is markedly lower in Franco's fascist Spain than it was in the days of the Republic?

Much of the debunking emphasis in research problem selection is possible for a reason pointed out in a recent study based on interviews with thirty leading American sociologists (Popovich, 1966): empirical research is not usually guided by systematic theory—which brings us to our next point.

THEORY-SHYNESS

Graduate training in any social science does not encourage one to be lavish in his expenditure of generalizations. Education called theory is often really concerned with the history of social thought—as if theory were something that has already happened. Most of our training in methodology rewards caution; the fledgling research scholar is asked whether he has met the assumptions required to use that statistic, and made to confess that he is not generalizing beyond the universe he sampled.

The consequences of such occupational socialization are readily evident in the lengthy disclaimers with which social scientists customarily conclude their contributions to the professional journals. Articles in the *American Journal of Sociology, Social Forces,* the *American Political Science Review,* the *Behavioral Scientist,* the *American Sociological Review,* and the like, often end with several paragraphs detailing the inadequacies of the author's research design and execution and denying any intention on his part to generalize about the findings, that is, to theorize. Perhaps we could inaugurate a FRIN-convention. Were editors to agree to print, in block caps, at the end of each article where the author deemed it appropriate, the letters F.R.I.N., we would all understand that further research is needed. The deletion of the several paragraphs per article devoted to a discussion of this fact might allow room for another article per issue. Better yet, editors might demand that each author have a try at a careful, imaginative interpretation of the likely meanings of his data. As Rupert Vance says:

In science as in poker, we realize we can play it one of two ways. We can play it close to the vest, that is, maximize description and minimize synthesis, or we can play it for maximum gains of human knowledge. In other words as Roger Nett says, the working scientist can be either a tight system builder or a loose system builder. A tight system has high validity and low generality. A line which twists and turns to touch a hundred points in a distribution is worth no more than the hundred points. A line which touches ten points and comes within hailing distance of 90 is usually worth more than the hundred points; it may give the scientist a curve of distribution or an equation of probability for his colleagues to test in a sequence of 100 analyses. "There exists a known tendency for all thought systems to be vulnerable." Accordingly the closer one sticks to his data, the less vulnerable are his generalizations and ofttimes the less important. A loose thought system sacrifices accuracy for the sake of generalization.

In science when one plays for double or nothing, he runs the risk of evolving a system of high generalizations and low validity. Obviously this represents high vulnerability and we are all cautious enough to dread the results. But we should remember there are two forms of maximum error: The first is a system that misses contact with the known facts at every point of observation. The second is no system at all. This is maximum error, for it equates with total ignorance. As a matter of fact, I am willing to make the claim that he who develops a theory capable of being proved invalid makes a contribution. In statistics the disproof of any hypothesis is accepted as a way station on the road to knowledge (1952).

In this context, what can we say of our next heading?

LABELS AND OTHER NONVARIABLE FRAMES OF REFERENCE

Research on the structure of racial segregation and the process of desegregation has led me to conclude that at least two concepts basic to contemporary social science theory sometimes do more to impede than to inform our insights. The concept of culture we too often use descriptively rather than analytically; we employ culture as a label rather than as a variable. The idea of culture, of course, has served a wonderfully valuable purpose in the development of social science, alerting us to the pitfalls of instinct theory and of biological determinism, and helping us to see and study the importance of socialization and normative structures.

It is not the use but the misuse of the concept of culture which I am deploring, the use of the word as a label, a substitute for structural analysis, as in "Why is there more racial discrimination in America than in France? Because France and the United States have different cultures."

I am not sure that the other concept I am concerned about is so much misused as miscast: the idea of social equilibrium. In social science, the notion of equilibrium often deflects analysis rather than guiding it. The use of the concept of equilibrium seems to me to provide a classic example of one of Herbert Blumer's criticisms of sociological theory:

It is remarkably susceptible to the importation of schemes from outside its own empirical field, as in the case of the organic analogy, the evolutionary doctrine, physicalism, the instinct doctrine, behaviorism, psychoanalysis, and the doctrine of the conditioned reflex (1954).

The aim of theory is the explanation of data. Theory works, then, by abstracting and generalizing from observations. A concept is useful to the extent that it subsumes a class of observations or a set of relationships between classes of observations. Let us examine the concepts of culture and of equilibrium within the framework of these criteria to see how useful they are to social scientists.

CULTURE AS A CLASS OF OBSERVATIONS

The classic characterization of culture refers to it as "that complex whole which includes knowledge, belief, art, morals, law, custom, and any other capabilities and habits acquired by man as a member of society" (Tylor, 1871). Culture, then, consists of commonly accepted and expected ideas, attitudes, values, and habits of individuals which they learn in connection with social living. For the individual in the early years of life, culture is an enormous aid in training him to get on more effectively in his world. Each new generation does not have to begin from scratch, but profits from those around it, who, in turn, learned how to adjust to the physical and social world largely from their progenitors. Later, this new generation passes on to the next generation what it has learned from the previous one and what it has added to the cultural whole.

Culture may be defined, then, simply as shared learned behavior.

The concept of culture is sometimes invoked to explain racial and ethnic discrimination. Black and Atkins take this approach.

"May it not be," we asked ourselves, "that what is often taken for prejudice in the Southerner may be just a 'learned-by-rote' set of definitions and rules regarding his relationship to a certain object (the Negro), much as we all learn by rote a certain set of definitions and rules regarding our relationship to the flag of our country?" By what metaphysical twist of logic is the one to be regarded as being prejudiced while the other is not? (1950.)

As Van der Zanden says:

> According to this approach, the southerner may not be using the Negro as a
> scapegoat for projecting personal frustration. He may not be misinformed or
> uninformed about the characteristics of the Negro. He may not be suffering from
> some personality or situational insecurity. He may not be an "authoritarian per-
> sonality." These are one group of factors advanced to explain prejudice. By the
> same token, the southerner may not be acting in response to widespread, external
> conditions of social or economic disorganization. Nor may he have a vested
> interest—political, economic, or status—in the prevailing intergroup structure.
>
> Rather, the individual can be viewed as functioning within a subculture in
> which racial prejudice and discrimination are prescribed by the prevailing norms.
> "The function which anti-Negro reactions serve for most citizens in the South
> is that of keeping them in harmony with their society—of gaining for them,
> social approval or at least averting for them social disapproval." (Black and
> Atkins, 1950.) Only when the southerner is viewed by "outside" standards is he
> a "deviant." But if he were to act in conformity with the "outside" standards, or
> if he were to internalize these norms, he would be "out of step" within his home
> society. Within the southern social framework the white supremacist is not a
> deviant; rather, the deviant is the white who no longer fully practices and
> follows the southern patterns (1966).

The trouble with this use of the concept of culture is that it describes a set
of shared, learned behaviors, but goes nowhere toward explaining them.

Barbados, in the British West Indies, has a cultural background almost
identical with that of the old Black Belt of America's Deep South. Like the
American South, Barbados had imported slaves from Africa and built a plan-
tation system of fields worked by Negroes and owned and operated by
Anglo-Saxons. Like American Negroes, Barbadians saw a century elapse
between formal emancipation and significant participation in political power.
If the concept of culture means anything analytically, we can surely say that
these two populations have virtually identical cultural *roots.*

Yet in Barbados, both whites and Negroes speak West Indianized English, while in the Deep South both whites and Negroes drawl American.
Descendents of Britishers serve afternoon tea in Barbados; descendents of
Britishers serve coffee in South Carolina. Descendents of Britishers and of
their African field hands play cricket in Barbados, but baseball in Alabama.
The concept of culture can be used as a summary description of the shared,
learned behaviors which link these two societies, or as a concept to summarize the behaviors which differentiate between the two. Culture describes
the patterns of behavior, but it does not explain what induces changes in
the patterns.

During years of residence and field work in the American South, I have
been assured many times that: "You can't make fast changes in our Way of
Life." (Way of Life, of course, is simply the layman's phrasing of the concept
of culture.) "When our children have been brought up in Our Way of Life,"

I have been told, "you just can't expect them to change overnight." Yet, as a football fan, I have watched a long procession of those children follow a career like that of Charlie Conerly, formerly of the New York Giants. Conerly was born and reared in Mississippi. He had a fair chance to be socialized into the Way of Life. He went to a segregated church, ate in segregated restaurants, attended segregated movies, graduated from a segregated high school. He went to the segregated University of Mississippi, where he became All-American. And then he accepted a contract from the New York Giants. Overnight he learned to work with Negroes, play with Negroes, eat with Negroes, accept blocking from Negroes, and collect his paycheck. What does the concept of culture tell us about the rapid changes in everyday behavior patterns to which Mr. Conerly and many of his fellow Southerners are subjected in professional athletics? Or in the military?

Culture not only fails to explain rapid changes in patterns of behavior, it is useless in the analysis of why some individuals and groups deviate from what are supposedly accepted social norms. Where do the Hodding Carters and the Ralph McGills and the Margaret Longs come from? Our inability to account for their existence or behavior within the framework of cultural analysis is a classic example of what Dennis Wrong has described as sociology's "oversocialized conception of man" (1961).

In the sense of providing an oversocialized conception of man, the use of the concept of culture confronts us with the risk, I believe, of an inherently conservative analytic framework. Because of this, it is related to the second concept, the use of which may be hazardous for sound empirical description and hence deleterious for the development of theory: equilibrium.

EQUILIBRIUM AS A NONEMPIRICAL FRAME OF REFERENCE

In his frequently cited "A Revised Analytical Approach to the Theory of Social Stratification," Parsons says:

It is a condition of the stability of social systems that there should be an integration of the value standards of the component units to constitute a "common value system." . . . The existence of such a pattern system as a point of reference for the analysis of social phenomena is a central assumption which follows directly from the frame of reference of actions as applied to the analysis of social system (1953).

If this means what I think it means, it is demonstrably false, as is shown by such empirical work as M. G. Smith's *Stratification in Grenada* (1965). Indeed, any intergroup conflict situation seems to me evidence that, within a given social system at a given time, there exists a lack of "integration of the value standards." Such difficulties as the current desegregation problems in the United States stem precisely from the lack of a common culture throughout the society, the absence of an agreed-upon set of shared norms.

If, on the other hand, this is not intended to be an empirically testable statement, that is another matter. If the quotation means that the fact of the stability of a social system proves the existence of "an integration of the value standards of the component units," then it is true by definition, and hence useless as a theoretical tool for guiding empirical social research.

There is nothing inhibiting to the study of change in functional analysis, if by functional analysis we mean the attempt to describe and understand social structures and their consequences. But when we move from structure-functional analysis to functionalism and an equilibrium model of society, the problem of change tends to wither away under the heat of the analyst's concentration on the "steady state" of the social system. Following W. B. Cannon's *Wisdom of the Body* (1932), Parsons and other equilibrium functionalists conceive of human society as a normative order which is not only stable but intrinsically harmonious. This assumption leads to such phrasing as that wherein conflict is "introduced into the system." (Parsons, 1951b.) Like Cannon's body, Parsons' society benefits from automatic corrections and adjustments when disturbed by either external or internal forces.

The principal weakness of the equilibrium functionalist's model of social order is its failure to correspond to observed social reality. This becomes apparent when Parsons himself turns to the analysis of revolution, conflict, or other change. As Gouldner has said:

Indeed, the extent to which Parsons' efforts at theoretical and empirical analysis of change suddenly lead him to enlist a body of Marxist concepts and assumptions is nothing less than bewildering. It almost seems as if two sets of books were being kept, one for the analysis of equilibrium and another for the envestigation of change (1956).

But this is because the equilibrium model tends to be an -ism rather than a scientific theory. "Instead of being a lens which sharpens our perspective and puts social reality in focus, it becomes a pair of rose-colored glasses which distort reality, screening out the harsh facts about conflict of purpose and interest in human affairs" (Inkeles, 1964). To be rid of its evils, there is no need also to throw out structure-function as a frame of reference; we can get at the study of change via a framework specifying social organization and its consequences.

THE PROMISE OF COMPARATIVE STRUCTURAL ANALYSIS

The burden of my argument is this: The concept of culture has served us magnificently as a sensitizing concept; we ought not to degrade it by using it as a label which substitutes for analysis. The concept of equilibrium has, if anything, turned us away from problems of deviance and dynamics which we ought to address.

Let me close with a little positive thinking. We see more and more evidence of the theoretical payoff in carefully executed empirical research designed to contrast different structures within a single cultural context or to generalize about comparable structures across differing cultures.

The work of Joseph Gusfield (1965) on misplaced polarities in the study of social change attacks persuasively what he calls "the all too common practice of pitting tradition and modernity against each other as paired opposites." Faunce and Smucker (1966) have demonstrated through an ingenious, quasi-experimental design that social structure is a better predictor than culture of patterns of interaction at different occupational prestige levels. By gathering comparable data on a Michigan industrial town and a nonindustrial Michigan village, and on an industrialized Costa Rican village and a nonindustrialized Guatemalan one, they have shown that Latin American and North American cultures are less valuable variables than industrialization and lack of it for understanding the relationship between work and community status. Inkeles and Rossi (1956) weighed the structural as opposed to the cultural variables influencing occupational prestige in six industrial societies by comparing societies with very different cultural traditions, such as Germany, Japan, and the United States, as to the distribution of occupational prestige. The intercorrelations ran from $+.84$ to $+.94$, with correlations as high as $+.93$ between the United States and Japan, and $+.97$ between Germany and Great Britain.

I am analyzing data we have gathered this year on desegregation of education in ten American communities. Racial segregation in schools is an institutional complex. The establishment of and maintenance of a system of segregated educational facilities depends upon segregation not only of pupils, but of teachers, administrators, and public officials. Segregated education depends upon and feeds upon segregated churches, segregated businesses, segregated recreational facilities, and segregated neighborhoods. Segregated education, in turn, reinforces segregation in churches, barber shops, parks, banks, and city halls. Where, as in some of these communities, a crack appears in one part of the segregated structure, the rest of it begins to crumble.

The size, social structure, and distribution of power in these communities tell us more about the process of desegregation than do variations by regional subculture.

If sociology is to fulfill its promise as a science of social organization, it will probably do so through careful comparisons of social structures and processes, intrasocietally and intersocietally.

Interdisciplinary efforts have contributed a great deal to the theoretical development of the social sciences in the past twenty years. (I hope it is clear by now that by theory I do not mean architectonic structures composed of concepts without empirical referents; by theory I mean an explanation of data, phrased with such care that we can test the validity of the explanation itself with another set of data.) Interdisciplinary contributions to social science theory seem to me to be the opposite of the weather situation: people are doing quite a bit about it, but nobody's talking about it. Such valuable ideas as that of the reference group in which Muzafer and Carolyn Sherif have accomplished both innovative and definitive work, are essentially the product of disciplinary cross-fertilization (1964).

As we begin to notice the payoff of interdisciplinary work, the products of having well-trained specialists in one discipline borrow ideas, techniques, or explanations of data from another field, perhaps we shall make progress toward abandoning the artificial division of theory and methodology into separate areas of learning. (In our own department, we no longer give separate doctoral qualifying examinations in theory and methodology; we give one examination in theory-hyphen-methodology.) As Kurt Vonnegut says in *Mother Night,* "We are what we pretend to be, so we must be very careful about what we pretend to be."

REFERENCES

BLACK, P., and R. D. ATKINS. 1950. Conformity versus prejudice as exemplified in white-Negro relations in the south: some methodological considerations. *Journal of Psychology,* 30 (7): 111.

BLUMER, H. 1954. What is wrong wtih social theory? *American Sociological Review,* 19 (2): 4.

CANNON, W. 1932. *The wisdom of the body.* New York: Norton.

CAPLOW, T. 1964. *Principles of organization.* New York: Harcourt, Brace and World.

———, and R. J. McGEE. 1962. *The academic marketplace.* New York: Basic Books, Table 5-5.

FAUNCE, W. A., and M. J. SMUCKER. 1966. Industrialization and community status structure. *American Sociological Review,* 31: 390–99.

GOULDNER, A. W. 1956. Some observations on systematic theory, 1945-55. *Sociology in the United States of America.* Paris: Unesco.

GUSFIELD, J. R. 1965. Tradition and modernity in India: misplaced polarities in the study of social change. Paper presented at the meetings of the American Sociological Association, Chicago, September 2.

INKELES, A. 1964. *What is sociology? An introduction to the discipline and profession.* Englewood Cliffs, N.J.: Prentice-Hall.

———, and P. H. ROSSI. 1956. National comparisons of occupational prestige. *American Journal of Sociology,* 61: 329–39.

MACK, R. W. 1954. The prestige system of an air base: squadron rankings and morale. *American Sociological Review,* 19 (6): 281–87.

PARSONS, T. 1951a. A revised analytical approach to the theory of social stratification. In R. Bendix and S. Lipset (Eds.), *Class, status and power: a reader in social stratification.* Glencoe, Ill.: Free Press (1953).

———. 1951b. *The social system.* Glencoe, Ill.: Free Press.

POPOVICH, M. 1966. What the American sociologists think about their science and its problems. *American Sociologist,* 1 (5): 133–35.

SHERIF, M., and C. W. SHERIF. 1964. *Reference groups.* New York: Harper and Row.

SMITH, M. G. 1965. *Stratification in Grenada.* Berkeley and Los Angeles: University of California Press.

TYLOR, E. B. 1871. *Primitive culture.* New York: Brentano's, 1924. First published in 1871.

VANCE, R. B. 1952. Is theory for demographers? *Social Forces,* 31:9–13.

VAN DER ZANDEN, J. W. 1966. *American minority relations: the sociology of race and ethnic groups.* (2d ed.) New York: Ronald Press.

WORSLEY, P. 1966. *The end of anthropology?* Paper for sociology and social Anthropology Working Group (6th World Congress of Sociology).

WRONG, D. H. 1961. The oversocialized conception of man. *American Sociological Review,* 26: (2) 183–93.

4

CONTIGUOUS PROBLEM ANALYSIS: AN APPROACH TO SYSTEMATIC THEORIES ABOUT SOCIAL ORGANIZATION

ROBERT DUBIN

It is the central thesis of this chapter that there is a good *methodological* reason why social science theory has not added up in the same productive manner that theory has grown in the natural sciences. In brief, the tendency for several scholars to focus on the same analytical problem has a stultifying consequence, the conditions of which are elaborated in the next several sections. This methodological constraint is especially noteworthy in interdisciplinary endeavors.

It is my purpose to demonstrate that we can improve the quality of interdisciplinary cooperation. The suggestion is advanced that scholars working in interdisciplinary cooperation give up the attempt to deal with a common analytical problem. As an alternative research and theory building strategy, the method of *contiguous problem analysis* is put forward.

THEORIES ABOUT SOCIAL ORGANIZATION

To provide the widest possible opportunity for citing examples of the issues involved, I will draw upon the area of social organization. The purpose is not to systematize this sprawling area of social theory, but rather to employ the successes and failures of interdisciplinary efforts in this analytical domain to illustrate the methodological issues I am raising.

Systematic theories about social organization have historically been focused on the analysis of whole societies. The fundamental analytical problem has been the evolution of such societies, or their cyclical development. I need only recall to your memory Maine's distinction between status- and contract-based societies (1861); Tönnies' distinction between *Gemeinschaft* and *Gesellschaft* societies (1887); Redfield's classification of cultures as folk and urban (1930); and Becker's contrast between sacred and secular societies (1950). Systematic models of social organization, of which these are just a few well-known examples, meet the tests of viability, which are that they be logically coherent and empirically grounded. Indeed one of the most ambitious empirical studies in the literature of the social sciences is Sorokin's analysis in *Social and Cultural Dynamics* (1937–43). In Sorokin, as in the other systematic theories about social organization, the basic analytical problem was the evolution of social systems.

These theories share several features. (1) They describe distinctive classes and/or stages of social organization. (2) They describe a dynamic by which a given social system moves from one class or stage to another in the course of its history.

What is most striking about these several theories (and their companions) is that these competing models of social systems, despite their author's contentious claims to be different from each other, turn out to be remarkably similar. Indeed, if one examines models like those illustrated in any detail, the differences among them are far less striking than their similarities.

I use these illustrations to introduce the fundamental analytical problem to which I address myself. The authors cited above, representing political economy, sociology and anthropology, have not produced theory that is additive. They have generated this consequence by focusing upon a single analytical problem. The result has been that the competing models developed turn out to be remarkably similar.

COMPETITION BETWEEN OR CONSENSUS ABOUT THEORY

We can raise, as this entire volume does, the issue of whether scientists coming from several intellectual disciplines, and therefore with different frames of reference, will not, willy-nilly, develop different and competing models in attacking the same analytical model. The answer so far seems very clearly to be "No." When students from several disciplines deal with the same analytical problem, there is considerable identity in the models they employ.

This similarity in the systematic theories developed around a shared problem is achieved in one of two ways: (1) By the point of view of a single discipline dominating the structure and content of the model developed. (2) By the reduction of a model to the lowest common denominator of shared variables and methodologies of the participating disciplines.

The dilemma which is therefore posed is a straightforward one. Does interdisciplinariness, when focused upon a shared analytical problem, lead to a homogenized theoretical model which contains few, if any, of the distinctive contributions expected from the cooperating disciplines? Another way to pose this dilemma is to ask whether or not concentrating men and resources from several disciplines upon a common analytical problem does not force them to "sing out of the same prayer book" in order that a minimum of cooperation may be achieved. I want to underscore this dilemma by restating it once more. Does a shared model of social organization utilized by several cooperating disciplines get built out of either the dominant analytical tools of a single discipline, or out of the lowest common denominator of the analytical tools of several disciplines?

My answer to this dilemma is direct and pessimistic. I will conclude that interdisciplinariness, when focused upon a common analytical problem, will produce no better results than if a single discipline had zeroed in on the same problem with its substantial professional talents. Indeed, the result could be substantially worse if several disciplines cooperate at the level of their lowest common denominator of discourse and mutual understanding. I therefore hold out very little hope for interdisciplinary research where the analytical problem is common to all members of the research team.

Before the conclusion is reached that I have only a negative message, let me hasten to add that interdisciplinary research as I will define it—by thinking of a series of coordinate analytical problems simultaneously attacked by scientists from several behavioral disciplines—has a high probability of being very productive of systematic theories of social organization. The critical point is that the cooperating behavioral scientists each choose their special analytical problems and together work over a coordinate body of data. Another way to put this conclusion is to suggest that science makes progress by competition and not by consensus, a position Karl Popper (1959) has made popular.

A systematic theory or model must define the units employed and the laws by which they interact with each other within a defined boundary, in order to qualify as a theory (Dubin, 1969). When this is done with respect to a single analytical problem, the units tend to be the same, as do the laws by which they are presumed to interact, and the boundaries within which the lawful relationship holds, regardless of the disciplines from which the theory builders come.

It follows that we get competing systematic theory primarily when we shift the analytical problem, and therefore have to change the components out of which we build the models. I will conclude that it is the shift in problem focus, however minor, that is the engine by which we make progress in the development of systematic theory of social organization. I will further argue that the separate disciplines are most distinctive from each other by virtue of their special discipline-bound analytical problems. This generates competing models which have high value in forcing empirical testing and critical evaluation in judging the relative merits of several theories about social organization. The most important consequence of all is that the shift in analytical focus permits models of social systems to "add up" in a manner not possible to achieve by any other means.

SYSTEMATIC THEORY

Until relatively recently, systematic theory usually meant the theory of a single writer which typically dealt with a broad and complicated analytical problem. The adequacy of such theories was judged by their internal logic and by their correspondence with the empirical world. This latter was usually demonstrated illustratively although there are notable exceptions, including the work of Sorokin, already mentioned. The exemplars of systematic theory about social organization, because of the very scale of the theories in which they dealt, often forced any potential competitors to deal at their level of generality in order to be considered an adequate antagonist.

This state of affairs in sociology reached a climax in the work of Parsons (1951) and Parsons and Shils (1951) whose systematic theories are not notably empirical. It is difficult, for example, to be critical of a grand system builder like Parsons, since he constructs his systems out of logic and the critic is forced to fault them on logical grounds primarily (Dubin, 1960). It is hard to believe that the four system problems that Parsons proposes as the focal point of social action, and whose solutions for a given social system test the conditions of its continued viability, constitute a set that truly comprises the range of human behavior or even a significant segment of it. Nevertheless, if one accepts his definition of these as the central problems of a social system, then Parsons makes a great deal of sense because the critic is forced to deal with his theory as though these were the only analytical problems that existed (see Black, 1961).

It is in this context that Merton's notion of theories of the middle range makes sense (1949). For the central meaning of the middle-range theory is that they are theories about the multiplicity of analytical problems. The middle range and the nether range of theorizing are the ranges in which more and more analytical problems come into focus. Indeed, it is precisely this fact which makes them middle and lower ranges of theorizing.

The problem of systematic theories at the middle and nether ranges of analytical problems involves two dimensions of coordination. On the one hand is the possibility that analytical problems will be fractured into so many pieces and parts that the scientific domain becomes a Balkanized region of research principalities. Under these conditions no attempt is made, nor is it even probable that a sensible attempt could be made, to bring order into the dispersed attention of theorists. The second problem of coordination has to do with the extent to which the nether-range theories and the middle-range theories in any way interlock to form a large theoretical structure at the upper or global range. This is the problem of the additivity of theories, one with the other. It is to both of these problems that I wish to call your attention, for their solution as a means for building theory will be found in what I will label the contiguous-problem approach.

As a necessary footnote I simply want to point out that broad-scale theories, middle-range theories, and nether-level theories cannot be distinguished from each other by any closeness to the empirical world. Any level of theory may be close to, or at a distance from, the world about which it seeks to make sense. The level of the theory is indifferent to its empirical relevance.

CONTIGUOUS-PROBLEM APPROACH

I want to suggest that interdisciplinary research is best pursued by attacking contiguous analytical problems. This approach involves defining analytical problems that lie close together and yet retain a significant individual identity. Several students, regardless of discipline, can attack these problems simultaneously. If they clearly understand that the boundary of each problem is contiguous with others, they can readily perceive the additivity of the results each will obtain from their theorizing and the subsequent research test of the theories. The major consequence is that one can predict in advance the connectedness of individual theories by noting that the boundary of its domain is contiguous with the boundary of the domain of another theory addressing a slightly different analytical problem.

The operating problem in doing contiguous-problem research is to be clear that the theory boundaries are indeed contiguous. Once this is established, then the linkage among areas of theory and their inter-relationships become quite clear. Furthermore, it then becomes possible to establish a temporal ordering of analytical problems to be attacked, insofar as the theoretical solution to one problem suggests means for grappling with a contiguous problem. Let me illustrate this by suggesting that a theory of pedagogy and a theory of learning are obviously contiguous analytical problems. They have, through much of the history of education, remained singularly noncontiguous in the view of many pedagogues. When learning theorists began to get curious about the contiguous problem of teaching, we developed revolutionary notions about pedagogy. Programmed instruction derives from a learning theory, and contemporary experimentation with early-infancy learning will undoubtedly have important consequences for the development of teaching theory in the pre-school as well as the school years. There seems to be a natural order in handling the contiguous analytical problems of learning and teaching, and that is to take them in precisely that order.

If one expands the space in which contiguous analytical problems are viewed to a three dimensional one, it becomes obvious that one may build upwards towards middle-range and even high-range theoretical models by following the contiguous-problem approach. It is also obvious that the analyst may move deductively from higher to lower levels of generality, linking each level through the contiguous analytical problems by which one level touches the other. Thus, the systematic work of Homans (1950, 1961) is an attempt to move between and among levels of generality with an unabashed contempt for any probable charges of reductionism of his sociology to a psychological level.

The special relevance of a contiguous problem approach to the subject matter of this volume is that it suggests a straightforward method whereby the several disciplines may cooperate with each other without either of the dire consequences which are the usual result of collaboration (the consequences noted at the beginning of this chapter).

Let us now turn to a more detailed look at the contiguous-problem approach. It involves three steps: (1) That at least two models or theories be under consideration simultaneously. (2) That the theorist-researchers be aware that two or more models are under test. (3) That the domains of the separate models be viewed as touching each other so that there are at least some common boundaries, or even areas of overlapping domains. When these three conditions are met, there is a high probability that the cooperating scientists will achieve some additivity in their results.

If what has already been said is understood, then the reason for the first condition is obvious. For there to be cooperation that is intellectually viable, it is necessary to have two or more different things that are joined in the cooperative effort. Failing that, if two or more researchers join forces to test a single model, they merely engage in a technical division of labor in the research operations. They may divide up the parts of the research operations among themselves for purposes of efficiency, but this is only a technical and not an intellectual basis of cooperation.

It may also seem obvious that the cooperating scientists be aware that two or more models are under investigation. What is obvious may not always be perceived, however. The pressures to appear to be employing the same model may actually lead to an artificial claim that what is different in fact, is asserted to be part of the same intellectual package. An excellent example of this is the volume *Toward a General Theory of Action* (Parsons and Shils, 1951) in which several authors, notably the psychologist Tolman, are dealing with contiguous (if not independent) problems under the guise of joining in production of a general theory. The casual reader might infer that the general theory had been realized.

The most difficult criterion to meet in contiguous-problem analysis is to insure that the analytical problems share a common boundary, or at least that they overlap. If my own analysis of theory building is accurate, this can be determined in at least four ways (Dubin, 1969).

1. The most obvious method is one in which the same units or variables, and laws by which they interact, are employed in several analyses. The only difference among the several analyses is that they separately focus on different states of the same system. What is contiguous here are the system states, and each may be separately studied by employing a common model. Thus, the sacred and secular are different system states of a society and may each be analyzed, employing the same units.

2. A second method for testing contiguity is to employ some common units. The contiguity is established when the same unit is seen as simultaneously or serially interacting with others so that the several domains of interaction either touch or overlap. For example, parental reports of how children are handled, and children's perceptions of such handling are contiguous analytical problems, having the child as a unit common to several domains (*cf.* Dubin and Dubin, 1965).

3. A third method for determining contiguity is through the formal definition of model boundaries. When the boundaries of a model are defined, it may turn out that they are contiguous. Thus, for example, the study of human response to extreme sensory deprivation has a domain boundary which is formally defined as the nature of response under conditions of minimal stimulus, and which is contiguous to each domain in which a particular sensory stimulus operates (*cf.* Solomon, *et al.,* 1961).

4. A fourth method for insuring contiguous-problem analysis is to have overlapping but nonidentical domains for several competing models. For example, this idea that lower-class juvenile delinquency is the product of valuing middle-class goals and styles of life but without the means available for their attainment (Cohen, 1955) must compete with an attempt to model this behavior as a group status-seeking phenomenon (Yablonsky, 1959). The variables or units employed in the competing models and the laws by which they interact are not the same, but the behaviors being predicted, juvenile delinquency, are shared between the two models.

I have suggested enough to indicate that the contiguous-problem analysis approach is readily identified in operational terms. More can be said on the subject but not within the limits of this chapter.

It should be added that contiguous-problem analysis does not require interdisciplinary sources of its practitioners. Indeed, an important source of *intra*discipline advance is the ability to add pieces of knowledge together because they are the product of contiguous-problem analysis. But it is especially important to note that this method is essential to interdisciplinary cooperation. If this method is not employed, then the disciplines remain genuinely separated and incapable of achieving coordination. The alternate result is to homogenize several disciplines with a loss of their distinctive contributions.

Another point of emphasis is that simultaneity is not a requisite of contiguous-problem analysis. Contiguous problems may be analyzed at quite different time periods with constructive results. Interdisciplinary cooperation is not time-bound and may, indeed, span long time periods and cooperation among scholars who never meet or engage in direct discourse. Thus, Lasswell (1931) and Freud, or Parsons (Parsons, Bales, and Shils, 1954) and Freud have worked on contiguous problems without contact and widely separated in time.

Finally, it should be clear that contiguous-problem analysis is not limited to model testing. It also applies to descriptive research. One of the important but lowly valued aspects of behavioral science is good description. Indeed, we make progress slowly because we value description so lowly. Nevertheless, good description proceeds in parts and the additivity of the described parts depends on their contiguity. None of the blind men feeling of the elephant has a sense of the others' area of search and cannot thereby gain a sense of the whole. The jigsaw puzzle is the appropriate analogy for contiguous-problem analysis at the descriptive level. The whole picture is revealed when the parts are exactly fitted to each other at their borders.

SOME ILLUSTRATIONS

It must be admitted immediately that the method of contiguous-problem analysis has been practiced, but it has not been named. It has not previously been recognized as a special method and for that reason, self-conscious practice of it is not readily to be found. I will therefore draw upon a number of examples, including several from my own work, to suggest for you how this method may prove useful.

Parsons (Parsons and Shils, 1951) developed the pattern variables as a model of how the person determines his course of action, an obvious analytical problem for a scientist interested in the structure of social action. I asked of his model (Dubin, 1960) the simple question: "How many different ways can a person act toward an object in the Parsonian model?" This was a question to which Parsons did not address himself but which is clearly contiguous to his analytical focus. When the implications of his model are worked out, the number of possible social acts exceeds a million—either a testament to the nonparsimony of his model, or a genuine reflection of the overwhelming complexity of human behavior. It was the contiguous-problem approach that led to this extension of a Parsonian model.

Merton (1938) presented sociology with a paradigm of deviant adaptations by individuals which suggested that there was only a limited range of four such adaptations. By modifying his model to analyze group as well as individual deviant adaptations, I expanded the number and types of adaptation, incorporating his in the larger group (Dubin, 1959a). Here we have again an example of contiguous-problem analysis that expands the range of scientific models.

A recurrent theme among students of the human consequences of modern industrial technology has been that man, the machine operative, is alienated from the work he does and may very well be alienated from the society in which he does it. My own studies (Dubin, 1958) make clear that work is not a central life interest for industrial workers, nor even for their supervisors and managers. Nevertheless, we *cannot* conclude that such people are alienated from society as a whole. The evidence indicates otherwise, namely, that they have central life interests outside the arena of work. Here, again, by dealing with a contiguous problem, the original area of analysis is better understood because a contiguous analytical problem was considered.

W. I. Thomas (1923) undertook to study the unadjusted girl and in the process came to grips with a central concern of social analysis, the motives for behavior. Out of this emerged his formulation of the four wishes, because he focused on the contiguous problem of what the unadjusted girl was seeking to satisfy.

It is somewhat more difficult to find examples of contiguous problem analysis in which several disciplines were involved. The great advance in the analysis of voting behavior came when sociologists and social psychologists turned attention to the processes of voter decision-making to complement the political scientists' analysis of electoral outcome and its demographic bases.

In the study of microsocial systems, the analyses of organization theorists of an early period have been supplemented by the work of behavioral scientists who focused on the human consequences of industrial systems. Both were later supplemented by the focus of system analysts who saw analytical problems of temporal order, mini-max strategies of decision-making, and bargaining techniques summarized under the heading of game theory.

Social psychologists, studying small social systems, have made it abundantly clear that norms are not points, but rather ranges of behavior and that consensus is an uncommon social phenomenon, contrary to the longtime accepted conclusions of anthropologists on this score.

Sherif (Sherif *et al.*, 1961), in his already classic study of the resolution of intergroup conflict, started from the social psychological concern with resolving conflict between two groups over a given issue. He rediscovered Sumner's (1906) conclusion about the consequences of outgroup threat for ingroup solidarity, and then made the insightful leap to the conclusion that two contesting groups could become a temporarily unified ingroup when confronted with a superordinate problem that neither could handle alone. The actual experiment confirmed the theory of intergroup cooperation by coalition formation.

In organization theory, the "assignment problem" deals with fitting people to the organization structure. Traditionally, the assignment problem is solved by maximizing the return to the organization through the "best" assignment of persons to jobs (Kuhn and Tucker, 1953). March and Simon (1958) revised this problem by declaring it to be the search for the minimum number of tasks required to perform the whole set of organization activities. I further modified the assignment problem by suggesting that the structure of interrelations among the jobs of an organization is another facet of the assignment problem (Dubin, 1959c). Thus, mathematicians, organization theorists, and a sociologist dealt with contiguous analytical problems so as to make their analyses additive.

The most comprehensive elaboration of a discipline-wide set of contiguous problems is revealed in the chapter prepared for this volume by Professor Mikesell. A careful reading of his chapter reveals the many-faceted ways in which geography is linked through contiguous-problem analysis with the social sciences. Mikesell has provided a most thoughtful analysis of these linkages, with many illustrations of the manner in which contiguous-problem analysis has served to bring geography into the realm of the social sciences.

By now you should have at least a dim notion of what I mean by contiguous-problem analysis. Furthermore, you should begin to see that this is not a time-bound or discipline-bound phenomenon. Finally, it should be apparent that contiguous-problem analysis is a structural feature of intellectual life rather than a consequence of interpersonal relations or collective decisions that interdisciplinary cooperation was necessary or desirable.

SOME OPPORTUNITIES

Before summarizing, let me briefly indicate some areas where contiguous-problem analysis gives every indication of providing some handsome payoffs. This will illustrate but scarcely exhaust a catalog of areas in which interdisciplinary cooperation gives every indication of productive results.

We have largely abandoned the formal analysis of institutions, although many analytical problems relating to them remain untouched. For example, we know next to nothing about the ways in which individuals enter new (to them) institutions. We are curiously ignorant of the manner in which several institutions articulate with each other. We are almost without knowledge of institutional isolation; about the possibility that there may be interstices between institutions in which new ones may develop; and about the linkages between organizations and the institutions whose functions they may carry out.

The linkages between behavior, motivation, and incentives have scarcely been elaborated, although each has been separately subjected to detailed analysis by specialists ranging from psychiatrists, to motion- and time-study experts. The possibilities that many areas of behavior may be necessary rather than voluntary raise a host of analytical problems about our models of motivation and incentives (Dubin, 1959b).

With moralistic fervor, and acting out our image of rational man eschewing the "law of the jungle," we have given inept attention to social conflict as a social process. Simply by shifting attention from what it *is* to what it *does,* we can illuminate the processes of group conflict, as Sherif did, and achieve a more sophisticated understanding of it (Coser, 1956; Dahrendorf, 1959).

The analysis of social stratification has severely suffered because sociologists have never recognized the significance of job evaluation, as developed by personnel specialists, for the stratification of occupations. In another dimension and for reasons which are only dimly understandable, sociologists, and social scientists generally, have abandoned a concern with class consciousness, although since Marx's time this surely must be considered a central problem of any model of social stratification.

Perhaps I have said enough to illustrate a few regions of the behavioral science landscape where we have immediately opportunities to enhance knowledge by adding to its store. It is my belief that this may be done with maximal effectiveness if we employ the method of contiguous-problem analysis so as to mobilize most effectively the contributions of all the behavioral sciences.

PERSPECTIVE AND PROSPECTS

It has been my argument that the traditional approach to inter-disciplinary cooperation has been singularly sterile in its consequences. This has not been for want of effort or sincerity of interest. My conclusion is that failure to move knowledge forward has resulted from a structural defect in the manner chosen to accomplish this goal through interdisciplinary efforts.

It is proposed that a method which involves an analysis of problems that lie side by side in an analytical field is a way to advance knowledge through the cooperation among several behavioral science disciplines. Some of the features of this method have been suggested. A few illustrations of how the method has worked in the past have been presented, as well as some suggestions of areas in which the method may profitably be employed in the future. The method is called contiguous-problem analysis.

REFERENCES

BECKER, H. 1950. *Through values to social interpretation.* Durham, N.C.: Duke University Press

BLACK, M. (Ed.). 1961. *The social theories of Talcott Parsons.* Englewood Cliffs, N.J.: Prentice-Hall.

COHEN, A. K. 1955. *Delinquent boys.* Glencoe, Ill.: Free Press.

COSER, L. 1956. *The functions of social conflict.* Glencoe, Ill.: Free Press.

DAHRENDORF, R. 1959. *Class and class conflict in industrial society.* Stanford: Stanford University Press.

DUBIN, R. 1958. *The world of work.* Englewood Cliffs, N.J.: Prentice-Hall.

————. 1959a. Deviant behavior and social structure: continuities in social theory. *American Sociological Review,* 24: 147–64.

————. 1959b. Industrial research and the discipline of sociology. *Proceedings of the Eleventh Annual Meeting,* Industrial Relations Research Association, Madison, Wis.

————. 1959c. Stability of human organizations. In Mason Haire (Ed.), *Modern organization theory.* New York: Wiley.

————. 1960. Parsons' actor: continuities in social theory. *American Sociological Review,* 25: 457–66.

————. 1969. *Theory building.* New York: Free Press.

————, and E. R. DUBIN. 1965. Children's social perceptions: a review of research. *Child Development,* 36: 809–838.

HOMANS, G. C. 1950. *The human group.* New York: Harcourt, Brace and World.

————. 1961. *Social behavior: its elementary forms.* New York: Harcourt, Brace and World.

KUHN, H. W., and A. W. TUCKER (Eds.). 1953. *Contributions to the theory of games,* vol. 2. Princeton, N.J.: Princeton University Press.

LASSWELL, H. 1931. *Psychopathology and politics.* Chicago: University of Chicago Press.

MAINE, H. S. 1861. *Ancient law.* London: J. Murray.

MARCH, J. G., and H. A. SIMON. 1958. *Organizations.* New York: Wiley.

MERTON, R. K. 1938. Social structure and anomie. *American Sociological Review,* 3: 672-82.

————. 1949. *Social theory and social structure.* Glencoe, Ill.: Free Press.

PARSONS, T. 1951. *The social system.* Glencoe, Ill.: Free Press.

————. 1954. *Social structure and personality.* Glencoe, Ill.: Free Press.

————, R. F. BALES, and E. A. SHILS. 1954. *Working papers in the theory of action.* Glencoe, Ill.: Free Press.

————, and E. A. SHILS (Eds.). 1951. *Toward a general theory of action.* Cambridge: Harvard University Press.

POPPER, K. R. 1959. *The logic of scientific discovery.* London: Hutchinson.

REDFIELD, R. 1930. *Tepoztlan: a Mexican village.* Chicago: University of Chicago Press.

SHERIF, M., O. J. HARVEY, B. J. WHITE, W. R. HOOD, and C. W. SHERIF. 1961. *Intergroup conflict and cooperation: the Robbers Cave experiment.* Norman: Institute of Group Relations, University of Oklahoma.

SOLOMON, P. (Ed.). 1961. *Sensory deprivation.* Cambridge: Harvard University Press.

SOROKIN, P. A. 1937–43. *Social and cultural dynamics,* 4 vol. New York: American Book.

SUMNER, W. G. 1906. *Folkways.* Boston: Ginn and Co.

THOMAS, W. I. 1923. *The unadjusted girl.* Boston: Little, Brown and Co.

TÖNNIES, F. 1887. *Community and society.* (Trans. and ed. by C. P. Loomis, 1957.) East Lansing: Michigan State University Press.

YABLONSKY, L. 1959. The delinquent gang as a near group. *Social Problems,* 7: 108–17.

5

MYTH AND INTERRELATIONSHIP IN SOCIAL SCIENCE: ILLUSTRATED THROUGH ANTHROPOLOGY AND SOCIOLOGY

Murray L. Wax

THE MYTH OF ETERNAL YOUTH

If we speak of "interdisciplinary relations," then we are at once propelled into such questions as the nature of each of these disciplines and how they are significantly distinct, one from the other. Further, we are propelled into asking how these several disciplines are, in turn, related to that master entity, "social science," and how it, itself, is to be defined or characterized. As "pure theory," the resultant discussions can be dull, since so often they represent either the ideology of the discipline or the ambitions of a scholar who wishes to impose upon his colleagues his program of investigation. It is more interesting and more likely to be helpful if we ask these same questions critically, rather than programmatically, and if we begin the response with an exercise in the sociology of knowledge and the "anthropology of knowledge"—to coin a new name for an old activity (for, if *Wissensoziologie,* wherefore not *Wissenanthropologie?*). Given the myths which, as social scientists, we all circulate about our disciplines, some demythologizing is likely to remind us not only of the human focus of our researches, but also of the human nature of ourselves as researchers.

Consider as a principal theme of this mythology, the notion that the social sciences are "young." Disregarding for the moment its possible truth, we note that this self-characterization has many uses: predominantly it permits social scientists to cherish the eschatological vision of a science that will predict and control, and to maintain the plausibility of this vision in the face, not so much of utter failure, as of paltry successes. Likewise, by emphasizing the novelty and modernity of these sciences, their practitioners are enabled to dismiss as worthless much of the traditional learning that might otherwise be regarded as germane. For, if the subject matter of sociology was invented by Comte (aided perhaps by a few of his contemporaries), and if a similar pattern of invention holds for the other social-scientific disciplines, then the work of earlier scholars has only the relevance that Aristotle is seen by natural scientists to have had for Galileo, namely, being the author of some deluded (nonempirical) theorizations. Likewise, the wisdom that might be inherent in folk conceptions (or common sense) can not only be disregarded, but ridiculed and attacked, since its basis does not rest with the youthful science (e.g., note how courses in introductory psychology instruct students that their folks skills are delusionary in such vital matters as judging character from people's faces or observing rapid and complex events).

Yet the notion of the social sciences as "youthful" is only tenable by some adroit maneuvering with words, as if physics were to be considered as having just emerged in the nineteenth century when it acquired its present name, so that the long history of investigations conducted by medieval Europeans, Arabs, Hindus, Hellenistic peoples, etc., could be relegated to the category of prehistoric lore. Surely, if prediction and control are the goals of science (and I am far from thinking this to be so, but only assuming for the sake and pleasure of argument), then, anthropologically speaking, the most signal and basic of such achievements was that associated with the process by which man domesticated himself and transformed his existence from that of primate into that of gabbling human. With the development of human language, there went, concomitantly, the emergence of human culture and the child-rearing that leads to self-awareness and self-control. These were (and continue as) tremendous feats of social engineering, and they can be dismissed from consideration only by verbal maneuvers and by an attitude of scientistic elitism which reserves the label "social engineering" for those changes which are directed by cadres of especially trained modern men. Like the notion that scientific investigations can only be conducted by scientists, the notion that engineering can only be performed by engineers is elitism or obscurantism. From his appearance as human, man has repeatedly and sometimes with marked success attempted to control his own conduct, that of his neighbors, and of the groups in which he participated. True, his failures have sometimes been spectacular, but his successes are often underestimated (particularly by the apostles of the "new sciences"). Thus, to speak only of the post-Reformation West, the notions of rationally and consciously designed national constitutions, codes of law, economic and fiscal systems, systems of military organization, etc., constitute not merely social innovations but attempts at social engineering, and the consequences are palpably visible. We live today, not as inhabitants of manorial society somehow encumbered with a more complex technology, but as participants in huge, complexly organized, industrial societies. Whether it was Calvin reorganizing the society of Geneva, or Jefferson, Adams, *et al.* organizing the United States, or Lenin, Trotsky, *et al.* organizing the USSR, much of the nature of modern society is the consequence of the attempts of social engineering by thoughtful and learned men who set out to produce a particular kind of society distinguished by particular kinds of virtues. Judged by their own values, none of these men was more than partially successful, but their efforts are not more to be scorned than those of a contemporary U.S. business executive who with the aid of the findings from the latest market research launches a campaign to create a market for a new product.

The myth of the social sciences as youthful is likewise challenged by the sage remark of Alfred Kroeber that it is not the human capacity for creative innovation that serves to distinguish man from his animal kin, but rather his ability to transmit from one generation to the next that which has been innovated, tried, and proven valuable. In the sciences this is particularly true, for while the mythology that is preached to the young emphasizes the individual culture heroes of the scientific adventure and how they challenged the received truths of their age, in actuality, as Polanyi (1964), Kuhn (1962), and others have argued, the core of science is its continuity and its cumulation about the cooperative and disciplined search for truth.[1]

THE ROUTINIZATION OF ACADEMIC DISCIPLINES

In contemporary times, this search has been institutionalized in the form of the various scientific disciplines, and it is appropriate that we note the resultant characteristics. Indeed the *organizational* is the only meaningful sense in which we can say that either science, generally, or social science particularly, is youthful. Not the search for truth, nor the systematic teaching, writing, and cooperative efforts with disciples, but the complexly developed and bureaucratically organized system of scientific societies, universities, and professional journals and conferences, are the true novelties and the truly youthful entities. Their consequences have been both beneficial and detrimental.

As the pursuit of scientific truth has become enmeshed with the graduate school of the university within a mass educational system, it has been increasingly subjected to the bureaucratic patterns affecting the whole. Knowledge is assumed to be divided into fixed quanta, marked by the discipline and the subdiscipline (or field), the course, the class period, the textbook lesson, and the examination. These quanta are summable as credit hours, and

1. Reading the foregoing section in its draft form, Muzafer Sherif pointed out that the word "youthful" is ambiguous, referring on the one hand to chronological age, on the other hand to conduct. Commenting on this point, Sherif sees the social sciences as acting youthfully in the sense of their being erratic and immature. Continuing in the same vein, one might describe the social sciences as behaving like adolescents in their subjugation to fad and fashion—their shift from one methodological orientation or research technique to another, because of extrinsic considerations. In his class lectures, Herbert Blumer used to illustrate this adolescent behavior by outlining the methodological presuppositions of the various schools of social psychology and pointing out that these had seldom been disproven but had simply gone out of fashion.

when sufficient accrue to the individual, he is certified with a degree. Plainly, that knowledge which fits best into this Procrustean frame is dead knowledge, fixed and finished, consisting either of a body of texts composed by scholars long deceased, or of a body of propositions forming a closed formal system, such as classical mechanics within physics. Equally plainly, much of sociology and its sister disciplines does not yet fit that description (indeed, it can be argued that a healthy and developing science is always hard to categorize into fixed pigeonholes).

University deans, on the one hand, and grand theorists, on the other—not to mention the other organized interests, such as benevolent foundations and publishing houses—have each attempted to structure the social-scientific disciplines into a set of mutually exclusive and exhaustive enterprises. Their task is not so much impossible as it is destructive. For, from the viewpoint of a systematic and logical division of scientific labor, the very existence of the disciplines or sciences that are taken to constitute the social or behavioral sciences makes but little sense. Sociology, anthropology, and their siblings are not the outgrowths of a systematic division of social-scientific labor, but are instead the arbitrary consequences of particular social processes. From sociology onward, the more recent entrants (e.g., human relations, social work, speech, child development) into the university system have represented the consolidation of social movements which have been oriented about particular programs for the solution of social problems, and which thus constitute further exceptions to any rational division of social-scientific labor. Sociology itself was initially an amalgam of interests in partial reform, total societal reorganization, and theoretical science. Especially within the English-speaking countries it was markedly associated with programs for meliorating the condition of the urban poor, and as it became more high-toned and theoretical and less interested in immediate and local reform, it left room for the later entrants into the professional community. (The pattern seems strikingly similar to the temporal succession among religious sects, where, as the earlier emergent becomes denominationalized and respectably great traditional, vacancies are created which are then filled by the emerging of new orders or sects.)

As sociology elbowed its way into the universities of the United States, it had to assume the deportment of the more ancient disciplines of economics, political science, and history while, at the same time, it had to claim that it was concerned with something other than those senior colleagues. Sociologists based their claim upon a concern with the social problems associated with industrialization and urbanization, particularly the problems of urban poverty, crime, and familial disorganization, as well as of the social transitions associated with migration, especially from rural to urban settings. These kinds of problems were worthy of detailed empirical investigation and they had been slighted by the existing disciplines, but, from the point of view of a systematic division of social-scientific labor, the resultant differentiation among the disciplines has never made any sense. How can one study poverty without studying the framework of production and trade in which people are poor; and, conversely, how can one study the economy without studying how it encourages the displacement and migration of peoples and their location as urban poor? How can one study crime without studying the political machinery that defines crimes and labels men as criminal; and, conversely, how can one study the state without studying the ways in which people resist the authority and edicts of the governors?

Once we appreciate the historical facts which show that the various disciplines of social science have come into existence as the resultant of social movements or other arbitrary social processes, we must also confess that if we try to view the relationship among these disciplines as if it were or could easily become a rational division of social-scientific labor, then we are indulging in mythology or ideology. We deal not with a set of logically integrated scientific disciplines, but with a set of scientific societies (professional associations) which have, as a result of particular social processes, managed each to gain for itself some mandate to study the body social (*cf.* Hughes, 1959). Thus, in terms of a logical and systematic division of social-scientific labor, social psychology, ethnopsychology, and psychological sociology ought to be grouped together as the one discipline that they seem to be; and, if economics deserved to be a separate discipline, then there should be no need for economic anthropology and industrial sociology—and so on.

Yet, as social scientists, we realize that logic is seldom the best organizer of social relationships and that, given that scholars are human beings and not instruments of inquiry, it may be best that the social sciences are chaotically organized and that the various disciplines are professional rivals for the same subject areas. Scholars with different backgrounds who come to study the same subject areas will perceive and organize their materials differently. While one may regret that economics and political science developed parochially in relationship to the problems of Western national societies, yet, given that this has occurred, it may then have been well that other sciences (especially anthropology and comparative sociology) appeared quite independently as compensatory movements for the ethnocentric bias of their senior colleagues. In any case, I would argue that, given the nature of the social-scientific disciplines and given the nature of the task of social research, then the defect of our present division of labor is not too much overlap but too little. The fault is not that several different disciplines are each studying the same subject matter, while giving different labels to their activities, but that the gaps among our disciplines are much too large. The most abysmal is the separation of anthropology from history (*cf.* Evans-Pritchard, 1964), of political science (or government) from law (usually considered a professional school), and of sociology from them all. As a result, many sociologists still continue to draw their imagery of the Protestant Reformation from Max Weber, although professional historians have long since relegated his theories to the dustbin. In the same way, sociologists long continued to draw their imagery of primitive societies from *Patterns of Culture* far after the time when anthropologists had dismissed Benedict's ethnographic depictions as quite misleading. In neither case does the rejection of the work deny the intriguing quality of the conceptual scheme, but it does brand the specific historical or ethnographic accounts as so fallacious empirically that the concepts would not be utilized without the most careful reconsideration. And, both cases serve to illustrate how the gap between disciplines has lead to one of them relying upon theories and data which are quite invalidated among the originating discipline.

FUCTIONALISM AS INTERDISCIPLINARY BORROWING

Because anthropology secured the mandate to study "primitive peoples" and because few other scholars were equipped or interested in so doing, anthropologists were placed in the position where they were encouraged to study the entire round of life of small, relatively isolated, homogeneous little communities (Redfield, 1960). Where Western man and his societies had been divided into bits and pieces among the practitioners of the several social-scientific disciplines, these little communities came to be studied by individual researchers, who thus were afforded the opportunity to perceive and depict each one of them as a natural whole (a microcosm). The earliest practitioners of this anthropological art were men (Malinowski, Radcliffe-Brown) of high intelligence, considerable learning and a marked gift for essay and polemic, so that their pioneering studies were, not only scientific accomplishments, but recognized and lauded by the general intelligentsia. As the format of the community study developed it could accommodate both those who wished to concentrate on rigorously defined problems with tight investigational procedures as well as those whose interests were more esthetic and novelistic, and in general it forced both factions toward an academic accommodation. Most important, it encouraged each field worker to investigate and describe every significant aspect of the life of this particular community, so that, unrestrained by disciplinary boundaries, he had to record and comment upon its economy, politico-jural organization, social structure, modes of personal interaction, language patterns, and the like. Yet, the field worker was able to execute this achievement only at a price, for these little communities could be investigated only because they had come into the scope of trade, missionization, pacification and colonial administration of the great Western powers, while anthropologists had come to define their mandate (or academic subject matter) as excluding these very penetrations. In their fieldwork and scholarship, ethnographers chose to ignore the linkages between the little communities of their researches and the greater societies enveloping them; and, when they could not accomplish this isolation in the ongoing system of activities, they retreated into an idealistic past, "the ethnographic present," where the little communities could be considered as relating, if at all, only to each other, but not to the emissaries and potentates of the greater societies.

Among the various disciplines of the social sciences, there was none which might logically have 'had the responsibility for correcting the distortion implicit in these anthropological studies. Insofar as the linkages to the greater societies were economic or political, it might conceivably have been the representatives of economics or political science who took advantage of the occasion, but in fact these disciplines remained focused on the internal affairs of the Western nations. It might also have been the sociologists, except that, despite such glittering ancestral stars as Max Weber, the field of comparative sociology has been relatively neglected within the United States, at least until the period of World War II. Instead, then, of rushing to reprove the anthropologists for their colonialist (Maquet, 1964) blindness, the sociologists were so impressed with the yield of the community study as a research procedure (Arensberg, 1961; Stein, 1964) that an increasing number of them came to apply it to whatever in modern North America was sufficiently small and isolable to possess some of the qualities of a little community. Small towns (Middletown, Yankee City, Cantonville), ethnic neighborhoods (Cornerville), prisons, asylums for the insane, were among the major types of entities thus investigated by sociologists (and "deviant anthropologists") and the results in many cases were landmarks for the social sciences (*cf.* discussion and bibliography in Vidich, Bensman, and Stein, 1964).

From their inception, the studies of the exotic little community had been contributory to the development of a simple and powerful theoretical system —*functionalism,*[2] in which the exotic community was treated as an isolated system balanced in dynamic equilibrium (homeostasis). Many of those who (later) came to perform community studies within North America were likewise moved to adopt a modified form of the functionalist mode of conceptualization, and, consequently, their findings contained a magnified form of the distortion noted above. To regard a Trobriand village as an isolated whole might be considered a minor error; to do the same for a New England city was an error of far greater magnitude. In the case of William Lloyd Warner's interpretation of the causes of labor difficulties within Yankee City, the distortion was recognized quickly, particularly by those filiated to Euro-

---

2. Radcliffe-Brown had been led toward functionalism under the influence of Durkheim. The point I wish to stress is not the novelty of functionalism as a theoretical scheme, since the orientation can be considered quite old, but rather that it is an especially congenial scheme for characterizing the small community, so that researchers are naturally led toward employing it. On the other hand, the application to the national state—as if this, too, were a self-contained society—involves the dangers of extrapolation; the consequent errors are illustrated in that work of Durkheim's which used national societies as cases.

pean theories of social conflict, and scholarly debate on the issue provided the opportunity for public correction. However, in other cases, such as prisons and asylums for the insane, the distortion was more hidden until social scientists attempted to inaugurate programs for reform, or, in parallel cases among rural communities of impoverished persons until they attempted to guide programs for community development. For, in these types of cases, the social researchers and reformers found themselves repeatedly thwarted in their planned reconstruction by the intricacies of the linkages between the supposedly isolated target community and the agencies of power, wealth, and influence within the greater society (*cf.* Willner, 1964; Reining, 1966). While few of the thwarted reformers perceived that their problem lay in their simplistic theoretical conceptualizations about the nature of communities in the modern world (many chose to attribute responsibility to interfering agencies, or "betrayal" by clients, or the intractable nature of the subject people), still these episodes constituted an empirical and pragmatic refutation of the applicability of the functionalist schema. The lessons were visibly there for the learning.

Meanwhile, on the level of grand theory, the functionalist conceptualization had been embraced and elaborated by other scholars, notably among them being two men who were to come to be considered as the intellectual fountainheads for "structural functionalism" in North American sociology, Robert K. Merton and Talcott Parsons. Both saw in functionalism a way of guiding the study of modern, industrial and urban societies, and both followed Durkheim in adopting, as their fundamental unit for functionalist interpretation, the social system of the national state, in particular, the United States. Their usage of functionalism won them numerous disciples, but it also triggered much criticism. On the one hand, those who followed in the path of Robert E. Park, W. I. Thomas, and the "Chicago School," had regarded the city as frontier, an area where different peoples met, competed for scarce resources (particularly space), sometimes fought, and sometimes reached an accommodation with each other. These scholars saw in "National Functionalism" (if I may refer to it by this phrase), an over-simplifying of the cultural, social, and ecological complexities of the metropolis. Note, for example, the contrast between their approach and that of Merton to the study of delinquency: the latter framed his analysis in terms of the way in which the delinquent relates to the national norms (the delinquent utilizes illegitimate means to reach approved ends), whereas the "Chicagoans" framed their analysis in terms of delinquent (and criminal) subcultures (or occupations) and the process by which the youngster is socialized into them (and so learns norms that are contrary to those of "middleclass society"). A second variety of criticism of National Functionalism issued from those who followed the intellectual tradition of regarding the nation state as rooted in conflict; for, from the perspective of that tradition, to treat the national society as if it were a community in functionalist equilibrium appeared as either

political naivete or as ideological conservatism, and in either case as obfus-
cating the study of social conflict and change. Accordingly, the "Chicago
School" and the "Conflict Theorists" shared not only an opposition to the
application of functionalist conceptualizations to the nation, but a vision of
that nation (and especially its urban areas) as composed of a diversity of
groups—social classes, ethnic communities, bohemians, etc.—groups which
were distinctive in their interests, norms, and values. Yet, for the Conflict
Theorists, the issue was not necessarily functionalism as a theoretical schema
since, for example, one of their leading scholars, Lewis Coser, has attempted
to enlarge and modify functionalism by incorporating within it a Simmel
notion of "the functions of social conflict."

The disagreement between the "National Functionalists" and the "Conflict
Theorists" is illustrated well by the following criticism of the interpretation
of the English industrial revolution that was advanced by the Parsonian sociologist Neil Smelser on the possibility of a minimum wage law. Thompson
(1966) is forced to protest that—

The difficulty lay, not (as Professor Smelser has it) in the "dominant value
system of the day," but in the strong opposition of a minority of masters and in
the mood of Parliament (which Professor Smelser commends for its success in
"handling" and "channelling" the weavers' "unjustified disturbance symptoms")
(p. 300).

By the very nature of their approach to the national state, the National
Functionalists have detached themselves from much of the Western tradition
of political philosophy. The exception is their extraordinary concern with
"the problem of Hobbes"; since, like that observer of the English Reformation and of the growth of the modern nation state, they perceive the state as
an organism that is fragile yet utterly essential to the maintenance of organized social life.[3] In effect, by regarding the national state as conterminous
with "society" (or the "social system"), these theorists have come to be indis-
tinguishable politically from conservative nationalists. In this respect they
are loyal disciples of Max Weber (*cf.* Mayer's portrait, 1955). It is ironic to
reflect that Weber's own analysis of the English Reformation would likely
have been more in the form of Thompson's with its concern for organized
political power, and less in the form of Smelser's with its talk about systems.

MYTH AND SCIENCE

We have reviewed briefly the following myths purveyed by the social sciences: that these sciences are young; that the various disciplines represent
a rational and systematic division of scientific labor; that the national society
can be considered as a community or system in homeostatic equilibrium. As

3. The limitations of this kind of focus on Hobbes are exposed in MacPherson (1964).

social scientists contemplating ourselves, we can perhaps adjudge that we too require some myths to sustain us in our work and to facilitate those patterns of cooperation and competition which are helpful in any organized activity; and we can feel that these are not the most vicious of myths nor the most delusionary. Then, too, our need for myth and ideology is not completely of our own making. For the social sciences are very much a part of the world about them, and, within the U. S. the support for social research derives from other institutions: the agencies of the federal government, benevolent foundations, universities; and these have considerable roles in tempting us to sustain these myths in order to enjoy their momentary favors. Archetypical of these myths and of the blandishments for accepting them is that which says that, if the social sciences would model themselves rigorously after the natural sciences, then they, too, would achieve the status of being true sciences. Thus, the American Association for the Advancement of Science awards annually a prize of $1,000 "in order to encourage in social inquiry the development and application of dependable methodology analogous to the methods that have proven so fruitful in the natural sciences." The existence of such an award exposes clearly the mythical nature of the goal. Surely, the test of methodology is its consequence: those methods are better which yield better results. Surely, also, the natural sciences enjoy their prominence and respect because of their achievements, not because of the purity and dependability of their methodology. To my knowledge, no prizes of significance are awarded within the natural sciences because of the methodology of the investigator but rather because he has solved a troublesome problem or achieved an elegant conclusion. Surely, again, no investigator would deliberately choose a "non-dependable methodology" for his researches; all other things being equal, and he being a sensible man, he would choose methods that held promise of helping him to win significant and dependable results.

The consequence of emphasizing methodology—as if it could be judged and evaluated apart from the total investigation and apart from the consequences of employing it—has served to convert social-scientific activity from systematic learning into acts of ritual piety. The goal becomes, not the study of human beings, their interactions, their societies, etc., but instead the performing of a set of ritualized exercises (*cf.* Blumer, 1954; Sherif, 1967); necessarily these rites are sustained, not by their accomplishments within the mundane world, but by an eschatological vision—the coming of the Kingdom of Behavioral Science. As but one tiny symptom of this, let me refer to my own recent experience serving upon the editorial board of a reputable journal in the social sciences. A surprising number of papers reaching me for editorial review have been simply methodological programs; not, mind you, proposals to do specific research, but, instead, grand outlines for social research generally. Reading these papers, I gain little feeling that the authors are genuinely interested in studying any particular kind of social phenomena, but rather that, like some of the theologians of the Reformation, they are so preoccupied with formulating the right doctrine they have no time to be interested in actual human beings and societies. I suppose that these reformers of social science may think of themselves as being latterday incarnations of Galileo, Kepler, and Copernicus, but, if so, they seem to be forgetting the long hours of observation and computation, patient and detailed to the point of drudgery, which these forefathers invested in their researches and which laid the groundwork for their revolutionary findings.

Ironically, if we were to review the history of social science over the past two centuries, I think we would be struck by the number of its exponents who thought of themselves as ushering in the scientific millenium by applying the methods and rigor of the natural sciences. Comte and Pareto, Freud and Watson, Radcliffe-Brown and Boas—just to single out some diverse theorists within the same discipline—each of these men thought of himself as study- ing human conduct in a fashion akin to the way that the natural scientist had been studying the nonhuman world. Each of these men elaborated not merely, a theory, but a program, and each was successful in recruiting dis- ciples to help launch the program. Yet where are the social sciences today? The scientistic critics of the AAAS seem to believe that very little progress has been made, else they would not be offering prizes for researches employ- ing dependable methodologies. But, if in fact we have made so little of that type of progress despite the efforts of such brilliant, energetic, and magnetic individuals, then perhaps it is not unreasonable to surmise that the pursuit of natural scientific methodologies is a pernicious delusion.

Returning to the sextet of ancestors listed above, it could be argued that the worst aspect of their researches was the influence of natural science ide- ologies and models, so that, for example, Freud's findings about human rela- tionships would have been clearer, simpler, and therefore more accurate had he not been obsessed with an attempt to locate great natural forces akin to electromagnetism. Likewise, the critics of Boas (including myself, 1956) have contended that the largely negative, incomplete, and simply naïve character of his cultural anthropological researches is only intelligible in terms of the rigor and constriction of his methodological beliefs, so that his manifest abilities and great energy were thwarted by his simplistic empirical creed.

THREE RIVAL METHODOLOGIES

I have argued that the disciplinary boundaries among the social sciences do not represent a systematic division of labor; I could equally have argued that the significant methodological differences do not follow the disciplinary boundaries but cut across them. Thus, by confining ourselves strictly to a consideration of relationships among disciplines we will fail to deal with significant issues of a methodological nature; and, so that these are not neglected, I shall here approach them directly. For economy of exposition I shall be focusing on three major methodological orientations which I see active in sociology and anthropology and some of their peripheral areas. By so focusing, I will be slighting some significant orientations, but, given the nature of this essay and the limitations of my studies, this procedure will be the best compromise. Following their sloganeering, I shall refer to the three orientations as symbolic interaction, systems theoretic, and ethnomethodological. Other labels would be possible, and my own interpretations may be such as to cause their disciples to think that I have compounded too much together. But, in any case, I see three orientations as distinctive in their conceptual schemes and their images of social scientific techniques and goals. Again on a sloganeering basis, I would say that, respectively, they are oriented toward: meaning and symbol; system and homeostasis; pattern and contrast.

The symbolic interactionist label has come to be associated with a school of social psychology that is integrated with a distinct philosophy of science; on the psychological side the school issues principally from G. H. Mead and C. H. Cooley, and on the philosophical side from Mead and J. Dewey. Within sociology, this approach has close affinity with the Germanic tradition of *verstehende Soziologie*. The approach postulates that distinctively human conduct occurs within a cultural environment composed of shared meanings. Hence, to comprehend any specific bit of conduct, the researcher must enter into that world of meanings; these are not treated as subjective, i.e. private or internal to the organism, but as present in the field of interaction and to be apprehended accordingly. In the Germanic tradition, the problems of elucidating meanings became entangled with that of imputing motives (Abel, 1953; Cahnman, 1964; Wax, 1967a), perhaps because the commonsensical and legal approach to the understanding of action has in Western cultures been equivalent to seeking for the motive of the actor. However, when the problem of elucidating meaning is so characterized, then the approach is justly to be criticized, for as C. W. Mills argued in a famous essay (1940), the imputing of motives is polemical and rhetorical rather than objective; and, as Dorothy D. Lee (1959) has reported, among many nonWestern peoples there is little or no effort to inpute motives (although these peoples certainly interact in a world of meanings). If the meaning of the act is thus detached from its spurious involvement with motivation, then the question still remains as to how the meaning is to be elucidated or inferred, and critics of *verstehende Soziologie* have accused it of lacking any reliable "operations" which, when rigidly applied, would yield valid meanings.

Notwithstanding its disinterest in developing special "operations" or instruments, symbolic interaction does lead to research techniques; these may appear unpretentious—ordinary forms of social inquiry—but the significant point is that they are conducted in a particularly systematic, disciplined, and self-conscious fashion. To the extent feasible, the emphasis is upon the immersion of the researcher in the cultural world of the people he is study-ing, or, barring that immersion, an intensive and prolonged interaction on his part with them. If he seeks to study a community, he will regard it as highly desirable to learn its languages or dialects, to observe or participate in its activities and ceremonies, and to talk with its folk about the topics of interest and concern to them. Beyond this, the researcher will keep careful records not only of the statements of the people of the community, but of his own personal reactions, and he will review these regularly in order to under-stand what changes have been occurring in himself and in his relationships with his subjects. In short, symbolic interaction leads the sociologist most naturally toward the techniques of participant observation (*cf.* R. H. Wax, 1968) and the anthropologists toward ethnographic (participating) field research; the psychologist, or at least the clinical psychologist, is led toward the interview in the spirit of Harry Stack Sullivan, who thought of the psychiatric interview as a variant of participant observation.

Especially if he has been influenced by the natural science image of what a science should be, the critic of symbolic interaction will contend, first, that the methodology does not lead anywhere, i.e. toward any general proposi-tions characteristic of scientific discoveries, and, second, that the methodol-ogy is not reliable, inasmuch as two students engaged in studying the same act, or the same people, may perceive different meanings (the most con-spicuous discrepancy being that two cultural anthropologists might compose two quite different reports about what are presumably the same or simi-lar people). The first point is fundamental, and researchers who might be classed within this methodological orientation have argued that social sci-ence is a moral science akin to history (Evans-Pritchard speaking specifically of anthropology in 1964), or is akin to art (Redfield 1948; Nisbet 1965, despite himself), or akin to philosophy (Winch 1958), and in short should not be compared with the natural sciences as an ideal. Correspondingly, it could be argued that some of the finest achievements of social sciences to date have been either the elucidation of meanings among a people (or within a situation) foreign to ourselves or a demythologizing nearer to home (*cf.* Seeley, 1965, 1967). Thus, the epitome of this type of research would be Evans-Pritchard's analysis of magic and witchcraft among the Azande (Gluckman, 1944), or the analysis of a pathologically disordered child by Bruno Bettelheim, or of opiate addiction by A. R. Lindesmith. The second point of the critic is deserving of a better and more direct answer than it has had in the literature. It is clearly true that different researchers studying what appears to be the same people, or the same phenomena, have com-posed quite different reports and have emphasized different constellations of meaning. This is inevitable, given that meaning is an outgrowth of human interaction and to be apprehended differently by persons who, coming from different backgrounds, experience different interactions in the course of their researches (Seeley, 1965, pp. 64–65). Yet, the significant fact is that a field such as cultural anthropology, which has relied primarily upon field research carried out via participant observation, has in fact made significant progress. For, the fact that different observers submit different reports does not leave the matter in stalemate, but instead has stimulated a process of controversy during the course of which the contrary reports and data are examined, reexamined, compared with similar materials from elsewhere, and thoroughly debated. Further and more exact field research may then be carried out, subject only to the ever-present limitations of time and money—and the continued survival of the people in question. Thus, issues can be resolved, or clarified toward resolution, and the course of investigation fulfill the basic requirements of being a science.

It is intelligible that the symbolic interaction orientation should not satisfy those with more ambitious theoretical goals and, especially, those whose ideal is represented by the natural sciences. Some of these scientists have taken as their scientific goal the formal logical system which, in propositional or mathematical form, generates an abstract model. While the elements of the system need not correspond exactly with observable social entities, the homeostatic functioning of the model is intended to provide a guide to the functioning of actual societies. Classical economics provides a convenient illustration: it postulates a population of "economic men," isolated individuals, motivated solely by rational economic self-interest, and completely knowledgeable about the market. Whether or not human beings actually conform to this postulate, the theoretical model is useful to the extent that its workings provide guidance to the behavior of actual economic systems. Such systems-theoretic orientations can also be employed in dealing with individual human beings, as when psychologists attempt to program computers to simulate the learning and response patterns of human subjects; the issue is not whether the neural processes of the brain and the switching patterns of the computer are in correspondence, but rather whether or not the outputs are usefully similar.

The foregoing somewhat overstates the case. Most systems theorists have found it, not only convenient, but necessary to construct their models so as to provide a correspondence—limited, to be sure—between the elements of their model and social reality. It was not misguided foolishness that led Adam Smith to insist that human beings did act like economic men (although he, himself, had described human conduct far more richly in his non-economic essays—cf. Truzzi, 1966). Working within a systems-theoretic orientation, structural functionalists have sought to follow the lead of the economists. Their problem, of course, is that if their model is to be general, they cannot afford to be concerned with meanings that vary from individual to individual or from group to group. Hence, like Adam Smith, they seek for what presumptively are universal varieties of human behavior. Durkheim was a pioneer in this regard; he contended, for example, that all societies recognized a "religion" which they distinguished from a "magic." On this basis, he proceeded to erect a theoretical model for religion which would be applicable to all societies. In like manner, he argued about *suicide* as if it were a phenomenon which members of all societies could agree in chara terizing. (Thus, "John committed suicide" is a proposition which, in accord with the basic postulates of Durkheim's argument, should be capable of unequivocal translation into every natural language.) Other social scientists have perceived the universal variety of human behavior in rational action, so that, in Aristotelean fashion, all acts could be classified in terms of the choice of means in relationship to ends. Just as economists have postulated an "economic man," rational in his pursuit of gain, so sociologists have postulated a "social man" who was rational in his role behaviors. Since the totality of social life is far more complex than that segment associated with the market, sociologists have been driven toward more complex models for rational conduct and for dealing with the nonrational residues (*cf.* Max Weber, 1947, trans. 1964), and only when they are dealing with such limited and structured situations as a game—with formalized rules, goals, and tactics—could they operate in a fashion approximating the elegance of the economists with their models.

Unhappily for the systems theorists and structural functionalists, the problems of meaning cannot be so easily evaded. Although himself a functionalist, Radcliffe-Brown was forced to challenge the theoretical system for religion that had been advanced by Durkheim on the grounds that as a matter of ethnographic fact the *sacred/profane* and *religion/magic* dichotomies were not distinguished by members of exotic cultures and so the phenomena were not universally present in human societies (*cf.* Goody, 1961; Wax, 1967b). More recently, another scholar (Douglas, 1966) had made a similar attack upon the concept of "suicide." Since Durkheim's theories presume that the peoples in question themselves recognize and respond to these categories of acts and events, these criticisms are damaging. A parallel criticism can be made of the contemporary structural functionalism of Talcott Parsons, as Parsons was a student of Malinowski and built his model of social interaction upon the image of man which he inherited from his teacher.[4] In his theory of *magic,* Malinowski had argued that the primitive

---

4. Parsons' scientific goal is neatly summed in his judgment (1964, p. 20) upon Weber: "He did not perceive that starting from the frame of reference of subjectively interpreted individual action . . . it was possible by functional analysis to develop a generalized outline of social systems of action." In order for Parsons to accomplish this goal, he found it necessary to argue (1949, p. 425 and citing A. D. Nock) that "men do not in general 'believe' their religious ideas in quite the same sense that they believe the sun rises every morning." The confirmation of this disjunction he found (1949, p. 425) in Malinowski's essay on "Magic, Science, and Religion," which "satisfactorily demonstrated the existence of such an empirical distinction in the senses in which primitive men believe in the efficacy on the one hand of magical manipulations, on the other of rational techniques." Parsons thought at the time that "Malinowski's view in this respect has been widely accepted by anthropologists," and certainly it was accepted by some of them. The pendu-

(i.e., the Trobriand Islander) recognizes a clear distinction between the "empirical" and the "nonempirical," using native "science" in the first area and magic in the second. In fact, this was a misleading categorization on his part (Leach in Firth, 1956; Gluckman, 1944; Wax, 1967b), and one which he utilized in order to belabor Lucien Lévy-Bruhl, whom, he felt, was derogating the mentality of primitive peoples. In the heat of his polemical rebuttal, Malinowski had converted the Trobriander (and all other "primitives") into a species of Western man. This error of Malinowski's proved highly convenient to later functionalists, not only Parsons but Merton—who, together with his students, repeatedly cites the celebrated comparison of fishing in the lagoon and the sea—and they made it basic to their schema of human action. For, if all men agreed in distinguishing the "empirical" from the "nonempirical," then, for example, the task of constructing a universal theory of magic and religion was greatly simplified, and so too was the task of constructing a model of rational action. Unfortunately, the facts are that the distinction is far from universal, so that incorporating it into the very foundations of structural-functionalist theories has built in a most pernicious error.

The ethnomethodologists have attempted to steer a course between the symbolic interactionist's reliance on meaning for the actor and the systems theorist's hope of universal categories of acts and events. This they do by focusing not on meanings, but on patterns and contrasts in the language or communicative code. The development of the methodology of linguistic analysis is taken as an exemplar (just as certain fields in economics have been regarded as the exemplars by Talcott Parsons and other systems theorists), and a quasi-linguistic procedure for collecting data is being followed. Items are always viewed in natural context (or linguistic environment) and one mode of inquiry is by systematically observing which variations of discourse elicit differences in response of the subject. If, for instance, one were studying kinship usages in the English language, he might arrive at the patterned role of "father," and its contrast with "mother," "brother," etc., through a series of systematized interrogations involving such terms as "father," "mother," "grandmother," "great-grandfather," etc. Kinship usages have, in fact, been the principal area where the ethnomethodologists have worked, and where they have achieved their most elegantly formal results. And, as in linguistic analysis proper, the consequence of their labors often seems more elegant, precise, and, thereby intriguing, than it does of useful import. Indeed, the most eminent scholar who might be associated with this

lum has since swung far in the other direction. As always, much depends on how the issue is phrased; doubtless, it is possible to demonstrate for some peoples a distinction between their belief in some item such a "the sun will rise tomorrow" and a creation myth; but their conduct and their discussion of a matter such as a death in the community, or a crop failure, quickly reveals that the neat distinction between "empirical" and "nonempirical" is in the eyes of the Western observer, not in theirs.

A forceful critique of Malinowski's position on these questions will be found in the essay by E. R. Leach (1964).

methodological orientation, Claude Lévi-Strauss, has emphatically disclaimed any practical consequence to his formal investigations.

The ethnomethodological approach is applicable to the extent that the investigator can locate and delineate a cultural production (such as a natural language or a terminology for kinship relations) which is a closed system crescively developed of unconscious cultural patterns. It would seem likely that the approach will therefore find its most significant employment among highly integrated—therefore isolated and ancient—cultures. It will illuminate the ability of such peoples to abstract and conceptualize in ways very different than has been characteristic of Western societies. On the other hand, the symbolic-interactionist critic will be impatient of its abstention from issues of meaning: he believes that the analysis of syntactic systems of kinship terms should lead to an understanding of patterns of action among those people and he is impatient with a sterile precisionism.

RELATION TO HISTORY

Seeking to bridge the rival methodologies of his time, Max Weber saw in sociology

a science which aims at the interpretative understanding of social conduct and thus at the explanation of its causes, its course, and its effects (Weber, 1966, p. 1). [*eine Wissenschaft, welche soziales Handelen deutend verstehen und dadurch in seinem Ablauf und seinen Wirkungen ursächlich erklären will* (Weber, 1947, p. 1).]

Operating from this strategic posture, Weber was able to produce a brilliant interpretive (*verstehende*) study of the Reformation, while embedding it as strategic case example in a structure of concepts and propositions that were designed to be applicable to the widest range of societies. Such spectacular and encyclopedic achievements were to have a lasting impact upon sociology or, more precisely, were to contribute markedly to the emergence of sociology as a distinctive discipline. Meanwhile, however, Weber's essays on the Reformation were to arouse a flood of discussion and criticism within the general scholarly community. By the present date, most European historians (whether economic, social, or religious) have agreed that the basic argument of *The Protestant Ethic and the Spirit of Capitalism* is, not so much debatable or wrong, as it is occupied with a spurious question. Chadwick, for example, speaks (1966, p. 184) of "an alleged connexion of puritanism and capitalism" while Elton (1966) is even more emphatic:

There is no good reason for linking Protestantism and capitalism in the significant relationship for so long accepted as certain . . . Looked at with an open mind, the whole idea of a meaningful correlation—even geographic coincidence—of these historical phenomena simply disappears. Answers have been devised for non-existent questions (p. 318).

For any student of interdisciplinary relationships, the response of sociologists (and anthropologists, indirectly) to these devastating judgments by
eminent historians must be of the greatest signficance. Yet, most sociologists
have continued to formulate the issues in the terms of Weber's own day:
they believe that a connection or correlation has empirically been established beyond disproof, and that the issue is whether Weber's analysis is
correct—thus yielding an idealistic interpretation of history—or whether his
analysis is incorrect and a historical materialistic interpretaton must follow. This phrasing of the issue is manifest even in the elucidations of the
Weberian corpus by so sophisticated a sociologist as Bendix (1962). Especially is it noteworthy that, while Bendix feels it appropriate to amend
Weber's portrait of ancient Judaism with judicious selections from the work
of subsequent scholars, such as William F. Albright, he feels no kindred
necessity in the case of Weber's portrait of the Reformation. That strategic
case thus tends to remove itself from an empirical foundation in historical
materials and to slide into the abstract world of analytic theory. Parsons
(1963) is even more explicit in this orientation:

In the Protestant Ethic, Weber raised a set of theoretical problems in the field
of human social action of the very first order of importance. The central problem
was whether men's conceptions of the cosmic universe, including those of Divinity and men's religious interests within such a conceptual framework could
influence or shape their concrete actions and social relationships, particularly in
the very mundane field of economic action. This possibility was entertained seriously, and the question of *how* to conceive the operation of religious ideas
became central. In the case of the relation between Protestantism and capitalism,
the study of the operation of religious ideas led to questions of historical interpretation. But Weber early became acutely aware, as many participants in
discussion still are not, that the problem of causation involved an *analytical*
problem, one of the isolation of variables and the testing of their significance in
situations where they can be shown to vary independently of each other. The
purely "historical" method, seeking ever more detailed knowledge of the "ideal"
and "material" historical antecedents of modern economic organization, is inherently circular. It was only by establishing a methodological equivalent of
experimental method, in which it is possible to hold certain factors constant, that
even the beginnings of an escape from circularity was possible (p. XXI).

But it is Parsons here who misunderstands the nature of the historians'
critique. They are not at all concerned with the ancient idealistic/material-
istic debate, but rather (Elton, 1966) point out that—

Weber started with an axiom which was simply not true: that a special kind of
capitalist spirit distinguished post-Reformation Europe and was most marked in
Protestant countries. Neither the view that the outburst of material improvement
and commercial enterprise, which characterized the centuries after 1600, in some
way emanated from the new cast of mind which had also produced Protestantism
(Weber), nor the view that capitalism exploited the peculiarities of the Protes-

tant form of Christianity to free itself from all restraint (Tawṇey) is borne out or required by the facts (p. 318).

More disturbing than his misinterpretations of this criticism is Parsons' assertation that further historical investigations can be disregarded (because of their inherent circularity), since, to my thinking, this would deprive the scholarly discussion of empirical foundation and, would furthermore, make meaningless the historical researches of Weber himself. Parsons is correct in urging that students who wish *to understand Weber* must view his essays on the Reformation in relationship to the total corpus of his writings; but surely it does not follow that essays which were published as independent journal articles and which advanced particular propositions about European history can be removed from historical examination and criticsm (*cf.* also Samuelsson, 1961; its review by Parsons, 1962; and the appraisal of Samuelsson by Elton, 1966, p. 312).

For purposes of the present discussion, we can note that the systems-theoretic orientation of Parsons would serve to foreclose meaningful collaboration between the sociologist and the historian. We might also comment that the consequence for sociologists of elevating Weber to the position of deified ancestor has been to trans-substantiate historical and comparative researches from empirical to analytical status, so that while they have the "accidents of factuality," their "essence" is pure theory.

SOME CONCLUDING REMARKS

While some social scientific disciplines—linguistic analysis (philology) and political economy—are respectably ancient, sociology and anthropology and psychology have appeared as organized entities only within the past two centuries. In the more ideological versions of their origins, emphasis is placed upon the application to social phenomena of that new and master tool—the scientific method (*cf.* Nisbet, 1965, p. 150). This explanation, I have argued (1965, 1966), downrates the observations and studies of the previous millenia, while distorting the role of recent Western history. Sociology arose as a response to the Industrial Revolution—to the emergence and growth of new and peculiar social forms. The new military technology, the vastly improved systems of transportation and communication, combined with the exploitation of inanimate sources of power and with the increasing specialization and division of labor, all these were facilitating the emergence of new social arrangements in which human beings were being associated together in larger numbers and for more complex operations than ever before. At the same time, the quality of human associations had been changing drastically, so that more and more people were now associating with, or interdependent upon, others who were not their kith and kin. Marxism and sociology can both be regarded as reflexes of this social revolution—as attempts by the more reflective minds to comprehend these developments and to confront and direct them in a conscious and moral fashion.

The same period of history also saw the mutation which led to the emergence of classical economics. Let us recall that this theoretical model was predicated upon the most crude portrait of human nature and of social interaction; as compared to the heritage of Western political and moral philosophy, classical economics represented a retrogression. Yet its crudity was essential to its task, namely that of characterizing the operations of an institutional system based upon partial or degraded human relationships. This crudity and degradation must sharply be distinguished from the abstracting process of classical mechanics in which an apple can, as a falling body, be treated as a mass concentrated as a point, ignoring its flavor, taste, color, and irregularities of shape. For the apple never loses its property of mass, while human beings do and, often, engage in behavior that escapes the paradigms of classical economics. To say this is not to derogate that discipline, either in its original form or in its much revised modern versions, but to remind us that these models are necessarily and inevitably untrue, and that this poses a terrible danger. For economics is not intended just as a pure science but as a guide to action. To the extent that the student encases himself within that model as if it were the total of social reality, then he converts a heuristic approximation into an ideology with far-reaching moral implications. (Classical economics was used to justify the most terrible and inhuman treatment of the lower classes during the Industrial Revolution in England and on the Continent.)

During the course of this essay I have several times singled out for attack the functionalist school in its nationalist and structuralist variants: one reason for my animus is that, like classical economics, functionalist systems lend themselves to the combination of being scientific model and ideological creed, so that the label of "pure science" protects the ideology from political or moral counterattack, while the abstraction necessitated by model building permits a distortion that can serve one group of interests at the expense of others (cf. Seeley 1965, 1967). As but one illustration, consider that nationalist functionalism leads the student toward focusing on national societies as isolated and autonomous units in an age when the great national powers (the United States and the USSR) are intervening actively and powerfully in the affairs of most of the peoples of the world. As a consequence, social scientists are in the position of discussing "development" as if it were a matter of isolated national social structures and values when, in fact, the activities of the great powers are of such significance that they cannot be dismissed. Moreover, as I have argued above, the very disparateness of the social-scientific disciplines reinforces such distortions and omissions.

In a world which now includes billions of peoples who are associated together in national and international linkages of economic, religious, military, scientific, and other varieties, we cannot avoid the processes of abstraction and of isolating arbitrary fields for investigation. The task of description and of understanding is staggering. How much simpler it all was for the Hellenic philosophers who could focus on their small quasi-tribal societies, and no wonder that today we find so limited a range of applicability to their observations and reflections. Contrary to the current mythos of social science, its students are faced, not by the growth of a new and youthful science, but by the desperate struggles of an ancient science to keep descriptive pace with the human capacity to create and manipulate complex webs of social relationships. Where the mythos claims a revolution in man's understanding of man, I would note instead the revolution in human societies—in the emergence of mass, industrial, urban societies, globally interdependent.

Structural functionalism or some other varieties of systems-theoretical approaches are undoubtedly necessary as conceptual instruments for descriptively coping with this overwhelming challenge. Yet, if they are to be scientific rather than ideological counterparts of the nationalistic and imperialistic developments of the United States (and other Western societies) then social-scientists must become far more conscious of the arbitrariness, deliberate bias, and ethnocentricity of their initial assumptions.

Given a variety of disciplines in such rivalry with each other that they do not respect disciplinary boundaries, given also a variety of styles of research, and given, especially, a sufficient quantity of research which requires the student to immerse himself in the world of exotic peoples, then we can hope that the social-scientific dialogue will limit the excessive growth of distorted and ethnocentric models. On the other hand, the argument of this essay has shown that myths and ideologies are continuing to flourish within the social sciences, and that the seeming accomplishments of one discipline can be embraced uncritically by a neighbor and then maintained with such vigor as to ignore the process of criticism which begins at home. From this example, I would judge that 'the dialogue among the disciplines is still deficient and inadequately critical.

REFERENCES

ABEL, T. 1953. The operation called *Verstehen.* In H. Feigl and M. Brodbeck (Eds.), *Readings in the philosophy of science.* New York: Appleton-Century-Crofts.

ARENSBERG, C. 1961. The community as object and as sample. *American Anthropologist,* 63: 241–64.

BENDIX, R. 1962. *Max Weber: an intellectual portrait.* Garden City, N.Y.: Doubleday Anchor.

BLUMER, H. 1954. What is wrong with social theory. *American Sociological Review,* 19: 3–10.

CAHNMAN, W. J. 1964. Max Weber and the methodological controversy in the social sciences. In W. J. Cahnman and A. Boskoff (Eds.), *Sociology and history.* New York: Free Press of Glencoe.

CHADWICK, O. 1966. *The Reformation*. ("The Pelican History of the Church," O. Chadwick, ed., vol. 3.) Baltimore: Penguin Books.

DOUGLAS, J. D. 1966. The social meaning of suicide. Paper presented to annual meetings, American Sociological Association, Miami Beach, September.

ELTON, G. R. 1966. *Reformation Europe: 1517–1559*. ("History of Europe" series, J. H. Plumb, ed.) New York: Harper Torchbook.

EVANS-PRITCHARD, E. E. 1964. Social anthropology: past and present. In *Social anthropology and other essays*. New York: Free Press of Glencoe.

FIRTH, R., (Ed.). 1956. *Man and culture: an evaluation of the work of Bronislaw Malinowski*. New York: Harper Torchbook.

GLUCKMAN, M. 1944. *The logic of African science and witchcraft: an appreciation of Evans-Pritchard's "Witchcraft Oracles and Magic among the Azande" of the Sudan*. Indianapolis: Bobbs-Merrill.

GOODY, J. 1961. Religion and ritual: the definitional problem. *British Journal of Sociology*, 12: 142–64.

HUGHES, E. C. 1951. Work and the self. In J. Rohrer and M. Sherif (Eds.), *Social psychology at the crossroads*. New York: Harper.

––––––. 1958. *Men and their work*. Glencoe, Ill.: Free Press.

––––––. 1959. The dual mandate of social science: remarks on the academic division of labor. *Canadian Journal of Economics and Political Science*, 25: 401–410.

KUHN, T. S. 1962. *The structure of scientific revolutions*. Chicago: University of Chicago Press (Phoenix Books).

LEACH, E. R. 1964. The epistemological background to Malinowski's empiricism. In R. Firth (Ed.), *Man and culture*. New York: Harper Torchbook.

LEE, D. D. 1959. *Freedom and culture*. Englewood Cliffs, N.J.: Prentice-Hall (Spectrum Books).

MAQUET, J. J. 1964. Objectivity in anthropology. *Current Anthropology*, 5: 47–55.

MACPHERSON, C. B. 1964. *The political theory of possessive individualism: Hobbes to Locke*. Oxford: Clarendon Press.

MAYER, L. P. 1955. *Max Weber and German politics*. London: Faber & Faber.

MILLS, C. W. 1940. *Situated actions and vocabularies of motive*. Indianapolis: Bobbs-Merrill.

NISBET, R. 1965. Sociology as an art form. In M. Stein and A. Vidich (Eds.), *Sociology on trial*. Englewood Cliffs, N.J.: Prentice-Hall (Spectrum Books).

PARSONS, T. 1949. *The structure of social action*. Glencoe, Ill.: Free Press.

––––––. 1962. Review: *Religion and economic action* by Kurt Samuelsson. *Journal for the Scientific Study of Religion*, 1: 226–27.

––––––. 1963. Introduction to *The sociology of religion*, by Max Weber, trans. by E. Fischoff. Boston: Beacon Press.

––––––. 1964. Introduction to M. Weber, *The theory of social and economic organization* (trans. by T. Parsons and A. M. Henderson). New York: Free Press.

POLANYI, M. 1964. *Science, faith and society*. Chicago: University of Chicago Press (Phoenix Books).

REDFIELD, R. 1948. The art of social science. *American Journal of Sociology*, 54: 181–190.

_____. 1960. *The little community.* Chicago: University of Chicago Press (Phoenix Books).

REINING, C. C. 1966. *The Zande scheme.* Evanston, Ill.: Northwestern University Press.

SAMUELSSON, K. 1961. *Religion and economic action.* Trans. by E. Geoffrey French. New York: Basic Books.

SEELEY, J. R. 1965. Social science? some probative problems. In M. Stein and A. Vidich (Eds.), *Sociology on trial.* Englewood Cliffs, N.J.: Prentice-Hall (Spectrum Books).

_____. 1967. Social problems: toward an ethical stance. *Social Problems,* 14: 382–89.

SHERIF, M. 1967. If basic research is to have bearing on actualities . . . In *Social Interaction.* Chicago: Aldine Publishing Company.

_____, and B. L. KOSLIN. 1960. The "institutional" and "behavioral" controversy in social science with special reference to political science. Norman: Institute of Group Relations, University of Oklahoma. (Mimeo.)

STEIN, M. R. 1964. *The eclipse of community.* New York: Harper Torchbook.

THOMPSON, E. P. 1966. *The making of the English working class.* New York: Random House (Vintage Books).

TRUZZI, M. 1966. Adam Smith and contemporary issues in social psychology. *Journal of the History of the Behavioral Sciences,* 2: 221–24.

VIDICH, A. J., J. BENSMAN, and M. R. STEIN. 1964. *Reflections on community studies.* New York: Wiley.

WAX, M. L. 1956. The limitations of Boas' anthropology. *American Anthropologist,* 58: 63–74.

_____. 1965. The tree of social knowledge. *Psychiatry,* 28: 99–106.

_____. 1966. Some dialectical tensions within sociology and anthropology. Paper presented to annual meetings, American Anthropological Association, Pittsburgh, November.

_____. 1967a. On misunderstanding Verstehen: a reply to Abel. *Sociology and Social Research,* 51: 323–33.

_____. 1967b. Religion and magic. In J. Clifton (Ed.), *Introductory cultural anthropology.* Boston: Houghton Mifflin.

WAX, R. H. 1968. Participant observation. *International Encyclopedia of the Social Sciences.* New York: Free Press of Glencoe.

WEBER, M. 1947. Wirtschaft und Gesellschaft. ("Grundriss der Sozialökonomik" III. Abteilung.) Tübingen: J. C. B. Mohr.

_____. 1963. *The sociology of religion.* Trans. by Ephraim Fischoff. Boston: Beacon Press.

_____. 1964. *The theory of social and economic organization.* Trans. and ed. by A. M. Henderson and T. Parsons. New York: Free Press of Glencoe.

_____. 1966. *Max Weber on law in economy and society.* Trans. by E. Shils and M. Rheinstein. Cambridge: Harvard University Press.

WILLNER, D. 1964. Organizational dissonance and directed change. Paper presented to annual meetings, American Anthropological Association, Detroit, November.

WINCH, P. 1958. *The idea of a social science.* London: Routledge and Kegan Paul.

PART II
Illustrative Problem Areas

6

INTERDISCIPLINARY THINKING AND THE SMALL WORLD PROBLEM

Stanley Milgram

When a social scientist frees himself from the narrow grooves of his academic discipline, a new range of intellectual problems is made accessible to him, and new paths of inquiry open. I have seen this time and again among colleagues and graduate students, and am beginning to believe that just as cross-pressures in voting free the individual from following the traditional choices of his social group, intellectual cross-pressures generated by an interdisciplinary outlook liberate a person's thinking from the limiting assumptions of his own professional group, and stimulate fresh vision.

To say that a problem is treated in an interdisciplinary fashion can mean a number of different things, depending on the exact point in the process of inquiry at which interdisciplinary thinking is introduced. (1) To begin, it may enter into the formulation of the problem chosen for study: one may conceive a problem in such a way that it lies astride two or more disciplines. Not every phenomenon of nature has contours that match the boundaries of university departments. (2) Once a problem is posed, an investigator must decide what research techniques and procedures will be used to study it, and again, an interdisciplinary outlook can be helpful. Research procedures typical of one discipline may be usefully applied to certain problems posed by another discipline. In the study described below, an experimental style derived from laboratory social psychology is brought to bear on an investigation of large-scale social structure. (3) Even late in the research, interdisciplinary thinking may be introduced. Sometimes an investigator working solely within the traditions of his discipline comes across a fact that cannot be explained with the concepts available to him, and he must search in a neighboring field for the needed explanatory principle. (4) Finally, in its applications, a finding, insight, or concept generated solely within a single discipline may achieve interdisciplinary breadth. As in the case of Shannon's information theory, even ideas yielded by a highly technical

103

specialty may have broad application (see Mann, 1963).

Although interdisciplinary thinking may play a part in the *formulation, method of investigation, explanation,* or *application* of a study, the earlier in the research process such thinking is introduced, the less superficial it is likely to be, and the more likely it will confer meaningful intellectual benefits.

As a substantive contribution to this volume, I offer an account of research that does not fit neatly into any single discipline; rather it deals with a phenomenon possessing numerous facets and that can be treated by psychology, sociology, and political science. The problem concerns the manner in which individuals are linked, through bonds of kinship and acquaintance, into complex networks, and the means of devising efficient paths connecting any two points within the network. For the sake of simplicity, let us call this "the small world problem," a phrase long current in our language, but first employed in the social sciences by Ithiel Pool (cited in Rand, 1964).

The simplest way of formulating the small world problem is: "Starting with any two people in the world, what is the probability that they will know one another?" A somewhat more complex formulation, however, takes account of the fact that while persons X and Z may not know each other directly, they may share a mutual acquaintance—that is, a person who knows both of them. One can then think of an acquaintance chain with X knowing Y and Y knowing Z. Moreover, one can imagine circumstances in which X is linked to Z not by a single link, but by a series of links, that is, X-a-b-c-d---y-Z. That is to say, person X knows person a who in turn knows person b, who knows c, . . . who knows y, who knows Z.

Therefore, another question one may ask is: given any two people in the world, person X and person Z, how many intermediate acquaintance links are needed before X and Z are connected? There are two general philosophical views on the small world problem. Some people feel that any two people in the world, no matter how remote from each other, can be linked in terms of intermediate acquaintances, and that the number of such intermediate links is relatively small.

There is, however, a contrasting view that sees unbridgeable gaps between various groups. Given any two people in the world, they will never link up, because people have circles of acquaintances which will not necessarily intersect. A message will circulate in a particular cluster of acquaintances, but may never be able to make the jump to another cluster. This view sees the world in terms of isolated clusters of acquaintances. The earlier view sees acquaintances in terms of an infinitely intersecting arrangement that permits movement from any social grouping to another through a series of connecting links.

Concern with the small world problem is not new, nor is it limited to social psychologists like myself. Historians, political scientists, and even city planners have spoken of the matter in quite unambiguous terms. Jane Jacobs

(1961) who has written on city planning, expressed it in terms that many of us have entertained as children.

When my sister and I first came to New York from a small city, we used to amuse ourselves with a game we called Messages. The idea was to pick two wildly dissimilar individuals—say a head hunter in the Solomon Islands and a cobbler in Rock Island, Illinois—and assume that one had to get a message to the other by word of mouth; then we would each silently figure out a plausible, or at least possible, chain of persons through which the message could go. The one who could make the shortest plausible chain of messengers won. The head hunter would speak to the head man of his village, who would speak to the trader who came to buy copra, who would speak to the Australian patrol officer when he came through, who would tell the man who was next slated to go to Melbourne on leave, etc. Down at the other end, the cobbler would hear from his priest, who got it from the mayor, who got it from a state senator, who got it from the governor, etc. We soon had these close-to-home messengers down to a routine for almost everybody we could conjure up (pp. 134–35).

The importance of the problem does not lie in these entertaining aspects, but in the fact that it brings under discussion a certain mathematical structure in society, a structure that often plays a part, whether recognized or not, in many discussions of history, sociology, and other disciplines. For example, Henri Pirenne (1925) and George Duby (1958), make the point that in the dark ages communication broke down between cities of western Europe. They became isolated and simply did not have contact with each other. The network of acquaintances of individuals became constricted. The disintegration of society was expressed in the growing isolation of communities, and the infrequent contact with those living outside a person's immediate place of residence.

THE UNDERLYING STRUCTURE

Sometimes it is useful to visualize the abstract properties of a scientific problem before studying it in detail; that is, we construct a model of the main features of the phenomenon as we understand them. Graph theory, which is concerned with the mathematical treatment of networks, provides a convenient way of representing the structure of acquaintanceships. (Harary, Norman, and Cartwright, 1965)

Let us represent all the people in the United States by a number of points. Each point represents a person, while lines connecting two points show that the two persons are acquainted. Each person has a certain number of first-hand acquaintances, which we shall represent by the letters a, b, c, . . . n. Each acquaintance in turn has his own acquaintances, connected to still other points (see Figs. 1a and 1b).

The exact number of lines radiating from any point depends on the size of a person's circle of acquaintances. The entire structure takes on the form of a complex network of 200,000,000 points, with complicated connections

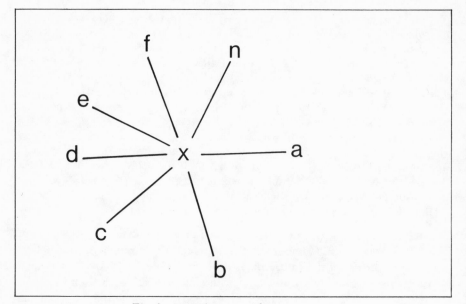

Fig. 1a Acquaintances of x, a . . . n

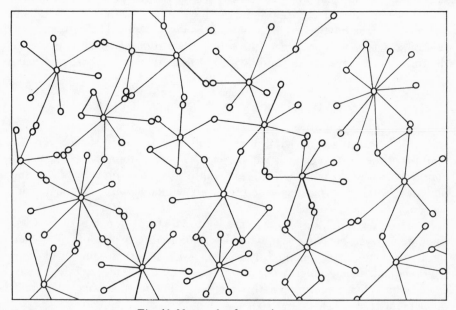

Fig. 1b Network of acquaintances

between them. One way of restating the small world problem in these terms is this: given any two of these points chosen at random from this universe, through how many intermediate points would we pass before they could be connected by the shortest possible path?

There are many ways to go about the study of the small world problem, and I shall soon present my own approach to it. But first, let us consider the contributions of a group of workers at MIT under the leadership of Ithiel de Sola Pool. Pool, working closely with Manfred Kochen of IBM decided to build a theoretical model of the small world, and the model parallels closely the idea of points and lines shown in Figure 1. To build such a model certain information needs to be known. First, you have to know how many acquaintances the average man has. Surprisingly, though this is a basic question, no reliable answers could be found in the social science literature. So the information had to be obtained, and Dr. Michael Gurevitch, then a graduate student at MIT, set about this task. Gurevitch (1961) asked a variety of men and women to keep a record of all the persons they came in contact with in the course of 100 days. It turned out that on the average, these people recorded names of roughly 500 persons, so that this figure could be used as the basis of the theoretical model. If every person knows 500 other people, what are the chances that any two people will know each other? Making a set of rather simple assumptions, it turns out that there is only about one chance in 200,000 that any two Americans chosen at random will know each other. However, the odds drop precipitously when you ask the chances of their having a mutual acquaintance. And there is better than a 50-50 chance that any two people can be linked up with two intermediate acquaintances.

Of course, the investigators were aware of the fact that even if a man has 500 acquaintances, there may be a lot of inbreeding. That is, many of the 500 friends of my friend may be actually among the people I know anyway, so that they do not really contribute to a widening net of acquaintances. Figure 2 illustrates the phenomenon of inbreeding by showing how the acquaintances of X feed back into his circle of acquaintances and do not bring any new contacts into the structure.

It is a fairly straightforward job to check up on the amount of inbreeding using one or two circles of acquaintances, but it becomes almost impossible when the acquaintance chain stretches far and wide. There are just too many people involved to make a count practical.

So the main obstacle in applying a model of this sort is the problem of social structure. Although poor people always have acquaintances, it probably turns out that they tend to be among other poor people, while the rich speak mostly to the rich. It is exceedingly difficult to assess the impact of social structure on a model of this sort. If you could think of the American population as only 200,000,000 points, each with 500 *random* connections, the model would work. But the contours of social structure make this a perilous assumption, for society is not built on random connections among per-

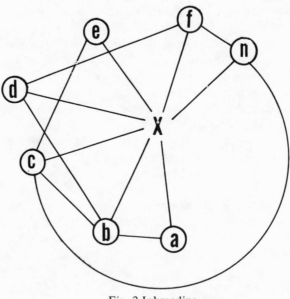

Fig. 2 Inbreeding

sons, but tends toward fragmentation into social classes and cliques.

But could the problem admit of a more direct experimental solution? The Laboratory of Social Relations at Harvard gave me $680 to prove this was the case. My approach was to try to find an experimental method whereby if two persons were chosen at random, it would be possible to trace a line of acquaintances that linked the two.

Let us assume for the moment that the actual process of establishing the linkages between two persons runs only one way: from person A to person Z. Let us call person A the *starting* person, since he will initiate the process, and person B the *target* person, since he is the person to be reached. All that would be necessary, therefore, would be to choose a *starting* person at random from the 200,000,000 persons who live in the United States, and then randomly choose a *target* person. Then we would ask the starting person to try to establish contact with the target person using only a chain of friends and acquaintances. We could then see how long the chain was, and study many of its other properties. Of course, the starting person cannot, at the outset, know what the complete chain looks like: he cannot see beyond the circle of his immediate acquaintances, and the chance that anyone of his immediate acquaintances would know the target person is small. The starting person cannot see beyond the first link, he can only start the process on its way, by moving it one step toward the target.

The general procedure was to obtain a sample of men and women from varied walks of life. Each of these persons was given the name and address of "Target Person" (that is, an individual chosen at random living somewhere in the United States). Each of the participants was asked to move a message towards the target person using only a chain of friends and acquaintances. Each person could transmit the message to one friend or acquaintance who would be more likely to know the target person than he was. The friend would repeat the process until the message reached the target person. Messages may only move to persons who know each other on a first-name basis.

As a crude beginning, we thought it best to draw our starting people from some distant city such as Wichita, Kansas, or Omaha, Nebraska (from Cambridge, these cities seem vaguely "out there," on the Great Plains or somewhere). So letters of solicitation were sent to residents in these cities asking them to participate in a study of social contact in American society. (For certain purposes, residents of the Boston area were also used.) It was necessary to select a target person and the first individual to serve in this capacity was the wife of a Divinity School student living in Cambridge. In a second study, carried out in collaboration with Jeffrey Travers, the target person was a stock broker who worked in Boston and lived in Sharon, Massachusetts. To keep matters straight, I will refer to the first study as the Kansas study and the second study as the Nebraska study. These terms indicate merely where the starting persons were drawn from. Each person who volunteered to serve as a starting person was sent a document, which is the main tool of the investigation (see Fig. 3). I suggest that it be scrutinized to learn the flavor and details of the procedure, but let us quickly review its main contents. The document contains:

1. The name of the target person as well as certain information about him. This orients the participant toward a specific individual.

2. A set of rules for reaching the target person. Perhaps, the most important rule is stated in box 4; *"if you do not know the target person on a personal basis, do not try to contact him directly. Instead, mail this folder . . . to a personal acquaintance who is more likely than you to know the target person . . . it must be someone you know on a first-name basis."* This rule sets the document into motion, moving it from one participant to the next, until it is sent to someone who knows the target person. Then, rule 3 takes over and the chain is completed.

3. A roster on which the subject affixes his name. This tells the person who receives the letter exactly who sent it to him. The roster also has another practical effect; it prevents endless looping of the document through a participant who has already been an earlier link in the chain. For each participant can see exactly what sequence of persons has led up to his own participation.

4. A stack of fifteen business reply cards.

Several other features of the procedure need to be emphasized. First, the

COMMUNICATIONS PROJECT

322 EMERSON HALL   HARVARD UNIVERSITY   CAMBRIDGE, MASSACHUSETTS 02138

We need your help in an unusual scientific study carried out at Harvard University. We are studying the nature of social contact in American society. Could you, as an active American, contact another American citizen regardless of his walk of life? If the name of an American citizen were picked out of a hat, could you get to know that person using only your network of friends and acquaintances? Just how open is our "open society"? To answer these questions, which are very important to our research, we ask for your help.

You will notice that this letter has come to you from a friend. He has aided this study by sending this folder on to you. He hopes that you will aid the study by forwarding this folder to someone else. The name of the person who sent you this folder is listed on the Roster at the bottom of this sheet.

In the box to the right you will find the name and address of an American citizen who has agreed to serve as the "target person" in this study. The idea of the study is to transmit this folder to the target person using only a chain of friends and acquaintances.

TARGET PERSON

Name, address, and information about the target person is placed here.

HOW TO TAKE PART IN THIS STUDY

1 ADD YOUR NAME TO THE ROSTER AT THE BOTTOM OF THIS SHEET, so that the next person who receives this letter will know who it came from.

2 DETACH ONE POSTCARD. FILL IT OUT AND RETURN IT TO HARVARD UNIVERSITY. No stamp is needed. The postcard is very important. It allows us to keep track of the progress of the folder as it moves toward the target person.

3 IF YOU KNOW THE TARGET PERSON ON A PERSONAL BASIS, MAIL THIS FOLDER DIRECTLY TO HIM (HER). Do this only if you have previously met the target person and know each other on a first name basis.

4 IF YOU DO NOT KNOW THE TARGET PERSON ON A PERSONAL BASIS, DO NOT TRY TO CONTACT HIM DIRECTLY. INSTEAD, MAIL THIS FOLDER (POST CARDS AND ALL) TO A PERSONAL ACQUAINTANCE WHO IS MORE LIKELY THAN YOU TO KNOW THE TARGET PERSON. You may send the folder on to a friend, relative, or acquaintance, but it must be someone you know on a first name basis.

Remember, the aim is to move this folder toward the target person using only a chain of friends and acquaintances. On first thought you may feel you do not know anyone who is acquainted with the target person. This is natural, but at least you can start it moving in the right direction! Who among your acquaintances might conceivably move in the same social circles as the target person? The real challenge is to identify among your friends and acquaintances a person who can advance the folder toward the target person. It may take several steps beyond your friend to get to the target person, but what counts most is to start the folder on its way! The person who receives this folder will then repeat the process until the folder is received by the target person. May we ask you to begin!

Every person who participates in this study and returns the post card to us will receive a certificate of apprecia-tion from the Communications Project. All participants are entitled to a report describing the results of the study.

Please transmit this folder within 24 hours. Your help is greatly appreciated.

Yours sincerely,

Stanley Milgram, Ph. D.
Director, Communications Project

ROSTER

1
2
3
4
5
6
7
8
9
10
11
12
13
14
15

SIGN YOUR NAME HERE.

PLEASE FILL IN THIS
INFORMATION ABOUT YOURSELF

MY NAME:

MY ADDRESS:

MY OCCUPATION:

AGE _____ SEX _____

DETACH ONE POSTCARD.
FILL IT OUT AND RETURN IT TO HARVARD UNIVERSITY.

PLEASE FILL IN THE FOLLOWING INFORMATION ABOUT
THE PERSON TO WHOM YOU ARE SENDING THE FOLDER.

HIS (HER) NAME:

HIS (HER) ADDRESS

HIS OCCUPATION:

APPROXIMATE AGE _____ SEX _____

NATURE OF HIS RELATIONSHIP TO YOU

_____ (PLEASE EXPLAIN WHETHER

HE IS A FRIEND, ACQUAINTANCE, RELATIVE, ETC.)

subject operates under the restriction that he can send the folder on only to one other person. Thus, the efficiency with which the chain is completed depends in part on the wisdom of his choice in this matter. Second, by means of the business reply card, we have continuous feedback on the progress of each chain. The cards are coded so we know which chain it comes from and which link in the chain has been completed. The card also provides us with relevant sociological characteristics of the sender and receiver of the card. Thus, we know the characteristics of completed, as well as incomplete, chains. Third, the procedure permits experimental variation at many points.

In short, the device possesses some of the features of a chain letter, though it does not pyramid in any way; moreover it is oriented toward a specific target, zeros in on the target through the cooperation of a sequence of participants, and contains a tracer that allows us to keep track of its progress at all times.

The question that plagued us most in undertaking this study was simply: Would the procedure work? Would any chains started in Kansas actually reach our target person in Massachusetts? The answer came fairly quickly. Within a few days after initiating chains in Kansas, one of the documents was returned to the target person, the wife of a Divinity School student. The document had started with a wheat farmer in Kansas. He passed it on to an Episcopal minister in his home town, who sent it to a minister who taught in Cambridge, who gave it to the target person. Altogether the number of intermediate links between starting person and target person amounted to *two!*

As it turned out this was one of the shortest chains we were ever to receive, for as more tracers and documents came in, we learned that chains varied from 3–10 intermediate acquaintances, with the median at 5.5. Figure 4 shows what may be regarded as the main finding of the study; the distribution of 42 chain lengths from our Nebraska study, in which 160 persons started in an attempt to reach a stock broker who resided in Sharon, Massachusetts. The median number of intermediate persons is 5.5, in certain ways, impressive, considering the distances traversed. Recently, I asked a person of intelligence how many steps he thought it would take, and he said it would require 100 intermediate persons, or more, to move from Nebraska to Sharon. Many people make somewhat similar approximations, and are surprised to learn that only 5.5 intermediaries will—on the average—suffice. Somehow it does not accord with intuition. Later, I shall try to explain the basis of the discrepancy between intuition and fact.

It is reasonable to assume that the theoretically pure number of links needed to complete the chains is even less than that shown by our findings. First, since our participants can only send the folder on to one of their 500 possible contacts, it is unlikely that even through careful selection they will necessarily, and at all times, select a contact best able to advance the chain to the target. On the whole they probably make pretty good guesses, but surely, from time to time, they overlook certain possibilities for shortcuts.

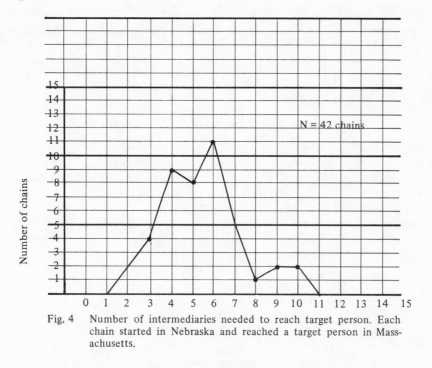

Fig. 4   Number of intermediaries needed to reach target person. Each
chain started in Nebraska and reached a target person in Massachusetts.

The chains obtained in our empirical study are less efficient than those generated theoretically.

Secondly, the only basis for moving the folder to the target person is to
work along certain highly rational lines. That is, a certain amount of information about the target person concerning his place of employment, place
of residence, schooling, etc., is given to the starting subject, and it is on the
basis of this information alone that he selects the next recipient of the folder.
Yet, in real life, we sometimes know a person because we chance to meet him
on an ocean liner, or we spend a summer in camp together as teenagers, yet
these haphazard bases of acquaintanceship cannot be fully exploited by the
participants.

There is one factor that could, conceivably, work in the opposite direction,
that is, give us the illusion that the chains are shorter than they really are.
There is a certain decay in the number of active chains over each remove
even when they do not drop out because of reaching the target person. Of
160 chains that started in Nebraska, 42 were completed and 128 dropped
out. These chains die before completion because a certain proportion of
participants simply do not cooperate and fail to send on the folder on each
remove. Thus, the results we obtained on the distribution of chain lengths,
occurred within the general drift of a decay curve. It is possible that some
of the completed chains would have been longer than those that did get

completed. To account for this possibility, Professor Harrison White of Harvard has constructed a mathematical model to show what the distribution of chain lengths would look like if all chains went through to completion. In terms of this model there is a transformation of the data, yielding longer chains.

EXAMINING THE CHAINS

There are several features of the chain worth examining, for they tell us something about the pattern of contact in American society. Consider, for example, the very pronounced tendency in our Kansas study for female participants to send the folder on to females, while males tended to send the folder on to other males. For a total of 145 subjects involved in the study, we find:

Female ⟶ Female	56
Male ⟶ Male	58
Female ⟶ Male	18
Male ⟶ Female	13

that is, subjects were three times as likely to send the folder on to someone of the same sex as someone of the opposite sex. This is true when the target person is female, less true when the target person is a male. Exactly why this is so, is not easy to determine, but it suggests that certain kinds of communication are conditioned strongly by sex roles.

Subjects also indicated on the tracer cards whether they were sending the folder on to friends, relatives, or acquaintances. In this same series, 123 cards were sent to friends and acquaintances, while only 22 were sent to relatives. Cross-cultural comparison would seem useful here. It is quite likely that in societies which possess extended kinship systems, relatives will be more heavily represented in the communication network than is true in the United States. In American society, where extended kinship links are not maintained, acquaintance and friendship links provide the preponderant basis for reaching the target person. I would guess, further, within certain ethnic groups in the United States, a higher proportion of familial links would be found in the data. Probably, if the study were limited to persons of Italian extraction, one would get a higher proportion of relatives in the chain. This illustrates, I hope, how the small world technique may usefully illuminate varied aspects of social structure, as well as cultural topics.

In Figure 5 we show what kind of people were involved in some typical chains that stretched from Nebraska to Massachusetts.

Each of us is embedded in a potential small world structure. It is not enough to say, however, that each acquaintance constitutes an equally important basis of contact with the larger social world. For it is obvious

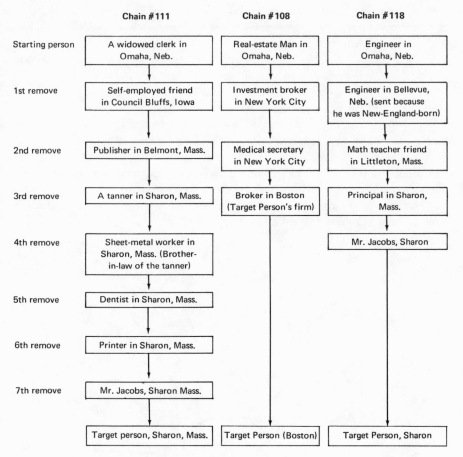

Fig. 5: Typical chains in the Nebraska study

that some acquaintances are more important in establishing contacts with broader social realms: some friends are relatively isolated; others possess a wide circle of acquaintances, and contact with them brings the individual into a far-ranging network of additional persons.

Let us consider in detail the pattern of convergence crystallizing around the target person of our second target person, a stock broker living in Sharon, Massachusetts, and working in Boston. A total of 62 chains reached him,[1] 24 of these at his place of residence in a small town outside of Boston. Within Sharon, fully sixteen were given to the target person by Mr. Jacobs, a clothing merchant in town. He served as the principal point of mediation between the target person and the larger world, a fact that came as a considerable

1. This includes the 42 originating in Nebraska and 20 additional chains originating in the Boston area.

surprise, and even something of a shock for the target person. At his place of work in a Boston brokerage house, ten of the chains passed through Mr. Jones, and five through Mr. Brown, business colleagues of the target person. Indeed, 48 per cent of the chains to reach the target person were moved on to him by three persons: Jacobs, Jones, and Brown. Between Jacobs and Jones there is an interesting division of labor. Jacobs mediates the chains advancing to the target person by virtue of his residence. Jones performs a similar function in the occupational domain, and moves 10 chains enmeshed in the investment-brokerage network to the target person (Fig. 6).

More detail thus comes to fill out the picture of the small world. First, we learn that the target is not surrounded by acquaintance points each equally likely to feed into an outside contact; rather, there appear to be highly popular channels for the transmission of the chain. Second, there is differentiation among these commonly used channels, so that certain of them provide the

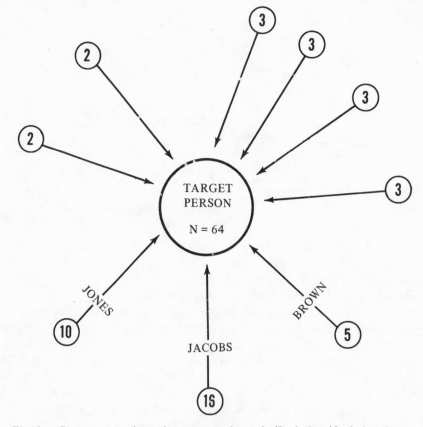

Fig. 6   Convergence through common channels (Includes 42 chains that
            started in Nebraska and 22 that started in the Boston area)

chief points of transmission in regard to residential contact, while others have specialized contact possibilities in the occupational domain. For each possible realm of activity in which the target is active, there is likely to emerge a sociometric star with specialized contact possibilities.

GEOGRAPHIC MOVEMENT

Geographic movement from the state of Nebraska to Massachusetts is striking over the several links. Figure 7 shows the progressive closing in on the target area with each new person added to the chain. There are some cases, however, in which a chain moves all the way from Nebraska to the very neighborhood in which the target person resides, but never quite makes the necessary contact to complete the chain. Some chains have died only a few hundred feet from the target person's house, after a successful transmission of 1000 miles. Social communication is sometimes restricted less by physical distance than by social distance.

1305 miles	(starting position)
710 miles	first remove
356 miles	second remove
210 miles	third remove
79 miles	fourth remove
44 miles	fifth remove
20 miles	sixth remove
Target area	seventh remove

The chains progress toward the target area with each remove. Figure 7 shows the number of miles from the target area with each remove averaged over all chains, completed as well as incompleted. For example, by the sixth remove, the average chain (assuming it is still active) is 20 miles from the target area. The target area is defined as any location less than 20 miles from Boston.

Fig. 7 Geographic movement from Nebraska to Massachusetts

The major research focus for future inquiry calls for changing the relationship between the starting person and the target person. If the two are drawn from different class backgrounds, does this decrease the probability of completing the chain? Does it increase the number of links?

In collaboration with Charles Korte, I am now applying the small world method to the study of communications in subgroups in American society; namely, Negro and white persons. We will have Negro starting persons and target persons, and white starting persons, and try to trace the lines of communication between them. We would first like to ask: In what degree are the racial lines surmounted? Can any sizeable fraction of the communications get through the racial barrier? If the answer is affirmative, what is the typical locus of transition? Does it occur at the neighborhood level? At the place of work? We are particularly interested in the persons who serve as links between Negro and white groups. In what way do they differ from others in the chain? Do they tend to occupy particular professional categories, such as minister, teacher, etc.? Is there any easier flow between Negroes and whites in Northern or Southern locales? Perhaps some new light can be cast on the structural relationships between Negro and white communities by probing with the small world method.

As stated previously, many people were surprised to learn that only 5.5 intermediaries will, on the average, suffice to link randomly chosen individuals, no matter where each lives in the United States. We ought to try to explain the discrepancy between intuition and fact.

The first point to remember is that although we deal directly with only 5.5 intermediaries, behind each of them stands a much larger group of from 500 to 2500 persons. That is, each participant selects from an acquaintance pool of 500 to 2500 persons the individual he thinks is in the best position to advance the chain, and we deal only with the end product of a radical screening procedure. Second, there is an element of geometric progression implicit in the search procedure, and there is nothing more alien to mathematically untutored intuition than this form of thinking. As youngsters, many of us were asked the question: If you earned a penny a day and the sum were doubled each day, how much would you have earned by the end of a 30-day working period. Most frequently people give answers on the order of $1.87 or $6.45, when in fact the sum is more than $10,000,000 for one 30-day working period, the last day alone yielding $5,368,709.12 in wages. Elements of geometric progression with an increase rate far more powerful than mere doubling underlies the small world search procedure, and thus, with only a few removes, the search extends to an enormous number of persons.

Finally, when we state there are only 5.5 intermediate acquaintances, this connotes a closeness between the position of the starting person and the target persons, but this is in large measure misleading, a confusion of two entirely different frames of reference. If two persons are 5.5 removes apart, they are far apart indeed. Almost anyone in the United States is but a few removes from the President, or from Nelson Rockefeller, but this is only as seen from a particular mathematical slant and does not, in any practical sense, integrate our lives with that of Nelson Rockefeller. Thus, when we speak of five intermediaries we are talking about an enormous psychological distance between the starting and target points, a distance which only seems small because we customarily regard "5" as a small manageable quantity. We should think of the two points as being not five persons apart, but five "circles of acquaintances" apart—five "structures" apart. This helps to set it in its proper perspective.

There is an interesting theorem based on the model of the small world. It states that if persons from two different populations cannot make contact, that no one within the entire population in which each is embedded can make contact with any person in the other population. Said differently, given person a embedded in population A (which consists of his circle of acquaintances), and person b embedded in population B, if a cannot make contact with b, then:

1. No other individual in A can make contact with b.
2. No other individual in A can make contact with any other individual in B.
3. In other words, the two subpopulations are completely isolated from one another.

Conceivably, this could happen if one of the populations were on an island never visited by the outside world. In principle, any person in the United States can be contacted by any other in relatively few steps, unless one of them is a complete and total hermit and then he could not be contacted at all.

In sum, perhaps the most important accomplishment of the research described here is that—although people have talked about small world connections, and have even theorized about it—these are, to my knowledge, the first empirically created connections between persons chosen at random from a major national population.

Although the study started with a specific set of questions arising from the small world problem, the procedure illuminates a far wider set of topics. It reveals a potential communication structure whose characteristics have yet to be exposed. When we understand the structure of this potential communication net, we shall understand a good deal more about the integration of society in general. While many studies in social science show how the individual is alienated and cut off from the rest of society, from the perspective of this study a different view emerges: in some sense, at least, we are all bound together in a tightly knit social fabric.

The small world problem is a relatively new topic of investigation, and thus has not yet been "claimed" as the exclusive property of any one discipline. Communications specialists, city planners, social psychologists, mathematical sociologists, political scientists, and historians have felt free to talk about the problem. Let us hope that it does not become "private property" claimed by any single discipline, which then posts "no trespassing" notices on it, and thereby denies it the benefit of new insights from a variety of sources.

REFERENCES

Duby, G., and R. Mandrou. 1958. *Histoire de la civilisation française*. Paris: Colin.
Gurevitch, M. 1961. The social structure of acquaintanceship networks. Unpublished Ph.D. dissertation, Massachusetts Institute of Technology.

HARARY, F., R. Z. NORMAN, and D. CARTWRIGHT. 1965. *Structural models: an introduction to the theory of directed graphs.* New York: Wiley.

JACOBS, J. 1961. *The death and life of great American cities.* New York: Random House.

MANN, J. 1963. *Frontiers of psychology.* New York: Macmillan.

PIRENNE, H. 1925. *Medieval cities; their origins and the revival of trade.* Princeton, N.J.: Princeton University Press.

POOL, I. DE S. Unpublished memorandum, Massachusetts Institute of Technology.

RAND, C. 1964. *Cambridge, U.S.A.: hub of a new world.* New York: Oxford University Press.

7

BIOLOGICAL BASIS OF HUMAN WARFARE: AN INTERDISCIPLINARY PROBLEM

JOHN PAUL SCOTT

INTRODUCTION

A perennial problem in human affairs is that of warfare; and since human beings are living organisms, it seems logical to suppose that at least some of the bases of warfare lie in the biological organization of *Homo sapiens*. From time to time biologists have proposed such hypotheses, and one of the reasons that these have never been widely accepted is that they have been stated in overgeneralized forms, such as that all fighting is instinctive. If biologists wish to speak meaningfully regarding human problems, they must be sophisticated in other sciences as well as their own, or at least agree to speak in unison with members of other branches of science. Conversely, it is never safe to propose general theories affecting human problems without considering the biological basis of human behavior. In this paper I shall first review what is now known about the biological basis of group fighting and then go ahead to relate this to knowledge derived from other fields.

In the first place, warfare always contains a large element of agonistic behavior. By this we mean behavior which arises from a situation of conflict between two members of the same species. Agonistic behavior may include fighting, running away, threats, postures of dominance and submission, and freezing. Occasionally these patterns of behavior may be extended to another species, usually a similar species or one to which an individual has been foster-reared, but in any case the behavior is quite distinct from predation, in which a predator attacks its prey for the purpose of securing food. In animals which regularly prey upon other species, as do wolves, the two kinds of patterns of behavior are quite different. When a wolf pack attacks a moose, the wolves attempt to get around behind the animal and hamstring it; whereas in social fighting the approach is always head to head, and the two wolves attempt to seize each other by the back of their necks.

In addition to agonistic behavior (i.e., fighting directed against members

121

of the same species), human warfare has another universal characteristic: it consists of organized fighting between two groups of individuals. Therefore, if we look for analogues or homologues of warfare in other parts of the animal kingdom, we must look for examples of organized group attacks on other groups of the same species. Such behavior, incidentally, is very difficult to find in species other than our own.

THE EVOLUTION OF AGONISTIC BEHAVIOR

THE ADAPTIVE NATURE OF AGONISTIC BEHAVIOR

It is one of the canons of evolutionary theory that behavior which is disadvantageous to the survival of a group will tend to be selected against and disappear. Hence agonistic behavior should have survival value for the species under the conditions in which it normally lives, and we would expect that most cases of agonistic behavior would have a useful function for the species. However, the assumption that any particular example of agonistic behavior is adaptive should not be accepted without proof, as there may now be in existence many animal species in which agonistic behavior is nonadaptive and in which either the behavior or the species itself is on the way to eventual extinction.

CONDITIONS FOR THE EXISTENCE OF ADAPTIVE AGONISTIC BEHAVIOR

If we make a survey of reported cases of social fighting in the animal kingdom, we find that these are almost entirely confined to two phyla, the vertebrates and the arthropods. The reasons for this are fairly obvious. One is that the animals engaged in social fighting must have the sensory equipment enabling them to discriminate between individuals, or at least between classes of individuals of the same species, in order to employ agonistic behavior in a useful fashion. Indiscriminate attacks on all members of the same species would be of little adaptive value. Second, a species must have the motor equipment to make such attacks effectively. Among vertebrates, agonistic behavior is extremely uncommon among members of the class Amphibia, which have neither teeth nor claws. In one of the few known examples (Test, 1954), frogs of a South American species do attack each other, but their only method of fighting is jumping on top of another sitting frog.

RITUALIZATION OF AGONISTIC BEHAVIOR

J. S. Huxley (1923) long ago observed that some of the courtship activities of birds consist of ritualized forms of nonsexual behavior such as preening. Hence this behavior is reduced to a signaling function. Many authors have since observed that fighting under natural conditions is frequently reduced to a form that is little more than a symbolic representation of the behavior and that, therefore, does very little harm to the combatants. Lorenz (1966) in particular has made the assumption that such behavior is entirely evolved and that fighting or its lack is determined by the exchange of appropriate innate signals. This leaves out of consideration the well-known phenomenon of the dominance hierarchy. Dominance-subordination relationships are not determined by evolutionary antecedents but by the experience of particular individuals with each other. When strange hens are introduced to each other, the first reaction is a downright fight. It is only after a winner and loser have been determined that the behavior of threat and avoidance is substituted for fighting itself.

In the dog, dominance develops over a long period as the members of a litter grow up together, beginning with playful fighting behavior at the age of 3 or 4 weeks (Pawlowski and Scott, 1956; Scott and Fuller, 1965). In some cases this develops into actual fighting, and the result is settled much as it is between hens, but with very little damage to the contestants because of their small teeth and undeveloped muscles. Between female puppies, dominance frequently develops as a result of threats, with no actual fighting ever occurring. Furthermore, the final relationship developed between any pair of animals may take many forms. In the highest degree of dominance, the subordinate animal never comes near the dominant one, with the result that the relationship is very nearly completely peaceful, with threats or attacks being almost never observed. Other individuals may work out a pattern of mutual threat in which both individuals growl and bark, but neither is actually dominant over the other. Still other individuals may adopt an extremely subordinate posture whenever threatened, and others may simply pay no attention to a threat but go on about their business.

It is obvious that there is an ontogenetic history of ritualized behavior as well as an evolutionary one. A species may have evolved the capacities for exhibiting such patterns of agonistic behavior, but they only reach their final expression through the developmental history of the individual. In the course of development they are subject to variation resulting from environmental stimulation and the process of learning, as well as that resulting from individual genetic differences.

From all these considerations, it is obvious that any evolutionary interpretation of agonistic behavior is meaningful only within the context of the particular kind or kinds of social organization that are developed by that species. With this in mind, I shall review some of the instances of fighting that have now been thoroughly studied in various animal societies.

AGONISTIC BEHAVIOR BETWEEN INDIVIDUALS

INVERTEBRATES

As indicated above, all of the reported instances of social fighting among invertebrates occur in the phylum Arthropoda. Mild fighting occurs between male dragon flies as they fly about above the ponds which are their breeding grounds (Jacobs, 1955). The result is that each male tends to be confined to a certain small but not definitely marked area. This behavior is maintained for a few hours, after which the males fly away. There are two possible interpretations with respect to adaptive function. One is that the agonistic behavior serves to produce a mating territory within which individuals do not interfere with each other, and another possibility is that this behavior helps to distinguish the two sexes, thus preventing energy being wasted on sterile sexual behavior. Individual fighting is also well known in certain crustaceans such as crayfish and lobsters, and between males of certain species of crickets. In most cases the general adaptive function of the behavior is unknown. In addition, there are thousands of species of arthropods in which fighting has never been reported.

FISH

Agonistic behavior is a well-established phenomenon in many species of bony fish. As an example, during the breeding season a male sunfish moves to an area of shallow water and establishes a small territory by driving other males away. Within this area mating takes place and the eggs are fertilized. The net result is to establish an area within which the somewhat complicated process of external fertilization can take place without interference and where the eggs can be protected once they are laid. Similar nesting and territorial behavior occurs in a wide variety of freshwater fish.

BIRDS

Because of their diurnal habits and conspicuous appearance, agonistic behavior has been observed in a large number of bird species. One well-known example is that of the European starling, now a common pest in this country. Like many other passerine birds, this species forms flocks outside the breeding season. In the fall, the male and female each defend a nest hole from members of the same sex. In the spring, courtship behavior occurs and the pair uses one nest hole. While in flocks, the starlings have a dominance-subordination arrangement (Davis, 1963). This is a somewhat unusual situation among passerine birds in that most migratory species show very little agonistic behavior during the flocking season, living and feeding together in an apparently peaceful fashion. Many species of perching birds will attack a hawk or owl as a group (the "mobbing" reaction, as the English ornithologists call it), but they never attack an individual of their own kind in this fashion.

REPTILES

These animals have not been studied with the same thoroughness as birds, but many species of lizards seem to react in a fashion similar to bird societies, setting up small territories and exhibiting threats and other ritualized fighting behavior during the breeding season.

MAMMALS

The agonistic behavior of mice and rats has been thoroughly studied in the laboratory and to some extent under natural conditions (Scott, 1966). Like many species of small mammals, mice are nocturnal in their habits and hence are incapable of guarding large territories effectively. In this species, animals reared together show almost no fighting, but strangers fight vigorously. In a confined situation strange mice are not able to develop good dominance-subordination relationships in which fighting is reduced to nonharmful levels, but in a free situation the result of such a fight is that the losing individual escapes and does not return. The general result is that mice are able to live in high concentrations where individuals grow up together close to a plentiful food supply, but individuals from other areas cannot move in. Another result is that mice are able to move only into areas that are empty of other mice.

Woodchucks (Bronson, 1964) show more agonistic behavior than mice and will not tolerate each other except for brief periods while mating and while the female is caring for her young. Adults of both sexes attack on sight, with the result that individual woodchucks always live some distance apart and maintain a continual pressure on each other to move into uninhabited areas. While this constant display of agonistic behavior has unfavorable results on the physiology of individuals (woodchucks show an unusually high rate of heart disease), the species as a whole is quite successful. Since these are relatively large herbivorous rodents, the spacing resulting from agonistic behavior assures each animal an adequate food supply.

One of the most highly social rodents is the so-called prairie dog, in reality a large ground squirrel (King, 1955). Unlike many rodents, these animals are chiefly active in the daytime. They live in large colonies which often contain thousands of individuals. The area in which the colony lives is divided up into territories, the inhabitants of each usually including one male and two or more females with their young. There is very little overt fighting, but if a neighboring animal strays over the boundary line, it is threatened and pursued until the line is reached.

After a litter of young has been raised, the older animals move out to the edge of the colony in the following spring and construct a new burrow, leaving the old one for the younger generation. This means that the oldest and most exierienced animals are located on the outskirts of the colony and thus are best able to warn the rest of predators and escape from them. Compared to woodchucks, there is a great deemphasis of fighting.

Agonistic behavior forms an important part of the social organization of the highly social herd mammals, and mountain sheep are an interesting example. During most of the year the males and females travel in separate flocks (Scott, 1945). In a group of males, evidence for a dominance order is seen when animals compete for bedding places. The dominant animal will butt the subordinate one out of the way with a single push, which is often avoided. In the mating season, however, a different kind of competitive behavior appears. The males join the females and begin to fight. This takes place in such a ceremonious fashion that it has often been described as "jousting." Two males back off and then run toward each other headlong, striking their heavy horns together with a tremendous clash. After a few tries one of them usually gives up and goes away, leaving the stronger and more hard-headed individual in the company of the females. There is never any instance of a group of males attacking a single animal, in spite of the fact that the greater part of the life of a sheep is spent in concerted activity.

Individual fighting is likewise the rule for members of both the cow family (Bovidae) and deer family (Cervidae). Muskoxen will form a tight defensive group against predators of other species, but they never attack each other in this fashion.

Thus in the great majority of cases in which agonistic behavior is a prominent part of social organization, it is confined to fighting between individuals. This is definitely not the case in human warfare, and our choice of possible models in the animal kingdom is correspondingly limited.

AGONISTIC BEHAVIOR BETWEEN GROUPS

ANT "WARS"

An ant society, or colony, is formed of the descendents of a single mated pair, and thus is essentially a very large family group, composed for the most part of neuter females, or workers. There is almost no agonistic behavior within the group and seldom any agonistic behavior directed toward members outside the group. However, ants will attack a strange individual who enters the colony, the stranger being identified on the basis of odor. Haskins (1939) describes a species of South American ant that shows regular inter-colony conflicts. Each colony lives in a space hollowed out of a tree, and as the colonies are enlarged they break into one anothers living space. The result is a fight, with the winning colony taking over the young and pupae of the beaten group. The net result is not destruction but fusion of the two groups, and eventually the whole tree may be occupied by one colony.

Because it occurs so rarely, inter-colony conflict in other species of ants has been little studied except in casual observations. Once the fighting gets started, it spreads to involve many individuals. Seen from above, the activity consists of many small struggles, usually between two or three individuals, and a great deal of scurrying around and general excitement. The ants are exposed on top of the ground to predators, and in the end the ground may be littered with corpses. The behavior can be explained as exaggerated form of a colony attempt to defend the nest (Brian, 1965). Although entomologists have in the past frequently identified this activity with human warfare, there are many obvious differences in the degree of coordination of the groups concerned.

GROUP ATTACKS BY WOLVES

Wolves normally live in packs, moving out from the den area to hunt in the surrounding area and bringing back food for the young. A limited area around the den is defended as a territory against strange animals, and the pack wanders over a much larger area during its hunting activities (Murie, 1944). During the winter months the animals may not return to the den but wander through the hunting range, finding and killing prey animals as they go. Within a normal well-organized pack there is almost no overt fighting, but considerable evidence of a dominance order with respect to eating. Although there have been no reported cases of one wolf pack attacking another, if a strange wolf approaches the den he may be attacked by the entire group and driven off. Behavior similar to that of wolves is seen in domestic dogs allowed to run in packs. When sufficiently excited, a group may attack an individual, often with fatal results.

GROUP FIGHTING AMONG PRIMATES

In many ways baboons form a good model of precultural human social life (Hall and DeVore, 1965). These are plains-living primates, and they normally live their whole lives in a close social group, including many individuals of all ages and both sexes. There is a strong dominance order between males, and if a fight breaks out between two young individuals, the nearest dominant male will threaten both and break up the fight. There are no instances of group attacks on individuals, nor do attacks take place between different bands, even when they come close together at water holes. On the other hand, if a group is threatened by a predator, the nearest animal gives an alarm cry and all of the males band together to attack and threaten. While this behavior is directed against a member of another species, it is conceivable that fighting between human groups could be a distortion of a similar reaction.

Rhesus monkeys are a more quarrelsome relative of baboons, and show somewhat different kinds of behavior directed toward each other (Southwick *et al.*, 1965). The rhesus under normal conditions live in bands like baboons but in more wooded areas. There are no definite territorial boundaries. Each band lives in a core area and wanders out from this to feed in a more extensive range which usually overlaps with that of neighboring groups. The various bands avoid each other when they meet and there is ordinarily no conflict. However, when rhesus monkeys live in cities, two bands may meet each other without warning and serious fighting may break out, often with considerable injury to the participants. Usually one group is dominant over the other, and the subordinate one flees as quickly as possible.

This instance of fighting between groups in rhesus monkeys is perhaps the closest approach to human fighting between groups that is now known. It results in part from social disorganization, in this case brought about by the conditions of the human city environment which permits strange animals to come into contact with each other without warning. There are differences between this and human group combat in that the behavior of individuals is not precisely organized in any way, and that no rhesus group ever sets forth with the ovbious intention of finding another group to fight.

On the other hand, it does resemble human warfare in that the behavior is adaptive under certain circumstances, that is, the dominant troop may be left in possession of the accumulated food set out for animals in an Indian temple. This is, however, an unusual circumstance produced by human alteration of the environment. Southwick (1966) found that if he produced a food shortage in a captive group whose food was widely distributed, as it is under normal conditions in the wild, fighting within the group was actually reduced because of the constant efforts of the individuals to find food. However, if he concentrated the food in a few spots, a situation that normally occurs only with human intervention, fighting was increased.

There are no known instances of fighting between groups in man's closest biological relatives, the anthropoid apes. Among themselves, chimpanzees seem to be a mild-mannered lot, confining most of their agonistic behavior to threats and vocalization (Goodall, 1965), and the same thing appears to be true of gorillas (Schaller, 1963).

CONCLUSION

From this brief survey of agonistic behavior in the animal kingdom it is clear that the great majority of cases of social fighting take place between individuals rather than groups. Such fighting has a wide distribution in two of the higher animal phyla and has equally wide forms of adaptive significance. In any case it rarely results in death or serious injury to the participants and is often reduced to threats and other forms of "ritualized" behavior in the course of the development of a dominance hierarchy.

On the other hand, group fighting directed against an individual of the same species is relatively rare, and organized fighting between groups is almost nonexistent. Of the cases that do exist, such as the inter-colony conflicts between ants and the inter-group fights in rhesus monkeys, there is none which provides a good analogue of human warfare, and certainly none which can be considered a homologue. Social fighting in primates has diverged in form and function just as it has in other species of animals, and because behavior leaves no fossils, there is no way in which we can trace the genetic and evolutionary history of human warfare back beyond historical times, although we can infer from such artifacts as armor and swords that it existed somewhat earlier.

There are two conclusions that can be reached from our current information regarding agonistic behavior in other animals. One is that we cannot justify the existence of human warfare on the basis of a general evolutionary tendency, because there is no evidence that such a tendency exists. Rather, agonistic behavior has evolved in a great variety of ways, related in each case to the social organization typical of the species. The second conclusion is that if we are to understand human behavior from the biological viewpoint, we must study human beings as human beings and not try to derive all our information from distantly related animals.

THE BIOLOGICAL NATURE OF MAN

WARFARE IN PRECULTURAL MAN

Precultural man no longer exists, and we can infer his behavior only from the fossil remains of skeletons and from such crude artifacts as now exist. The evidence now available indicates that our early ancestors lived on the warm dry plains of South Africa. Leakey (1967), the anthropologist who has been responsible for the discovery of many of these fossils, points out that these early hominids were not the brutal heavy-jawed cave men of fiction, but rather had skeletons much like our own, with small jaws and teeth, light bones, and erect posture. They had no natural weapons that equipped them for either predation or destructive social fighting. Indeed, Leakey wonders how they could have survived at all in competition with the large predators such as lions.

It is now known from the studies of Goodall (1965) that chimpanzees devise and use simple tools and that they also catch and eat other smaller animals on rare occasions. Living under similar conditions, our own human ancestors must have learned to use tools at an early date, and Leakey has found artifacts that suggest the use of stones used as knives and stones tied together by cords that could be thrown like a modern bolo. Once tools were available that could be used for hunting other species, it is obvious that these could also be used for killing fellow members of the same species.

Killing by means of tools does not necessarily involve organized group fighting, but it does lead to a useful hypothesis that throws considerable light on the nature of warfare in historical man. Man, as we know, is *par excellence* a tool-using animal. We can by extension think of organized group fighting as a tool, in the sense that it is, under certain circumstances, a useful device. It is obvious that a well-organized group can overcome any individual, and that it can usually overcome a more poorly organized group, with or without the use of weapons. It is likewise obvious from the history of warfare that the issue of conflict between two equally well-organized groups is often determined by the possession of superior weapons by one group.

We traditionally think of weapons as the tools of war, but we can also think of warfare itself as a tool. It follows that as long as people have this tool available and can attain what they consider desirable ends with it, there is a high probability that warfare will exist. In order to reduce this probability, we must extend the old principle of "taking the profit out of war" far beyond its original sense. Many other things can be obtained through warfare besides economic profit, such as, for example, the elimination of people who happen to have different sets of ideas. Human beings are, and will probably remain, extremely adroit at using tools. Therefore, in order to keep people from using warfare we must either make the tool of organized fighting unavailable or organize the world in such a way that it no longer works.

THE BEHAVIORIAL ANALYSIS OF MODERN WARFARE

Warfare does include a certain amount of agonistic behavior, or social fighting, of the kinds that we have seen in animals, and at various periods in history it has been culturally ritualized so that the element of fatality is greatly reduced, as it was in the chivalric fighting of the Middle Ages (at least among the upper classes, who were worth much more alive than dead). However, if one looks at the actual behavior of a modern soldier, it is obvious that a very small amount of his time is spent in active conflict. Of a two-year term in the Army, a soldier in Vietnam may spend only a few hours in actual fighting, and even while killing others may never come into direct contact with them. The greatest part of his time is spent in behavior that can only be described as allelomimetic.

By allelomimetic behavior we mean behavior in which two or more individuals do the same thing at the same time, with some degree of mutual stimulation. It is highly characteristic of schools of fishes, flocks of birds, herds of mammals, and troops of primates, and is no less characteristic of the human species.

Most of the activity of a soldier consists of this kind of behavior and, in fact, is a deliberate part of military training. Consequently, human warfare is based on more than one motivational system. The motivational states directly connected with agonistic behavior are there, but even more important are those connected with allelomimetic behavior.

It is unfortunate that the physiological basis of allelomimetic behavior in man is almost completely unknown, but in dogs we are beginning to gain some knowledge of the nature of this motivational system. Beginning at about 3 weeks of age, young puppies will begin to show great emotional distress when placed in strange situations apart from familiar objects and individuals. This is almost an automatic reaction, dependent on experience only in that the young animal must remain in contact with certain places and individuals long enough so that they become familiar to him and he can thus discriminate between them and unfamiliar situations and animals. In the course of normal experience, the young puppy quickly learns that if he leaves familiar individuals, he becomes distressed, and that his distress is relieved when he returns to them. This happens over and over again, with the result that this primary emotional reaction becomes magnified by learning into a very strong form of motivation. In order to avoid distress, the puppy must stay with other individuals, and in order to stay with them he must do what they do, or perform allelomimetic behavior. There may also be a positive pleasant emotion associated with allelomimetic behavior, but we have no direct evidence on this point.

There is considerable evidence that similar motivational mechanisms are present in human beings. Young babies cry when left alone in strange places, beginning at about 2 months of age, and we have all experienced the punishing effects of being forcibly or accidentally isolated from a group. Assuming that this motivational system is present and can be definitely established in human beings, it would follow that warfare can be fun, given the circumstances that one's own side is winning and nobody gets seriously injured or killed. Dealing with this element of enjoyment of warfare, which was more evident in the nineteenth century than it is today, was the chief concern of William James (1910) in his essay, "The Moral Equivalent of War."

James thought of this motivation as a serious danger because it offers a constant temptation to go to war simply because it would be fun, and he suggests various sorts of constructive equivalents into which the motivation could be channeled. His idea has since been put to productive use several times in such organizations as the Civilian Conservation Corps and the Peace Corps. While these activities may have had a desirable result by reducing the occurrence of violence within our society, and certainly have afforded a great deal of emotional satisfaction to the participants, there is no evidence that they have had any effect in reducing international conflict. In other words, there are many other causes for war besides the emotional satisfaction derived from certain kinds of military activities.

More than this, in both agonistic and allelomimetic behavior, the principal behavioral components of warfare, there are no physiological mechanisms which would produce stimulation through internal metabolic changes, such as occurs in hunger. In allelomimetic behavior the emotional distress caused by isolation is a direct reaction to the situation. Likewise, in the case of agonistic behavior, the emotion of anger arises from external situations. Anatomically this reaction is located in the central nervous system, in the hypothalamus, and it serves to magnify and prolong the effects of external stimulation. There is no physiological evidence of a mechanism which would cause this emotion to be stimulated from within (Scott, 1958). Indeed, since fighting is an emergency reaction and one which brings the individual into situations of considerable danger, there is every reason to expect that there would be selection against any individual that showed such an internal mechanism if it should ever arise (Scott, 1966). This is quite a different situation from that with respect to eating and sexual behavior, where an internal source of motivation would contribute to individual and genetic survival.

Even these motivational systems, similar as they are in some ways, have physiological bases very different from each other. The older instinct theories of social fighting are based on crude analogies with the kind of motivation seen in hunger and sex and should be discarded.

DESTRUCTIVE FIGHTING THE RESULT OF SOCIAL DISORGANIZATION

As we saw earlier, baboons observed in well-organized societies in their native habitats show very little destructive fighting within their own groups, and indeed, often show behavior that would be labeled cooperative and even altruistic if observed in a human social group.

This picture contrasts greatly with a group of baboons studied by Zuckerman (1932) in the London Zoo. This was one of the first attempts to present animals to the public in semi-natural surroundings, and the zoo officials gathered together a large group of wild-caught male baboons and a few females and placed them together in an enclosure, large by the old standards of zoo cages but much smaller than the normal range of a free troop. The original animals undoubtedly came from several troops and so were strange to each other. Under these conditions the males began to fight each other and continued to fight throughout the two-year period in which Zuckerman watched them. At one point the numbers were reduced because of the severe casualties, and the zoo officials introduced another group of strange animals. During the entire two-year period, only one infant baboon ever survived.

Zuckerman concluded that his observations demonstrated the native ferocity of these beasts, and that this was their normal behavior in the wild. It was not until Washburn and DeVore (1961) observed these animals in well-organized groups that a truer picture of baboon behavior began to emerge. The baboons in the London Zoo were a disorganized group consisting mostly of a group of strange males held together in confinement and unable to escape from each other and influenced also by an abnormally small number of females. Under these conditions they developed ferocious and destructive behavior toward each other instead of the cooperative and even altruistic behavior of which they are capable in a well-organized social group in a favorable and free environment.

This suggests that a major cause of destructive social fighting in animal societies is social disorganization. This theory, while supported by many other instances of accidental disorganization and cases of disorganization produced by experiments concerned with other factors, has been subjected to relatively few direct experimental tests. Guhl and Allee (1944) deliberately produced social disorganization in flocks of chickens by removing certain birds and substituting strange ones. They were chiefly interested in the adverse physiological effects of this treatment, such as lowering of egg production, but they also observed considerable increase of fighting as a result of the disruption of dominance hierarchy. Recently Gottier (1967) performed an experiment with groups of cichlid fishes, first allowing them to attain stable dominance order in a large aquarium and then substituting a strange fish for one of the regular group each day. Under these conditions the numbers of threats and attacks was consistently higher by about 200 per cent. In short, the theory that destructive fighting is the result of social disorganization is both tenable and testable, and all experiments completed at this date have given strong positive results.

Does this theory apply to the occurrence of destructive violence in human societies? As I have pointed out elsewhere (Scott, 1962), there is considerable evidence that many high crime-rate areas in our own cities are occupied by recent immigrants, and the violence taking place within them has been blamed on this or that culture or race as each has migrated in large numbers to the cities. Actually, the situation is very similar to that in which the baboons found themselves in the London Zoo. While speaking the same language, the new immigrants are strangers to each other, are more often males than females so that family organization breaks down, and are forced to live together in crowded conditions by poverty and the social barriers of the ghetto.

Further, there is in our society a built-in period of developmental social disorganization. Around the age of adolescence both males and females in our society, but more particularly males, begin to leave their primary families and do not reestablish new family ties for a period that may be as long as ten years or so. Going along with this are figures that demonstrate that the age of 18 to 25 is the high crime age, the age of highest accident rates for automobiles, and so on. It will not escape notice that this is the age that is most frequently involved in riots in the streets, although older individuals sometimes join in.

This is not, however, an explanation for human warfare. Warfare consists of highly organized fighting, and while its results may produce social disorganization in the end, it begins with a group well organized for military purposes. As I have pointed out earlier, the effectiveness of warfare as a tool depends upon its degree of organization. Thus, while social disorganization may result in destructive violence within a society, it is also possible for a group to be organized for the direct purpose of destruction and violence. The same principle holds in certain kinds of organized crime, such as juvenile gangs and gangs of more adult criminals. In fact, one well-known way in which a political leader can unify a partially disorganized human society is to start a war, or invent some sort of threat from without.

The factor of social disorganization has relevance to human warfare only in this respect, that human societies as now constituted may be well organized from within but are very crudely organized, if at all, between themselves. The obvious remedy is international organization, and we should not allow the partial failures along these lines, such as the League of Nations and the United Nations, to deter us from further efforts. Every theoretical consideration supports this general viewpoint, and the principal practical difficulties are concerned with achieving a workable and effective world organization consisting of many disparate cultural elements.

THE ANALYSIS AND CONTROL OF HUMAN WARFARE: AN INTERDISCIPLINARY PROJECT

If we consider the theoretical factors that affect the behavior of an individual from any species, we can see that behavior is affected by factors operating on every major level of organization (see Table 1). Behavior is modified by heredity, by physiological factors, by psychological factors such as learning, by social organization, and finally on the highest level by factors arising from ecological organization. In addition, there are influences that are not apparent from this scheme and which act at every level of organization—the evolutionary history of the species and the developmental history of the individual.

TABLE 1

THE STUDY OF ANIMAL BEHAVIOR

Level of Organization	Scientific Discipline	Phenomena Studied (Examples)
Ecological	Ecology	Population organization
Societal	Sociobiology	Social organization
Organismic	Psychology, Animal Behavior	Behavior
Physiological	Physiology, Biochemistry	Physiology of behavior; emotions
Genetic	Genetics	Inheritance of behavioral capacities

To be more specific, social fighting is affected by major factors on every level of organization. There is no way in which one can allocate a percentage of variance attributable to each level except for specific situations, for none of these factors operate independently, but are always an integral part of the operation of all of them.

The levels of organization correspond to the subject matter of major academic disciplines, and it is obvious that if we are ever to achieve real understanding of human behavior, and especially such complex behavior as that involved in warfare, it must be through the combined efforts of all scientific disciplines.

In the broadest sense, all of these levels of organization are biological, although certain ones such as the organismic and social levels have been taken over by specialized sciences applied to the psychology and sociology of the human species. It is therefore the particular province of the biologist to present an overall long-range picture of human behavior framed in each of these levels of organization and coordinated through evolutionary and developmental history. However, the biologist who does this must be a broadly trained and widely sophisticated individual rather than a narrow specialist. The person who attempts to draw such a picture from the base of a narrow speciality such as genetics or organic evolution can only give a partial answer, and because his answer is obviously incomplete it is likely to be rejected entirely.

The picture of the hierarchy of the sciences that I have given in Table 1 provides a convenient way of measuring the adequacy of statements in this interdisciplinary area, even for one who is at home in only one. If any major area is omitted, you may be sure that you are dealing with an overconfident enthusiast. It will not escape your attention that the highest of these levels of organization is the ecological one, and this provides a real challenge to the future biologist. Because it is so global and complex, biologists have often found it more practical to work with simpler and more easily controlled variables in the genetic and physiological levels of organization. The future, however, belongs to explorations on the higher levels.

REFERENCES

BRIAN, M. V. 1965. *Social insect populations.* New York: Academic Press.

BRONSON, F. H. 1964. Agonistic behavior in woodchucks. *Animal Behavior,* 12 (4): 470–78.

DAVIS, D. E. 1963. The physiological analysis of aggressive behavior. In W. Etkin (Ed.), *Social behavior and organization among vertebrates.* Chicago: University of Chicago Press.

GOODALL, J. 1965. Chimpanzees of the Gombe Stream Reserve. In I. DeVore (Ed.), *Primate behavior.* New York: Holt, Rinehart and Winston.

GOTTIER, R. F. 1967. The frequency of aggressive attack as a function of social disorganization. Paper read at Midwestern Psychological Association, Chicago, May.

GUHL, A. M., and W. C. ALLEE. 1944. Some measurable effects of social organization in flocks of hens. *Physiological Zoology,* 17: 320–47.

HALL, K. R. L., and I. DeVORE. 1965. Baboon social behavior. In I. DeVore (Ed.), *Primate behavior.* New York: Holt, Rinehart and Winston.

HASKINS, C. P. 1939. *Of ants and men.* New York: Prentice-Hall.

HUXLEY, J. S. 1923. Courtship activities of the red-throated diver *(Colymbus stellatus* Pontopp.); together with a discussion on the evolution of courtship in birds. *Journal of the Linnaean Society,* 35: 253–93.

JACOBS, M. E. 1955. Study on territorialism and sexual selection in dragonflies. *Ecology,* 36: 566–86.

JAMES, W. 1910. The moral equivalent of war. *Popular Science Monthly,* 77: 400–12.

KING, J. A. 1955. *Social behavior, social organization and population dynamics in a black-tailed prairie dog town in the Black Hills of South Dakota.* ("Contributions from the Laboratory of Vertebrate Biology," No. 67.) Ann Arbor: University of Michigan Press.

LEAKEY, L. S. B. 1967. In D. B. Lindsley (Ed.), *Brain function*. Vol. 4, *Brain function and learning*. Los Angeles and Berkeley: University of California Press.

LORENZ, K. 1966. *On aggression*. New York: Harcourt, Brace and World.

MURIE, A. 1944. *The wolves of Mt. McKinley*. U.S.D.I. Fauna Series No. 4. Washington, D.C.: U.S. Government Printing Office.

PAWLOWSKI, A. A. and J. P. SCOTT. 1956. Hereditary differences in the development of dominance in litters of puppies. *Journal of Comparative Physiology and Psychology*, 49: 353–58.

SCHALLER, G. B. 1963. *The mountain gorilla*. Chicago: University of Chicago Press.

SCOTT, J. P. 1945. Social behavior, organization and leadership in a small flock of domestic sheep. *Comparative Psychology Monographs*, 18(4): 1–29.

———. 1958. *Aggression*. Chicago: University of Chicago Press.

———. 1962. Hostility and aggression in animals. In E. L. Bliss (Ed.), *Roots of behavior*. New York: Harper.

———. 1966. Agonistic behavior of mice and rats: a review. *American Zoologist*, 6: 683–701.

———, and J. L. FULLER. 1965. *Genetics and the social behavior of the dog*. Chicago: University of Chicago Press.

SOUTHWICK, C. H. 1966. Experimental studies of intragroup aggression in Rhesus monkeys. *American Zoologist*, 6: 301.

———, MIRZA ASHAN BEG, and M. RAFIQ. SIDDIQUI. 1965. Rhesus monkeys in North India. In I. DeVore (Ed.), *Primate behavior*. New York: Holt, Rinehart and Winston.

TEST, F. H. 1954. Social aggressiveness in an amphibian. *Science*, 120: 140–41.

WASHBURN, S. L., and I. DeVORE. 1961. Social behavior of baboons and early man. In S. L. Washburn (Ed.), *Social life of early man*. Chicago: Aldine Publishing Company.

ZUCKERMAN, S. 1932. *The social life of monkeys and apes*. New York: Harcourt, Brace, and World.

8

THE FORMATION OF NATIONAL ATTITUDES:
A SOCIAL-PSYCHOLOGICAL PERSPECTIVE

HENRI TAJFEL

INTRODUCTION

It is not the aim of this paper to attempt a general analysis of modern nationalism or a general approach to its study. Nationalism cannot be described or "explained" in terms which would stress any one set of its causal factors or components—be they historical, economic, political, psychological or social—at the expense of others. The complexity of nationalism and its universality in the modern world are reflected in the difficulty of defining it; the enormous literature on the subject is full of competing definitions. The social psychologist could perhaps adopt provisionally the simple statement that, whatever else it may be, nationalism is an attitude shared by millions of people in a large variety of cultural contexts. But this simplicity is achieved at the cost of ignoring, or bypassing important problems and difficulties. An attitude is a compound of opinions, beliefs, value judgments and emotional involvement. What is the "object" of the attitude that we call nationalism? Is it an attitude at all, the sense of a coherent affective and cognitive orientation of an individual towards an immense group of people? It would not be difficult for anyone who loves his family to define, however informally, the object of his love. The same holds true of many other groups towards which there is some degree of attitudinal involvement: religious, social or political groups, associations large or small, formal or informal. "Nation" is a shadowy concept, and its ambiguity is best seen in the diversity of attempts to catch its substance made by historians, political scientists, sociologists, and writers of all persuasions. The conclusion reached by Zangwill

This paper is a version of an introduction to a book on national attitudes in children in preparation by the author, N. B. Johnson, and their collaborators, to be published by Academic Press, London. It was written when the author was Fellow at the Center for Advanced Study in the Behavioral Sciences, Stanford, California.

in 1917 still holds: "Thus, then, it appears, neither identity of race, nor of language, nor of religion, nor of territory, nor of interests, nor of soul, is indispensable to a Nationality" (p. 44). "And yet"—he continues—"Nationality is no illusion, no accident. . . . It is a psychological phenomenon, having its regular laws of origin, development and decay" (p. 45). It is "a state of mind corresponding to a political fact" (p. 46).

Zangwill does not refer to nationalism but to nationality, not to the attitude but to its object. The diversification of national units in the world since the last war would make the general definition of a nation based on any set of selected criteria even more difficult than in Zangwill's time. However, when one considers the phenomenon from the point of view of the "state of mind" that it represents, it is possible to assert that the best definition would be one which is purely tautological: a nation is that human group towards which a large proportion of its individual members display the attiutde of nationalism.

Despite its tautological lack of respectability, this kind of definition may have its points. The character of nationalism and of the nation to which it applies varies as a function of a large number of social, historical, economic, and political factors. But when—within this welter of complexities—one considers purely the relation between nationalism as an attitude and the definitions of their nation that are used by those who share that attitude, then the following statement appears far from implausible: it is the definition of nation that varies with certain characteristics of the attitude towards it rather than the other way round.

Examples abound of the various ways in which nations have been defined in the past by the articulate nationalist elites. Shafer (1955) devotes several chapters of his book to a review of numerous "illusions concerning the basis of nations and nationalities" which he classifies into types of "myths": metaphysical, physical, and cultural. The "illusory" character of these various notions about the origins and basis of national entities is not in that they are *all* necessarily false but that each of them taken separately presents a gross oversimplification. The range is wide, from nation being seen as a "creation of God, nature and mystical forces" to its conception "as the product of the bourgeoisie and their demand for markets and status." In between these supernatural and economic extremes are located ideas about nationhood as determined by racial and "blood" bonds, a common past, a social "need," a common language, unity in the face of adversity, and many others.

It is not our purpose here (nor would it be within our competence) to present a historical perspective of the development of national ideologies. Many historians place the origin of modern nations in Europe of the eighteenth and nineteenth centuries, particularly in the effects of the French Revolution. From the psychological point of view, the most interesting aspect of the subsequent rapid development of nationalism is the search for "justifications" in which nationalist elites engaged in an ever-increasing number of countries. As mentioned, most of Shafer's "myths" were created by these elites. And, as he points out, "historians and patriots often have tended to see forces which later might develop into nationalism as the thing itself" (p. 60).

These "justifications" were needed in order to create or foster the very thing the existence of which they were supposed to have explained. This is not an unfamiliar pattern today; in many new nations the need is felt to stress or create common bonds in the past in order to force the pace of the development of nationhood. The forging of bonds need not be of a "racial" kind, though it has often been of this nature, particularly in the young European nationalisms of the nineteenth century. The phenomenon is even clearer in racism, old or new; the racist ideologies have always been characterized by a frantic search of common bonds of an "innate" or "instinctive" nature in the distant past so as to provide a justification for the claim of the special sort of unity that the racial group is supposed to have and of its inherent and immutable differences from other such groups.

The staggering complexity of man's social environment has always led him towards attempts to simplify for the sake of understanding. There is in existence an enormous literature concerned with peoples' stereotypes about their own and other human groups (see Duijker and Frijda, 1960, for an extensive bibliography). Perhaps one of the most fundamental generic characteristics of stereotypes is their creation of simple and easily conceived differences between human groups whenever the clear perception of such differences fulfills some function in the context of social or individual needs. The less ambiguous these assumed differences between groups are, the more permanent and inherent they appear to be, the better fitted they are for their tasks of simplification, justification, and unification. In one of his discussions of the emergence of European nationalisms, Kohn (1962) distinguishes two separate strands, both clearly discernible (though at slightly different times) during the French Revolution: the "twofold heritage" of liberal and nationalistic ideas. There is little doubt that the second won the battle more often than the first. There must have been many good historical reasons for this; but it is also true that, as compared with "liberal" views, the "nationalistic" ideology with its usual stress on the uniqueness of the ingroup based on simple and distinctive criteria is conceptually easier, as it presents a view of the world sharply drawn in black and white with hardly any room for uncomfortable gray shadows which are not clearly one thing or the other.

Thus, it seems that definitions of nation inherent in many varieties of nationalism fulfill a psychological function which has two interdependent aspects: emotional and cognitive. This "functional" consideration of nationalism may help to specify in a preliminary way the contribution that can be made by social psychology to the general analysis of the phenomenon. There is a duality to this contribution that seems somewhat paradoxical. On the one hand, there is a psychology of nationalism which consists of describing the psychological assumptions that are being made by its proponents and ideologists. An excellent example of this sort of careful psychological anatomy of nationalism can be found in various sections of Doob's (1964) book on the subject. There is also the psychology of the psychology of nationalism which consists of an analysis of the processes responsible for the development of national affiliation and identity. The latter includes the former.

This duality can be illustrated by reference to a related concept, that of "national character." The idea of national character can be used in the manner described above as a justification for the existence of a nation, of its distinctiveness. But the sequence can also be reversed, so that nation-building and its attendant rise of nationalism are seen as facilitating the creation of certain similarities of attitudes and behavior displayed by a group which is going through the process of becoming a nation (e.g., Pye, 1962). The search for these similarities is based on the notion that they arise as a function of the group being exposed to a set of common social, political, economic, cultural, and psychological influences. National character a (of the first kind) is used as a sort of independent variable made responsible for national unity, the need for it, its course of development, etc. National character b (of the second kind) is seen as a modal phenomenon (see, e.g., Inkeles and Levinson, 1954; Inkeles, 1963) which stands itself in need of an explanation. National character a is a psychological device; national character b is a controversial concept in the social sciences. The emergence of *ideas* about national character a, as distinct from its function, is mainly a problem for the historian; the emergence of ideas about national character b is part of the development of concepts in the social sciences.

Nationalism considered as a subject matter for psychological inquiry presents some parallels with the issue of national character. There are three general causal directions that the study of nationalism can take. One consists of analyzing its historical determinants; another in assessing its role as a causal factor in political action; and the third in asking questions about how individuals come to feel themselves members of their national group. The first two need to use a level of historical and political analysis in which indiscriminate "psychologizing" would prove of little help; the third is part of the general problem (as is national character b) of accounting for psychological uniformities observed (or assumed to exist) within social structures.

If we now go back to the definitions of nationalism, it soon appears that an attempt to account for its psychological causes—as distinct from its historical and political causes and effects—is unavoidable. The one common element in the innumerable definitions is in their reference to nationalism as an attitude, a psychological phenomenon shared by large masses of individuals. Nationalism for the authors of the report published in 1939 by the Royal Institute of International Affairs was "a consciousness, on the part of the individuals or groups, of membership in a nation, and of a desire to forward the strength, liberty or prosperity of a nation"; and one of the six defining characteristics of a nation, "a certain degree of common feeling or will, associated with a picture of the nation in the minds of individual members." An emotional overtone is added to this by Rosenblatt (1964) who, basing himself on an extensive survey of the literature, wrote that nationalism is "an individual disposition involving intense feelings of loyalty to a perceived sovereign political entity" (p. 131). To Graham Wailas (1908) "the modern state exists as an entity of the mind, a symbol"; and Kohn, like Zangwill, defines nationalism as a state of mind and finds its historical changes to be a reflection of changes in "communal psychology." In view of all these and many other definitions, Klineberg (1964) is justified in proposing his "extreme statement" that "nationalism exists in the minds of men, and that its influence upon the course of events will depend upon the meaning those minds give to it" (p. 54).

No useful purpose would be served in multiplying these examples. One need not agree with Kohn that historical changes in nationalism are a *reflection* of changes in "communal psychology"—views such as these totter dangerously on the brink of reviving the idea of a "group mind" as a causal factor in historical events; and one may feel that Klineberg's statement, far from being "extreme," is expressing an undeniable truth since it would be difficult to find any other place for nationalism to be in than "the minds of men," and that if it is true that nationalism influences the course of events, then it can do so only by virtue of its meaning to the people involved. The full circle has been finally completed by Emerson (1960) who proposed a definition to end all definitions: "The simplest statement that can be made about a nation is that it is a body of people who feel that they are a nation; and it may be that when all the fine-spun analysis is concluded this will be the ultimate statement as well" (p. 102). An extension of Emerson's definition from nation to nationalism could thus read as follows: nationalism is an attitude displayed by a body of people who are a nation because they feel that they are a nation. And so we come back to the tautology that we proposed earlier as a possible approach to a psychological definition of nationalism.

Three features seem to characterize all these various definitions of nationalism, though not all of them appear in all the definitions. Nationalism as an attitude implies some conception of a nation of which one is a member; an emotional significance given to that membership; and the sharing of these conceptual and emotional identifications by large masses of people. The first characteristic is a necessary condition for the existence of nationalism. Emotional identification implies some idea, however crude and implicit it may be, of the object with which one identifies; the "idea of a nation" alone, devoid of all emotional significance, could hardly account for the countless actions, political and personal, which have been associated for generations with the awareness of national membership. The third characteristic, the sharing of national attitudes by millions of people, is more in the nature of a working hypothesis than of a necessary condition for the existence of nationalism. It is true that this "common consciousness" pervades most of the definitions quoted above and very many others. It is also true that, as we have seen, to many scholars this spread of nationalism becomes a criterion of the very existence of a nation. One of Shafer's (1955) statements is characteristic of this view: "Before a nation could come fully into being there had also to be a people who consciously possessed some common customs and ideas, some common history and hopes" (p. 74).

One of the striking aspects of the rise of modern nations from the second half of the eighteenth century is to be found in the desperate efforts of the various nationalist minorities to spread the gospel, to awake their compatriots to an awareness of national identity. Both the liberal and the militant strands of nationalism which we previously mentioned spread rapidly from France to other countries, one or the other becoming predominant in various countries at various times. In 1848, writes Kohn (1962), "the renewed revolution carried everywhere the two-fold heritage of 1789—liberalism and nationalism. As far as the latter survived on the European continent, it put itself into the service of militant nationalism" (p. 8). Romantic movements were at that time intensely nationalistic in central Europe; and a generation earlier, in the aftermath of Napoleonic wars in Germany, nationalism slowly began to transform its *Weltbürgertum* ideals into the "blood" conceptions of nations popular at mid-century and still very much alive in the first half of the twentieth century—which also saw a further extension of national ideas to other continents. A survey of this powerful trend enabled Kohn (1962) to write: "National self-assertiveness has become today a universal phenomenon; it is the outstanding characteristic of the age" (p. 121). There is little doubt that a glance at the recent developments in Africa, Asia, and Latin America, and the revival of policies of national separateness in eastern Europe provide abundant confirmation of Kohn's assertion of universality.

But what sort of universality is it? Nationalism is an important facet of the history of ideas in the last two centuries, and also one of the causal factors in political action. From the point of view of social psychology, two questions arise to which answers cannot be obtained from any amount of evidence concerning these two aspects of nationalism. First, is it true that nationalism was an attitude which spread from writers, leaders of opinion, and politicians to the common man in their societies? And, second, if so, what were the psychological and social processes responsible for this deep penetration?

Despite the existence of some excellent analyses of the spread of popular culture (e.g., Hoggart, 1957; Lowenthal, 1961; Williams, 1958) there is no available documentation which would trace systematically the spread of national ideas. This is hardly surprising; attitude and public opinion surveys are a recent device, and the common man of the past was not in the position to leave behind much usable evidence of the extent or intensity of his national feelings. A temporary increase or decrease in the frequency or intensity of nationalist writing is no evidence of a parallel rise or fall of nationalism at large.

The absence of this kind of evidence points to an important aspect of the psychologist's approach to the problem of national attitudes. The historical analysis of nationalism traces the connection between the various conditions of the development of a political movement and the characteristics of that movement; it also establishes the links between the political phenomenon of nationalism and the nature of its effects on subsequent historical events. There is ample documentation for all the stages of this analysis; but any "psychological" inferences that are drawn from it, or any assumptions of "psychological" causation, remain strictly in the realm of exciting specula-tion. The serious part of the job is in the establishment of causal chains of historical events; none of it is based on reliable psychological data. Such data may exist in the case of individual historical figures; but in the case of political movements of the past, inferences to and from psychological proc-esses, quite apart from being untestable, imply some form of a simple cor-respondence between historical events and a summation of the motives and cognitions of millions of people. Even if such a procedure could be logically defended, it would be empirically unjustified in view of much recent evi-dence (see, e.g., Zajonc, 1968) of the frequent lack of predictive value that assessments of attitudes have for social behavior that would seem relevant to these attitudes. The problem has been well stated by Deutsch (1966) in a slightly different context:

"consciousness" and "will" cannot be used without considerable danger in political science. The danger is that the political scientist will try to describe nationalism and nationality with the help of those words, in the belief that he has made a meaning-ful statement. But what is the meaning of such statements, and how and by whom are they to be tested? The political scientist has passed the baby to psychology, but the psychologist does not seem eager to take it (p. 26).

Some of the reasons for this lack of eagerness can perhaps be inferred from the difficulties just discussed. The psychological analysis of national attitudes must remain in the here-and-now, it must remain a-historical. But a-histori-cal does not mean a-social; the gathering of evidence that national attitudes exist at large must be followed by a description of their features (*cf.* Doob, 1964) and the consideration of their psychological causation and functions in relation to the contextual social variables in which they are embedded. However, beyond and above the cultural differences in national attitudes which need to be related to their social background, nationalism presents two distinctive features which appear in all of its varieties and whose unique combination distinguishes it from most other social affiliations. A nation is the largest, the most complex and abstract human membership group; and it is also a group which seems to be able to command at times a greater intensity of attachment than almost any other. As Emerson (1960) wrote :

The nation today is the largest community which, when the chips are down, effectively commands men's loyalty, overriding the claims both of lesser communities within it and those which cut across it or potentially enfold it within a still greater society, reaching ultimately to mankind as a whole. In this sense, the nation can be called a "terminal community," with the implication that it is for present purposes the effective end for man as a social animal, the end point of working solidarity between men (p. 95).

THE PSYCHOLOGICAL APPROACHES

The attempts to account psychologically for the development of national attitudes have been primarily concerned with two questions: first, how does an individual come to identify with his national group in the conceptual and emotional sense indicated earlier? And, second, how do these identifications become the common property of very large numbers of people in a large number of countries? A survey of these attempts allows for their rough classification in terms of the kind of assumptions that they took for their point of departure. Three types of general approaches can be distinguished: postulation of some form of an instinctive or biological basis for the development of national affiliation; analysis of this affiliation in terms of its role in personality functioning; and a search for general cognitive and motivational processes which would account for the origin and development of national affiliation.

BIOLOGY AND PSEUDO-BIOLOGY

The biological views of the growth of national identity have two main versions, at least one of which more properly deserves the label of pseudo-biological. Neither of them would have to be taken very seriously today had it not been for the fact that both survive in the form of indestructible "myths" such as those to which Shafer (1955) was referring in his book. The pseudo-biological approach can be characterized as the attribution of an individual's national affiliation to some species of an instinct bringing men together in common endeavor and common defense against others. Its importance lies in the fact that one of Freud's most explicit statements of his own views on the subject was made against the background of these earlier views and as a reaction against them (Freud, 1922). The second approach enjoys an increasing popularity today as one of the numerous attempts to transplant the new insights of the ethologists from the realm of animal social behavior to various aspects of the social behavior of man.

The pseudo-biological view has a history almost as long as mankind, and certainly longer than modern nationalism. It is, in Ginsberg's words (Ginsberg, 1942, p. 197), "the habit of those who explain national character in terms of race to refer highly complex institutions to specific innate tendencies." McDougall's theory of group mind (1920) provides Ginsberg justifiably with some of his favorite examples—such as the explanation of the "prevalence of centralized system of government in France mainly by the supposed intensity of the gregarious instinct in the Mediterranean and Alpine races"; but, surely, complains Ginsberg, there is a far cry from gregariousness to centralized government.

There is perhaps an equally far cry from centralized government to processes of national identification. This gap is bridged by McDougall with the help of notions some of which have a surprisingly contemporary ring. In his account of the three classical theories of "group psychology"—those of Le Bon, McDougall, and Trotter—Freud (1922) points out that while Le Bon was concerned with transient group formation and Trotter with the "permanent herd," McDougall's interest was in stable associations. These are the most likely of the three to be relevant to the formation of national bonds. And it is here, in his specification of the conditions under which gregariousness would lead to the formation of a stable group consciousness, that McDougall falls back on concepts which are very close to those used today in the descriptions of the formation of social norms. He assumes a set of basic similarities between the members of a group in their outlooks, interests, and emotional biases; and further, comes very near to stating that these similarities are responsible for a high level of reciprocal influence which in turn enhances unity.

For this reason, McDougall's conceptual jump is not nearly as breathtaking as some which have been made almost half a century later. In several important recent publications (e.g., Carthy and Ebling, 1964: Lorenz, 1966; de Reuck and Knight, 1966) attempts can be found to draw fairly direct inferences from a functional and evolutionary analysis of animal societies to human social behavior. Most of these discussions are devoted to the problem of roots of aggression in society; they are relevant to the issue of national affiliation only to the extent to which this affiliation is seen as one of the effects of intergroup hostility. There is, however, a more specific aspect to this view: animal intraspecific aggression cannot be understood without a careful consideration of animal territoriality. Thus, several links are easily established; they amount to a chain of inferences which encompass human and animal aggression, human and animal territoriality, the universal human institution of property rights, and "my country, right or wrong."

The result is a bizarre concoction presented by Ardrey (1966) in which the size of conceptual jumps is only matched by the amount of care exercised in the selection of heterogeneous bits of supporting evidence. Some of Ardrey's statements about the psychological roots of nationalism will convey the general flavor of his presentation. Discussing the contribution made by scientists to the development of an increasingly more effective machinery for the conduct of war, he concludes: "In the language of this inquiry we should say that he [the scientist] fills out from the particularity of his learning to the generality of that open instinct, the territorial imperative; and, having done so, he will act according to the finished pattern with the predictability of a Capricorn beetle" (p. 28). More generally, "if we defend the title to our land or the sovereignty of our country, we do it for reasons no different, no less innate, no less ineradicable, than do lower animals" (p. 5). "The territorial nature of man"—we are told by Ardrey—"is genetic and ineradicable. We shall see, farther along in our inquiry, a larger and older demonstration of its power in our devotion to country above even home" (p. 116). What we do see, both nearer and farther along in the book, is the attribution to the workings of the "territorial imperative" of the greater efficiency of American private farming as compared with the state-controlled Soviet farming, a similar assertion about the private farms and the kibbutzim in Israel, a description of the strong emotion with which the author greeted the news about Pearl Harbor, and a curious classification of modern nations into "true nations" and "*noyaux*." "All forces in a true nation work for compromise and inner peace; all forces in a true *noyau* for division and emotional mayhem" (p. 185). Italy is selected as a prime example of a *noyau*—the "society of inward antagonism" which "cannot tolerate loyalty, honesty, trust. It forbids that total abandonment known as friendship" (p. 187)—and it cannot be considered a "true nation" since its antagonisms are not primarily outward-directed.

It may be argued that Ardrey's dramatic conclusions do not deserve the attention that is given to them in this review. This would undoubtedly be justified but for the fact that the book is socially important: it represents the return of the myth, dressed up this time in shining new clothes borrowed at random from the promising recent studies of animal behavior. We referred previously to the need for simplifying the social environment and to its relation to the constantly recurring popular themes of "inherent" national identity and distinctiveness. It would be a grave mistake to assume that this is a matter of the past. Ardrey is the present-day equivalent of the nineteenth-century nationalist writer and journalist with new "scientific" weapons at his disposal. His importance is not in *how* he explains, but in the fact that he is an able new representative of a long social and intellectual tradition in which the use of a certain kind of "psychological" explanation never seems to lose its capacity for rebirth from its own ashes.

PERSONALITY FUNCTIONING

It is in some ways paradoxical that Freud's attack on the problems of group —including national—identity represented a reaction against some of the "instinctive" doctrines outlined above, and perhaps the first serious attempt to include explicitly social factors in a psychological analysis of the phenomenon. For Freud (1922), group psychology was "concerned with the individual man as a member of a race, of a nation, of a caste, of a profession, of an institution, or as a component part of a crowd of people who have been organized into a group at some particular time for some definite purpose" (p. 3). His analysis of group identifications is not specifically concerned with the issue of nationalism. In *Group Psychology and the Analysis of the Ego,* the church and the army are the two institutional groupings to which he devotes special attention. It is clear, however, that in his view the treatment of these two applies to the problems presented by other large human groupings.

The two principal social factors that Freud introduces in his analysis are outgroup hostility and the role of a leader. They both act—simultaneously or in functional equivalence—to divert from the ingroup to the outgroup the "aversion and hostility" present in all human relations. The common tie with a leader enhances a perception of common qualities in the ingroup and also creates successful "partial identifications" with members of that group. Fundamental to Freud's reasoning is the assumption that, under these conditions, a transfer takes place of affective ties from primary to secondary group identifications, and it is in this form that his ideas were accepted as providing a theory of national identification. As Lasswell (1935) wrote: "Nations, classes, tribes and churches have been treated as collective symbols in the name of which the individual may indulge his elementary urges for supreme power, for omniscience, for amorality, for security."

This is admittedly an over-simplified version of the relevant aspects of Freud's "group psychology." Any interest that it may have is in considering these ideas in relation to the manner in which hypotheses deriving from them could be formulated and tested. The processes of "compensatory identification" were seen by Freud as leading to the formation of a self-concept of which national identification would be an inclusive part. He would presumably have no difficulties in allowing the processes of social influence to play their role as providing the means for the channeling of identification towards the national group rather than towards many other possible groups which theoretically would be equally plausible. Some difficulties arise, however, when an attempt is made to discover evidence for the specific hypotheses that could be extracted from the general body of Freudian ideas.

Consider the following examples: (a) identification with a national group will not take place unless it is related to the presence of charismatic leadership or of intense outgroup hostility; (b) in the absence of charismatic leadership, outgroup hostility is a necessary condition for the arousal of nationalism; (c) in the absence of intense hostility towards other national groups, the presence of a charismatic leader becomes a necessary condition. These hypotheses would have to be validated in a respectable sample of the political, social, and economic conditions under which the development of nationalism has taken place. The development of national attitudes in an individual would have to show already in childhood at least an incipient dependence upon outgroup hostility or the attachment to a national leader.

There is little doubt that we are dealing here with a rich and unexploited field for empirical explorations. In order to confirm Freud's basic ideas, evidence would have to be provided that a great variety of social, political, and economic contexts is psychologically equivalent in its production of national identification; the condition for this equivalence would be a basic similarity in the nature of leadership and of the relations with the outside world.

The vast post-war literature on the relations between personality and culture came into being partly in response to the need for providing a social context for Freud's ideas. There are several reasons why a good deal of it is not directly relevant to the psychological problems posed by modern nationalism. Most of the data came from observations of primitive societies; much of it was concerned with the establishment of modal similarities of psychological functioning in societies which were not characterized by rapid social change; and, finally, the specific problem of identification with a very large ingroup has not been given much prominence. One of the more recent and influential contributions to the movement (Erikson, 1963) can serve as an example. It is an impressive attempt to provide a broad canvas in which an individual's identity could be seen as an integration of the demands of his personal development from infancy to adulthood and of the conditions in which his society must survive. But it is not easy to derive from Erikson's treatment anything more than fairly obscure hints about the possible relations in a modern society between the course of a child's psychological development, the emotional context of a family structure characteristic of a culture, the problems that the surrounding society is facing, and the type of national identity that it produces. Erikson provides two fascinating accounts of individual development in the cultural environment of a large-scale complex society: the "legend of Hitler's childhood," and the "legend of Maxim Gorky's youth." But the pointers towards further empirical analysis are vague and unspecified. "On the stage of German history Hitler sensed to what extent it was safe to let his own personality represent with hysterical abandon what was alive in every German listener and reader" (p. 330). And, again:

For Germany the world is constantly changing its quality—and always to an extreme. The world is experienced either as vastly superior in age and wisdom, the goal of eternal longing and *Wanderlust;* or as a mean, treacherous, encircling encampment of enemies living for one aim—namely, the betrayal of Germany; or as mysterious *Lebensraum* to be won by Teutonic courage and to be used for a thousand years of adolescent aggrandizement (p. 340).

The distinctive psychological features of German nationalism seem to be explained by Erikson with the help of a set of not very clear relations between the role of the German father and mother in the family, the nature of Germany's political and *Lebensraum* problems, and a selective description of the cultural and historical background to the presumed German national character. The fact remains that some political scientists (e.g., Greenstein, 1965; Pye, 1961, 1962) have found Erikson's ideas useful in their analysis of the psychological correlates of political ideology and decision-making, particularly in transitional societies. This analysis is not usually concerned, however, with the progressive acquisition of national identity by masses of people who are neither actively involved in the political decision-making nor the articulate leaders of opinion in the transition from old loyalties to a wider national loyalty. "Indeed," as Pye (1962) writes, "the initiative for change comes more often than not from those in command of the arbitrarily introduced structures, and instead of the government responding to pressures from the society, the process is in many respects essentially reversed" (p. 43).

This reversal of the process does not, of course, mean that various aspects of the socialization process have no bearing on the development of national identity in the older and more stable nations, or that the leaders in new nations would ever succeed in their endeavors without a progressive formation of new sets of values congruent with the national ideology that they are trying to foster in the population. For Pye (1962), "the socialization process thus provides a link between personality and political change" (p. 52). The link is provided through three successive stages in which the "basic socialization process" is followed by political socialization (enabling the individual to develop "his awareness of his political world") and finally the stage of political recruitment is reached "when the individual goes beyond the passive role of citizen and observer to become an active participant and to assume a dynamic and recognized role in the political process" (pp. 45–46). The difference between stable and transitional societies is in the degree of coherence of the three processes.

The question of interest to us here is whether ideas such as these can become useful in the analysis of the development of national affiliation in a population at large. The abundance and variety of literature on national character and on the relations between personality and culture are such that a general statement is hardly possible. There is a core of agreement in all the various approaches that a common cultural background creates *some* degree of uniformity in individuals' manner of coping with *some* of their emotional problems. But beyond this, as Singer (1961) writes:

The contemporary theories differ in many significant respects: the particular psychological types employed, the number of personality types attributed to a given culture, the number of individuals who are supposed to bear a given type within a culture, how a particular type is learned, whether it is derived from cultural or psychological data, whether it is attributed to the culture as a whole as well as to individuals, by what causal theory it is related to the culture at a given time and historically, whether it applies only to primitive cultures or to modern nations as well (p. 22).

It is not surprising then that in their review, Duijker and Frijda (1960) identify six clearly different approaches to the study of national character, each
with a large number of subcategories.

Apart from the assumption of a certain degree of cultural uniformity
which is inherent in all these approaches, there is another statement (about
which there would be rather less general agreement) which can be made:
namely, that there is a continuity of childhood experience with the development of various crucial aspects of social identity. These two statements taken
together would imply: (1) that there may exist a possibility of specifying
certain aspects of the process of socialization which should lead hypotheti-
cally to various degrees of salience and intensity of national affiliation prevailing within a cultural milieu; and (2) that whenever these conditions
exist, some incipient signs of this type of affiliation should be found to exist
in childhood. To our knowledge, there exist two explicit attempts to relate in
this way the arousal of national identification to the psychological features
of the cultural background. One is to be found in the work on the authoritarian and ethnocentric personality (Adorno *et al.,* 1950); the other in a
recent (and still proceeding) cross-cultural research project on ethnocentrism (Campbell, 1965; Campbell and LeVine, 1961; LeVine, 1965).

Both these approaches concentrate on the outgroup hostility aspects of the
initial definition of ethnocentrism proposed by Summer (1906): "this view
of things in which one's own group is the center of everything, and all others
are scaled and rated with reference to it" (p. 13); the result of the scaling and rating is to excite contempt and scorn towards outsiders. Both
approaches are concerned with the development of ingroup identifications as
they relate to, and are determined by, various forms of outgroup hostility,
the roots of which are sought in turn in the socialization process. In the work
of Adorno and his colleagues, the stress has been on the background conditions of socialization leading to the development of a certain personality pattern in which the attitudes towards outgroup are one of the ways of coping
with emotional problems. In the work of Campbell and LeVine, an explicit
consideration of social structure variables has been included. They have
taken for their point of departure the views (1) that "intersocietal behavior
patterns can be thought of as modal personality characteristics which have
their ontogenetic source in the socialization process," and (2) that "variations in intergroup relations at the *intra*societal level cause variations in
imagery and behavior at the *inter*societal level" (LeVine, 1965, pp. 52–53).

The initial preoccupation of Adorno and his colleagues with anti-Semitism
led them to further studies of its more general attitudinal correlates, including attitudes towards minority groups other than Jews and towards the
"ingroup" of the United States and the "outgroups" of foreign nations. Significant intercorrelations were found between negative attitudes towards all
outgroups, and thus an authoritarian and ethnocentric personality syndrome

emerged, characterized not only by this generalized attitude towards out-groups but also by a cluster of other social and political attitudes. It is, however, the determination through clinical means of the relation of this syndrome to the manner of coping with emotional problems rooted in the socialization process that was for the authors "the most crucial result" of their studies. Thus, they wrote, "there is a close correspondence in the type of approach and outlook a subject is likely to have in a great variety of areas, ranging from the most intimate features of a family and sex adjustments, through relationships to other people in general, to religion and to social and political philosophy." In this last domain, correlations have been found between attitudes towards international relations and high scores on the F-scale. With regard to the more specific issue of national affiliation, Levinson (1957) found a positive correlation between scores on the F-scale and concern with power of his subjects' own nation; and Doise (1967) confirmed this in his European studies. He reported that the "high scorers" tend to keep the foreigners at a greater sociometric distance from their compatriots, that they perceive relatively greater differences between their own and foreign nations, that they show stronger adhesion to the political institutions of their own country, that their nationalism is more of a "closed" and excluding variety, not only with regard to their own country but also in relation to their ideas about the "closed" or "open" types of future European integration.

The link between this work and the previously discussed cultural uniformities of personality and attitudes is through the concept of "modal personality" (*cf.* Inkeles and Levinson, 1954). According to the authors' definition, "national character refers to relatively enduring personality characteristics and patterns that are modal among adult members of a society" (p. 983). In this view, national character is "related to the frequency distribution of personality patterns within a given society" (Duijker and Frijda, 1960, p. 14), amongst which the pattern exhibiting the highest frequency will be characterized as the national or cultural modal personality. In a subsequent paper, Inkeles (1963) discussed the logical grounds on which it can be expected that different human groups will show differences in the distribution and, by implication, modal points of the personality patterns of individuals composing them. He writes:

Even if the personality composition of any group is randomly determined, random assortment would not in fact guarantee the *same* personality composition in the membership of all institutions of a given type. On the contrary, the very fact of randomness implies that the outcome would approximate a normal distribution. Consequently, some of the groups would by chance have a personality composition profoundly different from others, with possibly marked effects on the functioning of the institutions involved. Furthermore, there is no convincing evidence that randomness *does* consistently describe the assignment of personality types to major social statuses (p. 354).

In addition to this, "societies will vary markedly both in the degree to which their institutions have either broad and general or highly specialized functions and in their particular combination of problems concentrated in any given institution" (p. 350).

The concept of ethnocentric personality links the development of national and other forms of ethnic identity to the processes responsible for intense outgroup hostility in a certain type of individuals. Frenkel-Brunswik (1949, 1954) was able to show that this link exists not only in adults but also in children. It may be assumed that different frequencies of the authoritarian and ethnocentric pattern would be encountered in different cultural habitats, and that the outgroup hostility component of national affiliation would vary consequently. Thus, the following sequence of statements may help us to assess the contribution that can be made by this body of work to the problem of development of national identification: *some* people will be intensely nationalistic in a large variety of situations; the form that their national-ism will take is outgroup hostility; their number is likely to vary from one cultural milieu to another.

The long history of jingoism and chauvinism in many countries (and of which the post-war American forms stimulated the authoritarian personality study) provides unquestionable evidence of the existence of such a category of people, though it does not validate the assumed causal sequence to per-sonality dynamics. But even if such evidence was not subject to any doubt, there are some fairly obvious reasons why the theory of authoritarian per-sonality cannot provide us with more than a segment of a general theory of the arousal of national identification. One is that under *some* conditions strong nationalism coupled with intense outgroup hostility becomes a widely shared norm in large populations whose members cannot all be assigned to the authoritarian and ethnocentric type; the second, that—at least in prin-ciple—there exists a possibility of national affiliations which are not inti-mately linked to strong outgroup hostility; the third, that variations over time in the mass manifestations of outgroup hostility and its attendant inten-sity of national affiliation can be related more parsimoniously to the social, economic, and political conditions of the moment than to any other set of factors. The links between these variations over time, and the conditions in which they take place, must be sought in general motivational and cognitive processes rather than in enduring and specific personality syndromes.

Some aspects of these limitations have been documented in recent empiri-cal studies. The problem of the relations between personality and socio-cultural factors in outgroup hostility has been ably discussed by Pettigrew (1958) in conjunction with his work on racial prejudice in South Africa and in the United States. He characterizes two extreme positions concerning this problem, one of which emphasizes "the personality of the bigot" and neglects his cultural milieu; the other neglects individual differences and views intolerance as "a mere reflection of cultural norms." The possibility of a theoretical compromise is provided by a functional analysis of attitudes suggested by Smith, Bruner, and White (1956) in which they distinguish between the cognitive, the social and the emotional aspects of the adjustment that an attitude may represent for an individual. The first consists of the appraisal of social reality as defined by the cultural context in which an individual lives; the second finds its roots in the network of an individual's reference groups and in his need to adjust his social *Weltanschauung* to his identifications with some groups and differentiations from others; and the third, which is closely parallel to the basic assumptions made by the studies on authoritarian personality, is the adoption of attitudes which represent "a transformed version of [an individual's] way of dealing with his inner difficulty."

When the development and the incidence of various forms of outgroup hostility are seen in this perspective, it soon becomes evident that neither the sociocultural factors reflected in the first two functions of attitudes nor the personality factors reflected in the third can provide by themselves a master key to the understanding of this hostility as a shared norm and as a mass phenomenon. Pettigrew summarizes a good deal of previous research, but perhaps the clearest examples come from his own data. In South Africa, he applied three attitude scales to his white subjects: an F-scale roughly comparable to the one used by Adorno *et al.*, a C (conformity) scale, and an A (anti-African) scale. The C-scale was nearly as predictive of the attitudes towards the Africans as was the F-scale; students born in Africa were found to be more prejudiced, but not more authoritarian, than those not born in Africa; the same was true of students belonging to the Nationalist party as compared with others; the Afrikaaners "are both more anti-African and more authoritarian, and, when the F-scale differences are corrected for, they remain significantly more hostile to the Africans" (p. 35). Results which point in the same direction were obtained in a comparison of four small towns in Georgia and North Carolina with four similar locations in New England; and, in comparisons made between various southern communities, those with "high Negro population ratios (38 and 45%) have significantly higher N (anti-Negro) scale means than the other communities sampled in the South with low Negro ratios (10 and 18%) though they are *not* different in authoritarianism and antisemitism" (p. 39). Pettigrew concludes that "in areas with historically embedded traditions of racial intolerance, externalizing personality factors underlying prejudice remain important, but sociocultural factors are unusually crucial and account for the heightened racial hostility" (p. 40).

Pettigrew's study has clear implications for the problem of the role played by outgroup hostility in the processes of national affiliation. If we follow the universally accepted assumption that the presence of acute outgroup hostility intensifies the ingroup identification, then it could be inferred that this identification is more intense among those categories of Pettigrew's subjects which are characterized by stronger prejudice. The possibility that this may be due exclusively to authoritarianism is ruled out by Pettigrew's data. There is, however, a remaining possibility of an indirect link which must not be overlooked: in his data from South Africa, Pettigrew found that the authoritarian pattern was relatively more prevalent amongst the Afrikaaners. There is a possible inference that this higher incidence affects the sociocultural milieu by creating stronger pressures towards conformity of hostile attitudes, and thus that the sociocultural factors serve as an intermediary link in a causal chain ranging from a certain modal personality pattern to outgroup hostility. This is a viable hypothesis, though it seems that a direct attribution of pressures towards conformity to the effects of social, economic, and political conditions is a more parsimonious explanation in view of the variation within the life-span of one generation in the intensity of the hostility directed at various outgroups. A prediction could still be made that, all else constant, a group including a greater proportion of "authoritarians" would produce stronger norms (affecting all its members) of intense outgroup hostility and ingroup affiliation. It is possibilities of this nature which point to the need for an eclectic approach to the study of national identification: the relative importance of various sets of causal factors can hardly be assessed on an *a priori* basis.

It is for the same reason that an exclusive concentration on the phenomenon of outgroup hostility is not likely to provide a satisfactory account of national affiliation. Campbell (1965) provided a stimulating new sideline to the problem of ethnocentrism by presenting an argument for the existence of "altruistic" components of outgroup hostility. Starting from an evolutionary point of view, he argues for the "very strong survival value in the pattern of social coordination." Coordination is obviously valuable to the group; to the individual, the membership of a social group presents basic advantages of which the most important are: "the economy of cognition" (i.e., the possibility to use for individual purposes the experience gained by others and socially transmitted); the economy of specialization and division of labor; and the economy of mutual defense. Campbell is mainly concerned with taking the universal phenomenon of ethnocentric hostility out of its usual context of what he refers to as "skin-deep hedonism" represented by most of the relevant psychological theories, of which he provides a long list. The same applies to the "rationalistic social-contract theories": they "saw social life as an intelligent decision on the part of totally selfish hedonistic calculators" and were never able to explain "the selfless behavior which makes lethal wars possible" (p. 303).

It is the possibility of this selfless behavior which is the principal riddle inherent in some aspects of national identification. Whether one does or does not accept Campbell's analogy between the selective processes of biological and sociocultural evolution (which, according to him, both led in their different ways to the development of "selfless ethnocentrism"), the fact remains that there is at least a possibility—which has not been often taken into account—of the existence of two sets of underlying motives for outgroup hostility, one of which need not be based on an "externalization of an individual's ways of dealing with his inner difficulties." If one continues Campbell's line of reasoning, it is possible to arrive at the conclusion that, though from the point of view of scientific rigor his enthusiasm may have run away with him, it has not run far enough in drawing speculative conclusions. If the various economies of functioning that a social group offers to an individual are capable of determining selectively certain *sui generis* altruistic forms of ethnocentrism, why can they not originate as well other forms of group identification which are not confined to outgroup hostility? Two of Campbell's three types of economy that a group offers to an individual need not be contingent upon the ingroup's relations with other groups. Is it, therefore, not possible to assume that some aspects of the development of national affiliation proceed quite independently of the existence of outgroups known to the individual to be in conflict with the ingroup and perceived as fundamentally hostile?

The research conducted by Campbell and LeVine remains, however, in the domain of intergroup hostility. Their hypotheses (some of which were referred to previously) differ from the more exclusive "personality" approach in their explicit introduction of variables inherent in the social structure of the ingroup. The principal aim is the study of ethnocentrism; as a result of this, the processes of ingroup identification are seen mainly in the context of the attitudes towards outgroups. But Campbell and LeVine are clearly aware of the relation of ethnocentrism to the aspects of social structure which determine ingroup affiliations, and they predict various types of relations between the intensity of outgroup hostility and the web of multiple loyalties determining the degree of internal integration of a society. In this way, their work is strongly influenced by the tradition represented in the writings of Simmel, and later of Gluckman (1955), Guetzkow (1955), and others "who have seen the cross-cutting ties of individuals to several groups as a politically integrating structural pattern" (LeVine, 1965, p. 54).

The main question that arises in considering all the work that has been discussed so far is whether outgroup hostility is a *necessary* adjunct of national affiliation. The importance of a "web of affiliations" in the integration of a large-scale society indicates that factors other than outgroup hostility may be equally crucial. Its ubiquity in the literature may be partly due to the fact that it has always been considered by the researchers as one of the first things which needs to be looked for. In a study reported by Christiansen (1959) there is some evidence that the development of national loyalties need not be related to outgroup hostility. Christiansen defines nationalism as "the investment of positive feelings onto national symbols." Such investment "may be based on a solicitous interest in one's own nation without such interest involving the rejection of other nations, or it may be based on the conception of one's own nation as superior to the rest of mankind. Depth psychological explanations have concentrated on the latter form of national-ism, which is frequently described as patriotism" (p. 201). In his attitude scales, Christiansen attempted to distinguish between "national idealization" ("a tendency to ascribe chiefly positive traits to one's own nation") and patriotism as just defined. He studied the relation between the two, and their correlations with attitudes towards foreign affairs. He found that "patriot-ism" was related to "the tendency to prefer aggressive national ways of react-ing in international conflict situations," while "national idealization" was not; and that there were no significant correlations between these two versions of national affiliation.

Findings such as these suggest that ethnocentrism (in its aspect of hostile attitudes towards outgroups), whether seen from a psychodynamic point of view or related to the social structure within which it arises, cannot be con-sidered *a priori* as the sole determinant of national identification. Campbell's "altruistic" motives need not be confined exclusively to situations of inter-group conflict; it is possible that intense and salient national identifications may develop without the presence of hostile outgroups onto which the indi-viduals may fasten and "externalize" their emotional problems. But we do not know; the reason for this ignorance has already been stated: the non-hostile ingredients of national identification have rarely been looked for in psychological research.

GENERAL MOTIVATIONAL AND COGNITIVE FACTORS

The various extrapolations that can be made, directly or indirectly, from theory and research in social psychology to the problem of national identity are not, on the whole, mutually exclusive. The reason for this is that there is no such thing as a psychological "theory of nationalism," and perhaps there cannot be. Nationalism can be all things to all people; which of its aspects are studied can be only a matter of emphasis determined by the general interests of the theorist and the researcher. We have already seen signs of eclecticism in Pettigrew's (1958) discussion of the balance of personality and sociocultural factors in the formation of prejudice; and in Campbell's and LeVine's (1961) synthesis of social structure and modal personality variables in their approach to the study of ethnocentrism. The same is true when one considers the inferences about nationalism that can be made from the work described in the previous section side by side with those deriving from the experimental study of small groups. The difference in emphasis is seen in a sharp focus by Sherif (1966) who writes:

The problem of group prejudice and stereotyped images of other groups is not a problem of the idiosyncratic hates and unfounded beliefs of a few separated individuals. It is the problem of hostilities and images shared, in varying degrees, by large numbers of persons belonging to the same human grouping (p. 24).

It may be argued, though, that the consideration of modal personality factors related to a sociocultural background is not necessarily a study of a "few separated individuals." It remains true, however, that many valid generalizations about group processes were obtained without any consideration of the personalities of the individuals composing the groups. Thus, in the context of the study of national affiliation, the emphasis on small group processes can be seen as placed halfway between the theoretical extremes of considering only the impact of personality factors, on the one hand, and only the characteristics of the underlying social structure, on the other. There is also another road which may be taken in generalizations about large groups in which the intermediary step of small group processes is omitted; in this, an assumption must be made that events in the outside world are perceived and reacted to in similar ways by large masses of individuals. In this postulation of general psychological processes capable of accounting for the causes and effects of identifications with large human groups, personality factors are implicitly considered as being reflected in the statistics of normal distribution of the intensity displayed by these general processes in a large population.

All motivational and cognitive processes entering into social behavior are relevant in one way or another to the study of national affiliation. In order to isolate those contributions which may have a more direct bearing on the problem we shall—at the risk of some repetition—lay down again certain selected requisites for relevance. For nationalism to come into being as a wide-scale social phenomenon, it is necessary that a large proportion of the individuals who are members of a nation: (1) perceive that nation as some form of an entity, however various individuals may define that entity to themselves; (2) feel to some extent emotionally identified with that entity; and (3) consequently share an involvement in the events affecting it. There can be obviously no uniformity in the population with regard to these three aspects of nationalism. The private definitions of the nation will vary from individual to individual or from group to group; emotional involvement will vary in its intensity; and the involvement in the events affecting the nation can take many forms.

One of the underlying conditions for the existence of these three aspects of nationalism must be sought in the existence of channels of social communication concerning the common national identity of the population and in the effectiveness of the messages transmitted through these channels. In other words, social communication must acquire the properties of social influence, and social influence must result in turn in social or cultural diffusion of attitudes pertaining to the nation and of ideas about the nature of the nation. The transition from communication to influence is possible only if the messages are acceptable to the population. This will depend on two general sets of factors: (1) the capacity of the messages to build up a cognitive structure which will be capable of coexisting with, or of dominating, the competing views of the world in which classifications of human groups in terms other than national are not seen as more salient and more important; and (2) the capacity of the messages to be congruent with an individual's motives.

The relation of the content of social communication to these two sets of factors is a complex one. National affiliation is characterized by a very wide range of emotional intensity. At one extreme there is a nonsalient (and often only latent) awareness that one is a member of a nation, without any need for this awareness to manifest itself in the daily routines of life. The salience of national membership may increase without necessarily acquiring a high degree of emotional intensity in situations in which this membership becomes one of the criteria differentiating an individual from others with whom he interacts—such as during travel abroad, at international meetings, or when meeting foreigners in one's own country. And finally, there are the situations in which national identity pervades most aspects of an individual's life and reaches to the core of his emotional functioning.

Most discussions of the psychological aspects of nationalism confined themselves to an analysis of its extreme forms. As we have seen, nationalism in its violent, chauvinistic, and hostile manifestations has drawn much more attention to itself than the "quieter" forms of national awareness. This was the aspect of the phenomenon that Freud attempted to explain; it is this also that provided the basis for the preoccupation with the authoritarian and ethnocentric syndromes; and that is also responsible for the overriding stress on the situations of acute crisis as determining national affiliation. It is, however, an untenable assumption that group identity of uncommonly high intensity can emerge from nowhere, that nationalist emotions can be whipped up to heights unknown in the case of most other human affiliations without being grounded in some previously existing structure of cognitions and preferences.

However, as the traditional approach to the psychology of nationalism has been mainly characterized by a predominant interest in its intense emotional forms, we shall first briefly review the main factors which were assumed to be responsible for their occurrence. This main feature of strong nationalism —its emotional intensity—determined the direction of search: the common denominator of these approaches is the assumption that, in some situations, an individual perceives a threat which applies directly to him and which he shares with others who are of his nationality. The fact that the existence of threat must have been socially communicated is usually taken for granted, though rarely analyzed in any detail. In other words, the analysis of the causes of intense nationalism has usually been made almost exclusively in terms of motivational factors without much attention being paid to the cognitive aspects of social influence.

Many examples of these "threat" generalizations can be found in Rosenblatt's (1964) extensive catalog of hypotheses about nationalism and ethnocentrism extracted from a wide survey of the literature. Here are a few:

To the extent that the group is perceived as a source of defense, nationalism and ethnocentrism increase in time of competition and threat (p. 132)—Needs for affiliation increase in time of threat (p. 136)—Frustration from outgroups produces and frustration from the ingroup may produce increased ethnocentric and nationalistic hostility (p. 138)—To some extent, within-group frustration produces ethnocentric or nationalistic hostility, the more so the more restraints there are on expressing hostility within the group (pp. 138-39)—There are needs to defend one's ego in the presence of one's nonsuccess. To the extent that nationalism and ethnocentrism provide an object to blame for nonsuccess, nationalism and ethnocentrism are rewarding (p. 136)—Needs to be related to something supraindividual, to have goals, or to belong increase in time of threat from outside the group (p. 134)—Such needs are greater among the obscure, incompetent, and unsuccessful. To the extent that these people find satisfactions in ethnocentrism or nationalism, they will tend to be more ethnocentric or nationalistic than the average group member (p. 134).

Despite their relative importance and high incidence, the threat generalizations are only a part of the large bundle collected by Rosenblatt. The entire collection lends itself to a classification in terms of two fundamental categories. Some of the causes and determining conditions relate to what may be called the "crisis" nationalism; others to a sort of *nationalisme quotidien*, the day-to-day latent attitude which may manifest itself in a variety of conditions not bearing the characteristics of a crisis. As will be clear from the examples just given, the crisis may be either national or personal, and it is with the latter that the "personality" explanations of nationalism are essentially concerned.

But there are two other trends of thought from which the crisis generalizations have originated: one is in the interpretation of historical events characterized by a rise of nationalism; the other, in the extrapolations from the experimental studies of small groups.

The interpretative literature is enormous, and we shall confine ourselves to one example which has the merit of attempting psychological inferences of a *general* nature. For Barbu (1966), "nationalism is a collective reaction to a deep crisis in the structure and self-image of a community" (pp. 184–85); it is also "a collective reaction to a series of disrupting social and psychological processes, the main trigger of which may be briefly described as a cultural lag" (p. 193). The "cultural lag" starts with the alienation of an elite group followed by guilt feelings, the consequent return of the group to the native culture, and "finally, the same emphatic self-reference of the whole community" (p. 195). It is not clear from Barbu's account how the elite succeed in infusing the population at large with its intense nationalistic ideology. For the first of his generalizations, he draws illustrative examples from the French Revolution and the rise of national socialism in Germany.

The Russian intelligentsia of the nineteenth century provides him with an example of the "cultural lag."

The attraction of generalizations such as these is that they make intuitive sense, both historically and psychologically. Their difficulties are fairly obvious, and they arise not only from the impossibility to test them, but also from the many alternative interpretations of the illustrative events which can be put forward without any firm criteria for deciding between them. Both these points emerged clearly in the discussion that followed Barbu's paper at the Ciba symposium on conflict in society. For example, Lapter argued that the development of intense chauvinism in nineteenth-century Russia did not originate in the alienated intelligentsia but in "the upper and middle classes of the Russian society of that time," while the intelligentsia "dissociated itself from the Tzar's regime and appealed to popularism rather than to nationalistic prejudices" (de Reuck and Knight, 1966, p. 198). The need for the establishment of quantitative empirical indices has been stressed in the same discussion by Rapoport:

If all the manifestations of nationalism are to be explained on the basis of your hypothesis you must show that nationalism exists whenever these conditions exist, and conversely that whenever these conditions do not exist nationalism does not occur either. If there were some quantitative index of nationalism which could be correlated with some index of social disorganization which is the backbone of your hypothesis, your argument would be strengthened (de Reuck and Knight, 1966, pp. 201–202).

Barbu's "crisis" hypothesis of nationalism relies on the determining conditions of social disorganization and social alienation. The problem then arises of the manner in which these two phenomena become transmuted into nationalist attitudes of the population at large. From the turn of Barbu's discussion and from his stated purpose "to consider nationalism as a source of socialized aggression" (p. 185), it is clear that we have taken here one more path which leads back to the domain of outgroup hostility. The assumed causal sequence may be schematized as follows:

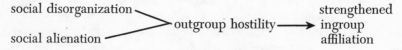

social disorganization
                          $\longrightarrow$ outgroup hostility $\longrightarrow$ strengthened
                                                                     ingroup
social alienation   affiliation

And thus, once again, displacement reactions are seen as a powerful determinant of the development of national affiliation. But there are many unresolved difficulties in the causal sequence shown above. From Berkowitz's (1962) review of the role of displacement reactions in intergroup relations, it is certainly possible to conclude that the first part of the sequence has no universal validity. The link from disorganization and alienation to the final intensification of internal cohesion can claim even less generality. Its shakiness has been well pointed out in Deutsch's reaction to Barbu's paper. He questions "the frequent assumption that a common enemy or common outgroup is necessary in order to increase the cohesion within a group" (de Reuck and Knight, 1966, p. 206). With the help of several examples he concludes that:

Scapegoating is thus not an instrument for integration but a symptom of the lack of it. The feedback from bad integration to scapegoating is strong, but the coupling from scapegoating to stronger integration is weak. I do not know of a badly integrated community which became lastingly integrated through resort to scapegoating (pp. 207–208).

Deutsch's examples suffer from the same weakness as Barbu's: there are always possibilities of alternative psychological interpretations of large-scale historical and political events. But the importance of his argument is in the fact that it points to a view of the determinants of group affiliation different from that represented in the above sequence, and to which not very much attention has been given in previous research. This is particularly true with regard to extrapolations from small group experiments to the development of national (or other large group) affiliation. The results of many of these experiments support some version of Barbu's sequence from outgroup hostility to ingroup integration. Some of these studies contain experimental arrangements which do not display the ambiguities shown by historical interpretations (*cf.* Berkowitz, 1962, for a review), and from which a sequence similar to Barbu's can be extracted:

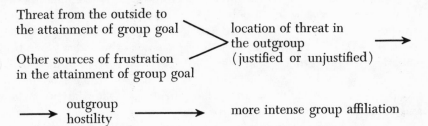

There is, however, a major difficulty here which relates to the point made by Deutsch. In most of the experimental situations there is no stable starting point of a strong initial level of group integration. In a field study in which such a starting point did exist (Festinger, Riecken, and Schachter, 1956), a disrupting event was followed by the group closing its ranks without the strong intervention of, or appeal to, outgroup hostility. When one considers a situation such as this, it becomes clear that even the experimental studies in which initial levels of various degrees of group integration have been introduced as one of the independent variables (e.g., Pepitone and Reichling, 1955) cannot hope to reproduce a long history of integration based on progressive formation of group norms, perception of common distinctive characteristics, and long-term cultural transmission. It is, therefore, fully possible that, *in the absence of all these long-term unifying processes,* outgroup hostility unavoidably comes to the fore when difficulties arise, since the group has no other means of cohesion at its disposal. Increase in group integration mediated by outgroup hostility usually arises in times of crisis. And, thus, in many of the extrapolations from small group experiments to the large-scale social phenomena we find an emphatic reaffirmation of the causal variables assumed to be responsible for what we referred to previously as the "crisis" version of nationalism; but this may be partly the result of finding in the data what has been built into them at the outset.

Some of the more general problems of the relevance of small group studies to political phenomena have been recently discussed by Verba (1961). He proposes "two ways in which the small group experimental model can be connected with actual social situations" (p. 246). The first is that the differences between the two must be systematic and "that they must be *known* differences" (p. 246). The second is "the use of realistic settings, and long-time spans so that groups can develop histories" (p. 247). One outstanding example of an attempt to use the second of these criteria is provided by the well-known series of Sherif's experimental field studies of intergroup relations (see Sherif, 1966, for a summary of his previous work on the subject). His results tend, on the whole, to support the "crisis" generalizations. In his camps for boys, an increased solidarity within each of the groups with its attendant changes of ingroup organization and practices followed after a period of intense conflict and competition between two groups. The reduction of intergroup hostility was not achieved through more contact between the groups; this was reached only when contact was combined with interdependence in a series of superordinate goals.

Many of Sherif's findings are directly applicable to the wider scene. Under conditions of intergroup conflict he was able to observe the development of stereotypes and unfavorable attitudes toward the members of the other group, an "overestimation of the achievements by fellow group members and lower estimates of the achievements by members of the outgroup" (p. 81), stronger pressures toward intolerance of deviant behavior, etc. Sherif's model has the merit of parsimony. The formation of the group is first determined by a number of common activities and common goals; its cohesiveness is then crucially enhanced because of the existence of a competing outgroup. In other words, it is possible to argue from Sherif's hypotheses and data that we have here *all* the necessary ingredients for the ingroup formation, and that, therefore, no other variables need to be taken into consideration for extrapolating to large-scale groups.

It is, however, one thing to conclude that Sherif's situations contain all the variables necessary for the formation of strong group affiliations and another to assume that no other paths are possible through which such affiliation could be developed. Intergroup conflict was, in the case of Sherif's studies, the main feature in the situation which cemented the groups' unity. Could these groups not have achieved strong attitudes of loyalty in their members if they developed and shared for a long time common goals, activities, norms, distinctive patterns of behavior, and sets of values without any intervention of an acute conflict with an outgroup? There are indications in Sherif's results that this may be possible: his groups became fairly cohesive and were able to modify the previously existing pattern of individual friendships during the short period of time when they lived peacefully. At this point, intergroup conflict erupted. We do not know what would have happened if this had not occurred and if the processes of peaceful integration had been allowed to pursue their course.

This brings us back to the distinction previously made between the historical and the a-historical approaches to the psychology of national affiliation. As Verba (1961) put it, differences between small groups and actual situations must be known differences. In the consideration of the development of national identity in individuals who are members of an already existing nation, the historical processes which had caused the formation of a nation must be taken for granted. It is fully possible that they consisted, in part at least, of the internal effects of conflicts with other groups. But when we consider the situation as it is at present, from the point of view of its effects on the individual members of a nation, then the degree of national integration *as it is now* becomes a *sui generis* independent variable in the arousal of national affiliation. The problem that we have is to specify the steps which make the transition between national integration and its psychological counterparts in the individual. However true it may be that conditions of crisis produce an intensification of ingroup affiliation, they do not account for its existence in other conditions; and, therefore, an exclusive reliance on them assumes that we are not dealing with an *intensification* of an attitude but with its *creation* out of nothing.

THE PROBLEM OF SOCIAL INFLUENCE

An explanation of the development of national affiliation in large masses of individuals must be directed at the two essential aspects of this affiliation which have been referred to earlier in this paper: the existence of concepts and ideas about the nation, and of a system of values and preferences concerning the nation. At one level, the problem is trivial: people develop ideas and preferences because they learn them from the surrounding society. At another level, this "triviality" is of the same kind as stating that a child can move about because he is endowed with an appropriate neuromuscular system which, in good time, will enable him to crawl, stand up, walk and run. Coordinated movements of the body present a problem to the physiologist and the psychologist only because they are able to consider an end result which appears intuitively "simple" as the outcome of complex underlying processes which are in need of detailed analysis. Every social scientist must be able to attain from time to time this perspective of a Martian visitor. One example will help to make this clear. In February, 1967, a prominent American politician, speaking about the Vietnam war to an audience of young people, stated that one American G.I. was more important to him than "the whole damn city of Hanoi." It is unlikely that this statement will do any harm to the political future of its author. It may be worth considering whether the same prediction could be made if the statement ran: "The preservation of a whole city, such as Hanoi, is more important to me than a few American G.I.'s." The fact that the first statement is less likely to harm a political career than the second is not "surprising"; but this lack of surprise can only be due to the taking for granted of an end result which stands in need of an explanation.

The sharing of the cognitive and affective content of national attitudes must be related to the processes of social influence; and the effects of these processes to the general features of an individual's conceptualization of the social world in which he lives. Social influence has been the subject of much theorizing and experimentation in social psychology. As in the case of the previously discussed issue of outgroup hostility, the empirical conclusions are based on experiments conducted in small group settings, with restricted crosscultural variations. It has been shown in hundreds of studies that substantial proportions of individuals tend to be influenced by groups of which they are members in their judgments about a great variety of issues, ranging from simple physical properties of objects to complex esthetic and attitudinal pronouncements. The theoretical analysis of social influence stressed two general sets of factors responsible for its effectiveness: the normative and the informational (cf. Tajfel, 1968 for a review). The normative factors relate to the motivational determinants of influence, such as the individual's involvement with the group, penalties for deviance, the cohesion of a group in its sharing of goals, etc.; the informational factors hinge on the fact that the social context in which an individual lives provides him with one of the most important sources of information about the world, and, therefore, that this social context acts as a filter through which much of the information about the outside world is received.

One of the important attempts to provide a synthesis of these two sets of factors has been Festinger's theory of social comparison processes (1954). Schachter (1959) provided the following summary statement of this position:

This notion of a "drive for self evaluation" has slowly emerged as the theoretical underpinning for a schema and body of research on social influence. Essentially it has been assumed that, given such a drive, tendencies exist to establish the "rightness" or "wrongness" of an opinion and the "goodness" or "badness" of an ability. If it is possible to check against physical reality or against authoritative sources, such evaluation may be forthright and simple. More often than not, however, such evaluation resources are nonexistent and it is possible to evaluate only by reference to other people . . . . Such social evaluation is possible, however, only when the comparison points are relatively close to one's own position . . . . A Jew does not evaluate the correctness of his opinions of Zionism by comparing them with those of an Arab nationalist . . . . This series of assumptions concerning the evaluation process leads to the expectation that when discrepancies of opinion or ability exist among the members of a group, tendencies will arise to reduce this discrepancy (p. 4).

The "drive for self-evaluation" can be understood to include in its effects an individual's view of many aspects of his social identity. It is not only his opinions and abilities that must be evaluated against those of "relevant" others; many of the criteria on which an individual's identity is based are entirely derived from a matrix of social categories. There is no other meaning to such membership groups as those related to social stratification, to ethnic differences, to occupational functions, to religious faith. In all these cases, an individual's identity must contain two aspects: defining his membership group and evaluating its position with regard to other groups.

The social origin of these aspects of self-identity allows for their comparison with an individual's "definition of the situation" in the much more restricted context of small groups used in experiments on social influence. When an individual is confronted with the unanimity of a small group concerning a specific issue, he finds himself in a closed system of social influence. As long as he is physically enclosed in the group, there is no recourse and no appeal to other sources of information. The results of this are sometimes quite dramatic: it has been shown again and again that many people in such situations yield to the judgment of the group even with regard to such issues of fact as differences in length between three lines (e.g., Asch, 1952). These are small and transient groups brought together for the purpose of the experiment and disbanded immediately afterwards. We may well ask what would be the effects of a nightmarish science-fiction situation in which an individual would live forever in such a closed system of social information. But there is no need to appeal to science fiction:

It may be expected that the effects of cultural background become more marked as a function of the complexity and ambiguity of the available information, and the opportunities that an individual has to engage in his own independent checking of what comes to him from social sources. This is parallel to the small group phenomena previously discussed. Thus, it is fairly obvious that supernatural beliefs or esthetic preferences will show more evidence of cultural impact than, for example, the perception of dimensional properties of the physical environment or the perceptual identification of objects. Between these two extremes in impact lie cultural differences concerning the rules about the amount and the nature of sensory information that is required in order to infer the existence of a physical phenomenom. One instance from Hallowell's (1951) work will make this clear. He transcribed an Ojibwa hunter's report of being pursued by a mythical hostile giant. As Hallowell pointed out, "auditory stimuli alone appear to have been the chief *physical* source of the subject's interpretation of the initial presence of a *windigo* and all his subsequent overt behavior . . . But in principle a succession of sounds is heard which, although they are physical, become significant to the perceiver because they also convey a conventional meaning" (p. 183) . . . There is no basis here for deciding how "immediate" to Adam Big Mouth was the perception of *windigo's* presence or how remote from physical cues was this inference. Because of the assumption of the existence of such mythical beings, the sequence of auditory cues was organized into a fully consistent and convincing pattern of evidence. There is no more evidence of "primitive thought" here than there is in our inferring the passage of a train when we are woken in the early morning by a crescendo of noise (Tajfel, 1968).

The question that arises is whether the modern nation presents, with regard to an individual's national identity, a relatively closed system of social information, so that its effects are comparable to those exercised by a small experimental group or by a cultural environment with a restricted range of cognitive alternatives. This problem has been extensively discussed by Deutsch (1966) who thus provides in his book a fundamental contribution to the social-psychological theory of nationalism.

The basic question to which Deutsch addresses himself is: how does a nation become a community? He adopts the definition of a society as "a group of individuals connected by an intense division of labor, and separated from other societies by a marked drop in this intensity" (p. 87). This is distinguished from both culture ("the habits, preferences and institutions as such, as if they were a configuration of disembodied ghosts") and community ("the collection of living individuals in whose minds and memories the habits and channels of culture are carried"). The members of a community share a culture in the sense of having "learned to communicate with each other and to understand each other well beyond the mere interchange of goods and services" (p. 91). This ability to communicate decreases sharply as the boundaries of a community are reached and members of one find themselves communicating with members of another.

It is Deutsch's contention that the modern state creates the conditions which help to transform its citizens into a community in the restricted sense of the term applying to their affiliation with the nation-state. This is done through the variety and complementarity of the numerous channels of communication concerning national identity. Complementarity consists of a functional equivalence of many different channels and of contents of their messages: "the same or a closely similar result may be reached by several different combinations of elements, or even by the entire replacement of some elements by others" (p. 96). And, thus, it is clear

. . . why all the usual descriptions of a people in terms of a community of languages, or character, or memories, or past history, are open to exception. For what counts is not the presence or absence of any single factor, but merely the presence of sufficient communication facilities with enough complementarity to produce the overall results (p. 97).

The creation of a community through channels of social communication is only possible when there are no strong competing alternatives which may determine an individual's adherence to another community. We know, however, that each individual in a complex society belongs to a number of communities; but this does not necessarily stand in contradiction to Deutsch's propositions. It is here that the existence of a relatively closed system of communication *with regard to national identity* becomes a crucial condition. The term "closed" is used here in a sense which is restricted in two ways: the first, that many other systems of communication concerning social identity which impinge on the individual are not competitive with the establishment of national identity; and the second, that in relevant conditions, the national system is dominant over other possible systems. The failure to satisfy either of these criteria would lead to the impossibility of forming a nation, or to the disintegration of one which already exists. For example, in a multinational state the various ethnic groups may hold on to their identity while preserving the overall national identity if the two affiliations are not incongruent. If they are, if the ethnic group attempts to create its own national identity in addition to its cultural, linguistic, or regional separateness, then the two systems of communication stand in direct competition, and a disintegration of one of them is possible, though the system which proves dominant will finally either way create or maintain a form of national identity. The criterion of dominance is crucial in yet another way: if under conditions of stress and crisis a national community cannot establish the priority of its influence over other communities, disintegration is also bound to follow.

The dominance of the national communication system over those which might possibly compete with it is established by what Deutsch terms its signal-to-noise ratio. The system is closed in the sense that other systems are not competitive with it because there are hardly any competing messages in the *relevant dimension* of national identity. The noise is practically nil; the signals are characterized not only by their variety and complementarity but also by the fact that an individual is bombarded by them from childhood to death. This virtual monopoly of communication is due not only to the fact that other channels are excluded, but also to the wide range of aspects of an individual's life that it covers. Processes of social comparison act at a multiplicity of levels. As Schachter (1959) pointed out, one of their most important features is that the yardstick against which an individual measures himself varies depending upon the reference point of the comparison which is being made. With regard to national affiliation to the manner in which an individual defines his identity at that particular level of his social framework, all the pressures focus in one direction to such an extent that it does not appear unreasonable to compare their effectiveness with the effectiveness of pressures acting upon an individual confronted with consistent unanimity in a small group setting.

Thus, the *conditions* determining national affiliation can be found in the system of social communication; their *effectiveness* in the processes of social influence, in the sense of an individual's acquisition of that part of his identity which is national through the process of social comparison. We now have to deal with the *content* of this identity, that is, with the formation of the cognitive structures and value systems which are its substance.

Many empirical studies concerned with messages which are assumed to induce national affiliation confine themselves to the effects of a few simple and concrete symbols of a nation, such as the flag, the anthem, or the person of a national leader. The implicit model is simple: the frequency of these symbols and the emotional significance that they are given in formal education, in the mass media, and in many other social contexts result in the arousal of positive attitudes toward the nation through the process of emotional conditioning. This seems a vastly oversimplified picture. The nation-state has its concrete symbols which are displayed at various occasions, and they undoubtedly help in creating the appropriate reactions of national piety. On the other hand, it would be a bold assumption that the effects of these symbols are able to account for the pervasiveness and the occasional intensity of national attitudes. The few concrete symbols of nation are embedded in a much wider structure of cognitions and value systems. Taken by themselves they would not be very different from some cases of persistent advertising. And, as Lazarsfeld and Merton (1949) wrote:

Advertising pays because it generally deals with a simple psychological situation. For Americans who have been socialized in the use of a toothbrush, it makes relatively little difference which brand of toothbrush they use. Once the pattern of behavior or the generic attitude has been established, it can be canalized in one direction or another (p. 477).

In the same way, the effectiveness of the explicitly concrete national symbols must be understood in relation to the background of "generic attitude" from which they take their meaning. The attitude itself is a result of widespread cultural diffusion of certain information and certain value systems; its content must be understood as a function of psychological mechanisms which transform the variety and multiplicity of social messages into a coherent cognitive and affective structure. One consists of simplifying, the other of "ideologizing" the relevant aspects of the social (and sometimes also physical) environment.

The process of simplification has been discussed by Barbichon and Moscovici (1965) in relation to the cultural diffusion of new scientific and technological information. One of its aspects is the reduction of complex phenomena to a level at which they can be dealt with in terms of a system of beliefs which are usually much simpler than the information which needs to be assimilated. In the case of technological innovation, a conflict remains between the preexisting system of beliefs and the knowledge that it is no longer adequate. In the case of ideas and beliefs about nations, the conflict hardly arises. The simple and straightforward views about the nature of one's own national group and its differences from others are not pitted against ubiquitous proofs of their inadequacy; and there is generally no shortage of social support for them.

We have already referred to this process of simplification when discussing some similarities between nationalist and racist ideologies. Its two main characteristics are: the attribution of certain clear-cut general properties to one's own national group, and, consequently, the perception of its clear-cut differences from other such groups. The articulateness of differences provides a basis for a firm belief in, and the justification of, national distinctiveness, of a unique national tradition which reaches far into the past, encompasses the present, and determines the lines of development for the future.

The categorization of mankind into distinctive national groups determines in turn a search for new characteristics which can be dichotomized within the same matrix of categories. Some striking examples of this can be found in the work of linguists. Fishman (1966) quotes evidence which is relevant: Wolff (1959) found that "West African groups speaking distinct, and, at times, unrelated languages, ignore the differences between them, at times reciprocally, and at times unilaterally." He "claims that mutual intelligibility is largely a function of intergroup attitudes" (Fishman, 1966, p. 10). Haugen (1966) provided similar evidence for Scandinavia. Linguistic findings of this kind fit in very well with more general experimental evidence that the imposing of a system of nonoverlapping categories on a series of stimuli which vary along a quantitative continuum results in an accentuation of perceived differences between the stimuli falling into distinct classes (Tajfel, 1959; Tajfel and Wilkes, 1963; Wilkes and Tajfel, 1966).

Thus, the information learned about the attributes of one's own nation and its differences from other nations is best assimilated as a series of clear-cut differentials which generalize from those that are genuine (such as language) to others (such as national "character," cultural products, aspects of everyday life, physical appearance, etc.) which in many cases present at best statistical distributions with a considerable degree of overlap. If the linguists are correct, the process goes even further: differences are not only perceived, accentuated, and generalized; they are also manufactured whenever necessary, and eliminated when this happens to fit the pattern of intergroup relations.

This elimination of differences is the obverse aspect of the phenomenon: the accentuation of similarities within the group. It must be clearly understood that this perceived internal unity of a nation, of its distinctive character, is not meant here to apply to the variety of interpersonal relations in which an individual engages every day of his life. The unifying and cohesive characteristics appear at an abstract "ideological" level. National acts and policies, whether discussed by political leaders, by the mass media, by school textbooks, or by individual citizens, are invariably referred to in the context of common national interest, common national fate, common values and mode of life, common traditions and cultural products, and the common character of the people who share so many bonds.

The cognitive aspects of national affiliation can thus be understood as resulting from the process of cognitive economy, of the ease with which the world can be fitted into a set of simple and distinct categories as compared with the difficulty of creating a system in which similarities and differences would be seen as embedded in a transitional, shifting, and complex matrix of overlapping categories. But this is not sufficient to account for the system of values and preferences which is an inherent feature of this affiliation. The simplification proceeds together with a concurrent process which sometimes has been described as "ideologizing." The distinctive features of one's own nation transcend mere description. In Doob's (1964) terms, "the people of every nation are convinced that their distinctiveness, no matter how small the area to which it pertains, is significant and virtually cosmic" (p. 92). The progressive inculcation of the virtues of distinctiveness, the ideologizing of the factual and fabricated features of the physical and social characteristics of a nation and of all that pertains to it, can be traced back all along the history of modern nations. There is little doubt that today, with the approaching universality of formal education and of the mass media, this process can become more effective than ever. In this, the concrete symbols such as the flag and the anthem are no more than the visible part of an iceberg; every aspect of national life has acquired, or is capable of acquiring, its own emotional charge. As Fishman (1966) puts it, the transition between ethnic group and nationality is based on an elaboration in which "the daily rounds of life that constitute traditional ethnicity (including ways of speaking, dressing, harvesting, cooking, celebrating, worshipping, etc.) come to be seen not as . . . localized and particularized 'innocent' acts, but rather as experiences of common history, common values, common missions, longings, goals, etc." (p. 3). In his paper, Fishman points out that, just as an ethnic group under certain conditions transforms itself in this way into a nationality, so does a multiethnic state when it is confronted with the need to create a common national bond. The process of ideologizing is likely to be similar in both cases.

The conjunction of effective social influence with ideologizing and simplifying throws some light not only on the cultural diffusion of national identity but also on some fundamental aspects of attitudes towards outgroups. There is a good deal of evidence in social psychology that perceived similarity to other people is correlated with an increased liking for them (e.g., Heider, 1958; Pepitone, 1966), though the causal direction of the process has never been made entirely clear. The

. . . emergence of norms seems . . . not only determined by the utility value of cooperating in order to remove a difficulty, but also as an emotionally autonomous consequence of affiliation with a group, whatever may be the original causes of the group coming together. . . . Shared needs and shared background lead to shared norms; shared norms lead to more shared background and to an emotional investment in the creation of more shared norms. All these interlocking processes result in the strengthening of group identification, and to the increased capacity for perceiving those who are in the same group as essentially similar to oneself. It will be obvious that this perception of similarity makes it much easier to adopt in any relevant situation the point of view of those who are categorized as being "in" in contrast to those who are perceived as being "out" (Tajfel, 1966, p. 82).

AN ATTEMPT TO SUMMARIZE

The informational content and the ideological features of national affiliation are determined by the social, political, economic, and historical factors which act upon the policies and decisions of states and statesmen; but they are equally determined by what is psychologically feasible and acceptable to the population at large. The success of many nation-forming movements of the past and the present has been partly based on the intuitive understanding by the leaders of what would be psychologically effective. The task of the social psychologist is to make these intuitions explicit in terms of general psychological processes. But the testing of his ensuing hypotheses is not possible without a return to the consideration of the network of social variables which form the context of the psychology of nation-building.

The review we undertook of the psychological approaches to the problem of national affiliation allows for a listing of the main variables which are likely to assume different degrees of importance depending upon the social context in which they make their appearance. They are as follows:

1. The salience of national affiliations in a sample of relevant research conditions;
2. The range and intensity of the outgroup hostility components of national affiliation;
3. The range and intensity of outgroup differentiations (as distinct from hostility) components of national affiliation;
4. The range and salience of ideologizing of national attributes;
5. The range and salience of simplification (stereotyping) of national attributes;
6. The range and salience of all the above in relation to the incidence of the authoritarian or ethnocentric syndrome;
7. The range and intensity of competing group affiliations:
    (a) inside the national group;
    (b) outside the national group;
    (c) cross-cutting the classification in terms of national criteria;
8. The areas and intensity of social pressures towards national affiliation as related to latitude for deviance.

The main contextual social variables which are capable of being set in direct predictive relations to these psychological variables appear to be: the existing level of national integration; and the dichotomy of "crisis–no crisis" situations. It will be obvious that these contextual variables must be defined and assessed independently of the assessment of the psychological variables.

A useful model for considering relations of this type has recently been pro-

TABLE 1

LEVELS OF ANALYSIS OF NATIONALISM (BASED ON KATZ, 1965)

Appropriate level of analysis		General category and its content		
Political and economic	1.	Types of national systems		
		Revolutionary society	Empire-building society	Technological bureaucratic society	"Blocked" society
Political and economic	2.	Functions of political state		
		Internal integration	Maximization of favorable input-output ratios	Survival and protection against external enemies
Political and psychological	3.	Ideologies sustaining (and sustained by) the above functions		
		Statism	Institutional nationalism	Cultural identity
Psychological and sociological	4.	Social instruments for the translation of ideology into shared norms (forms of social communication)		
		Family influences	Formal education	Mass media	Concrete forms of cultural traditions	Leaders
Psychological (process)	5.	Arousal of national affiliation		
		Emotional & behavioral conditioning to national symbols	Formation of self-concept as inclusive of national identity	Compensatory identification	Instrumental involvement in national structure
Psychological (finished product)	6.	Psychological dimensions of nationalism		
		Symbolic vs. reality oriented		Degree of emotional involvement	

vided by Katz (1965). He characterizes his approach as social psychological in the sense that it considers "both the nature of the social systems, national and international, and the nature of the psychological variables involved" (p. 356). He adds:

The personality theorist, in looking at belligerent national action, would see people showing aggression; the political scientist would see nations at war; and the social psychologist would see people playing their various roles in the national structure in relation to their needs and the social constraints of the situation (p. 357).

Katz's system of analysis is made on five interdependent levels. It is not our purpose here to reproduce the detail of his observations about each of these levels, but rather to paraphrase the system and to reallocate the levels of analysis in a way which seems most relevant to the present discussion. This has been done (see Table 1) by rearranging the system, specifying in each case the appropriate type of analysis and adding a sixth level ("social instruments").

A consideration of an analytic scheme of this nature (however tentative and oversimplified it may be) leads to several conclusions. The first is that a large number of hypotheses concerning the relations between the various levels can be derived from it; the second, that the testing of many of these hypotheses would obviously require a multi-disciplinary framework; the third, that the list of psychological variables which was previously presented could be used to expand and articulate the levels 3, 4, 5 and 6; and finally, that no single study of nationalism can hope to encompass the empirical problems arising from the scheme.

From the point of view of research in social psychology, this impossibility to encompass the problems within one study, however ambitious it may be, or within one discipline, does not mean that we have to sit and wait in a per-fectionist contemplation. There are at least two things that can be done with-out putting into gear an enormous multidisciplinary machinery. One is the provision of psychological data, both uni- and cross-cultural, which may establish the relations between the psychological variables previously listed, and from which further links to the contextual social variables can be postu-lated. The other is to create experimental conditions which would simulate, as far as it is possible, some of these contextual variables (such as various degrees of crisis, of long-term integration, of monopolistic social influence, of creation of distinctive group "ideologies"), and to determine in a prelimi-nary manner the extent to which the various "large-scale" hypotheses can be validated in simpler and better controlled conditions of research.

174 ILLUSTRATIVE PROBLEM AREAS

REFERENCES

ADORNO, T. W., E. FRENKEL-BRUNSWIK, D. J. LEVINSON, and R. N. SANFORD. 1950. *The authoritarian personality.* New York: Harper.

ARDREY, R. 1966. *The territorial imperative: a personal inquiry into the animal origins of property and nations.* New York: Atheneum.

ASCH, S. E. 1952. *Social psychology.* Englewood Cliffs, N.J.: Prentice-Hall.

BARBICHON, G., and S. MOSCOVICI. 1965. Diffusion des connaissances scientifiques. *Social Sciences Information,* 4: 7–22.

BARBU, Z. 1966. Nationalism as a source of aggression. In A. de Reuck and J. Knight (Eds.), *Conflict in society.* London: J. and A. Churchill.

BERKOWITZ, L. 1962. *Aggression: a social psychological analysis.* New York: McGraw-Hill.

CAMPBELL, D. T. 1965. Ethnocentric and other altruistic motives. In D. Levine (Ed.), *The Nebraska symposium on motivation.* Lincoln: University of Nebraska Press.

———, and R. A. LEVINE. 1961. A proposal for cooperative cross-cultural re-research on ethnocentrism. *Journal of Conflict Resolution,* 5: 82–108.

CARTHY, J. D., and F. J. EBLING (Eds.). 1964. *The natural history of aggression.* London: Academic Press.

CHRISTIANSEN, B. 1959. *Attitudes towards foreign affairs as a function of personality.* Oslo: Oslo University Press.

DEUTSCH, K. W. 1966. *Nationalism and social communication: an inquiry into the foundations of nationality.* (2d ed.) Cambridge: MIT Press.

DOISE, W. 1967. *Autoritarisme, dogmatisme et leur rapports avec des perceptions et attitudes dans le domaine des relations internationales.* Unpublished Ph.D. dissertation, University of Paris.

DOOB, L. W. 1964. *Patriotism and nationalism: their psychological foundations.* New Haven, Conn.: Yale University Press.

DUIJKER, H. C. J., and N. H. FRIJDA. 1960. *National character and national stereotypes.* Amsterdam: North Holland.

EMERSON, R. 1960. *From empire to nation.* Cambridge: Harvard University Press.

ERIKSON, E. H. 1963. *Childhood and society.* (2d. ed.) New York: W. W. Norton.

FESTINGER, L. 1954. A theory of social comparison processes. *Human Relations,* 7: 117–40.

———, H. W. RIECKEN, and S. SCHACHTER. 1956. *When prophecy fails.* Minneapolis: University of Minnesota Press.

FISHMAN, J. A. 1966. Nationality-nationalism and nation-nationism. Paper delivered at SSRC conference on *Language problems of developing nations.*

FRENKEL-BRUNSWIK, E. 1949. A study of prejudice in children. *Human Relations,* 1: 295–306.

———. 1954. Further explorations by a contributor to "The Authoritarian Personality." In R. Christie and M. Jahoda (Eds.), *Studies in the scope and method of "The authoritarian personality."* Glencoe, Ill.: Free Press.

FREUD, S. 1922. *Group psychology and the analysis of the ego.* London: International Psychoanalytic Press.

GINSBERG, M. 1942. National character. *British Journal of Psychology,* 32: 183–205.

GLUCKMAN, M. 1955. *Custom and conflict in Africa.* London: Oxford University Press.

GREENSTEIN, F. 1965. *Psychological aspects of politics.* Stanford: Center for Advanced Study in the Behavioral Sciences. (Mimeo.)

GUETZKOW, H. 1955. *Multiple loyalties: theoretical approach to a problem in international organization.* Princeton, N.J.: Princeton University Press.

HALLOWELL, A. I. 1951. Cultural factors in the structuralization of perception. In J. H. Rohrer and M. Sherif (Eds.), *Social psychology at the crossroads.* New York: Harper.

HAUGEN, E. 1966. Semicommunication: the language gap in Scandinavia. *Social Inquiry,* 36: 280–97.

HEIDER, F. 1958. *The psychology of interpersonal relations.* New York: Wiley.

HOGGART, R. 1957. *The uses of literacy: changing patterns in English mass culture.* London: Oxford University Press.

INKELES, A. 1963. Sociology and psychology. In S. Koch (Ed.), *Psychology: a study of a science.* Vol. 6: *Investigations of man as a socius: their place in psychology and the social sciences.* New York: McGraw-Hill.

――――, and D. J. LEVINSON. 1954. The study of modal personality and sociocultural systems. In G. Lindzey (Ed.), *Handbook of social psychology.* Vol. 2. Cambridge: Addison-Wesley.

KATZ, D. 1965. Nationalism and strategies of international conflict resolution. In H. C. Kelman (Ed.), *International behavior: a social psychological analysis.* New York: Holt, Rinehart and Winston.

KLINEBERG, O. 1964. *The human dimension in international relations.* New York: Holt, Rinehart and Winston.

KOHN, H. 1944. *The idea of nationalism.* New York: Macmillan.

――――. 1962. *The age of nationalism: the first era of global history.* New York: Harper.

LASSWELL, H. D. 1935. *World politics and personal insecurity: a contribution to political psychiatry.* New York: McGraw-Hill.

LAZARSFELD, P. F., and R. MERTON. 1949. Popular taste and organized social action. In W. Schramm (Ed.), *Mass communications.* Urbana: University of Illinois Press.

LeVINE, R. A. 1965. Socialization, social structure and intersocietal images. In H. C. Kelman (Ed.), *International behavior: a social psychological analysis.* New York: Holt, Rinehart and Winston.

LEVINSON, D. J. 1957. Authoritarian personality and foreign policy. *Journal of Conflict Resolution,* 1: 37–47.

LORENZ, K. 1966. *On aggression.* New York: Harcourt, Brace and World.

LOWENTHAL, L. 1961. *Literature, popular culture and society.* Englewood Cliffs, N.J.: Prentice-Hall.

McDOUGALL, W. 1920. *The group mind.* New York: Putnam.

PEPITONE, A. 1966. *Attraction and hostility.* London: Tavistock Publications.

――――, and G. REICHLING. 1955. Group cohesiveness and the expression of hostility. *Human Relations,* 8: 327–37.

PETTIGREW, T. F. 1958. Personality and sociocultural factors in intergroup attitudes: a cross-national comparison. *Journal of Conflict Resolution,* 2: 29–42.

PYE, L. W. 1961. Personal identity and political ideology. In D. Marvick (Ed.), *Political decision-makers*. Glencoe, Ill.: Free Press.

———. 1962. *Politics, personality and nation building: Burma's search for identity*. New Haven, Conn.: Yale University Press.

DE REUCK, A., and J. KNIGHT (Eds.). 1966. *Conflict in society*. London: J. and A. Churchill.

ROSENBLATT, P. C. 1964. Origins and effects of group ethnocentrism and nationalism. *Journal of Conflict Resolutions*, 8: 131–46.

Royal Institute of International Affairs. 1939. *Nationalism*. London: Oxford University Press.

SCHACHTER, S. 1959. *The psychology of affiliation*. Stanford: Stanford University Press.

SHAFER, B. C. 1955. *Nationalism: myth and reality*. New York: Harcourt, Brace and World.

SHERIF, M. 1966. *In common predicament: social psychology of intergroup conflict and cooperation*. Boston: Houghton Mifflin.

SINGER, M. 1961. A survey of culture and personality theory and research. In B. Kaplan (Ed.), *Studying personality cross-culturally*. Evanston, Ill.: Row, Peterson.

SMITH, M. B., J. S. BRUNER, and R. W. WHITE. 1956. *Opinions and personality*. New York: Wiley.

SUMNER, W. G. 1906. *Folkways*. Boston: Ginn.

TAJFEL, H. 1959. Quantitative judgment in social perception. *British Journal of Psychology*, 50: 16–29.

———. 1966. Cooperation between human groups. *Eugenics Review*, 58: 77–84.

———. 1968. Social and cultural factors in perception. In G. Lindzey and E. Aronson (Eds.), *Handbook of social psychology*. (2d ed.) Cambridge: Addison-Wesley.

———, and A. L. WILKES. 1963. Classification and quantitative judgment. *British Journal of Psychology*, 54: 101–114.

VERBA, S. 1961. *Small groups and political behavior*. Princeton, N. J.: Princeton University Press.

WALLAS, G. 1908. *Human nature in politics*. London: Constable.

WILKES, A. L., and H. TAJFEL. 1966. Types de classification et importance du contraste relatif. *Bulletin du C.E.R.P.* 15: 71–81.

WILLIAMS, R. 1958. *Culture and society*. London: Chatto and Windus.

WOLFF, H. 1959. Intelligibility and inter-ethnic attitudes. *Anthropological Linguistics*, 1: 34–41.

ZAJONC, R. B. 1968. Cognitive theories of social behavior. In G. Lindzey and E. Aronson (Eds.), *Handbook of social psychology*. (2d ed.) Cambridge: Addison-Wesley.

ZANGWILL, I. 1917. *The principle of nationalities*. London: Macmillan.

9

PHENOMENOLOGY AND CROSSCULTURAL RESEARCH

Robert B. MacLeod

One important field of interdisciplinary research is the comparative study of cultures, a field which we tend to regard as the special preserve of the anthropologist. In psychology the crosscultural approach is relatively new and extremely promising. Crosscultural psychology is usually treated as an extension of social psychology; understandably so, since the pioneer work of Wundt (1900–20) presented *Völkerpsychologie* as a supplement to the traditional analytic study of the individual mind, and most of the subsequent forays into the field have been concerned primarily with social processes. More properly, however, crosscultural psychology is a branch of a broadly defined comparative psychology. Mental processes can be studied comparatively across species (traditional animal psychology), across age groups (developmental psychology), through the comparison of individuals and subgroups within a culture, and through the systematic comparison of one culture with other cultures. This conception of comparative psychology is by no means new (*cf.*, for instance, Franz Kafka's almost forgotten *Handbuch der vergleichenden Psychologie*, 1922), but we need a frequent reminder that our central concern in psychology is with the understanding of mind (or behavior, if you prefer) and that this understanding will never be complete if the contexts within which we observe mental processes are arbitrarily restricted. In the study of animals, the reminder is perhaps less needed now than it was a few years ago when animal psychology was in danger of becoming the psychology of the laboratory rat; and there are hopeful signs in child psychology and even in the psychological study of the abnormal. We still need the reminder, however, that most of the psychology we write today is written within the context of a particular culture and that the generalizations we are now making may have to be revised as we learn more about mental processes in other cultures. The need for crosscultural study in psychology is obvious; my thesis in this paper is that some of the problems of

177

crosscultural study may be clarified, possibly even illuminated, through the adoption of a phenomenological approach.

That today's psychology is "culture-bound" needs little illustration. On a superficial level, it may be noted that there are now more psychologists in the United States than there are in the whole of the rest of the world, that psychological publications are overwhelmingly in the English language, that few of the writers of these can read with ease any language other than their own, and that still fewer can actually communicate in another language. "Parochial" might be a more appropriate word for this than "culture-bound"; twentieth-century psychology reflects predominantly the interests and prejudices of one national group. More disturbing, however, is the possibility that what we think of as a science of psychology may be bound to the implicit assumptions of a single culture. A science is distinguished by its questions, its data, its methods, and its explanatory constructs. If our interpretation of the human mind is based on the behavior of American college sophomores in artificially contrived situations and interpreted in terms of laws derived from domesticated rats and pigeons, then our psychology is truly culture-bound. The situation is not quite as bad as this, of course. Psychologists have long been aware of the dangers of illicit generalization. Especially in such fields as the testing of intelligence, it has become increasingly clear that a measure which has predictive value for one group may have little significance for another. Nevertheless the danger has been met all too frequently by a retreat from all generalization rather than by a serious effort to determine within which contexts valid generalization can take place. The facts of cultural difference, like those of individual difference, need not discourage the search for regularities in human behavior.

When I speak of adopting the phenomenological approach I refer, of course, to psychological rather than philosophical phenomenology; and I hasten to add, first, that mine is only one of many interpretations of phenomenology[1] and, secondly, that in the context of crosscultural research much of what we mean by psychological phenomenology is not far removed from what a good many anthropologists do in the ordinary course of their field work. In everyday language, psychological phenomenology includes the attempt to get, as it were, inside the world of the other person. It includes much more than this, of course, but in the study of other people what we are really trying to do is to understand the nature of the other person's identity, the structure and meaning of the world he lives in, and the ways in which he relates himself to that world.

The phenomenological problem which crosscultural study brings into focus is thus the problem of understanding directly the mental states and processes of "the other one" (*Fremdverständnis*), a problem which phenome-

1. For a discussion of the philosophical movement, see Spiegelberg (1965). For a review of recent trends in phenomenological and existentialist psychology, see Misiak and Sexton (1966).

nologists have long recognized (*cf.* Scheler, 1923) but from which experimentalists have tended to recoil. In principle it is the problem we face every day in ordinary communication. When two people speak and listen to one another, neither has assurance that what he intends to say is understood by the other in the way in which he intended. As Oliver Wendell Holmes pointed out whimsically in *The Autocrat of the Breakfast Table* (1884, p. 52 ff.), in any dyadic conversation there are at least six people involved. To put it in less felicitious language, there are: (1) the "real" speaker and (2) the "real" hearer, neither of whom truly communicates with the other, (3) the speaker as he apprehends himself, (4) the speaker as he is apprehended by the hearer, (5) the hearer as he is apprehended by the speaker, and (6) the hearer as he apprehends himself. If we allow the ghosts of the unconscious to materialize, this little platoon can become a veritable army of speakers and hearers, all talking at cross purposes with one another.

This is all very confusing, especially when we realize that the medium of spoken communication includes not only the structural components that we try to record in the dictionaries and the grammars of the language—sounds, phonemes, words, syntax, and so forth—but also all sorts of expressive variations, for example, speed, intensity, melody, and regularity of vocal utterance, plus accompanying facial expressions, manual gestures, and body postures, all of which may intentionally or unintentionally convey meaning. When we consider the fantastic complexity of the media of communication and the equally baffling complexity of the people involved, one wonders sometimes how it is that one person can ever speak to another person with the assurance that he will be understood.

If we push the problem of communication to its metaphysical limits, we must concede that it is incapable of solution. Each of us is playing around in his own private world and he can never know for sure what is going on in the world of the other one. As a matter of practical living, however, we always take comfort from the fact that there are times when we are quite sure that we have communicated our meaning satisfactorily to someone else. When I say to you "It looks like rain. You had better take your umbrella," and you do pick up your umbrella instead of a frying pan or a book of Shakespeare's sonnets, I feel reasonably sure that you have taken my prediction of rain seriously. If, however, instead of picking up the umbrella, you get down on your knees in an attitude of prayer or perform what looks like a ritualistic dance, I may still conclude that I have made you aware of rain as a probability; you simply believe that prayer and dancing will afford you better protection than will an umbrella. When I fully understand the nature of your belief and the conception of the world that lies behind it, I have come closer to an understanding of what it is that I have communicated to you.

It may be, of course, that you are reacting in a way which is completely meaningful to me, but that my apprehension of it is still completely wrong. For you the rain may not be a threat at all, but rather something to be desired; it may be that your ritualistic response to my prediction is not to ward off the rain but to encourage it. In this case I have communicated something to you, but not precisely what I thought I was communicating. My certainty provides no final guarantee, which is a good reason for the maintenance of a healthy state of skepticism. But the fact remains that at any given moment we have to act on the basis of our best hypotheses and that the consequences of minor misunderstandings are seldom catastrophic.

Traditional phenomenology has been concerned with a world in which "I" am a constant anchorage point. It is a world of colors and sounds, ideas and feelings as they appear to me or are experienced by me. To describe and analyze this world is a tough task, but an even tougher task is to shift the point of reference from the "I" to the "you" or the "he" and to reconstruct the world as it is there for the other person. One is tempted to use the term "private," and to talk of "my" private world or of peering into the private world of someone else. This, however, is a misleading way of speaking.

Every world is partly private or partly public. Unless we are content to escape into a solipsism, in which case all discussion is futile, you and I are agreed that we are surrounded by things and events that are public, even though we may apprehend them in slightly different ways. Your pain and my pleasure may be in a sense private, but I am prepared to defend the thesis that I can talk just as meaningfully, although with less certainty, about the pain you feel as about the color you see. In both cases I speak with less certainty than I do about the pain I feel and the color I see, but I contend that the phenomenological problem is in principle the same if I am the point of reference as it is if you are the point of reference; it is just a great deal more difficult to accept your point of view. Even when you and I are of the same species, age, sex, economic background, speak the same language, were at the same party last night, I still do not know *for sure* what is going on in the world which has you as its constant point of reference. Nevertheless, I can try to find out; and I can try to find out what is going on in the world of the child, or of a Swahili speaking African, or of an Irishman speaking English.

The experimental devices which enable me to learn more about "my own" world can be adapted to the exploration of worlds which differ radically from mine. Men like Edward Tolman have given us what might be called a phenomenology of the animal; Jean Piaget and his colleagues have been steadily charting out the world of the child; the existential psychotherapists, Binswanger for example, have been doing the same for the world of the psychotics; and our anthropological colleagues have given us much more than the beginnings of a phenomenology of the person in a different culture. All I am suggesting here is that those who are interested in psychological phenomenology should take full advantage of the insights provided by the study of other cultures. One might even hazard the guess that the phenomenology of the "other one" will actually be easier when we are dealing with people who are radically different from ourselves than when we stick with people of our own culture. As our clinical friends have demonstrated, the study of extreme deviations may make us aware of characteristics of the normal person which might otherwise have escaped our attention. Certainly when we try to fathom the thinking of a person in another culture we inevitably become aware of some of the unrecognized assumptions implicit in our own thinking.

May I say a word in passing about phenomenology and cultural relativism? When we talk loosely about phenomenology, as I have been doing, it might appear that phenomenology leads directly to a relativistic position. In one sense this is correct. If we oppose relativism to naïve realism, it would seem that any demonstration that my world is different from yours would tend to support the relativist. Segall, Campbell, and Herskovits, in introducing their interesting book *The Influence of Culture on Visual Perception* (1966), speak of "phenomenal absolutes." For any individual, and for that matter for any culture, certain phenomena are accepted as absolute. The objects about us retain their apparent size, shape, color, and position in space in spite of constantly changing conditions of stimulation, and similarly our conceptual structures, our stereotypes about other people, our standards of right and wrong, and so forth, are treated as though they were absolutes. To argue from phenomenal absolutism to epistemological absolutism, as many of us are prone to do, is obviously both illicit and dangerous. It leads to narrow-minded dogmatism and prejudice, and in our dealings with other peoples it fosters a vicious ethnocentrism. We owe much to Boas and his pupils for their stubborn and courageous fight against ethnocentrism. I submit that so far as the social sciences are concerned, this battle has been virtually won, even though ethnocentrism still rears its ugly head in politics and in the marketplace. The social scientist as citizen and as educator must continue his fight against the superficial philosophy of absolutism. The alternative, however, is not an equally superficial relativism. The relativism of the early Boas school was a healthy corrective, but it tended to become a positivism that was almost negativistic. Every culture is unique, it was claimed, and any crosscultural generalization is consequently irresponsible.

This, I think, is a defeatist position, and I suggest that a phenomenological approach may help us to find a way out. Phenomenal absolutes are facts. It is a fact that we live in a world of relatively stable objects, relatively fixed categories, and relatively firm beliefs. It would be impossible to survive in a world without any dependable anchorage points. The task of the scientists is not to settle the epistemological question, however, but rather to observe and describe the phenomena, to plot their regularities and, if possible, to formulate these as part of the corpus of natural law. What I have called a superficial relativism may involve either or both of two unacceptable assumptions: one, that the world is like a giant, chaotic inkblot on which we (the perceiver, the thinker) impose our categories; this is the fallacy of projection. The other, the fallacy of introjection, is that we are infinitely plastic lumps of putty on which the world imposes its structure. Not even the most dedicated Freudian nor the most evangelical Watsonian will defend the extremes of relativism. Both will concede, even insist, that behind the phenomena which invite a relativism there must be laws of human behavior consonant with the other laws of nature. Here is where the fact-oriented scientist must take another look at the phenomena of individual and cultural differences.

I find myself going back with considerable sympathy to the work of a much maligned anthropologist of an earlier generation, Lucien Lévy-Bruhl. In his three major works, *Les Fonctions Mentales dans les Sociétés Inférieures, La Mentalité Primitive,* and *L'Âme Primitive,* he argues from the observed facts of cultural difference to the conclusion that different cultures may represent different kinds of mentality. The primitive mind, he argued, does not use discursive thought or abstract reason. This is not necessarily because of a lack of aptitude but because of "an attachment to objects of sense" (1927, p. 3 ff.). He quoted with approval a missionary's report that "they don't believe what they cannot see" and therefore, the missionary concluded sadly, they refuse to believe in an invisible god. How unreasonable of them! Granted that Lévy-Bruhl may have been a little incautious in his use of sources and a little hasty in his willingness to generalize, he nevertheless makes an important point. If we are to understand the mentality of the so-called "primitive," we must suspend our own cultural biases and try to see the world as the "primitive" sees it. His conclusion that primitive thinking is based on a, for us, peculiar kind of pre-logic may be misleading. In pointing to an apparent breakdown of the logical laws of identity and non-contradiction, he is not necessarily challenging the normative laws of logic, but he is certainly raising questions about the psychological meaning of identity. He is really calling for a less culture-bound psychology of perception and thinking and, by implication, of all other fundamental psychological processes. There is no reason to believe that Lévy-Bruhl regarded himself as a phenomenologist. In my opinion, however, his approach was essentially phenomenological; and it is interesting to note that Husserl welcomed his contributions with what for Husserl was almost extravagant praise (Spiegelberg, 1965, p. 162).

THE PHENOMENOLOGICAL APPROACH

Let me now speak a little more technically about the phenomenological approach and suggest a few descriptive categories for a phenomenological psychology.

Psychological phenomenology calls for the bracketing of all presuppositions and the description of immediate experience in terms of its essential structures and attributes. This raises at once a number of questions, none of which can be answered simply and satisfactorily: (1) What do we mean by immediate experience? (2) Is it literally possible to suspend one's pre-suppositions? (3) Since description must be in terms of a language, what sort of language is required for a psychological phenomenology? Immediate experience is what the phenomenologist observes and describes. The adjective "immediate" usually connotes either "instantaneous" or "unmediated." We are obviously not limiting ourselves to instantaneous experience, not merely because the word has little psychological meaning but also because experience as we have it continues and develops through time. The notion of mediation is equally unsatisfactory; the psychologist is interested in every experience, whether or not, or however, it may be mediated. We must conse-quently scrap the adjective "immediate."

What then do we mean by experience? The Germans make a useful dis-tinction between *Erlebnis,* experience as we have it, and *Erfahrung,* past experience or experience as it has accumulated. The phenomenologist is con-cerned primarily with *Erlebnis,* for which there are such cognate terms as "consciousness" and "awareness." I suggest that for these terms there is no useful operational definition. Either we know what we mean when we say that we are conscious, or conscious of something, or we do not. We know the difference between red and blue, or we do not know it. The fact that we use verbal symbols to designate the difference is irrelevant. We could not use the symbols consistently if there were not differences in experience to which they refer.

Phenomenology must begin, then, with the assumption that we know what we mean by experience. It is probably better simply to use the word "phe-nomenon," in its correct sense as "that which appears." We are observing and attempting to describe phenomena, the world of appearances, accepting this world as it is, passing no epistemological judgments. The phenomenologist is interested in all phenomena, whether they be the sturdy, resistant things which surround him and thrust themselves at him as real objects in a real world or the wispy, imaginary, un-pin-downable images of dreams and fan-tasies. All are phenomena to be observed and to be described, eventually perhaps to be related meaningfully to the phenomena we call physical or physiological. The term "phenomenal world" as I am using it may at times be interchangeable with "phenomenal field," "psychological field," "behavi-oral world," or even "psychological life-space," as these have been used by other writers.

The bracketing of presuppositions required by Husserl's phenomenologi-cal reduction involved a very thorough housecleaning in which metaphysical ghosts of all sorts were swept out of the attic and hung on the clothesline for airing. Husserl was prepared to expose to the light even the most sacred pre-suppositions of science, religion, and everyday living. It would do the psy-chologist no harm if he were to be equally ruthless in his housecleaning (although if he were to do this I am not sure that there would be any psy-chology left). If we were to put all presuppositions in temporary brackets, our thinking might come to a stop, for we would be bracketing even the presupposition that thoughts are worth thinking. Husserl never went quite this far. He even wrote down his thoughts for the benefit of others and went through the agony of publishing them.

The bracketing procedure in psychological phenomenology is much more modest. In his role as scientist the psychologist is likely to leave unchallenged certain assumptions—about the possibility of observation, for instance, or about the rules of logical consistency—with which the philosopher must of necessity be concerned; but there is still ample room for the searching out and the identification of implicit assumptions which may be playing an unnoticed part in his observing and his theorizing. Titchener's caution against the stimulus error, while limited in its application, is still a healthy one; and so is the familiar caution against the confusion, so common in nineteenth-century associationism and in the early theories of instinct, between logical implication and psychological content. About twenty years ago (1947), I listed some of the "biases" commonly found in social psychological theory, among which were: the atomistic-reductive bias, the stimulus-receptor bias, the genetic bias, the logical bias, and the relativistic bias; and one could easily extend the list considerably. The word "bias" is probably an unfortunate one because of its association with prejudice, and might well be withdrawn. The point is that with a little effort and discipline the psychologist can become aware of some of the presuppositions that are silently present in his observation and thinking. The fact that totally presuppositionless thinking is an impossibility, and that at best presuppositions can be only partially and temporarily suspended, does not detract from the importance of the attempt to identify them.

Two further questions are frequently raised in connection with psychological phenomenology: (1) Does not the approach lead inevitably into a solipsism? (2) Is not the bracketing of presuppositions precisely what every scientist does as part of his scientific procedure? The first of these can be brushed aside. Solipsism is no more, and no less, a threat to the phenomenologist than it is to any other inquirer. Devising an escape from solipsism is a healthful exercise for the beginner, one of the more interesting escape routes being, I think, by way of a careful phenomenology.

The second question is to be answered with both a yes and a no: Yes, in that in his attack on a specific problem, the good scientist attempts to identify and challenge the implicit assumptions that are relevant to his problem; No, in that the scientist's interest is usually in the problem as set within the context of his science, not in the process of knowing as such. The phenomenological method might consequently be regarded, not as an alternative to the method of science, but rather as its extension. Again it must be noted that, while in principle a complete phenomenology is conceivable, any phenomenological description is subject to the limitations of the phenomenologist. This is ample ground for the conclusion that phenomenology will always remain an approach and will never yield a fully satisfactory theory.

DESCRIPTIVE CATEGORIES FOR A
PSYCHOLOGICAL PHENOMENOLOGY

Since a complete phenomenological description of experience is impossible, any proposed language of description must be quite tentative. The vocabulary and syntax of such a language should ideally be dictated by the phenomena themselves rather than impose their own structure on the phenomena. The only safeguard one can suggest is that we be constantly aware of linguistic constraints and be prepared to revise our descriptive categories in response to new observation. One useful question to ask might be the following: Supposing we were to attempt the impossible and invent a language which could faithfully and efficiently communicate all the essential data of experience, what would we have to build into that language to render such communication possible? Our concern is not with the structural elements of the language, e.g., the vocabulary, or with such devices as word order and intonation; we know from the comparative study of languages that similar meanings can be communicated with approximately equal efficiency in a wide variety of ways. We are asking, rather, for an identification of the forms and properties of the meanings themselves, however these may be represented in any given language; and this calls for a tearing aside of the screen of language and a direct scrutiny of the phenomena. An impossible task, we agree, yet a task that is worth attempting.

As a provisional framework for phenomenological description, I suggest that we begin with four crude categories, each of which will have to be subdivided further and no one of which is to be considered as more than a convenient label. The categories are (1) structures, (2) properties of structures, (3) relations among structures, and (4) phenomenal dimensions. The chief advantage of such a categorization is that it places in temporary brackets most of the traditional categories of psychological analysis, e.g., sensation, perception, memory, imagination, thinking, feeling, emotion, will, and encourages us to take a fresh look at the phenomena. Its drawback, of course, is that any system of categories runs the risk of reification. The proper way to avoid this is probably to keep revising one's categories. It may be that in the long run the attempt to classify is more rewarding than any particular classification which may be achieved.

Phenomenal Structures

Traditional Aristotelian theory, with the support of most of the empirical psychologies since Aristotle, has imposed on psychological description a set of categories based on the presumed sources of knowledge, or the channels through which knowledge is presumed to come, namely the senses. While the qualitative differences which we label as sensory are readily recognized, and may eventually be related to as yet unspecified subsystems of the organism, there is no *a priori* justification for their unique status and there is no empirical basis for their acceptance as descriptive units. The red-ness I see is not an object in itself but one of many properties of the objects I see. This is the familiar argument against sensations as psychological units, and it need not be repeated here.

For want of a better term I suggest that we designate as *structures* the identifiable entities of the phenomenal world. The word *Gestalt* would be equally good, were it not so closely associated with a particular theory.

Structures are not to be regarded as elements or units in any metric sense, for they vary in their properties and can be ordered along many dimensions. To assert that the phenomenal world is structured is merely to recognize that, except in hypothetical extreme cases, it is always organized in some form or other, even if that organization involves nothing more than a dim distinction between "me" and "not me." This point, too, is familiar from Gestalt psychology, and consequently needs no elaboration. What might be added, merely, is that the listing of phenomenal structures does not constitute an exhaustive description. Much of the phenomenal world is unstructured (William Stern speaks of *Ungestalt*) and the unstructured aspects of the world are as truly "there" as are the structures.

Phenomenal structures may be loosely classified into: (a) things, (b) events, and (c) selves, no one of which is to be totally differentiated from the other two. A phenomenal thing, event, or self is, however, a bounded, segregated structure of the phenomenal world which to some extent at least maintains its identity. Such structures are usually labeled in our language with nouns, although not all nouns represent structures.

Things[2] are probably the stablest of phenomenal structures. For humans, at least, they are characteristically spatial in organization, fairly clearly localized, enduring in time but not dependent on time. We see and feel and lift things; we apprehend them as "really there." Unless we are sophisticated, we think of the physical world as a world of things.

Events, by contrast, are characteristically time-bound. An event has a beginning, a course, and an end. It may have spatial location, but this is less essential to its structure than are the spatial characteristics of a thing. An event may also be apprehended as "really there," but, for humans at any rate, events seldom carry as much "reality" as do things.

In the traditional sensory classification, "things" might be regarded as primarily products of vision, touch, and kinesthesis, and "events" as products of "audition." While not to be disparaged, this distinction quickly loses its neatness when we observe the "event character" of visual movement and the "thing character" of certain noises. Furthermore, the distinction between thing and event begins to break down as we move into the modalities of smell, taste, temperature, and pain. In these categories, possibly, we have to do with *Ungestalt* rather than with *Gestalt*.

2. The word "object" is avoided here because of the more restricted use of the word "objective" below.

The self as a phenomenal structure has often been challenged but has never been completely banished. The stubbornness with which the first person (singular and plural) has maintained itself in every known human language would seem to support a firm place for it in a psychological phenomenology. I suspect that our objection to the self as phenomenal datum is grounded in metaphysics rather than in phenomenology and reflects a bias which, in itself, should be of interest to the phenomenologist. Granted that the self is inescapably "there" in experience, the main question is whether or not it deserves to be classified as distinct from things and events. Certainly the self possesses much in common with things and events. It is segregated, bounded, and localized in space, it has a recognizable if somewhat unclear temporal structure, and it maintains its identity in spite of change. Where it differs most from things and events is in the dynamic qualities which have invited such terms as *intentionality* and *free will*. This is not to suggest that phenomenal things and events are devoid of dynamic qualities, merely that in the self these are so much more prominent as to suggest a separate phenomenological category.

Things, events, and the self are usually presented as here, now, and real; and as such we usually refer to them as percepts. For a phenomenology, the traditional distinction between perception and memory, or between either of these and imagination, must be placed in brackets. A phenomenal structure is no less valid if it is then, there, and slightly unreal (a memory), or undated, unlocalized, and highly unreal (a fantasy). The tables and noises of memory and imagination are just as truly phenomenal structures as are the tables and noises of perception; and so may be the beliefs and concepts which at times, and with great reluctance, I have called "non-perceptual cognitive structues." As we move away from the here, now, and real of conventional perception, we are not forsaking one world and entering another. We are still in the phenomenal world, the structures, properties, and dimensions of which we continue to observe and describe.

PHENOMENAL PROPERTIES

Every phenomenal structure has a variety of properties, or attributes; and, for that matter, so do the unstructured components of the phenomenal world. These need not be listed in detail, since they can be found in any good textbook of experimental psychology. Things, for instance, usually have size and shape, and events have a temporal structure. Note, however, that the properties of phenomenal structures are not limited to the "sensory" attributes identified by the introspectionists, e.g., quality, intensity, extensity, duration, and clearness. Properties of things include modes of appearance, roughness, stability, and the like, and the structure of an event may include its velocity and its direction. The battle for the recognition of properties of organization as psychologically valid has seemingly been won.

One fact needs emphasis: Considerable progress has been made in the phenomenology of the more accessible forms of perceptual organization (particularly in vision, audition, and touch), but little more than a beginning has been made in the phenomenology of tertiary or physiognomic properties, of the traditional "higher thought processes," and of the affective and dynamic properties of the self. More about these presently.

PHENOMENAL RELATIONS

Within, between, and among phenomenal structures are such familiar relations as before-after, right-left, inside-outside, louder than, sweeter than, and so forth. These have traditionally been accorded a secondary status as special products of an act of judgment. So far as our psychophysics has been concerned, the consequences have not been catastrophic; the psychophysical curve is the same whether we treat the relation as a phenomenon or as an inference. In psychological theory, however, and in epistemology, this derogation of relations has been the source of considerable confusion; although, again, the bias it reveals is in itself of phenomenological interest. We owe a debt to William James (in his famous defense of the feelings of "if" and "and" and "but") for having restored relations to their legitimate place as valid psychological phenomena (1890, vol. 1, p. 195).

This becomes particularly important as we proceed from the study of the simple spatial, temporal, and intensive relations of classical psychophysics to relations which are less readily quantifiable. Gestalt psychology has stressed such relations as part to whole, thing to context, figure to ground, and some of the subtler relations of similarity; and such relations as those of phenomenal causality (Michotte, 1946, 1962) and phenomenal inherence (Benary, 1924) have been brought into the laboratory. Where phenomenology has been most timid, however, has been in its exploration of the dynamic relations of the self to other structures of the field, phenomena which we have tended to reserve for a special psychology of motivation. When we speak of desire or fear or regret, we refer to phenomenal relations between self and thing or event, and in love and hate we have a relation between self and another structure which is present as a "self." These relations are characterized by activity, tension, the release of force. When Lewin (1935) introduced the terms "valence" (*Aufforderungs charakter*) and "vector," he was distinguishing between the properties of the thing or event which command or release action and the resulting directedness of the self.

Lewin was evidently eager to restate as many as possible of the phenomena of motivation in terms of properties of structures, particularly of those which could be represented diagrammatically. This may have been an overreaction to Freud's neglect of phenomenology. The fact remains, however, that his diagrams also included needs, tensions, conflicts, and the like, which are not lodged in the self or in the thing but are rather relations in the field. One might argue, of course, that in the last analysis a relation is a property of a superordinate structure, the most all-inclusive structure being the whole phenomenal world. This might have the value of ridding us once and for all of such fictitious relations as "pure" space and time, but I suspect that before long we would find ourselves reinstating the more conventional use of the term.

The important point is that the phenomenologist must take another look at the phenomena of motivation. A simple paradigm of motivated behavior might involve a need, a goal, and certain conditions which sustain, regulate, or interfere with progress toward the goal. Insofar as these are phenomenally present, the need is there as a state of the self, but with a directedness beyond the self, and the goal is there as something other than the self, but with a valence. The relation between the two we call a desire, or a purpose, or a hope will depend on the characteristics of the need, of the goal, and of the other relevant conditions.

Before we begin to theorize about basic needs or ultimate goals, it will obviously be profitable to find out what happens to the self when it is in a state of need and what the phenomenal properties of a goal are. What is called for is the same sort of scrutiny of dynamic phenomena as that to which we have been subjecting the world of colors, sounds, and touches. Whether or not we can rest content with a mere phenomenology of motivation is another question. My own conviction is that, just as in the case of perception, we must transcend phenomenology if we are to develop a psychology, but that, as in the case of perception, it will be a better psychology if it is based on sound phenomenology.

DIMENSIONS

The familiar dimensions of psychophysics are space, time, intensity, and the like. Strictly speaking, these are not coordinate in a phenomenological description with structures, properties, and relations. We do not perceive space as such; we perceive objects as having such and such a size, separated from ourselves and from one another by such and such distances. If we are to be precise in our description, however, we find it necessary to order the phenomena along some sort of hypothetical continuum, even if all points in the continuum are not phenomenally present. Thus, although we recognize certain judgments of hue or pitch as phenomenally "absolute," i.e., as seemingly independent of anchorage points on a scale, we find it easier to specify them by assuming the existence of a scale on which they can be assigned a position. Description in terms of dimensions has the further value that it keeps reminding us of the constantly changing character of the phenomenal world. Although many phenomenal structures are characteristically stable, as we know from the studies of perceptual constancy, this stability may be maintained only at the expense of radical changes in their properties and relations.

When Boring (1933) discussed the "physical dimensions" of consciousness, he was obviously most interested in those psychological variables which can be coordinated more or less directly to the variables measured fairly simply by the physical scientist. Similarly, Gibson's (1966) attempt to coordinate more complex perceptual phenomena to "higher order" variables of stimulation also turns, although not as explicitly, to the physicist for psychological dimensions. The phenomenologist can have no quarrel with psychophysics, either in its classical or in its more recent form, provided that it does not claim to be giving an exhaustive account of all phenomenal dimensions. For the phenomenologist the dimensions of consciousness are to be discovered in the phenomena, not deduced from a prior analysis of the dimensions of the physical world. If physical (or anatomical or physiological) correlates can be established, so much the better; if not, the phenomenologist must continue his exploration of the phenomenal world without the aid of the physicist.

One might list, just as illustrations, a few frequently neglected dimensions which emerge in phenomenological analysis and which invite further study. These are best stated as pairs of opposites. Most of them can be scaled, at least crudely, but in some cases they may turn out to be multiple rather than single dimensions.

1. *Similarity-dissimilarity.* This is obviously a multiple dimension since "similar" is always "with respect to this or that feature." It is included merely because in most studies the relevant features are predetermined by the investigator. The most interesting judgments of similarity are those which are unanticipated.

2. *Reality-irreality.* The distinction has no necessary epistemological connotation. What is diagnosed as an hallucination, for instance, may be phenomenally as real as something judged to be a percept.

3. *Subjectivity-objectivity.* Again, there is no epistemological connotation. A pain is likely to be more subjective, i.e., more intimately a part or a property of the self, than is a visual object. A visual object, even an afterimage, is apprehended as "out there," not as "in me."

4. *Positive and negative affect,* or pleasantness-unpleasantness, or hedonic tone. Affect is most pronounced at the subjective end of the subject-object continuum, as in pain, warm, cold, and smell.

5. *Saliency-embeddedness.* Figure-ground demonstrations provide the most familiar illustrations, but the distinction is present in all phenomenal organization.

6. *Stability-instability.* This is also a characteristic of all phenomenal organization, emphasized in the studies of phenomenal constancy but even more important in the phenomenology of the self.

7. *Inherent-accidental.* The color of an object, for instance, may be phenomenally inherent in the object, whereas the shadow in which it is seen may be phenomenally accidental. The distinction goes back to Aristotle, and although it led Aristotle into physical errors, as in his assertion that weight is an inherent property, it is phenomenologically important.

Such a list could be extended almost indefinitely, but perhaps this is sufficient to indicate how even a somewhat casual phenomenology can suggest phenomenal dimensions that are worth exploring further. As we attempt to isolate dimensions, however, there are three points which might be kept in mind.

1. Dimensions emerge from free description, and the freer the better. Our language was not designed for phenomenological analysis, and it is often in the language of metaphor or of poetry, or in the frustrated search for the appropriate expression, that we gain our best insights. To decide on our dimensions in advance is to violate the phenomenological method.

2. As we move from the simpler phenomena of perception to the mercurial phenomena of motivation and thinking, we can no longer anchor our observations to controllable physical stimuli. Developments in scaling methodology, as in Osgood's semantic differential (1952), offer encouragement; but it is clear that if phenomenology is to become precise we must have sharper tools.

3. In the move from description to dimensional analysis, there is always the danger that dimensions may become reified. The phenomenologist's only safeguard is to keep returning to observation and description.

EXTENSION TO CROSS-CULTURAL STUDY

I have no easy formula for the extension of psychological phenomenology to the study of people in other cultures. The first step is usually to identify and bracket our biases. Since we have already suspended our ethnocentric bias, I suggest now that we suspend our relativistic bias. People differ from culture to culture—granted. Many of these differences are more closely related to culture than to genetic endowment, whatever genetic endowment may mean—also granted. But let us put in brackets for the time being the fruitless question: How much is inherited and how much is learned?—as though such a relationship could be quantified, and as though a reference to learning explained anything—and ask instead the more important question: *What are* these differences? How do people of one culture actually differ psychologically from those of another?

This is in principle an easy question to answer if we take our own culture as a constant point of reference and use our own standardized measuring devices. We have convenient instruments for the measurement of visual acuity, reaction time, susceptibility to geometric-optic illusions and other familiar laboratory phenomena, and we can even make comparative measures of responses to Rorschach inkblots. Studies such as these have been made, albeit all too infrequently, since the pioneering work of Rivers (1904) and his colleagues at the beginning of this century. In many cases we find no reliable crosscultural differences; in others, as in the report by Segall, Campbell, and Herskovits (1966), the differences found can be quite startling. To discover that the geometric-optic illusions are not responded to in the same way by all people is a healthy reminder that some of our cherished psychophysical laws may be somewhat culture-bound.

I am not disparaging this kind of study; in fact, I am inclined to recommend it as a first step in the direction of a psychology that is to take account of cultural differences. It is a humdrum sort of enterprise, but it would be most useful to have a painstaking inventory of abilities, aptitudes, habitual modes of response, and the like, of all sorts of people in all sorts of cultures, based explicitly on instruments which have been standardized in a known culture, namely our own. The results of such studies can be grossly misleading, of course, as was the case with the Army Intelligence Tests of World War I; but they need not be if, aware of the probable bias of the test, we are led to ask not only what it is measuring but also what it is *not* measuring. An example from neuropsychology can be found in the early studies of the effects of frontal lobotomy. Before–and–after tests with standard instruments revealed no substantial intellectual deficit, which pointed to the conclusion that the frontal lobes have no special function. Since this seemed implausible, the experimenters proceeded to explore with different and subtler tests, and found, as we all know, that the frontal lobes do indeed play an important role in, among other things, spatial and temporal orientation; a finding which in turn invites a revision of our traditional theories of brain localization.

A cruder example, but closer to our present concerns, might be found in the early attempts by well-meaning missionaries to translate the Bible into strange languages. If we are to believe the anecdotes, they proceeded on the assumption that for each English word there must be a counterpart in the other language, and the translations that resulted were sometimes quite ludicrous. No one would be guilty of such an error today, for we know, not only that precise semantic equivalents are rare even in closely related languages, but that language consists of much more than an array of words, each with its special meaning. The work of the lexicographer is not to be undervalued, and we can even learn something from the psychologists who in their innocence have assumed that learning a language is a matter of associating words with things. We now know that to understand a language fully one must study it within the context of living communication. As we learn to communicate in a language radically different from our own, one of the first discoveries is that for many structural units of English there are no simple counterparts in the other language. Then, more startling, comes the discovery that the other language contains expressions, and presumably corresponding cognitive structures, which cannot be translated directly into English.

For the linguist this is all quite commonplace, for he knows about the role of word order and syntax in communication. For the psychologist, however, whose concern is with the thought that lies behind language, there is the disturbing suspicion that in the other culture there may be thoughts which even with the aid of all the linguist's tricks are simply untranslatable. Sapir (1929) and Whorf (1956) raised this question, and long before them it was raised by Wilhelm von Humboldt (1830–35). Can it be that cultural differences cut so deep that understanding across cultures is in fact impossible? Whorf seemed to think so.

I have already hinted that in my opinion Whorf may have pushed his inference a little too far. The very fact that he felt he could write about the differences between the Hopi world and our own implies that he believed he had some comprehension of that difference. I like to think that Whorf's positive contribution was that he made us aware of some unrecognized assumptions in our thinking, assumptions related to the structure of our language. The proper conclusion, it seems to me, is not that language creates the structures, properties, relations, and dimensions of the world, but that language represents them, always imperfectly, in different ways in different cultures. William James said something like this in the final chapter of his *Principles*, and, if I am not mistaken, Plato had the same idea too.

I realize, of course, as I said at the beginning, that we can never know for sure that there are uncommunicable meanings in the world of another person. I am content to leave these meanings to the philosopher, if he wants them, just as I shall also let him worry, if he wishes, about the color off the ultraviolet end of the spectrum which the bee sees and we do not.

The phenomenologist's approach to crosscultural research would not involve the discarding of conventional methods of experimenting and testing; any tool that yields reliable results can be useful. It calls, rather, for a persistent focusing on questions for the answering of which we have no adequate tools. The history of science justifies the faith that if a question is asked often enough and clearly enough, an appropriate methodology will eventually be discovered. *Prudens quaestio dimidium scientiae.*

Let me limit myself to one example, and I choose this deliberately because it involves questions which are answerable but not yet answered. During recent years there has been mounting concern about the effects of chronic malnutrition on physical and mental health, especially in underdeveloped countries. One of the common deficiency syndromes, associated with a protein deficit, is Kwashiorkor (Brock and Autret, 1952). In addition to stunted growth, depigmentation, and other physical symptoms, the Kwashiorkor patient is characterized by emotional apathy and what seems to be intellectual retardation. The evidence is by no means complete, but it suggests that malnutriton during a critical period in early development may produce irreversible damage. What kinds and what degree of malnutrition? During what developmental period? Which functions are most seriously affected? What remedial procedures are possible and feasible? These and similar questions are researchable, and are now being attacked by psychologists, nutritionists, physiologists, and biochemists. There is no reason to doubt that before long we shall know enough about nutrition and behavior to be able to predict the more tangible consequences of malnutrition.

This kind of research can be conducted with little or no aid from phenomenology, and the findings will be significant and useful. Let us assume, however, that one of the predictable consequences of early malnutrition proves to be an inability to maintain orientation with respect to events in the remote past and future. This finding, too, might be reduced to formal measures. But the phenomenologist will wish to know something more. What, he will ask, is the world like for a person for whom past and future references have little meaning? Will it be a world in which there are no plans, no ambitions, no grudges, no guilt and anxiety neuroses, all of which rest on a finely articulated structure of time? Such questions require us to go beyond the rating of human performance against standards established within our own culture, to examine mental content as well as mental capacity or ability. If, for instance, motivation includes the ability to sustain goal-directedness over an extended period of time, then a full understanding of the motivation of people in another culture will depend on sympathetic insight into the goal and value structure of the world in which they live and behave. It may or may not be true that chronic malnutrition weakens the physiological basis of temporal orientation. This can be decided by research, *if the researcher knows what to look for.* The task of the phenomenologist is to penetrate the world of the other person, to describe it and analyze it in such a way that its structures, properties, relations, and dimensions can then be correlated meaningfully with independently defined physical, biological and social variables. Phenomenology in this sense is always propaedeutic to a science, never the science itself. Its scientific function is to generate questions, not to answer them.

The possible relation between malnutrition and time perspective is only one of many questions which begin to define themselves as we look phenomenologically at the experience of other people. Other questions are: the basis of phenomenal stability, which invites a crosscultural review of the many-faceted problem of phenomenal constancy; the meaning of personal identity, both individual and collective, which certainly varies from culture to culture; the nature of perceived and felt causality, already explored by anthropologists but scarcely touched by psychologists; the relation between short-term and long-term memory in nonliterate cultures. These, let it be said again, are in no sense new questions in psychology; all have been explored comparatively in the clinic, in the laboratory of child study, and even to some extent in the animal laboratory. The point to be emphasized here is merely that such questions will be still further clarified if they are examined again in the context of other cultures.

Phenomenology, to repeat, is not a substitute for other kinds of research; nor does it point uniquely to the comparative study of cultures. The comparative study of man in different cultures, however, has for the psychologist been a neglected field. I am convinced that cross cultural study, with or without a phenomenological orientation, will make for sounder psychological theory. But I like to think, too, that a psychology which includes a phenomenological emphasis will have special value for those who are attempting to understand the mentality of people in other cultures. I hold no brief for the particular descriptive categories I have suggested—phenomenal structures, properties, dimensions, and relations, with their various subcategories—but these represent, at least, one way in which we can ask the question: *What is there* in the phenomenal world of the other person?

REFERENCES

BENARY, W. 1924. Beobachtungen zu einem Experiment über Helligkeitskontrast. *Psychologische Forschung,* 5: 285–94.

BORING, E. G. 1933. *The physical dimensions of consciousness.* New York: Century.

BROCK, J. F., and M. AUTRET. 1952. *Kwashiorkor in Africa.* Monograph Series, no. 8. Geneva: World Health Organization.

GIBSON, J. J. 1966. *The senses considered as perceptual systems.* Boston: Houghton Mifflin.

HOLMES, O. W. 1884 (original edition, 1858). *The autocrat of the breakfast table.* Boston: Houghton Mifflin.

VON HUMBOLDT, W. 1963. Ueber die Verschiedenheit des menschlichen Sprachbaues und ihren Einfluss auf die geistige Entwicklung des Menschengeschlechtes (1830–35). Reproduced in A. Flitner and K. Giel (Eds.), *Wilhelm von Humboldts Werke,* Vol. 3. Stuttgart: Cotta'sche Buchhandlung.

JAMES, W. 1890. *Principles of psychology.* 2 vols. New York: Holt.

KAFKA, G. 1922. *Handbuch der vergleichenden Psychologie.* 3 vols. München: Reinhardt.

LÉVY-BRUHL, L. 1910 (Eng. trans., 1926). *Les fonctions mentales dans les sociétés inférieures.* Paris: Alcan.

———. 1922. (Eng. trans., 1923). *La mentalité primitive.* Paris: Alcan.

———. 1927 (Eng. trans., 1928). *L'âme primitive.* Paris: Alcan.

LEWIN, K. 1935. *A dynamic theory of personality.* New York: McGraw-Hill.

MACLEOD, R. B. 1947. The phenomenological approach to social psychology. *Psychological Review,* 54: 193–210.

———. 1952. British East Africa: some psychological aspects. *Rice Institute Pamphlet,* 39: 1–25.

MICHOTTE, A. 1946 (Eng. trans., 1963). *La perception de la causalité.* Paris: Vrin.

———. 1962. *Causalité, permanence et realité phénoménale.* Louvain: Publications Universitaires.

MISIAK, H., and V. S. SEXTON. 1966. *History of psychology.* New York: Grune and Stratton.

OSGOOD, C. E. 1952. The nature and measurement of meaning. *Psychological Bulletin,* 49: 197–237.

RIVERS, W. H. R. 1904. Observations on the senses of the Todas. *British Journal of Psychology*, 1: 321–96.

SAPIR, E. 1929. The status of linguistics as a science. *Language*, 5: 207–14. (Reprinted in D. G. Mandelbaum [Ed.]. 1949. *Selected writings of Edward Sapir*. Berkeley and Los Angeles: University of California Press.)

SCHELER, M. 1923 (Eng. trans., 1954). *Wesen und Formen der Sympathie*. Bonn: Friedrich Cohen.

SEGALL, M. H., D. T. CAMPBELL, and M. J. HERSKOVITS. 1966. *The influence of culture on visual perception*. New York: Bobbs-Merrill.

SPIEGELBERG, H. 1965. *The phenomenological moment*, 2 vols. (rev. ed.) The Hague: Nijhoff.

STERN, W. 1935 (Eng. trans., 1938). *Allgemeine Psychologie auf personalistischer Grundlage*. The Hague: Nijhoff.

WHORF, B. L. 1956. *Language, thought, and reality*. New York: Wiley.

WUNDT, W. 1900–20. *Völkerpsychologie*. 10 vols. Stuttgart: Kröner.

10

PERSONALITY THEORY AND SOCIAL SCIENCE

Silvan S. Tomkins

The major questions to which I will address myself are these: how interdisciplinary should we be—and why, or why not? How similar are the physical, biological, psychological and social systems? Can we tell without looking? How long should we look? Where should we look? Is there any reasonable basis for looking at this time for unifying concepts?[1]

Clearly the fact is that societies are composed of human beings and these are composed of tissues, muscles, bones, nerves and blood and these in turn are composed ultimately of elementary particles. This would not at once evoke any enthusiasm for a hyphenated research or training program entitled "Elementary Particle-Comparative Social Systematics." The fact that a man will fall through space at 32 feet per second is true but uninteresting as a basis for interdisciplinary concern. If man was not created in the image of *one* university department, neither would he be equally at home in any and all departments.

COEXISTENCE VERSUS INDEPENDENCE OF STATES

Let us examine at the outset some of the more obvious differences between biological, psychological and social systems. As a biological entity, man is not only differentiated but his separate characteristics have markedly different developmental histories. The familiar logistic growth curve is found more often in textbooks than in man. Consider first a characteristic which is roughly fitted by such a developmental curve—height. The embryo does grow very rapidly in height and does eventually reach an asymptote in the teens so that increases in height do not ordinarily occur after twenty nor are there marked *decreases* in height as the individual ages. But *weight*,

1. This work is supported in whole by a Public Health Research Career Award from the National Institute of Mental Health, 1-K6-MH-23, 797–01.

although it roughly conforms to the same curve of development as height, continues to increase, for some well into the thirties and alas for some to the end of their days, and for others varies with the spasmodic impulse to diet. Such characteristics as strength parallel the height curve, but then gradually decline with age. Such characteristics as sensory acuity reach a peak more rapidly but then fall off rather rapidly in the forties. The color of the eyes may begin blue and remain blue for the life span, or soon change to brown and so remain. The hair may begin sparsely, grow more dense and remain so, or become thin with variable rates ultimately to become bald or not. Hair color may begin blonde and remain so, or turn brown and then remain so, or become gradually gray and ultimately white or become white rather suddenly or never become white. We begin toothless, gradually acquire a set, then lose these and acquire another set which may remain intact the whole life span or which may be lost in toto or in part in different sequences for different individuals.

Different developmental curves for different subsystems would not distinguish biological from psychological or from social systems. More relevant for such comparison is the phenomenon of the relative *independence* of states for biological systems and the relative *coexistence* of states for psychological and social systems. Consider that if I lose my baby teeth and then get a second set of teeth I do not ordinarily possess both sets at the same time. If I then lose some of my second set, I do not also continue to have these teeth intact. If I gain weight and become obese—I am not *also* thin. If I lose weight by dieting, there does not remain an inner fat man. If my hair which was blonde turns brown, it is no longer blonde, and when it turns white it is no longer brown, and when it falls out—it is gone. Despite the tragic in some of these vicissitudes, it makes the way of the investigator relatively simple. Differentiated as the system is and changing as it does from moment to moment—it does *truly* change.

Consider by way of contrast the psychological domain (that subset of biological phenomena which we wish to treat for the moment as independent). By virtue of a storage system (the nature of which is still opaque), the person I was when I weighed fifty pounds more last year has not (like the weight) altogether evaporated into thin air. I am right now a most untidy aggregate of awareness of that once fat man—and possibly even a somewhat fatter man scornfully distorted in invidious comparison with my newly hard-won slender self and lurking uneasiness lest that fatter one materialize again unless vigilance is exercised. I am at the intersect not only of my several weights, but of many more of my many selves who have lived and said and felt and acted in many ways on many different occasions. This can be a cold war or at the very least a coexistence as perplexing to me as to you. Such a system is beset by problems of match and mismatch between several versions of every important variety of experience, by problems of isolation and loss of information—by problems of alternate magnification and attentuation of the same experience, by conflict between parts, by problems of integration of incommensurable parts and so on.

When we arrive at the social level, the order of magnitude of coexistence of relatively independent parts, both real and misremembered and misanticipated, grows toward infinity and the miracle is that these systems can be governed at all.

BIOLOGICAL VERSUS SOCIAL ADAPTATION

The phenomenon of biological evolution—improbable as it may seem—is much more probable than social adaptation, for a paradoxical reason. Man in society must adapt not only to his biological environment, which includes the animal man as well as other animals—but also to *society*—with all its artifacts and with all its men socialized to be adapted to other similarly socialized men—in short, to civilization. There is evidence that such adaptation is possible (though its price is still indeterminate), but in the nature of the case there can be no guarantee that it will necessarily continue to be possible. Biologically, men are mortal and some species of animals *have* become extinct.

At the psychological level there is evidence that aging is the rule. By psychological aging we mean a progressively diminishing contribution of new information to the transformation of the cumulative pool of stored, internalized information. I have called this the proaction-retroaction ratio, proaction referring to the transformation of new information by stored information, retroaction referring to the transformation of stored information in the light of new information. Although there does not appear to be an information death as such, the rate of growth of information characteristically parallels the logistic biological growth curve. Certainly there are instances, as with autistic children, of failures to develop at all.

At the social level too there is abundant evidence for hardening of the psychosocial arteries, with increasing aging and maladaptation to the environment. Civilizations appear in the past to have characteristically grown to maturity and to have become aged at the very least, if not in all cases to have died and become extinct. To this point in history the aging of succeeding civilizations has not been lethal for man in general, because other civilizations have developed in other places—and so man as a whole has continued to develop.

But there is some basis for supposing that psychosocial aging is not the consequence either of accident or willfulness of men. It is in part the result of the familiar exponential logistic growth curve (in this case of information) which radically increases the difficulty of restructuring the entire pool of programs which have been assembled over a lifetime for the individual—and over several centuries for a society. So, despite the fact that we have argued that biological, psychological, and social systems differ very significantly in complexity, we have here come full circle and suggested a basic *similarity*—namely, the phenomenon of limited growth ending in death.

But social aging and death is a function not only of the *internal* accumulation of rigid programs of information processing, but also of the fact that the *residues* of each set of successful problem solutions—the *artifacts* to which men in society must adapt—present a *new* and *different* set of problems which, in their totality may overwhelm the integrative capacities of any particular aging society. There is a worldwide malaise based, I think, upon the half-conscious intuition that every success in problem solution, every increase in knowledge, now *creates* problems more serious than the problem which it solved. The atom bomb is but one of many pyrrhic victories. We must confront the deadly possibility that the prevailing anxiety of contemporary man is a *rational* anxiety born out of information growth as malignant as tissue growth or the population explosion.

There are three distinct questions here: (1) Can man biologically tolerate the society he creates? (2) Can man psychologically tolerate this society? (3) Can society tolerate the kind of men it creates?

CAN MAN BIOLOGICALLY TOLERATE THE SOCIETY HE CREATES?

As our society becomes more complex and more competent, it appears to threaten the biological integrity of its members. Consider that increases in medical knowledge which have increased our capacity to deal with disease and threats to health has also produced, via the antibiotics, new drug-resistant strains which hold the possibility of new diseases to which man may have much greater vulnerability than he had to earlier diseases now controlled by antibiotics. Consider that in the solution of the problem of mobility via automobile and airplane, we have *produced* a new problem of immobility through the congestion of our freeways and our airports. That new forms of death on the highways and in the air have also thereby been created and that the threat of pollution of the air we breathe has also been created in part by our *solution* to the problem of mobility. Consider that the release of atomic energy not only has polluted our atmosphere but also threatens the destruction of all forms of life. Consider that our entire technology wastes our natural resources and pollutes our water sources at a rate which threatens our biological integrity. In short, in healing we hurt, in building we waste, in moving we become immobilized, and in releasing potential energy we threaten ultimate destruction.

CAN MAN PSYCHOLOGICALLY TOLERATE HIS SOCIETY?

As our society increases in complexity and competence, his psychological tolerance has also been seriously stressed. The increase in information has quickened the rate of change to such an extent that increasing numbers are experiencing a premature obsolescence of competence. The skilled human being, at all levels of skill, is becoming hopelessly outdated in shorter and shorter periods of time, and the end is not in sight. Such a rate of change not only produces obsolescence but also seriously undermines loyalties and commitments both to other human beings and to enduring ways of life. Further, it increases the fragmentation of society. Intergenerational conflict becomes a special case of a very general inability of individuals of one age to communicate with individuals a few years older or younger than themselves. Further, the increased rate of change, by virtue of our superb communication media, is brought with extreme vividness to the attention of more and more people, who share only their bewilderment and confusion at the increasing complexity and variety of the world in which they live. The very means which might have enhanced the quality of living now undermines the tolerance of its increasing audience for the strains of modern life. This is not to say that our TV, radio, press, magazines and books do *not* enhance the quality of our life, but rather to argue that they *also* create as many problems as they solve, and sometimes create more *severe* problems than those they solve.

CAN SOCIETY TOLERATE THE KIND OF MEN IT CREATES?

If there is a question whether biological man and psychological man can tolerate his own society, there is also the no less serious question whether any society can long endure which creates men who are in varying ways either over or under socialized. Modern man suffers alienation on the one hand and over-conformism on the other. He is exploitative, manipulative, and opportunistic but also oppressed, exploited, and manipulated. But most critical of all, can a society endure constituted of men who have suffered a failure of nerve—who have seen every success expose a more serious problem so that the whole idea of progress is undermined?

THE PRICE OF COMPLEXITY

In summary, complex systems whether they are personalities or societies suffer three critical vulnerabilities which are inherent in their growth. First, by virtue of their multiplicity of parts, they are vulnerable to mismatch and discoordination. Second, by virtue of the complexity reduction necessary to process rapidly changing information, increasing rigidities are introduced into stored programs which undermine adaptation to new information by transforming it into a variant of stored information. Third, the very quantity and rate of changing information which is *produced* by such a system may itself overstress the system which was its creator.

SOME ALTERNATIVES

There are, however, some more hopeful alternatives: (1) Particular societies will age and decline or become extinct, but other younger societies will
build upon these aging civilizations. (2) That society will continue to
grow which most nurtures its mutations, its dissident minorities who provide
it with new viable alternatives. (3) That civilization will be continued
through an international community which provides an ever-shifting set of
new models for the total world community.

International science may indeed be the most viable social institution man
has yet developed—and provide the requisite model for the other social
institutions. Despite the most severe conflict of interests and jealousies and
rigidities, it is said by theoretical physicists that opponents of a new theory
are never convinced but eventually die off, leaving the field to the young
Turks—who in turn later resist younger Turks—despite these familiar features of the human and social condition—there is also sufficient commitment
to a common aim, sufficient labor, sufficient pride and courage, to keep the
international scientific enterprise viable. (4) Last, and I hope not least,
social science may contribute sufficiently to our understanding of the nature
of human beings and the societies they create—to enable man not so much
to *predict* his own destiny, but to *control* it. This he has done in the physical
sciences where we have the paradox of primitive *prediction* of complex
nature in the raw (e.g., weather prediction) coupled with fine *control* over
nature through technology—the use and application of basic knowledge to
create artifacts (e.g., bridges, vehicles, TV transmitters and receivers).
These artifacts could not have been created without basic knowledge,
despite the fact that this knowledge is *insufficient* for understanding or predicting much of what happens in the teeming multidimensional domain of
nature. Happily, we may be able to *apply* somewhat inadequate, basic social
science to create more viable artifacts and social institutions.

It is to a brief consideration of some aspects of one such model that I now
wish to turn.

THE MEANS-END RELATIONSHIP AS ONE
UNIFYING CONCEPT FOR THE
SOCIAL SCIENCES

The relationships between individual human beings and their societies are
peculiarly complicated because this is a part-whole relationship in which any
part, formed by a whole (to varying degrees), may in turn modify that
whole (to varying degrees), which in turn may modify any part, which then
may further modify the whole, and so on and on. The part not only modifies
the remainder of the whole, but also thereby modifies itself. A small group of
American women who succeeded in modifying their society so that they

were given the legal right to vote changed at once *both* their society and *themselves* by changing their legal rights within that society. It is difficult therefore to disentangle cause and effect in such a field. If we cannot speak with precision about causal relationships between parts and wholes, perhaps we can speak of *similarities* between parts and wholes, between individuals and societies. It is to this strategy that I wish to turn your attention. There are numerous similarities between human nature writ small in individuals and human nature writ large in societies which I think it would be profitable for social science to examine. The means-end relationship is one of these.

Eventually we will have to construct many models to help build a bridge between personality theory and general social science. I have attempted to construct such models. But I would now like to examine a simpler and easier strategy. Are there any models *already* in use by several social sciences which represent a relatively unconscious consensus? I believe there is one, but it is somewhat masked by the specifics of each science. This is the means-end paradigm. All the social sciences rest heavily on the assumption of purposive behavior and its expected and unexpected consequences. In psychology this is known as *instrumental learning* (or "conditioning"). In politics it is known as *power*—"who gets what?" In economics it is known as *utility*— the means or end value of something for human beings. In sociology it is known as *structure-function* analysis—what collective purposes are served by social institutions. Is this not to readmit the long banished group mind? Yes and no.

Societies *are* in many ways *similar* to the human beings who collectively both create and are created by their cumulative product. It would be surprising if it were otherwise. But *human beings* are *also* similar to the society in which they live in several important respects. The rejection of the group mind was in part based on an excessively rationalistic and purposive view of human nature. If society is not always "conscious" of its intentions—neither is a human being. If such collective awareness as there is in society lacks unity and continuity of awareness—so too does the awareness of the single individual. If the society experiences many unintended transients—neither expected nor wished for—so does the individual. If there is a pluralism of selves in society, so may there be within the individual. If there is often conflict between these separate selves in society, so may there be within the individual. If there is competition between separate selves and classes within society, so may there be within the individual. In short, a society is more like an individual and an individual is more like a society than has been supposed. A society like an individual can commit itself or vacillate. It can mourn. It can learn or refuse to learn. It can become satiated. It can be humiliated and seek revenge.

This is not to say that when a nation suffers humiliating defeat in a war, or mourns the assassination of its leader, that it responds *exactly* as an individual would. But it is important nonetheless to examine the degree of similarity that *does* exist. It is our general impression that this very degree of similarity is itself a variable and an important one. Different societies act more or less like individuals in different sectors and at different times. Such an innovation as TV, for example, is radically increasing the communality of *shared individual* experience—most notably following the assassination of President Kennedy when almost all Americans spent about twelve hours daily looking at the same event and sharing each other's responses, to some extent in fact, and to some extent under the mistaken impression of consensus of response created both by the TV display and commentary.

We are suggesting that individuals and societies lend themselves equally well (or poorly) to analysis as feedback systems. Both individual and social feedback systems have awareness of goals or ends and criteria for determining goal achievement.

Let us turn now to an examination of the means-end relationship. Ralph Barton Perry defined value as any object of any interest. He was using the word interest as equivalent to any positive affect. I would suggest that we distinguish the concepts of value and end value. By value I will mean experience of any affect. Positive value would then be experience of any positive affect. Negative value would be experience of any negative affect.

The experience of affect is innately of value to the human being because this is his biological nature. It is a consequence of his evolution that he must innately prefer some states to other states. More specifically it is our belief that his affect system has been specialized to bias him toward and away from very general aspects of the world. This has been achieved through a rough correlation between the innate activators of affect—the profiles of density of neural firing (decreasing, increasing, and constant) so that he innately is equipped to *care*, either positively or negatively, whether events which are correlated with such patterns of neural firing occur or do not occur. Such events may be *anything* which increases in any way, which decreases in any way, or which remains constant at a nonoptimal overly intense way.

Next I will define *end value* as any object or activity which is perceived as per se evoking or reducing value (or any experience of affect). The distinction between value and end value is required because the experience of affect may be free floating—without any apparent cause or "object." I may feel afraid—but of nothing in particular, sad—but of nothing in particular, or happy—in general. When these experiences are related via cognitive recruitment to particular objects or activities so that I am now happy about being with you rather than simply happy, then we are dealing with what I have defined as an end value.

Then I will define *means value* as any object or activity which is perceived as evoking end value. Thus if I walk because I enjoy walking, this is an end value because walking *per se* evokes value or the experience of affect. If I walk in order to talk with you, which I enjoy as end value, then my walking in this case has means or instrumental value. This is not to say that I cannot enjoy *both* walking as end value *and* as means value, nor that I may not enjoy walking as end value just *because* it is a means to something else which is an end value.

What occurs when an end value is not freely available? When a means is interposed between the person and his enjoyment of an end value? What occurs is rather complicated—more so than we have supposed. Consider first that the interposition of a barrier immediately increases the intensity and duration of both positive and negative affect so that the individual now "wants" X, the end value, *more* and *longer* than he did the moment before he experienced a barrier. Second, ordinarily there is negative affect introduced by the presence of the barrier which would not have been experienced toward X if there had been no barrier. Third, there is negative affect introduced toward the *means* necessary to achieve X. Indeed if this means value is negative and stronger (in combination with negative end value of the barrier) than the positive end value of X, then the end may be renounced. Fourth, if the individual is to be persuaded to play the means-end game, he must *also* invest positive affect in the means-end activity.

There are many complications of this simple model which we will not have the time to examine here, but there are two of these outcomes I do wish to examine. One is the *attenuation* of awareness and reward for increasing skill in means-end achievement and the other is the increasing *magnification* of awareness and affect for increasing skill in means-end achievement. Both these outcomes create serious motivational problems for individuals and for societies.

Consider first the reduction in what I have called *ideo-affective density* consequent on the attainment of means-end skill. By ideo-affective density, I refer to the product of intensity and duration of affect, cognition, action, and awareness—in short, how much anything concerns and engages the awareness, the feelings, and the ideation as well as action by the individual. As I become more and more skilled in means-end activity, e.g. my daily shave in the morning, my awareness, my affect and conscious thought declines—so that I am hardly aware *that* I am shaving. It will *never* happen that I look in the mirror at the end and beam at myself—"You are an extraordinary human being—you have done it *again.*" We cannot be aware, let alone deeply enjoy *just* those achievements which are *most* skilled, because these result from the compression of information into programs which run off with minimal awareness and monitoring. Such reduction of ideo-affective density has the function of reducing the load on the channel, freeing it for new learning. The price of such a mechanism, however, may be quite severe because it results in the paradoxical consequence that we can be rewarded least by what should normally give us the greatest satisfaction, i.e. the achievement of our highest skill. As this occurs successively during a lifetime, it can result in a life which promises carrots which always proved eventually to be tasteless. If it is combined with a preponderance of negative affect during the earlier striving and learning, then the ensemble is a combination of bitter-sweet and tastelessness—issuing not infrequently in depression—for the individual and for the society. Individuals and societies alike must learn to enjoy the process of problem-solving if they are to experience enduring reward.

A second derivative of means-end analysis illuminates a motivational vulnerability which is exactly opposite to the one just described. It is a type of magnification, of slavery by seduction—a seduction in which means are converted into ends. Consider how this might happen. Let us begin with a child who wants to play with a toy—an end value. His parents now seize on his wish to teach him. They will permit him the toy he wants, but first he must clean his room. He may decide he does not want the toy that much, but if he plays this game, his wish for the toy has increased in intensity and certainly in total density, since even if the intensity of affect remained constant, its duration is prolonged by virtue of the interposed barrier. He has also learned to have a new wish—the wish to clean his room—though he may also detest the request, yet, to the extent to which he accepts this as a necessary means to the end he wishes, he has been taught to "want" something he might otherwise not have wanted. At this point he is in no danger of becoming an anal character. How could his character be so transformed? How could the means be transformed into an end? The doctrine of functional autonomy suggested that through long striving for ends, means often were so transformed by becoming eventually independent of the original end. The exact mechanism of such a transformation was never entirely clear. I believe that the interposition of time and enjoyment are not sufficient to account for it. What is necessary is to limit *all* other alternatives to the end, to make the end supremely attractive and then to place a barrier before the *means* to this end. Under such conditions the original means will be transformed into a new end value. Consider our former example. Having cleaned his room and enjoyed his toy, our hero is the next time confronted with the following ultimatum. "Yes, you cleaned your room very nicely but not quite so well as your brother does it. I am not sure that I will *let* you clean the room from now on unless you do it at least as well or better than your brother does. It is a privilege to clean your room which you must *earn* by doing it very well—*then* you may have the toy." If he will permit himself to be seduced further, he has taken the necessary step in the transformation of the original means into an end value. He will now compete for the privilege of doing what originally he did not wish to do. But so long as he continues to view *both* acts as *also* instrumental, the transformation is incomplete. We must draw out his effort in time and make it sufficiently arduous so that the winning of the competition itself produces such an intense and enduring affective reward that guaranteeing the sanctity of cleaning his room is heaven enough—with or without the further enjoyment of playing with his toy.

Lest this example be supposed to be entirely apochryphal, consider the wisdom of the classical economists, who knew better than psychologists how to transform the instrumental need for money into an end in itself. Their prescription was simplicity itself—let the number of workers exceed the number of jobs and men will not only work, but work for the lowest possible wage. During the last depression when a man had been unemployed for some years and one day returned home victorious—having just landed a job—he and his wife celebrated this victory. They did not ask—why do we really want the money this job will bring? Nor did they ask about how much money was involved, about job security, about fringe benefits, about the distance to be traveled to work and so on. Simply getting a job under these circumstances was reward enough. In order to understand this and similar motives, we must look more closely at the nature of that extraordinary human invention —money. If a means-end relationship is examined for its logical structure, we may distinguish two basic possibilities. The relationship may be a one-many, or a many-one relationship. If I wish to go to New York from Princeton, I may take the train, but if this is not possible, I may take the bus, or I may drive, or I may take an airplane, or failing all of these, I may walk. In such a case the means-end relationships have the many-one structure. Under such conditions the transformation of means into ends is very improbable for the simple reason that a barrier placed before one means is in no way constraining so long as alternatives exist and are known to exist.

Compare the many-one relationship with the one-many relationship. Money is means to many ends—standing in a one-many relationship. Further, it is often a means not only to many ends, but also to many *other* means. And finally it is a means to ends which I *now* have, but also a means to many *future* ends whose exact nature I do not now know, but I do know that money will be as useful to buy what I *may* want as it is right now to buy what I *do* want. Because of man's imagination, such a structure lends itself readily to endless *possible* expansion—and so this all-purpose means is invested with the power of endless possibility—and in this sense lends itself to worship. Money is in this sense all-powerful, just by virtue of its ambiguity. It will be remembered that I said for the transformation of means to ends to be completed the enjoyment of the *original* end had to be renounced and attenuated vis à vis the means. The ambiguity of the possible future enjoyment of money lends itself admirably to money worship as a possible savior, no matter what future ends become. In contrast to the freedom of the many-one means-end relationship, here we have the seduction of the human being *and* of his society by an unquestioning pursuit of a means which seems to offer ends of any and all kinds to satisfy every heart's desire of each and every individual in the same society. Since money can be used to buy anything—is a universal medium of exchange—then, despite vast individual differences between members of any society, they can unite in the same church of mammon because money is endlessly transformable. When then a barrier is placed before *such* a means, one can mobilize anyone to compete for it as though it had not only the property of an end, but of a set of all possible ends.

The same dynamic may transform *any* form of perceived power, be it intellectual power, political power, or economic power, into an all-consuming end in itself, to the impoverishment of all those ends for which such power may be sought.

11

GROWTH, DEVELOPMENT, AND POLITICAL MONUMENTS

Karl de Schweinitz, Jr.

In the developed societies of the Western world, economics is a self-sufficient discipline. Unlike political science, for example, which has been ranging widely through the other social sciences in search of itself, economics is methodologically at ease. The reason for this state of affairs is not hard to come by—economics works, at least moderately well. The phenomena with which it is concerned can be quantified, analyzed, and predicted. And if economists fall flat on their faces more often than they would like, it does not induce them to seek salvation in another social science. Rather they look to their models for inconsistencies, seek out new data, or rework the old data for a better fit. In so doing they have come to rely increasingly on mathematical, quantitative, and statistical techniques. Some economists have been seduced into mistaking the eloquence and rigor of these techniques for the substantive purposes of economics, but mostly they view them as tools for getting on with the job of improving our understanding of micro- and macro-economic performance. However much they succeed in this, they make economics a more formidable discipline and hence reinforce its self-sufficiency within the social sciences. Graduate students now must spend more time mastering the methods and techniques of economics and, therefore, have less time for reflective reading in cognate disciplines. The coming generation of economists will be better trained, but for precisely this reason they will be less qualified social scientists.

This is all very fine for societies where these conditions—social structure, political system, and so forth—which economics abstracts from or takes as given do not interfere unduly with the working out of the principles it articulates. But in newly formed societies where the economic system is not yet

1. I am indebted to my colleagues George I. Blanksten and Raymond W. Mack for valuable comments on an earlier draft of this paper.

generating self-sustaining growth and the polity is still an amorphous, unassimilated institution, it is not at all clear that these principles have the same validity. The literature of economic development, for example, abounds in arguments and theories which support the view that government must play a crucial role in accelerating the rate of growth in underdeveloped economies (for example, Baran, 1957, pp. 190–94; Bhatt, 1965; Higgins, 1959, p. 387; Hirschman, 1958, pp. 202–205; Lipton, 1962; Rosenstein-Rodan, 1943). Externalities, the scarcity of entrepreneurs, the instability of the demand for primary output, the adverse terms of trade, the need for import substitutes, etc., all suggest that the marginal changes a market is capable of mediating will not add up to a satisfactory rate of increase of per capita income. Government, it is contended, must take the initiative in stimulating growth because it has a sufficiently wide purview that it can account planfully for the externalities and interrelationships of economic activity and because it can alter the institutional conditions which inhibit growth.

It is equally true that there are many laments in the literature for the ineffectiveness of government and its failure to use resources wisely in the pursuit of growth objectives in the underdeveloped economies. At worst, public officials in the new governments may be corrupt and venal and divert resources from growth to their family fortunes (for example, Hagen, 1962, p. 453; Lewis, 1965, p. 3; Wraith and Simpkins, 1964). But even where personal motives are unexceptionable, development needs may be subverted by political expediency, local interests, the fortuitous influence of foreign experts or administrative officials with foreign experience, or the representatives of engineering firms (Watson and Dirlam, 1965, p. 169). Moreover, "development programs tend to overemphasize investment which takes the form of concentrated, large-scale projects which are spectacular rather than basic" (Singer, 1964, p. 115). In consequence, goods may be produced that fly in the face of resource availabilities and the principle of comparative advantage and capital imported that cannot be used optimally, given existing labor skills. Stadia, steel mills, convention halls, great dams, jet airlines may appear when less visible output more capable of responding to demand elasticities in international and domestic markets would have yielded greater impetus to further growth.

That the advocates of a forceful role for government in development have often been frustrated by and disillusioned in its performance is not surprising. For their expectations about governmental performance implicitly have depended upon conditions which may be taken for granted in the West but, more often than not, do not exist in the underdeveloped economies. The recommendation for the government to plan, to build social overhead capital, and so forth, cannot be acted upon successfully without a reasonably well-developed system of taxation and a cadre of technically competent civil servants instilled with some sense of commitment to the welfare of the society. These conditions, in turn, imply the existence of a legitimate political authority capable of enforcing its decisions and of a political community in which individual or group interests are muted by a sense of civil obligation. In the underdeveloped economies of the world, these conditions are conspicuously absent. The primordial attachments of clan, tribe or village dominate behavior, and the larger political community is an abstraction that has not yet become an important value motivating individuals (Geertz, 1963a, pp. 105–157). The Congo, Indonesia, and Ceylon are political communities in the making and still must contrive the means of transferring some of the commitment of these attachments to the polity. In short, economically underdeveloped societies are also likely to be politically underdeveloped, which is to say that government is no more nor less capable of generating growth than the market.

In these circumstances, the injunction to use governmental authority systematically to raise per capita income carries with it the need to develop the political community. In this paper I shall discuss how the simultaneity of these demands may restrict the applicability of conventional economic criteria. In order to do this, I should like in the next section to distinguish the concepts of growth and development and in the following section to consider the part that what I shall call "political monuments" may play in these processes.

GROWTH AND DEVELOPMENT

Economic growth may be distinguished from economic development.[2] The former refers narrowly to increasing income or output per capita, while the latter relates more broadly to the emergence in society of the attitudes, values, skills, and knowledge essential for sustained growth. Where the one stresses the quantitative output performance of an economic system, the other focuses attention on its qualitative input characteristics. While both are concerned with the same process, their different views of it stem from the quite different problems confronting underdeveloped and developed economies. The former want to create the conditions that will give rise to self-sustaining growth; having achieved this, the latter seek an optimal combination of growing output, increasing employment, and stable prices. Development economics is the progeny of the poor economies of Asia, Africa, and Latin America; growth economics, of the instability of rich capitalist economies.

For the greater part of world history, growth typically has been a short-lived phenomenon attributable to bountiful harvests, windfall gains in commerce, or the fortuitous acquisition of productive natural resources. It was not until the European community had passed through a long period of

2. This distinction has been made vividly for me by my colleagues who worked on the Northwestern University AID project in Liberia during 1961 and 1962. See Clower, Dalton, Harwitz, and Walters, 1966.

development that sustained growth became possible. The actual timing of the "take-off" into self-sustained growth varied from country to country, but in each case had been prepared by pervasive transformations in the institutions affecting economic attitudes and opportunities. Where development lagged, as in Russia, the onset of accelerated growth was delayed and when it appeared was less vigorous than in Western Europe. In the non-Western world, the industrialization of the Japanese economy following the Meiji Restoration was made possible by the development that took place during the Tokugawa era. Elsewhere in Asia and Africa the persistence of traditional values and institutions inhibited development so that indigenous growth remained stillborn and the growth that did occur in the nineteenth and early twentieth centuries was confined to enclave sectors established by Western entrepreneurs and colonial administrators.

If growth follows development in historical sequence, it hardly lags as a widely accepted value or goal. However diverse the background and cultural traditions of tribal West Africans, Malayan peasants, and Latin American *mestizos,* they can all agree that it is better to have more than less output. One does not need to be a Utilitarian to believe that the individual (village, tribe, extended family) is better off if there is an increase in the quantity and an improvement in the quality of goods he consumes. Indeed, the revolution of rising expectations that one hears so much about in the underdeveloped economies is a consequence of a spreading belief in the virtues of growth. And the special problems these economies face are caused in part by the hiatus between the aspirations stimulated by such belief and their development capabilities.

No one believes that these problems can be solved easily. A poor economy does not achieve steady growth simply by having foreign exchange made available to it through lending and aid programs and by importing certain allegedly key types of capital with the complementary technical expertise. The distinction between growth and development points up the fact that the initiation of acceleration of the former in traditional societies requires the creation of a population that will respond energetically and productively to economic opportunity. This involves not only the refurbishing of the environment through the improvement of transportation and other overhead, but the training and education of the population in the skills, cognitions, values, and drives essential for productive activity. Clearly, the requisite behavioral characteristics cannot be acquired quickly, any more than personalities can be formed quickly. Development must take generations, if not centuries.

However gradually it occurs, it is nonetheless possible to devise coherent investment programs for development, the relative merits of which can be argued about and evaluated on the basis of their anticipated impact on output. Just what the substantive content of such an investment program would be it is not my intention to discuss. The point I wish to emphasize for subsequent comparison with political development is that the measures men may take to speed development are rational in that cost-benefit calculations, albeit crude ones, may be made for the relevant alternatives. To that extent, the scope of intuitive decision-making, or policy-by-hunch, may be restricted. To put it another way, economic growth is the consequence of activities which have meaning to individuals as individuals. Development planning may attempt to expand those activities in which individual interest will have a maximum payoff in terms of expanding social output.

When the concepts of growth and development are applied to the evolution of political systems, some contrasts to economic evolution come to mind. Political growth may be defined narrowly as an increase in the size of a political entity as measured by the extent of the territory and population over which rulers govern. Political development may be thought of as the creation of attitudes and values and the building of institutions which raise the efficiency, somehow measured, with which rulers transform the inputs of a political system into its outputs.[3] Growth is a short-run phenomenon that may occur at any moment in history. Polities have grown through conquests, annexations, and population explosions. We are likely to be cognizant of of historical dates and events which mark changes in the rate and direction of growth. Military campaigns and peace settlements are perhaps the most familiar occasion of discrete political growth. At the conclusion of wars, new states may be formed, old states may become larger, or smaller—or, indeed, disappear. But in the sweep of world history we have no difficulty in identifying growing polities, e.g., the formation of the Athenian city-state in classical Greece, the dynastic expansions of the Chinese empire, the emergence of the nation-state in Europe. Nor do we have any difficulty in observing declining polities, e.g., the break-up of the Roman, Austro-Hungarian, or Ottoman empires.

It is patent that in politics, unlike economics, growth precedes development. States have typically acquired additional territory and population without a concomitant development of the attitudes and institutions necessary for increasing governmental efficiency. The lag between growth and development occurs, for one reason, because of the power struggles that have occupied men in positions of authority since the beginning of time. In all societies there is a class of men variously recruited—a leadership elite—whose preferences incorporate the state or the commonweal and whose satisfactions are derived from maximizing state interest. For them, political growth may be an end, a value worth pursuing regardless of how it relates to the values of individuals. Their preference-functions may well contain a

3. There is a diffuse and highly suggestive literature on political development which is laden with sociological and psychological concepts. It seems to be increasing exponentially and the references which follow do not pretend to be complete: Almond and Coleman, 1960; Apter, 1965; Binder, 1964; Eisenstadt, 1964; Geertz, 1963b; Huntington, 1965, 1966; Kautsky, 1962; La Palombara and Weiner, 1966; Lerner, 1958; Packenham, 1966; Pye, 1962; Pye and Verba, 1965; Shils, 1960; Ward and Rustow, 1964; Weiner, 1962.

heavily weighted need for power. Or they may have an acute sensitivity to the social welfare which leads them to believe that they know better than individual citizens what is in their interests. Whatever it is that sets them apart, the preferences of political rulers are different from those of the ruled.[4] In consequence, they have not hesitated to aggrandize state power. Throughout history the growth aspirations of rulers have been constrained less by the internal problems of effective political organization than by the similar ambitions of their peers in competing polities. Moreover, until recent times political growth did not require the expenditure of vast resources. Leaders bent on expansion have been able to accomplish prodigious feats without having to engage the full energies of society and with only the direct involvement of relatively few men, e.g., the growth of the British empire in India. And, finally, in the contemporary era accelerated population growth has increased the size of polities willy-nilly. All states have grown together from this cause.

However widespread its impact, political growth differs from economic growth in that it is not a widely affirmed value. Anyone can appreciate and desire more output; it is most unlikely that many people other than political leaders want a larger state. As states grow larger, their benefits become more diffuse, though the costs of generating them—taxation and military service, for example—remain as much as ever a clear individual liability. It is, therefore, difficult for individuals to measure the advantages of membership in the polity. For this reason, the rational citizen may be expected to resist the obligations of membership. He knows, for example, that, given the large numbers of people organized in the state, if he does not pay taxes or perform military service, others will and the resulting benefits will still be available to him. The rational citizen neither pays taxes nor joins up voluntarily (Olson, 1965). He must be coerced into accepting the obligations of the state and this becomes increasingly the case the larger the polity. One cannot, then, expect individuals to acquire spontaneously the beliefs that will induce them to affirm political growth. On the contrary, it would appear to be the case that small polities are in some sense "natural" and that there is ever present in political life a centrifugal tendency that threatens negative growth.

Turning now to political development, it would not be inconsistent with the definition already given to assert that an extended family or tribal community is a highly developed polity. One may imagine that since both are closely knit, face-to-face societies, there is effective communication between rulers and ruled who share a consensus on fundamental values at once facilitating the articulation of interests, for example, and the management of conflict. Inputs may be transformed into outputs in these communities with a

---

4. In particular, political rulers are likely to have lower time preferences than the ruled insofar as they represent an entity—the state—which has a longer life, and, therefore, a longer planning horizon, than a private individual.

high degree of efficiency. This view is hardly consistent with the main thrust of contemporary analysis of political development, and the reason is obvious. It ignores the mass dimension of modern society. Polities have grown beyond the stage where they can be managed in face-to-face contact. Political development involves the socialization of individuals to an acceptance of political entities with which they have little or no sensory contact and whose governors are remote and seldom seen in the flesh. Somehow they must be integrated into an impersonal polity; they must come to believe that it symbolizes their mutuality, interdependence, and uniqueness and that there is, therefore, a community whose interests governors may legitimately represent.

In the modern era, the integration of mass society and the legitimation of the polity are especially acute problems of political development. Democratic and socialist ideologies pervade the world and the view is widely held that society ought to be organized in the interests of the masses. No longer is it possible for governors to claim royal prerogative, divine right, or some other transcendent principle of legitimacy. Nor is it possible to exclude from polities certain groups of people on the grounds that they do not own property or that their class or lineage is improper or that the labor they perform is menial. Everyone now must be brought into the polity; the legitimacy of the state must be established and affirmed through substantive or symbolic political participation (Edelman, 1964). Yet, an increase in the number of politically active people exacerbates the conflicts inherent in the diverse interests of individuals and places a heavy burden on the political order.[5] This will be all the more true if, as in many of the new states of Asia and Africa, society is torn by linguistic, religious, ethnic, or tribal differences that limit its consensual potential. Political development in these states, as James Coleman has put it, involves the governing elites in attempts

to create by an act of will, an integrated process of political socialization in which at all levels there is an inculcation of positive sentiments of respect, loyalty, and pride in the new polities. Their efforts are being met with strong resistance. . . . Moreover, there are distinct limits to which a political culture can be deliberately created in a single generation; such a culture is a reflection of the ensemble of predispositions and orientations toward authority and politics, most of which are the product of socializing experiences and influences antedating the contemporary drive toward modernization (Almond and Coleman, 1960, p. 545).

It is when one contemplates the difficulties of deliberately and consciously seeking to promote political development in the new states that one becomes aware of a possible conflict with economic growth. It is not simply a matter of political outputs drawing scarce resources away from economic outputs. No doubt the creation of a state bureaucracy, the building of a military

5. Alternatively one may say that it makes the voting paradox more acute. *Cf.* Arrow, 1950, 1951; Riker, 1961.

establishment, or the promotion of a party system, if these facilitate political development, consumes resources with alternative uses. But it also may turn out that the economic sector itself plays a part in the process of political socialization. This possibility reflects an aspect of political development that distinguished it sharply from economic development, namely, the need to subordinate individual preferences and values to the polity, the governing efficiency of which it is the task of development to promote. Expenditures on the bureaucracy are clearly necessary, but how does one create the "predispositions and orientations toward authority and politics" that will render the responsibilities of bureaucrats more manageable? How does one make the ruled more amenable to the demands that the "unseen" rulers may impose on them? There is implicit in these questions a nonrational answer, for they relate to the needs of the polity for legitimacy, rather than to individual needs, to values and beliefs that are more easily absorbed in growing up than consciously learned.[6]

In order to show how growth in the economic sector may be limited by the nonrational demands of political development, it will be convenient now to develop the concept of political monuments.

POLITICAL MONUMENTS

Political monuments are public goods which articulate and reify the state or nation and facilitate the process of political socialization.[7] Unlike private goods, their consumption is not restricted to the individuals who purchase them. They are consumed jointly and one person's use of them is not constrained by the consumption of others. They also differ from public goods like parks because their consumption cannot be understood solely in terms of private satisfactions. Rather they evoke in the beholder a complex set of reactions, some of which serve to identify him with the values and achievements of the community, state or nation. I call them monuments because the examples that come most readily to mind are public structures like the Lincoln Memorial, the Washington Monument, the Nelson Column, the Arc de Triomphe, and so on. While these monuments have significance for private satisfactions through their impact on architectural and esthetic values, they also may inspire in individuals a sense of awe and respect for the polity by deifying the statesmen and soldiers who, in the past, have performed heroi-

6. On the application of psychological learning theory to the development of legitimacy, see Merelman, 1966.
7. On public goods see Musgrave, 1959, and Samuelson, 1954, 1955, 1958. Political socialization has been defined as "the process of induction into the political culture. Its end product is a set of attitudes—cognitions, value standards, and feelings—toward the political system, its various roles, and role incumbents. It also includes knowledge of, values affecting, and feelings toward the inputs of demands and claims into the system, and its authoritative outputs" (Almond and Coleman, 1960, pp. 27–28).

cally in its interests.[8] They help to invest the political offices of the state with a legitimacy that facilitates the tasks of governing for the present holders of the offices.

But political monuments are not restricted to memorials of the kind discussed in the previous paragraph. The more remote the seat of governmental authority from the daily lives of individuals, the more massive, elegant, or ornate are the buildings that house legislators, judges, and administrators in order that citizens may acquire a physical sense of the presence of government and, perhaps, respect for the functions it performs. The annual pilgrimage to Washington or the Kremlin is a more successful instrument of political socialization because the structures there are imposing enough to set government and the political community somewhat apart from the private concerns of the individual.

Memorials, statuary, and public buildings do not exhaust the manifestations that political monuments may assume. The accouterments of the military establishment, for example, symbolize the collective needs of the community for defense. In the new states where the elements of cohesion and the sources of governmental legitimacy are weak, "the military constitutes more than a group of professional specialists. As compared with business entrepreneurs and even with civil service, its personnel become fused into an active political ingredient, because they reflect and incorporate dramatically and visibly, national aspirations" (Janowitz, 1964, p. 44). It is also possible that the resources allocated to the production of output with an ostensible economic rationale also fulfill a political purpose. Myint has observed of backward countries that "people seem to desire up-to-date factories and other trappings of modern industrialism, not so much for the strictly material returns they are expected to yield as for the fact that they are in themselves symbols of national prestige and economic development" (1954, p. 149). Visible industrial outputs, like steel mills and jet airplanes, however uneconomic by neoclassical criteria, may as political monuments respond to this desire and give the polity purposeful representation.

If political monuments are embodied in industrial outputs in the underdeveloped economies, it is because of the simultaneous pressures on them to grow economically and develop politically. In the Western world, political development preceded economic growth; industrialization took place in

8. The dictionary defines *awe* as "respectful or reverential fear, inspired by what is grand or sublime." That this nonrational element is essential for legitimation is pointed up by Talcott Parsons in a discussion of cultural legitimation: "By explicit cultural legitimation, I mean the emergence of an institutional cultural definition of the society of reference, namely, a referent of 'we' . . . which is differentiated, historically or comparatively or both, from other societies, while the merit of we-ness is asserted in a normative context. This definition has to be religious in some sense, e.g., stated in terms of a particular sacred tradition of relations to gods or holy places. It may also ascribe various meritorious features to the group, e.g., physical beauty, warlike prowess, faithful trusteeship of a sacred territory or tradition, etc." (Parsons, 1964, p. 345).

states where the capacity to govern was highly developed. In these circumstances, political monuments assumed orthodox forms. For one reason, the use of resources by government for political socialization was held to a minimum by the strength of private forces working to this end.[9] Within the family, the church, benevolent associations, and other social organizations, the individual from birth to death was enveloped by the symbols of the political community. The history of the United States, for example, has generated a plethora of statesmen, military leaders, documents, battles, and other events which may serve as symbols for communicating to individuals a sense of their common political origins. And these, of course, are readily communicated, for their use is free. No school is prevented from declaiming on the virtues of the Declaration of Independence, the Constitution, or Washington's Farewell Address because other schools are doing likewise. Indeed, the effectiveness of such symbols lies precisely in their unrestricted consumption. For another reason, economic growth occurred in the private sector where relative costs and resource availabilities could be ignored only at the risk of the profitability of enterprise. Output was produced in response to the demand of the market, not to political demands.

Moreover, where political communities have evolved gradually over time prior to the onset of industrialization or accelerated growth, there are frequent occasions when outputs originally produced as private goods subsequently become public goods. Mount Vernon and Versailles are examples of this kind of transformation. Further, there are opportunities for public-minded associations to provide services which have some of the characteristics of political monuments. Thus, Williamsburg, Virginia, New Salem, Illinois, and Upper Canada Village, Ontario, help give the polity historical depth by linking the present generation with past generations.

The creation of political monuments out of the previous history of a society suggests that political development, like economic growth, may be subject to increasing returns. At some level of per capita income economic growth becomes self-sustaining. The conditions—high consumption propensities, poor investment opportunities, explosive population potential—which impose a low-level equilibrium trap on a country may be removed by the growth of income of some magnitude. In other words, the more growth, the easier it is to obtain further growth. Similarly, the longer a continuous existence the political community already has behind it, the easier it may be for private households and groups to disseminate the symbols that create the cohesiveness of the political community.[10] The customs, traditions, and val-

---

9. Or to use Gabriel Almond's terminology, the tasks of manifest political socialization have been minimized by the effectiveness of latent political socialization. See Almond and Coleman, 1960, p. 28.

10. The "may be" in the sentence should be underscored. The case of France is a salutary reminder that history transmits to the present symbols of dissension as well as symbols of consensus.

ues that constrain individual (group) self-regarding motives can only be formed in the passage of time. So far as the state is concerned, in the beginning these scarcely exist; they come into being as society begins to act, creatin a record of events out of which a consciousness of the political commur may grow.

As the political community acquires a past, increasing returns become manifest in the higher value the society places on a New Salem or an Upper Canada Village. Moreover, there are markets for private goods created which have a complementary relationship with political monuments and so work to increase the consciousness of the latter. Manufacturers produce log cabin building sets, White House models, picture histories of world wars, popular biographies and histories of important persons and events that may be consumed privately even while they add to the stock of political symbols that households accumulate in common.

Unlike the United States and other nations in the Western world, the state in the underdeveloped economies cannot depend upon private households to disseminate symbols that facilitate political socialization and acceptance of the legitimacy of its authority to govern. First of all, appropriate symbols may be in short supply. The newly independent states of Sub-Saharan Africa, for example, have little history on which they can draw to heighten citizens' consciousness of their mutual political origins. Because the boundaries of these states often reflect the imperial conflicts of European nations more than tribal or ethnic groupings, they may in fact have no past which can be used to give an abstract polity—Ghana, Nigeria, the Congo—political substance. Secondly, the network of autonomous communication so important in the formation of private attitudes may not be coterminus with the limits of the states' domain, inhibiting the flow of unifying symbols. Tribal differences as in West Africa, or linguistic and religious differences as in India and Ceylon, splinter the political community and so render more difficult the emergence of a consensus in the give and take of private individual (group) conduct.

If, then, the underdeveloped economies must consciously attempt to develop the polity at the same time that they must consciously attempt to accelerate economic growth, in circumstances where the autonomous forces making for unity are weak, their use of resources uneconomically in the industrial or the governmental sectors may reflect the dilemma of these twin imperatives rather than the corruption, willfulness, or stupidity of political leaders. When political development cannot be initiated or sustained on the basis of an historical consciousness of a polity, it must be sought in the future, in the promise of development itself. The primordial attachments which inhibit the formation of the polity may lose some of their force in competition with a broader civil attachment that has associated with it the potential benefits of the modern world. The elite of the underdeveloped economies—the lawyers, civil servants, teachers, military leaders—who have been educated in the Western world and infected by the virus of modernity are the first to become aware that these benefits can only be attained in a state capable of mobilizing the latent energies of a fragmented and backward people. It is they who led the independence movements during the decline of the Western imperial systems and it is they who form the concept of the polity and take responsibility for establishing its legitimacy in the community as independence becomes reality.[11]

Economic growth is a link with the future and it is not implausible to look upon it as a means of achieving the legitimacy of the political order that otherwise does not form autonomously. But it is not the material payoff alone that is important in this connection. Indeed, increased income per capita, *ceteris paribus,* may simply strengthen primordial groupings at the expense of the larger community. If the village or tribe can improve its economic condition within existing institutional arrangements, the pressures for changing these become less compelling. What is at issue is the possibility that economic growth may raise the consciousness of the social or collective purpose of the polity in the scale of values motivating individuals so that parochial loyalties no longer dominate behavior.

Thus far I have suggested that large, dramatic, and visible outputs in the underdeveloped economies have some of the characteristics of political monuments in that they symbolize the collective purpose of the polity. So also may the economic system. This will be least true of market forms of economic organization, for in their very nature they do not communicate to those who interact in them a sense of system with which one can easily identify. While economists themselves typically are strongly committed to the systemic or general equilibrium features of market economies, they make it abundantly clear that the virtues of these systems depend precisely on individuals who act as microcosms independently of one another and without regard to their impact on the economic order. In perfect competition, individuals are price takers adapting to the constellation of prices generated in the system, which is to say that the system does not enter their consciousness. Because this is so, the justification and purpose of market economies are not self-evident. Schumpeter, for example, feared that capitalism even when growing dynamically, could not survive. The masses, burdened by the short-run annoyances of the market and blind to its long-run advantages, were susceptible to the carping criticisms of the "scribbling set" and the organizational demands of its enemies (Schumpeter, 1950, pp. 143–55). No

11. Not all the elites of the underdeveloped economies are anxious to stimulate political development. In Liberia, for example, the ruling Americo-Liberians use their monopoly of political power to minimize the benefits tribal Liberians receive from the revenues their labor for the foreign rubber and iron ore concessionaires make possible. Nothing could be further from their minds than an enlargement of the political community which might impose obligations on them inconsistent with the exploitation of tribal Liberians for personal profit; *cf.* Dalton, 1965, pp. 569–90.

doubt it is for this reason that economists in recent years have become increasingly concerned about economic literacy and interested in economic education in secondary schools.

The elusiveness of the systemic features of market economies is one reason why political leaders bent on achieving both economic growth and political development find some variant of planning attractive. For planning has the purposiveness that makes political monuments out of economic organization. Consider, for the moment, the five-year plans in Russia. By conventional economic criteria they cannot be said to have received very high marks. Critics in the Western world had no difficulty in pointing out the many micro-economic irrationalities that prevented the system from maximizing income. The peculiar ideological aversion to the use of the rate of interest in capital planning led to capital waste in the drawing up of investment projects. A multiplicity of prices, none of which accurately reflected scarcity values, made it difficult for planners to assess resource availabilities and firms to economize scarce materials. Administrative rigidities blocked the flow of economic information and facilitated the emergence of ministerial autarchy, thus preventing the attainment of optimal specialization.[12] Had Western economists been afforded the opportunity of participating in the great debates of the twenties on the future course of Soviet economic growth,[13] they surely would have confronted Trotsky and the advocates of so-called teleological planning with these and other problems; they would have stood squarely with the right wing in urging that planning be based on a modification of the market relationships that were evolving during the New Economic Policy.

Yet, for a politically backward society like Russia, the long-run production targets articulated by central planners imparted to the polity a collective purpose. They gave the political leadership a claim to legitimacy that so frequently in the past eluded Russia's rulers. The repressions, purges, and terror associated with Stalinism should not blind one to the political value of the Russian economic system.[14] That the society survived the excesses of Stalin attests to this; however much he dissipated his claim to legitimacy by paranoiac political machinations, he had the promise of the economic order to support him.

12. For a discussion of these and other problems in the management of the Soviet economy, see Nove, 1961.

13. I use the adjective "great" advisedly, for seldom has there been as vibrant a discussion in the history of economics of the issues central to economic growth. See Erlich, 1960; Spulber, 1964.

14. See, for example, the favorable attitudes towards the Soviet economic system reported in Bauer, Inkeles, and Kluckhohn, 1956, pp. 135–37. In view of the fact that these attitudes were expressed by post-World War II emigrants from Russia who might otherwise be expected to overstress their hostilities to the system they had left, their testimony in favor of the economy is all the more impressive.

CONCLUSION

If it is granted that planning and industrial outputs have some of the characteristics of political monuments in underdeveloped economies, what then? This question is as frustrating as it is terse. For the truth of the matter is that we have no calculus that allows us to measure the productivity of resources used in this manner. Steel mills and great dams have quantifiable economic payoffs and it is possible to compare them with rates of return on alternative investment projects. But how does one measure the payoff of a steel mill in the building of the political community? Who can advise governors about the political rate of return of resources in this use relative to others? Advising is at best a risky profession, difficult enough where the elements of consensus have widely permeated society. When these have to be consciously constructed, political leaders and their advisers must transcend the limits of systematic knowledge. Political development, unlike economic growth and development, is a non-rational process, which is to say that historical knowledge of the old states which have achieved it is not necessarily relevant to the new states. We can tell stories about how it has been done, but stories are not the same thing as theories. In short, political development is an art, and as in the world of the fine arts we must suffer much mediocrity to get a masterpiece. The governments of the new states may offend orthodox economic criteria in building political monuments in the industrial sector, but we at least must entertain the possibility that occasionally these may facilitate the development of the political community and the conditions in which the utilization of scarce resources can be more responsive to economic rationale.

REFERENCES

ALMOND, G. A., and J. S. COLEMAN (Eds.). 1960. *The politics of developing areas.* Princeton, N.J.: Princeton University Press.

APTER, D. E. 1965. *The politics of modernization.* Chicago: University of Chicago Press.

ARROW, K. J. 1950. A difficulty in the concept of social welfare. *Journal of Political Economy,* 58(4): 328–46.

——. 1951. *Social choice and individual values.* New York: Wiley.

BARAN, P. A. 1957. *The political economy of backwardness.* New York: Monthly Review Press.

BAUER, R. A., A. INKELES, and C. KLUCKHOHN. 1956. *How the Soviet system works.* Cambridge: Harvard University Press.

BHATT, V. V. 1965. Some notes on balanced and unbalanced growth. *Economic Journal.*

BINDER, L. 1964. National integration and political development. *American Political Science Review,* 57: 622–31.

CLOWER, R. W., G. DALTON, M. HARWITZ, and A. A. WALTERS. 1966. *Growth without development.* Evanston, Ill.: Northwestern University Press.

DALTON, G. 1965. History, politics, and economic development in Liberia. *Journal of Economic History*, 25(4): 569–90.

EDELMAN, M. 1964. *The symbolic uses of politics.* Urbana: University of Illinois Press.

EISENSTADT, S. N. 1964. Breakdowns of modernization. *Economic development and cultural change*, 12(4): 345–67.

ERLICH, A. 1960. *The Soviet industrialization debate, 1924–1928.* Cambridge: Harvard University Press.

GEERTZ, C. 1963a. The integration revolution-primordial sentiments and civil politics in the new states. In C. Geertz (Ed.), *Old societies and new states.* New York: Free Press of Glencoe.

——— (Ed.). 1963b. *Old societies and new states: the quest for modernity in Asia and Africa.* New York: Free Press of Glencoe.

HAGAN, E. E. 1962. *On the theory of social change.* Homewood, Ill.: Dorsey Press.

HIGGINS, B. H. 1959. *Economic development.* New York: Norton.

HIRSCHMAN, A. O. 1958. *The strategy of economic development.* New Haven, Conn.: Yale University Press.

HUNTINGTON, S. P. 1965. Political development and political decay. *World Politics*, 17(3): 386–430.

———. 1966. Political modernization: America vs. Europe. *World Politics*, 18(3): 378–414.

JANOWITZ, M. 1964. *The military in the political development of new nations.* Chicago: University of Chicago Press.

KAUTSKY, J. H. (Ed.). 1962. *Political change in underdeveloped countries.* New York: Wiley.

LAPALOMBARA, J., and M. WEINER (Eds.). 1966. *Political parties and political development.* Princeton, N.J.: Princeton University Press.

LERNER, D. 1958. *The passing of traditional society.* Glencoe, Ill.: Free Press.

LEWIS, W. A. 1965. Beyond African dictatorship—the crisis of the one-party state. *Encounter*, 25(2): 3.

LIPTON, M. 1962. Balanced and unbalanced growth in underdeveloped countries. *Economic Journal*, 72(287): 641–57.

MERELMAN, R. M. 1966. Learning and legitimacy. *American Political Science Review*, 60(3): 548–561.

MUSGRAVE, R. 1959. *The theory of public finance.* New York: McGraw-Hill.

MYINT, H. 1954. An interpretation of economic backwardness. *Oxford Economic Papers*, N.S., 6(6): 149.

NOVE, A. 1961. *The Soviet economy—an introduction.* New York: Praeger.

OLSON, M. JR. 1965. *The logic of collective action.* Cambridge: Harvard University Press.

PACKENHAM, R. 1966. Political-development doctrines in the American foreign aid program. *World Politics*, 18(2): 194–235.

PARSONS, T. 1964. Evolutionary universals in society. *American Sociological Review*, 29(3): 345.

PYE, L. W. 1962. *Politics, personality, and nation building: Burma's search for identity.* New Haven, Conn.: Yale University Press.

————, and S. VERBA (Ed.). 1965. *Political culture and political development.* Princeton, N.J.: Princeton University Press.

RIKER, W. H. 1961. Voting and the summation of preferences: and interpretive bibliographical review of selected developments during the last decade. *American Political Science Review,* 55(4): 900–911.

ROSENSTEIN-RODAN, P. N. 1943. Problems of industrialization of Eastern and South-Eastern Europe. *Economic Journal,* 53(210–11): 202–211.

SAMUELSON, P. A. 1954. The pure theory of public expenditure. *Review of Economics and Statistics,* 36(4): 387–90.

————. 1955. Diagrammatic exposition of a theory of public expenditure. *Review of Economics and Statistics,* 37(4): 350–56.

————. 1958. Aspects of public expenditure theories. *Review of Economics and Statistics,* 40(4): 332–38.

SCHUMPETER, J. 1950. *Capitalism, socialism, and democracy.* (3d ed.) New York: Harper.

SHILS, E. 1960a. Political development in the new states (I). *Comparative Studies in Society and History,* 2(3): 265–92.

————. 1960b. Political development in the new states (II). *Comparative Studies in Society and History,* 2(4): 379–411.

SINGER, H. W. 1964. *International development: growth and change.* New York: McGraw-Hill.

SPULBER, N. 1964. *Soviet strategy for economic growth.* Bloomington: Indiana University Press.

WARD, R. E., and D. A. RUSTOW (Eds.). 1964. *Political modernization in Japan and Turkey.* Princeton, N.J.: Princeton University Press.

WATSON, A., and J. B. DIRLAM. 1965. The impact of underdevelopment in economic planning. *Quarterly Journal of Economics,* No. 2, 169.

WEINER, M. 1962. *The politics of scarcity.* Chicago: University of Chicago Press.

WRAITH, R., and E. SIMPKINS. 1964. *Corruption in developing countries.* New York: Norton.

PART III
Perspectives across Disciplines

12

THE BORDERLANDS OF GEOGRAPHY AS A
SOCIAL SCIENCE

Marvin W. Mikesell

In the context of this volume, geography is best described as a mosaic within a mosaic (Merton, 1963). To say that geography is both a natural and a social science is to identify the basic feature of its complexity, but this dichotomy masks more than it reveals. The character of modern geography is more clearly revealed if one recognizes that its subdivisions imply a pattern of interdisciplinary relations extending from anthropology to zoology. However, this statement is also misleading, for geographers are not distributed evenly or randomly across the vast spectrum of their enterprise. Cultural geographers oriented toward anthropology are far more numerous than biogeographers oriented toward zoology, and the external orientation of cultural geographers differs from that of economic or political geographers.

Perhaps it is best, therefore, to postpone discussion of the diverse interests of geographers and state simply that the geographic profession now includes a substantial, if not dominant, group of scholars who hope to see their subject ranked alongside anthropology, economics, political science, psychology, and sociology as a social or behavioral science. This expectation is based upon a growing awareness of geography's past and potential contributions as well as its indebtedness. Regardless of the tradition they follow or the methodology employed in the definition of their role, most human geographers have no hesitation in identifying themselves as social scientists. However, because of its diverse origins, singular evolution, and persistent pluralism, the problem of effective communication is especially acute in geography. Consideration of this problem is best approached indirectly by means of an historical survey, for geography did not begin as a social science nor is it universally recognized as such today.

FROM PHYSIOGRAPHY TO AREAL DIFFERENTIATION

In the United States, geography evolved out of geology, a consequence of the development of interest among physiographers in the influence of natural environment on mankind. In Germany, geography evolved out of eighteenth-century cosmography and can still be regarded as a comprehensive "earth science" (*Erdkunde*). Geography's antecedents in France can be traced to interests aroused by that country's commitments abroad and, in a more narrow academic sense, to an evolution from history. In Britain, the first scholars to identify themselves with geography were conscious of the contribution they might make in the clarification of Britain's role in the world and the management of its Empire. From these diverse beginnings geography gradually moved away from its original home in natural science and the humanities, seeking to function first as a bridge between nature and culture and then as an autonomous but pluralistic enterprise devoted to man-land relations, area studies, spatial structure or location theory, and to physical geography as a component of earth science (Pattison, 1964).

When the first department of geography in the United States was established at the University of Chicago in 1903, its announced function was "to occupy the ground intermediate between geology and climatology, on the one hand, and history, sociology, political economy, and biology, on the other." Three years later the first president of the Association of American Geographers proclaimed that "any statement is of geographic quality if it contains . . . some relation between an element of inorganic control and one of organic response" (Davis, 1906, p. 71). The conception of geography as occupying an intermediate position between natural and social science was appealing to the first generation of American geographers, who were trained for the most part as geologists and hoped to apply this knowledge in the study of mankind. The logical culmination of this rationale was expressed by Barrows (1923), for whom geography was the study of mutual relations between man and his natural environment or "human ecology." However, Barrows differed from Davis in asserting that geographers, as thus identified, could abandon their responsibility to conduct original research in physiography and climatology. Barrows' conception of the scope of geography represented a further narrowing of previous views, for the "ecology" that he proclaimed was to be based primarily upon economic geography.

Meanwhile, Fenneman (1919), who like Davis was known mainly for his physiographic studies, surveyed the position of geography among the sciences and asserted that the field should be designated by its core rather than its periphery. In Fenneman's view, that core was regional study, for the common bond among geographers was an interest in places, areas, and regions. This argument was carried further by Sauer (1925) who announced that geography could not claim an independent status if it were preoccupied with a particular causal relation and thus failed to provide an explanatory description of a definite class of data. In his view, the movement from physiography to human geography had followed two divergent paths. The first entailed a shift of interest from an objective analysis of the variable surface of the earth to an attempt to proclaim a causal relationship between nature and culture. The second trend, more fully developed in the European literature, entailed no radical reorientation of method or rationale but merely a shift of attention from the works of nature to the works of mankind. According to the latter interpretation, the genetic and comparative procedures of physiography could also be applied to culture, or at least to material culture, and there was no need to proclaim a deterministic doctrine. In other words, the goal of human geography should be an understanding of the cultural processes that produce "cultural landscapes," just as physiography had sought to understand the natural processes that produce "natural landscapes."

Sauer's statement had considerable influence in the development of American geography. However, the redefinition of geography as the study of landscape proved to have serious practical difficulties, and Sauer repudiated many features of his initial programmatic statement in later publications (Sauer, 1963). Perhaps the most serious weakness of his argument of 1925 was the assumption that geographers should begin their inquiry by reconstructing the pre-human or natural condition of an area. In a world nearly devoid of undisturbed natural landscapes, the difficulties entailed in such a task are forbidding (Thomas, 1956), and geographers concerned primarily with the present landscape were understandably reluctant to begin their studies in antiquity. Moreover, the genetic-morphological method proved uncongenial to economic geographers whose studies tended to develop along generic and functional lines (Platt, 1962). In addition, many geographers felt that it could not be maintained that the study and interpretation of landscapes is the exclusive preserve of the geographer or that landscape, however defined, contains all that is geographical (Broek, 1965, pp. 77–78).

In 1939 Hartshorne presented a more comprehensive statement on the nature of geography in which emphasis was placed on the concept of "areal differentiation." Since geography could not be defined in reference to an explicit class of data, as botany could be defined in reference to plants or political science in reference to politics, it seemed preferable to describe its task as one of integration. According to this view, which had long been evident in the German literature (Hettner, 1927), geography stood apart from the systematic sciences, and its function was to integrate through space as history integrates through time. As the facts of history are time facts and their association can be expressed by the concept of period, so the facts of geography are place facts and their association could be expressed by the concepts of location and area. Since the surface of the earth is infinitely varied and no two places or areas are alike, geographers were presented with a logically defined field of study and had every reason to be confident that their discipline would achieve appropriate recognition as an empirical science.

THE EXTERNAL ORIENTATIONS OF HUMAN GEOGRAPHY

Hartshorne's meticulous review was the culmination of attempts by American geographers to define their subject as an integrated and autonomous field. By the time of World War II, human geographers, always subject to strong centrifugal forces, had created several subfields. Insofar as these were defined phenomenologically—i.e., in reference to land use, settlements, industry, commerce, transportation, and so on—the methodologies designed to support geography's independence were not challenged. However, human geographers began increasingly to define their interests in reference to one or more of the neighboring fields of social science. When the Association of American Geographers sponsored the publication of a comprehensive survey (James and Jones, 1954), one could point to well-developed subfields of economic, historical, and political geography. In addition, urban geographers had been influenced by the "human ecology" school in sociology, and cultural geographers had drawn support from anthropology. Today one can also speak of population geographers oriented toward demography and a growing desire of geographers interested in environmental perception to employ the data and concepts of psychology. The remainder of this paper is devoted to an exploratory examination of each of these "borderlands."

GEOGRAPHY AND ANTHROPOLOGY

The problem of communication between these two fields is unusually complex, for the concept of culture is implicit in all of human geography and explicit in the subfield of cultural geography. The position taken by Wagner and Mikesell (1962) that cultural geographers are identified by their preoccupation with four research themes—"culture area," "culture history," "cultural landscape," and "cultural ecology"—underscores the status of cultural geography as an interdisciplinary field, for each of these themes is shared with anthropology. As I have tried to show elsewhere (Mikesell, 1967), geographers probably have most to learn from anthropologists on social organization, the delimitation and classification of culture areas, and the processes that produce culture change. They may have most to offer in return on settlement patterns, land tenure and land use, and the more general issue of cultural ecology. Since no clear distinction can be made between these two general categories of interest, it is not surprising that substantive studies show a pattern of convergence and that philosophical or methodological writings show a pattern of parallel development.

These two trends can be illustrated by reference to common work in cultural ecology. As already indicated, concern for the relations of nature and culture formed the first explicit rationale of American geography. Interest in this relationship waned as a result of the criticism of the environmentalist doctrines proclaimed in the twenties and thirties (Tatham, 1951). Since prescriptive rather than philosophical arguments were the main basis for this rejection—i.e., geography should not be defined in reference to a particular causal relationship—it is not an exaggeration to suggest that environmentalism was disapproved rather than disproved (Rostlund, 1962; Lewthwaite, 1966). The principal failing of the environmentalists was that they tried to describe nature and culture as separate entities or opposing forces. The philosophy developed in response to criticism of this effort represented a retreat from determinism to the relative security of "possibilism." Simultaneously, physical and human geographers were drifting apart, and the latter tended increasingly to minimize the influence of natural environment. For example, the comprehensive survey mentioned above includes chapters devoted to nature and chapters devoted to culture but none devoted to their relationship (James and Jones, 1954). Actually, geographers had not abandoned this inquiry but rather had placed emphasis on processes of environmental modification, such as deforestation and erosion (Thomas, 1956). Enriched by this experience, they have tried in recent years to develop a more sophisticated philosophy of man-land relations in which emphasis is placed on nature and culture as interlocking components of a system (Eyre and Jones, 1966; Wagner, 1960).

The first attempts of American anthropologists to work out a philosophy of man-land relations were empirical and inductive, a consequence of efforts to delimit and classify culture areas (Kroeber, 1939; Wissler, 1926). Since careful examination of the distribution of elements of nature and culture produced no clear evidence of causation, anthropologists embraced a cautious philosophy roughly comparable to the geographic concept of possibilism. Subsequent research has developed along three lines: Some anthropologists have sought to establish a connection between environment and exploitative technology and between exploitative technology and social organization (Steward, 1955). Others have sought a more accurate functional explanation of the activities of particular groups exploiting particular ecological niches (Barth, 1956; Leach, 1954). Still others have reconsidered the question of whether environment has a limiting effect on the evolution of cultures (Ferdon, 1959; Meggers, 1954, 1957).

Taken as a whole, the ecological commitment of geographers shows relative sophistication in examinations of land and livelihood and relative naiveté in examinations of social structure (Brookfield, 1964). Anthropological studies display strength and weakness in the reverse direction (Mikesell, 1967). The complementary nature of the respective disciplines is obvious. Nevertheless, examples of cooperation are few (Brookfield and Brown, 1963), and only one case can be cited of a substantive research problem that has been attacked with equal vigor by members of both disciplines (Conklin, 1961; Spencer, 1966).

One could discuss other examples of convergent interest or parallel development, but the case of cultural ecology is sufficiently clear to illustrate the general pattern. Cultural geographers and anthropologists are like brothers separated in infancy and taught to speak different languages. Faced with the challenge of a wide range of common problems, they may yet realize that they are natural allies.

GEOGRAPHY AND SOCIOLOGY

Communication between geography and sociology has been more effective than that between geography and any other social science. However, one must add a qualification, for sociologists appear to have restricted their attention very largely to the work of urban geographers. Moreover, this relationship has been sustained primarily by the school in American sociology known as "human ecology." That this school should have been influenced primarily by urban geographers is ironical, for no field of modern geography is less ecological. However, the irony is more apparent than real, for the sociological definition of ecology differs notably from the essentially biological (i.e., etymologically conservative) use of the term in the literature of anthropology and cultural geography. For sociologists, "ecological" studies are those that deal explicitly with the spatial dimension of social structure. For anthropologists and cultural geographers, ecology refers to the relationship between natural environment and culture. But this is a digression, useful only as a warning that the various meanings assigned to "ecology" and "ecological" constitute one of the most perplexing semantic problems in social science. For the purpose of this essay, it is sufficient to indicate that "ecological" sociologists and urban geographers are both concerned with the form, function, and organization of modern cities, and that each group has profited from the other.

Indeed, it is probably safe to suggest that most urban geographers are aware of the work of the more prominent contributors to "human ecology" (e.g., Park, Burgess, Wirth, Hawley, Duncan, Foley, Firey, and Schnore). Sociologists, in turn, seem to be well aware of the environmentalist tradition that once prevailed in American geography (Thomas, 1925; Sorokin, 1928) and have taken account of various articles published in their journals by geographers (Harris, 1943; Harris and Ullman, 1945; Platt, 1948; Ullman. 1941). Recent studies by two other geographers (Berry and Garrison, 1958a, 1958b) have been reprinted by the Bobbs-Merrill Company in a series devoted to sociology. Conversely, the first general work on spatial statistics, ironically entitled *Statistical Geography*, was produced by sociologists rather than geographers (Duncan, Cuzzort, and Duncan, 1961). However, geographic research on this topic is probably relatively more advanced at the present time (Berry and Marble, 1967; Chorley and Haggett, 1967; Gregory, 1963; Haggett, 1966).

While impressive, these illustrations of overlapping interest cannot be taken as proof that the flow of information between the two fields is un-impeded or that comprehension is not frustrated to some extent by intro-spective methodologies. For example, although it is safe to assume that a geographer specializing in urban analysis will be reasonably well informed on the postulates of "classical human ecology," it would be rash to assume that he would be able to differentiate between what is "classical" or "neo-othodox" (Theodorson, 1961), or that he would understand the rationale for the placement of geographic studies in anthologies edited by sociologists (Hatt and Reiss, 1957; Theodorson, 1961). Moreover, with a few notable exceptions (Duncan, 1964; Schnore, 1961), it would be hard to prove that "human ecologists" are well aware of the evolution of geographic thought in recent years or, as indicated previously, that they are well aware of geo-graphic research conducted outside the subfield of urban geography. Con-versely, references to the work of rural sociologists seldom appear in the writings of American geographers. The last point gains added significance from the fact that a more comprehensive view of the interaction of human geography and sociology is evident in the writings of European geographers (Sorre, 1957).

In short, the relation between geography and sociology seems to illus-trate a general principle. When scholars trained in different fields recognize their commitment to a common substantive issue, the communication bar-riers created by independent academic status tend to disappear or at least be reduced to less formidable size. However, this does not mean that mem-bers of a particular discipline will have an accurate overall impression of the interests or traditions of their neighbors. In the case of geography and soci-ology, the narrowness of the bridge between the two disciplines is explained in large part by the failure of American geographers to develop a field of social geography and by the preoccupation of American sociologists with the urban environment of modern America.

GEOGRAPHY AND POLITICAL SCIENCE

In their lighthearted moments geographers sometimes claim Napoleon Bona-parte as the founder of their discipline, for the political realignments re-sulting from the Napoleonic Wars forced geographers to develop a more comprehensive view of regional geography. However, the nation state has remained the chief focus of interest for political geographers. The rationale of this interest has varied notably. For Ratzel, author of the first general treatise on political geography (1897), states could be likened to organisms subject to natural laws of growth or decay. Later scholars sought to apply geographic concepts in studies of military strategy and international rela-tions. Although the elaborate theoretical structures built up with these inter-ests in mind intoxicated a generation of geographers, and even a few political scientists (Sprout and Sprout, 1965; Spykmann, 1942), each was subject eventually to destructive criticism. For example, the German school of "geopolitics" was condemned as a pseudo-science designed to provide a geographic justification for national expansion. And, more generally, geopolitics was exposed as being divided logically into as many different schools as there are independent states or national ideologies (Hartshorne, 1954). Correspondingly, the famous "heartland theory" of Mackinder (1904), according to which control of the Eurasian landmass was the essential basis of political predominance in the Old World, was challenged successively by theories that placed greater stress on sea and air power.

As a consequence of its early excesses and inherent ambiguity, political geography has suffered more than any other field of geography from pessimistic views of its potential. In 1927 Sauer described it as "the wayward child of the geographic family." In 1954 the scholar most responsible for attempts to recast political geography in an empirical and inductive mold felt obliged to complain that in political geography more than in any other field of geography, the attempt to teach others had gone far ahead of the pursuit of learning by teachers (Hartshorne, 1954, p. 170). Criticism of this sort encouraged a reassessment of the role of political geography, and in recent years political geographers have tended to abandon their traditional quest for principles to explain international relations in favor of a more modest role. For example, the objective of most of the current textbooks in political geography is to provide a disciplined interpretation of the areal expression of political phenomena. Moreover, recent methodological statements have encouraged attempts to treat political areas as "systems," and in this regard political geographers have moved closer to political science (Jackson, 1964). For example, the stress placed on communication efficiency as a crucial process of political integration in the work of Deutsch (1935a, 1953b) has a counterpart in the emphasis placed on circulation, interaction, and the relative importance of centrifugal and centripetal forces in the work of political geographers (Gottmann, 1951, 1952; Hartshorne, 1950; Jones, 1954). Similarly, the spate of recent studies of electoral geography (Kasperson, 1965; Lewis, 1965; Prescott, 1959) has brought geographers into one of the central issues of political science. Finally, concern for the role of decision-making in the management of resources has created a new interdisciplinary field in which political geography merges with economic geography, and political theory is enriched by the concepts of social psychology (Burton and Kates, 1965).

Whether the "new" political geography will be more respectable than its ancestors remains to be seen, but there is no doubt that it will be more self-consciously scientific. Now as in the past, the essential challenge of political geography is to understand the role of government in shaping the character of areas, for what one sees in a particular landscape, whether in France, Mongolia, or the United States, can seldom be understood without reference to ideology, authority, and institutional structure.

GEOGRAPHY AND ECONOMICS

Economic geography is not only the most populous field of human geography, it is also the field that has been most affected by technological innovations in recent years. Whether geography as a whole has been transformed by a "quantitative revolution" (Burton, 1963) seems doubtful, but there is abundant evidence that infusion of quantitative techniques is producing a new breed of economic geographer (Smith, Taaffe, and King, 1968). However, in methodological terms the character of economic geography remains unchanged, for traditionalists, moderate reformers, and even "revolutionaries" share a common interest in the spatial or locational aspects of economic activity.

The persistent lack of mutual interaction between geographers and economists is best explained in the same terms, for spatial or locational problems have not been central to the interests of economists, and geographers have seldom claimed to offer new insights into the nature of economic activity. For example, Chisholm assesses his recent work on *Geography and Economics* (1966, p. 3) in these terms: "The economist may find applications and implications of fundamental ideas which will at least put some things in a new light and, in particular, he may find some interest in the diversity of spatial implications of quite ordinary economic concepts." In other words, the personality of the statistically sophisticated and theoretically oriented economic geographer is frankly schizoid: confident in his discourse with fellow geographers, he tends to be diffident in the company of economists.

The reason for this attitude is easy to explain, for prior to World War II economic geographers shared the introspective viewpoint of most human geographers. Textbooks in this field were devoted to descriptive, indeed encyclopedic, accounts of the zonation of land use, the location of industrial raw materials, and patterns of production and exchange. The new tendency in economic geography differs from the old in seeking functional rather than historical or ecological understanding and in striving to be more deductive and theoretical (McCarty and Lindberg, 1966). The principal sources of support for this development have been the writings of five economists—Von Thünen (1826), Weber (1909), Lösch (1939), Hoover (1948), and Isard (1956a, 1960)—and one geographer (Christaller, 1933) which, collectively, provide the foundation for location theories that embrace agricultural, industrial, and commercial activities. Perhaps the most highly regarded formulation of this character is "central-place theory," which relates the size and spacing of urban settlements to functional complexity and the areal range of demand for goods (Berry and Pred, 1961). Economic geographers have also made substantial contributions to the theory of industrial location (Harris, 1954; Pred, 1966), have laid the foundation for a more effective theory of rural land use (Chisholm, 1962), have tried to identify and correlate indices of economic development (Ginsburg, 1960, 1961), and have continued to perfect their methods of economic regionalization (Harris, 1964).

But the problem of effective communication with economics remains, and the extent to which it is being solved is explained in part by the function of the Regional Science Association as a mediating agent between geographers and other social scientists devoted to locational analysis. In his presidential address, the founder of this Association relegated geographers to a subsidiary role (Isard, 1956b). They were to conduct inductive and empirical studies useful in the model-building of "regional scientists." That this subordinate assignment was not accepted by geographers is evident in the prominent role they have since played in the Regional Science Association and the frequency of their contributions to its publications. By compensating in large part for the previous weakness of its external ties, the Regional Science Association has substantially aided the recent development of economic geography. Indeed, in the meetings and publications of this association, geographers have an opportunity to present studies accomplished with the aid of quantitative techniques borrowed from fields as diverse as botany and civil engineering to an audience that includes "human ecologists," econometricians, and planners. The "hybrid vigor" developed in response to these stimuli has been a potent force in the recent evolution of economic geography. However, it seems likely that this evolution will take a more independent course in the future, for the appearance in 1969 of a new quarterly publication, *Geographic Analysis: An International Journal of Theoretical Geography*, suggests that geographers devoted to model building and mathematical or statistical analysis are now sufficiently numerous and productive to sustain an autonomous enterprise.

GEOGRAPHY AND DEMOGRAPHY

In his pioneer treatise of 1910 Jean Brunhes suggested that the essential task of human geography might be described in reference to two maps, one showing the general distribution of rainfall and the other showing the distribution of human population. Although most geographers have ceased to feel that they are obliged to proclaim a causal connection between these two distributions, Brunhes' suggestion is useful in demonstrating an early commitment to population geography. However, it was only in the 1950's that this commitment became explicit. Responsibility for the growth of population geography in the United States belongs primarily to Trewartha (1953) and Hooson (1960), who demonstrated the logical position of such study within the framework of human geography, and to Zelinsky (1962, 1966), who clarified the scope and rationale of population geography, its relations to other fields of geography, and to other social sciences. Population geography has also shown a notable development in Europe and especially in France (Beaujeu-Garnier, 1956–58; George, 1959).

According to Zelinsky, the relatively late development of population geography is explained by the dearth of statistics, maps, and other data required for such study and the ambiguous position of demography as a companion science. The growth of population geography has also been frustrated by the persistent tendency of human geographers to regard the works of man rather than man himself as the primary object of their concern. The decline of this inhibiting philosophy can be attributed to a growing awareness that the "population explosion" of the twentieth century is a compelling subject for geographic research, and also to the belated recognition of demography as a social science.

Since demographers and population geographers have the same general interest, the distinction between the two disciplines is best described as a reflection of academic tradition. "The demographer is ultimately concerned with the intrinsic nature, the universal attributes of populations, with the systematic principles governing their composition, socioeconomic correlates, behavior, and changes" (Zelinsky, 1966, p. 3). Population geographers share these concerns, while adding the significant dimension of space, which is only incidental to the central purpose of demography.

Given its spatial perspective, population geography is concerned with three levels of discourse: (1) the simple description of the location of population numbers and characteristics; (2) the explanation of the spatial configurations of these numbers and characteristics; and (3) the geographic analysis of population phenomena, which includes a quest for scientific explanation of population distribution and correlation of population data with other features of geographic concern (Zelinsky, 1966, pp. 5–6).

This statement demonstrates the importance of population geography to other fields of geography and the intricate reciprocal relationship of geography and demography. Since both fields have extraordinarily complex patterns of interdisciplinary contact, it is obvious that academic nationalism in this case would be a contradiction in terms.

GEOGRAPHY AND PSYCHOLOGY

Concern for the psychological dimensions of human geography is more deeply rooted in the history of geography than is commonly realized. As early as 1917 Hellpach sought to demonstrate the effects of natural environment on behavior, and a persuasive statement on the relevance of psychological studies for human geography was presented by Sorre in 1954. But the research potentials implied by this relationship have received general recognition only in recent years (Kates and Wohlwill, 1966; Lowenthal, 1967). The key concept in this development is "perception," which implies a recognition that the objective reality of natural or artificial environments may be less significant in geographic research than the perception of such environments by groups or individuals. As Lowenthal (1961, p. 60) suggests,

"The surface of the earth is shaped for each person by refraction through cultural and personal lenses of custom and fancy."

The rationale behind the recent interest in perception is varied. For some it is derived from attempts to work out a more comprehensive and durable geographic epistemology (Lowenthal, 1961; Kirk, 1963). For others, studies of environmental perception are the logical consequence of attempts to transform cultural geography into a behavioral science (Sonnenfeld, 1967). Still others have used the concept to clarify issues in the history of ideas (Tuan, 1967). In addition, geographers have examined the perception of floods and other natural hazards (Kates, 1962; Saarinen, 1966). Perhaps the most effective demonstration of the importance of perception in geographic analysis is offered in two studies by Lowenthal and Prince (1964, 1965), in which an attempt is made to determine the effect of landscape taste on landscape evolution. Taken together, these several studies have sustained the argument of Lowenthal (1961) and Kirk (1963) that geographers must accept the challenge of dealing with a behavioral as well as a phenomenal environment.

For example, it seems clear that understanding of erosion requires consideration of how this process is perceived as well as its physical manifestations (Blaut, 1959). Similarly, for geographers interested in resource management or conservation, knowledge of how or even why a resource is utilized may be less significant than knowledge of the perception of cause and effect by the peoples or agencies responsible for such utilization. Moreover, there is abundant evidence that culture areas delimited objectively by statistical or cartographic analysis may differ notably from subjective areas as viewed from within (Weiss, 1962). Needless to say, cultural geographers, in common with all students of culture, are also well aware that an innovation may be accepted or rejected not on the basis of its form or function but because it is identified with desirable or undesirable neighbors.

Geographers will perhaps continue to be concerned primarily with concrete objects—roads, houses, fields, irrigation works, and so on—but there seems to be a growing awareness that comprehension of what is where must be based upon a disciplined consideration of the determinants of behavior. In this regard, geographers will draw from and hopefully also contribute to the neighboring field of psychology.

GEOGRAPHY AND HISTORY

The relationship of geography and history is not basic to geography's status as a social science. Nevertheless, this connection has attracted more attention than any other external tie (Broek, 1941; Clark, 1954, 1960; Darby, 1953; Hartshorne, 1939, 1959; Merrens, 1965; Mikesell, 1960; Sorre, 1962). Historical geography is linked to history by a common historiographic commitment. Historical geography differs from history in its explicit attempt to regard the earth itself, as well as written documents, as a source of information about the past. It is not surprising that the borderland between geography and history is broad in extent and poorly defined. Historical geographers have been strongly influenced by historians and historians, in turn, have derived some benefit from the work of historical geographers. However, the effectiveness of the interchange has been impeded, at least in the United States, by the lack of general awareness among historians of the nature of geography. Historical geographers have been moved more than once to complain that the only geographical thought of wide currency among historians is the obsolete work of the environmentalists.

The several patterns of relationship between the two disciplines have been outlined by Darby (1953), who distinguishes primarily between a concern for the "geography behind history" and the "history behind geography." Until recently, historical geographers devoted most of their effort to the former theme, which is perhaps best illustrated by Vidal de la Blache's *Tableau de la géographie de la France* (1911). This rationale is also evident in works of Semple (1903, 1931) and Whittlesey (1949). However, in recent years historical geographers have tended to reject this rather subordinate assignment, preferring instead to deal with the geography of past periods or the processes that produce geographic change. The research strategies employed in these efforts range from comprehensive reconstruction at a particular period (Brown, 1943; Darby, 1952–67) or succession of periods (Whittlesey, 1929) to attempts to deal with the impact of particular innovations (Clark, 1949) or the evolution of landscape features (McManis, 1964). In addition, many historical geographers have sought to work out a pattern of influence, such as the impact of survey systems on settlement morphology (Harris, 1966; Thrower, 1966).

Since historical geographers, in common with most geographers, are concerned primarily with man's use of the earth, it is not surprising that their main external orientation has been toward economic rather than social, political, or intellectual history (Brown, 1948; Darby, 1936). However, their principal allies within geography have been cultural rather than economic geographers, for their interest in economic activity is less binding than their interest in the processes that produce geographic change (Sauer, 1941). Although historical geographers are well aware of their identity, their subject cannot be defined in phenomenological terms. All geography is potentially historical because there is an historical dimension to all geographic problems. Nevertheless, the commitment to interpret past periods of time or changes through time imposes special training requirements that unite this group more effectively than most in modern geography. The basis of this unity is a general agreement on the role of historiography as an internal bond and of historians as allies. However, to conclude on this note would be misleading, for the historiographic competence shared with historians provides technical support rather than theoretical orientation, and the specific research interests of historical geographers oblige them to move toward one or more of the neighboring fields of social science.

POSTSCRIPT: GEOGRAPHY AND AREA STUDIES

Although the relations between the various topical specializations of geography and neighboring fields are most important to geography's development as a social science, the most extensive pattern of interdisciplinary communication has probably been created by geographers concerned with foreign areas. A geographer with this interest will subscribe to and occasionally contribute to journals devoted to his area. If he is well trained in the language or languages of his area, the extent of his commitment may include the specialized studies of Arabists, Sinologists, and so on. He will undoubtedly try to be informed about a wide range of social science research in his area and he may review such studies for the geographic journals.

However, although regional geography is often described as the "last citadel" of general human geography, most geographers with regional interests tend to be committed to a particular topical specialization, e.g., historical geography of Latin America, economic geography of East Asia, cultural geography of Africa, and so on. In this respect, concern for the language and civilization of a particular region is like the historiographic commitment of historical geographers: it provides a foundation or context for research rather than a theoretical orientation. Consequently, the training requirements of foreign-area specialists entail a double or even triple program. They must have a working knowledge of a particular language, be liberally educated in the history of a particular civilization, and also have effective control of the data and concepts of a topical field. The difficulties entailed in this task are forbidding. Yet many geographers have elected to follow this course, and they may have established geography's most effective alliance with scholars trained in other fields.

The full range of geographic contributions to area studies has not yet been described in detail, although one can point to surveys devoted to Latin America (Parsons, 1964), Africa (Thomas, 1965), and the Soviet Union (Harris, 1962, 1965), and also to a recent re-examination of the theory and practice of regional geography (Minshull, 1967).

CONCLUDING REMARKS

This paper opened with a comment on the inherent complexity of geography, sought to explain that complexity by reviewing the evolution of geography in the United States, and then considered geography's relations with neighboring fields. Taken together, the discussion of these relations reveals that imports are more prominent than exports. In addition, it is probably fair to say that most of the geographic works known to scholars in other fields are not regarded by geographers themselves as indicative of their current interests. Among anthropologists and historians, the voice of American geography is undoubtedly Ellsworth Huntington (1876–1947), whose theories of climatic influence have been obsolete for more than thirty years. Among political scientists, geography is most commonly identified with the various schools of "geopolitics" that flourished in the 1940's and are no longer taken seriously by political geographers. It would be difficult to prove that geographic thought is more clearly perceived by economists, although central-place theory and other formulations of location theory have some currency among economists concerned with urban and regional planning (Friedmann and Alonso, 1964). Sociologists are perhaps unique among social scientists in having a more accurate perception of modern trends in geographic research, although this awareness is confined very largely to the work of urban geographers.

While discouraging, this situation is not surprising, given the small size of the geographic profession, which has at best a few dozen productive scholars in each of its subfields, and the relatively recent commitment of geographers to function as social scientists. Needless to say, examples of export or more effective communication could be multiplied considerably if one took full account of the contribution of geographers to area studies or if attention were directed to particular processes rather than the more rigid framework of recognized subfields—e.g., urbanization (Hauser and Schnore, 1965), economic development (Wood and Thoman, 1965), or cultural ecology (Fosberg, 1965).

In any case, the emphasis placed on external connections should not be taken as an indication that there is a perfect flow of information within the field. Like most of the social sciences, geography has its schools and factions and, correspondingly, a considerable programmatic literature. In recent years passions have been aroused primarily by a debate between advocates of deductive logic, model building, and quantification and those who have faith that inductive field studies lead eventually to a comprehensive personal wisdom. It is difficult, to say the least, for someone who thinks that regional synthesis represents the highest expression of the geographic "art" to enjoy cordial discussion with a colleague who condemns this tradition as being "unscientific." Spokesmen for these *complementary* positions view each other in a harsh and distorting light: the model builder becomes a "mechanic" and the champion of regional synthesis is exposed as a "mystic."

Moreover, the emotional methodologies that have been presented to geographers in recent years have their counterpart in a series of practical or operational distinctions that are deeply rooted in American geography. For example, cultural geographers prefer in general to study non-Western or at least pre-industrial societies, tend to seek historical understanding, and habitually elect to deal with rural rather than urban landscapes. It is not surprising, therefore, that they have shown little interest in studies, however

sophisticated, that are devoted to the shopping habits of American house-
wives. On the other hand, concern for technique may create a situation that
makes a student of industrial location feel more comfortable conversing with
a statistically competent climatologist than with an economic geographer
who does not use statistical techniques. However, to state that these situations exist is not to prove that they constitute a serious problem, for geographers, like most social scientists, can also be divided into those who regard
the fragmentation of their field as a threat to its integrity and those who welcome such development as a sign of maturity.

REFERENCES

BARROWS, H. H. 1923. Geography as human ecology. *Annals of the Association of
American Geographers,* 13: 1–14.

BARTH, F. 1956. Ecologic relationships of ethnic groups in Swat, North Pakistan.
American Anthropologist, 58: 1079–89.

BEAUJEU-GARNIER, J. 1956–58. *Géographie de la population.* 2 vols. Paris: Li-
brairie de Médicis.

BERRY, B. J. L., and W. L. GARRISON. 1958a. The functional basis of the central-
place hierarchy. *Economic Geography,* 34: 145–54.

———, ———. 1958b. Alternate explanations of urban rank-size relationships.
Annals of the Association of American Geographers, 48: 83–91.

———, and D. F. MARBLE (Eds.). 1967. *Spatial analysis: a reader in statistical
geography.* Englewood Cliffs, N.J.: Prentice-Hall.

———, and A. PRED. 1961. *Central place studies: a bibliography of theory and
applications.* Philadelphia: Regional Science Association.

BLAUT, J. 1959. A study of the cultural determinants of soil erosion and conservation in the Blue Mountains of Jamaica. *Social and Economic Studies,* 8:
402–420.

BROEK, J. O. M. 1941. The relations between history and geography. *Pacific Historical Review,* 10: 321–25.

———. 1965. *Geography: its scope and spirit.* Columbus: Merrill Books.

BROOKFIELD, H. C. 1964. Questions on the human frontiers of geography. *Econo-
nomic Geography,* 40: 283–303.

———, and P. BROWN. 1963. *Struggle for land: agriculture and group territories
among the Chimbu of the New Guinea highlands.* Melbourne: Oxford
University Press.

BROWN, R. H. 1943. *Mirror for Americans: likeness of the Eastern seaboard, 1810.*
New York: American Geographical Society.

———. 1948. *Historical geography of the United States.* New York: Harcourt,
Brace and World.

BRUNHES, J. 1910. *La géographie humaine.* Paris: Alcan. (Trans. by T. C. Le
Compte as *Human geography.* Chicago: Rand McNally, 1920.)

BURTON, I. 1963. The quantitative revolution and theoretical geography. *Canadian
Geographer,* 7: 151–62.

————, and R. W. KATES (Eds.). 1965. *Readings in resource management and conservation.* Chicago: University of Chicago Press.

CHISHOLM, L. 1966. *Geography and economics.* New York: Praeger.

CHISHOLM, M. 1962. *Rural settlement and land use.* London: Hutchinson.

CHORLEY, R. J., and P. HAGGETT. 1967. *Models in geography.* London: Methuen.

CHRISTALLER, W. 1933. *Die zentralen Orte in Süddeutschland.* Jena: Fischer. (Trans. by C. W. Baskin as *Central Places in Southern Germany.* Englewood Cliffs, N.J.: Prentice-Hall, 1966.)

CLARK, A. H. 1949. *The invasion of New Zealand by peoples, plants, and animals.* New Brunswick: Rutgers University Press.

————. 1954. Historical geography. In P. E. James and C. F. Jones (Eds.), *American geography: inventory and prospect.* Syracuse: Syracuse University Press.

————. 1960. Geographical change: a theme for economic history. *Journal of Economic History,* 20: 607–13.

CONKLIN, H. C. 1961. The study of shifting cultivation. *Current Anthropology,* 2: 27–61.

DARBY, H. C. 1952–67. *The Domesday geography of England.* 5 vols. Cambridge: Cambridge University Press.

————. 1953. On the relations of geography and history. *Transactions and Papers, Institute of British Geographers,* 29: 1–11.

————. (Ed.). 1936. *An historical geography of England before A.D. 1800.* Cambridge: Cambridge University Press.

DAVIS, W. M. 1906. An inductive study of the content of geography. *Bulletin of the American Geographical Society,* 38: 67–84.

DEUTSCH, K. W. 1953a. *Nationalism and social communication.* New York: Wiley.

————. 1953b. The growth of nations: some recurrent patterns of political and social integration. *World Politics,* 5: 168–95.

DUNCAN, O. D. 1964. Social organization and the ecosystem. In R. E. L. Faris (Ed.), *Handbook of modern sociology.* Chicago: Rand McNally.

————, R. P. CUZZORT, and B. DUNCAN. 1961. *Statistical geography: problems in analyzing areal data.* New York: Free Press.

EYRE, S. R., and G. R. JONES (Eds.). 1966. *Geography as human ecology: methodology by example.* London: Arnold.

FENNEMAN, N. M. 1919. The circumference of geography. *Annals of the Association of American Geographers,* 9: 3–11.

FERDON, E. N., JR. 1959. Agricultural potential and the development of cultures. *Southwestern Journal of Anthropology,* 15: 1–19.

FOSBERG, F. R. (Ed.). 1965. *Man's place in the island ecosystem.* Honolulu: Bishop Museum Press.

FRIEDMANN, J., and W. ALONSO (Eds.). 1964. *Regional development and planning.* Cambridge: MIT Press.

GEORGE, P. 1959. *Questions de géographie de la population.* Paris: Presses Universitaires de France.

GINSBURG, N. S. 1961. *Atlas of economic development.* Chicago: University of Chicago Press.

———— (Ed.). 1960. *Essays on geography and economic development.* Chicago: University of Chicago, Department of Geography Research Paper No. 62.

GOTTMANN, J. 1951. Geography and international relations. *World Politics,* 3: 153–73.

———. 1952. The political partitioning of our world: an attempt at analysis. *World Politics,* 4: 512–19.

GREGORY, S. 1963. *Statistical methods and the geographer.* London: Longmans, Green.

HAGGETT, P. 1966. *Locational analysis in human geography.* New York: St. Martin's.

HARRIS, C. D. 1943. Suburbs. *American Journal of Sociology,* 49: 1–13.

———. 1954. The market as a factor in the localization of industry in the United States. *Annals of the Association of American Geographers,* 44: 315–48.

———. 1962. The land. In P. L. Horecky (Ed.), *Basic Russian publications: an annotated bibliography on Russia and the Soviet Union.* Chicago: University of Chicago Press.

———. 1964. Methods of research in economic regionalization. *Geographia Polonica,* 4: 59–86.

———. 1965. The land. In P. L. Horecky (Ed.), *Russia and the Soviet Union: a bibliographic guide to Western-language publications.* Chicago: University of Chicago Press.

———, and E. ULLMAN. 1945. The nature of cities. *Annals of the American Academy of Political and Social Science,* 242: 7–17.

HARRIS, R. C. 1966. *The seigneurial system in early Canada.* Madison: University of Wisconsin Press.

HARTSHORNE, R. 1939. The nature of geography. *Annals of the Association of American Geographers,* 29: 171–658.

———. 1950. The functional approach in political geography. *Annals of the Association of American Geographers,* 40: 95–130.

———. 1954. Political geography. In P. E. James and C. F. Jones (Eds.), *American geography: inventory and prospect.* Syracuse: Syracuse University Press.

———. 1959. *Perspective on the nature of geography.* Chicago: Rand McNally.

HATT, P. K., and A. J. REISS, JR. (Eds). 1957. *Cities and society: the revised reader in urban sociology.* Glencoe, Ill.: Free Press.

HAUSER, P. M., and L. F. SCHNORE (Eds.). 1965. *The study of urbanization.* New York: Wiley.

HELLPACH, W. 1917. *Die geopsychischen Erscheinungen.* Leipsig: Engelmann.

HETTNER, A. 1927. *Die Geographie, ihre Geschichte, ihr Wesen und ihre Methoden.* Breslau: Hirt.

HOOSEN, D. J. M. 1960. The distribution of population as the essential geographical expression. *Canadian Geographer,* 17: 10–20.

HOOVER, E. M. 1948. *The location of economic activity.* New York: McGraw-Hill.

ISARD, W. 1956a. *Location and space-economy.* New York: Wiley.

———. 1956b. Regional science, the concept of region, and regional structure. *Papers and Proceedings of the Regional Science Association,* 2: 13–39.

———. 1960. *Methods of regional analysis: an introduction to regional science.* New York: Wiley.

JACKSON, W. A. D. (Ed.). 1964. *Politics and geographic relationships: readings on the nature of political geography.* Englewood Cliffs, N.J.: Prentice-Hall.

JAMES, P. E., and C. F. JONES (Eds.). 1954. *American geography: inventory and prospect.* Syracuse: Syracuse University Press.

JONES, S. B. 1954. A unified field theory of political geography. *Annals of the Association of American Geographers,* 44: 111–23.

KASPERSON, R. E. 1965. Toward a geography of urban politics: Chicago, a case study. *Economic Geography,* 41: 95–107.

KATES, R. W. 1962. *Hazard and choice perception in flood plain management.* Chicago: University of Chicago, Department of Geography Research Paper No. 78.

————, and J. F. WOHLWILL (Eds.). 1966. Man's response to the physical environment. *Journal of Social Issues,* 22: 1–136.

KIRK, W. 1963. Problems of geography. *Geography,* 48: 357–71.

KROEBER, A. L. 1939. *Cultural and natural areas of native North America.* University of California Publications in American Archaeology and Ethnology, No. 38.

LEACH, E. R. 1954. *Political systems of highland Burma.* Cambridge: Harvard University Press.

LEWIS, P. F. 1965. Impact of Negro migration on the electoral geography of Flint, Michigan, 1932–62. *Annals of the Association of American Geographers,* 55: 1–25.

LEWTHWAITE, G. R. 1966. Environmentalism and determinism: a search for clarification. *Annals of the Association of American Geographers,* 56: 1–23.

LÖSCH, A. 1939. *Die räumliche Ordnung der Wirtschaft.* Jena: Fischer. (Trans. by W. H. Woglom and W. F. Stolper as *The economics of location.* New Haven, Conn.: Yale University Press, 1954.)

LOWENTHAL, D. 1961. Geography, experience, and imagination: towards a geographic epistemology. *Annals of the Association of American Geographers,* 51: 241–60.

———— (Ed.). 1967. *Environmental perception and behavior.* Chicago: University of Chicago, Department of Geography Research Paper No. 109.

————, and H. C. PRINCE. 1964. The English landscape. *Geographical Review,* 54: 309–46.

————, and H. C. PRINCE. 1965. English landscape tastes. *Geographical Review,* 55: 186–222.

MACKINDER, H. J. 1904. The geographical pivot of history. *Geographical Journal,* 23: 421–44.

MCCARTY, H. H., and J. B. LINDBERG. 1966. *A preface to economic geography.* Englewood Cliffs, N.J.: Prentice-Hall.

MCMANIS, D. R. 1964. *The initial evaluation and utilization of the Illinois prairies, 1815–1840.* Chicago: University of Chicago, Department of Geography Research Paper No. 94.

MEGGERS, B. J. 1954. Environmental limitations on the development of culture. *American Anthropologist,* 56: 801–24.

————. 1957. Environment and culture in the Amazon Basin: an appraisal of the theory of environmental determinism. In *Studies in human ecology,* Social Science Monographs, 3. Washington, D.C.: Pan American Union.

MERRENS, H. R. 1965. Historical geography and early American history. *William and Mary Quarterly,* 22: 529–48.

MERTON, R. K. 1963. The mosaic of the behavioral sciences. In B. Berelson (Ed.), *The behavioral sciences today*. New York: Basic Books.

MIKESELL, M. W. 1960. Comparative studies in frontier history. *Annals of the Association of American Geographers*, 50: 62–74.

———. 1967. Geographic perspectives in anthropology. *Annals of the Association of American Geographers*, 57: 617–34.

MINSHULL, R. 1967. *Regional geography: theory and practice*. Chicago: Aldine Publishing Company.

PARSONS, J. J. 1964. The contribution of geography to Latin American studies. In C. Wagley (Ed.), *Social science research on Latin America*. New York: Columbia University Press.

PATTISON, W. D. 1964. The four traditions of geography. *Journal of Geography*, 63: 211–16.

PLATT, R. S. 1948. Environmentalism versus geography. *American Journal of Sociology*, 43: 351–58.

———. 1962. The rise of cultural geography in America. In P. L. Wagner and M. W. Mikesell (Eds.), *Readings in cultural geography*. Chicago: University of Chicago Press.

PRED, A. 1966. *The spatial dynamics of U. S. urban-industrial growth*. Cambridge: MIT Press.

PRESCOTT, J. R. V. 1959. The function and methods of electoral geography. *Annals of the Association of American Geographers*, 49: 296–304.

RATZEL, F. 1897. *Politische Geographie*. Munich and Leipzig: Oldenbourg.

ROSTLUND, E. 1962. Twentieth century magic. In P. L. Wagner and M. W. Mikesell (Eds.), *Readings in cultural geography*. Chicago: University of Chicago Press.

SAARINEN, T. F. 1966. *Perception of the drought hazard on the Great Plains*. Chicago: University of Chicago, Department of Geography Research Paper No. 106.

SAUER, C. O. 1925.*The morphology of landscape*. University of California Publications in Geography, 2: 19–53.

———. 1927. Recent developments in cultural geography. In E. C. Hayes (Ed.), *Recent developments in the social sciences*. Philadelphia: Lippincott.

———. 1941. Foreword to Historical Geography. *Annals of the Association of American Geographers*, 31: 1–24.

———. 1963. *Land and life: selections from the writings of Carl Ortwin Sauer*. Ed. by J. Leighly. Berkeley and Los Angeles: University of California Press.

SCHNORE, L. F. 1961. Geography and human ecology. *Economic Geography*, 37: 207–17.

SEMPLE, E. C. 1903. *American history and its geographic conditions*. Boston: Houghton, Mifflin.

———. 1931. *The geography of the Mediterranean region: its relation to ancient history*. New York: Holt.

SMITH, R. H. T., E. J. TAAFFE, and L. J. KING (Eds.). 1968. *Readings in economic geography: the location of economic activity*. Chicago: Rand McNally.

SONNENFELD, J. 1967. Environment perception and adaption level in the Arctic. In D. Lowenthal (Ed.), *Environmental perception and behavior*. Chicago:

University of Chicago, Department of Geography Research Paper No. 109.

SOROKIN, P. 1928. *Contemporary sociology theories.* New York: Harper and Row.

SORRE, M. 1954. *La géographie psychologique: L'Adaptation au milieu climatique et biosocial.* Paris: Presses Universitaires de France.

———. 1957. *Rencontres de la géographie et de la sociologie.* Paris: Rivière.

———. 1962. The role of historical explanation in human geography. In P. L. Wagner and M. W. Mikesell (Eds.), *Readings in cultural geography.* Chicago: University of Chicago Press.

SPENCER, J. E. 1966. *Shifting cultivation in Southeastern Asia.* University of California Publications in Geography, 19.

SPROUT, H., and M. SPROUT. 1965. *The ecological perspective on human affairs, with special reference to international politics.* Princeton, N.J.: Princeton University Press.

SPYKMAN, N. J. 1942. *America's strategy in world politics: the United States and the balance of power.* New York: Harcourt, Brace.

STEWARD, J. H. 1955. *Theory of culture change.* Urbana: University of Illinois Press.

TATHAM, G. 1951. Environmentalism and possibilism. In G. Taylor (Ed.), *Geography in the twentieth century.* New York: Philosophical Library.

THEODORSON, G. A. (Ed.). 1961. *Studies in human ecology.* Evanston, Ill.: Row, Peterson.

THOMAS, B. E. 1965. Geography. In R. A. Lystad (Ed.), *The African world: a survey of social research.* New York: Praeger.

THOMAS, F. 1925. *The environmental basis of society.* New York: Century.

THOMAS, W. L., JR. (Ed.). 1956. *Man's role in changing the face of the earth.* Chicago: University of Chicago Press.

THROWER, N. J. W. 1966. *Original survey and land subdivision.* Chicago: Rand McNally.

THÜNEN, J. H. VON. 1826. *Der isolierte Staat in Beziehung auf Landwirtschaft und Nationalökonomie.* Rostock: Leopold. (Trans. by C. M. Wartenberg and P. Hall as *Von Thünen's Isolated State.* London: Pergamon Press, 1966.)

TREWARTHA, G. T. 1953. The case for population geography. *Annals of the Association of American Geographers,* 43: 71–97.

TUAN, YI-FU. 1967. Attitudes toward environment: themes and approaches. In D. Lowenthal (Ed.), *Environmental perception and behavior.* Chicago: University of Chicago, Department of Geography Research Paper No. 109.

ULLMAN, E. 1941. A theory of location for cities. *American Journal of Sociology,* 46: 835–64.

VIDAL DE LA BLACHE, P. 1911. *Tableau de la géographie de la France.* Vol. 1, part 1, of E. Lavisse (Ed.), *Histoire de France Illustrée.* Paris: Hachette.

WAGNER, P. L. 1960. *The human use of the earth.* Glencoe, Ill.: Free Press.

———, and M. W. MIKESELL (Eds.). 1962. *Readings in cultural geography.* Chicago: University of Chicago Press.

WEBER, A. 1909. *Über den Standort der Industrien.* Tübingen. (Trans. by C. J. Friedrich as *Alfred Weber's theory of the location of industries.* Chicago: University of Chicago Press, 1929.)

WEISS, R. 1962. Cultural boundaries and ethnographic maps. In P. L. Wagner and

M. W. Mikesell (Eds.), *Readings in cultural geography*. Chicago: University of Chicago Press.

WHITTLESEY, D. 1929. Sequent occupance. *Annals of the Association of American Geographers*, 19: 162–65.

————. 1949. *Environmental foundations of European history*. New York: Appleton-Century-Crofts.

WISSLER, C. 1926. *The relation of nature to man in aboriginal North America*. New York: Oxford University Press.

WOOD, W. D., and R. S. THOMAN (Eds.). 1965. *Areas of economic stress in Canada*. Kingston: Industrial Relations Centre, Queen's University.

ZELINSKY, W. 1962. *A bibliographic guide to population geography*. Chicago: University of Chicago, Department of Geography Research Paper No. 80.

————. 1966. *A prologue to population geography*. Englewood Cliffs, N.J.: Prentice-Hall.

13

HUMAN GEOGRAPHY AND NEIGHBORING DISCIPLINES

RAYMOND E. CRIST

Geographic awareness of the relations between man and the land or water bodies from which he makes his living is and will always be greater than the sum of the efforts of those who labor within the walls of Geography. The art of seeing how land and life have come to differ from one part of the earth to another has interested man since the dawn of history. Man may well be the only animal who is aware that he will die, although fortunately he is never aware of when or whence the poisoned dart will strike; he is also an animal who is interested in appraisal of the resources of the earth, including himself and his capacities, as he spreads over the regions of the earth and uses them in accordance with the techniques evolved in whatever historical period or phase he finds himself.

The right of a body of knowledge to separate existence, with a name of its own, depends on the cultivation, by those who work with it, of that part of the field which is not overlapped by others. As each worker becomes familiar with the central core of his field, he may and often does, find himself working more and more in the border areas.

MALARIA CONTROL AND GEOGRAPHY

It is impossible to bypass the essential stages of painstaking work in the core area of the field so that observed physical and human phenomena can be carefully recorded in words or on maps—and it should be pointed out that many developing nations have no maps at all or very inadequate ones—as necessary steps in the analysis and subsequent synthesis required to make up a body of geographic literature.

The geographer needs aids and tools and cooperation from many sources, as will be indicated by the following discussion.

AFRICA

Professor R. Mansell Prothero (1965), points out the lack of geographic reconnaissance in health work in Africa, where international boundaries frequently divide tribal groups; however, when people of the same group live on either side of a boundary there will inevitably be considerable movement backwards and forwards across it. Hence official and unofficial attitudes to boundaries at the present day are important. When present national boundaries delimited colonial territories, they were regarded by Africans as the unwanted creations of the European powers. The anomalies and inconsistencies associated with them were continually, and quite rightly, criticized. Now that the majority of the colonial territories are independent states with the same boundaries which were formerly criticized, the governments of these states have shown great reluctance to consider any changes in them. Where there are major boundary problems, as for example between Ethiopia and Somalia, Ghana and Togo, Algeria and Morocco, the prospects of revision seem very slight. Inevitably these problems engender poor relations between the countries concerned and thus reduce the likelihood of achieving effective cooperation in malaria eradication and in other fields of development.

In 1960 a public health mission reviewed at some length the factors which had been responsible for malaria eradication projects failing to achieve the success that had been hoped for. Under the heading of *technical failures,* the lack of appreciation of the importance of human habits and socioeconomic conditions were listed, with population mobility as the factor that was most frequently the cause of failure. *Operational failures* included "deficient geographical reconnaissance" which resulted in "deficient coverage in spraying operations," and "difficulties in communications" due to faulty or inadequate information on transport and its problems in project areas.

Geographical reconnaissance has progressively come to be regarded as an essential element in malaria eradication. Some of the data required are readily available for areas where eradication is being planned, but for the most part this is uncommon. The major malarious areas of the world are deficient in most kinds of data, or else these are so superficial as to be useless. It is essential to ensure that all available information is brought together and checked. Those responsible for geographical reconnaissance in malaria eradication should be in close contact with the various technical services in the countries in which they are working, in the likely event that they may be able to supply some of the information required on such things as agriculture, irrigation, water supply, trade, and communications.

THE GUAJIRA PENINSULA

A decade ago I was engaged in a reconnaissance study of the Guarjira Peninsula north of Maracaibo, which is inhabited by the largely unaccultured Guajiro Indians; it is dissected unequally by a modern political boundary line, Venezuela having the smaller portion. The Guajiro Indians have lived a semi-nomadic existence on their wind-swept, desertic peninsula for centuries, long before any such thing as a modern nation state had come into being. Both Venezuela and Colombia are now interested in eradicating diseases such as malaria, for which a mosquito is the vector, and Chagas disease, for which the vector is the *pito,* an out-size bedbug that is very much at home in the thatch roofs or adobe walls of those having semi-permanent dwellings, and is even carried in clothing and blankets.

It is very important to have an accurate census of people on both sides of this frontier, and to know those who migrate back and forth across it. But how is this to be done? Few Guajiros speak Spanish; they still live according to tribal laws, and think of themselves as Guajiros and not as Venezuelans or Colombians. The first step attempted by the central governments was to issue identity cards, on which a picture of the carrier was to be pasted. The reply of the Guajiros to the card-issuing mission was that they did not need to have identity cards, as everybody knew everybody else anyhow, and, as for paying the small fee to have their pictures taken, *they* were used to being paid to have their pictures taken! So the plan to provide everyone with an identity card was given up. The sanitation teams decided to spray as effectively as possible all houses, temporary camps, clothing and blankets, and the like. In general, however, public health missions everywhere are apt to have no member who is specifically concerned with geographical reconnaissance and is adequately trained for it. Thus, for example, while the medical aspects of malaria are investigated by a fully trained and experienced malariologist, and the mosquito vectors are studied by a specialist entomologist, no specialist is assigned to the collection, analysis and evaluation of data on vital geographical, and particularly human, factors.

The need for geographical reconnaissance has been generally recognized, but the means for undertaking it are inadequate, and until these are provided, geographical factors will not receive the attention that they require. If persons were appointed specifically to undertake the tasks of geographical reconnaissance, they would work in the closest association with malariologists and entomologists to produce fully integrated assessments of the complex relationships between the three elements which produce malaria—parasites, mosquitoes, and men. At the present time inadequate consideration is being given to *men* and to the *environments* in which they live.

MAN'S ROLE AS VIEWED BY TWO GEOGRAPHERS

In 1955 an International Symposium on "Man's Role in Changing the Face of the Earth" was held in Princeton, New Jersey. The subject of the Symposium was the idea of the geographer, Dr. William L. Thomas, Jr., at that time Assistant Director of the Wenner-Gren Foundation; he also acted as organizer of the symposium and edited the volume of papers that were given there. Of the seventy participants from all over the world sixteen were geographers.

The keynote paper in the monumental volume on *Man's Role in Changing the Face of the Earth,* entitled "The Agency of Man on the Earth," was given by the dean of American geographers, Professor Carl Ortwin Sauer. His two concluding paragraphs deserve the attention of us all:

The road we are laying out for the world is paved with good intentions, but do we know where it leads? On the material side we are hastening the depletion of resources. Our programs of agricultural aid pay little attention to native ways and products. Instead of going out to learn what their experiences and preferences are, we go forth to introduce our ways and consider backward what is not according to our pattern. Spade and hoe and mixed plantings are an affront to our faith in progress. We promote mechanization. At the least, we hold, others should be taught to use steel plows that turn neat furrows, though we have no idea how long the soil will stay on well-plowed slopes planted to annuals. We want more fields of maize, rice, beans of kinds familiar to us, products amenable to statistical determination and available for commercial distribution. To increase production, we prescribe dressing with commercial fertilizers. In unnoticed contrast to our own experience these are to be applied in large measure to lands of low productivity and perhaps of low effectiveness of fertilizers. Industrialization is recommended to take care of the surplus populations. We present and recommend to the world a blueprint of what works well with us at the moment, heedless that we may be destroying wise and durable native systems of living with the land. The modern industrial mood (I hesitate to add intellectual mood) is insensitive to other ways and values.

For the present, living beyond one's means has become civic virtue, increase of "output" the goal of society. The prophets of a new world by material progress may be stopped by economic limits of physical matter. They may fail because people grow tired of getting and spending as measure and mode of living. They may be checked because men come to fear the requisite growing power of government over the individual and the community. The high moments of history have come not when man was most concerned with the comforts and displays of the flesh but when his spirit was moved to grow in grace. What we need more perhaps is an ethic and aesthetic under which man, practicing the qualities of prudence and moderation, may indeed pass on to posterity a good Earth (1956, p. 68).

Professor Pierre Gourou, the outstanding French geographer, author of *Les Pays Tropicaux* (translated as *The Tropical World,* 1965), gave a brilliant paper on the evaluation of land use practices of tropical cultivators (pp. 336–49.) He also rewards his readers with some profound reflections on the influence of civilization on landscape:

Density of population is a good basis for the study of human geography. A detailed map of the density of the population asks many questions: Why so few inhabitants here? Why so many there? Answers may be given by climate, physiography, soils, diseases, history, or techniques (of production and of spatial organization). Each particular question may be the field of specialists. But the weight of a population over a particular area is not explained by the juxtaposition of specialized studies; it must be explained by geographical appreciation of the interdependence of multiple factors.

Civilization is not a product of the physical environment, nor is it a product of a choice oriented by a finality. If a human group selected a certain type of exploitation of some resources, the choice was undetermined. Man has made himself, without knowing where he was willing to go. He has made himself by the making of himself. There was no physical determination, finalistic predestination, or conscious decision; there was a necessity for an undetermined choice and, consequently, a departure into a future. This geographical interpretation of the position of man on earth and in history is full of hope. The future, good or bad, will be in the work of man and not the result of physical constraints (1965, p. 346).

AGRICULTURAL ORIGINS AND DISPERSALS: COOPERATIVE INVESTIGATIONS

One of the problems that has been under investigation by geographers for decades has been that of agricultural origins and dispersals, in the process of which the geographer has had to call on the expertise of many disciplines (Sauer, 1952). One botanist gathers together the available data on the uses, native habitats, wild ancestors, chromosome numbers, and history of cultivation of scores of cultivated plants (Zukovskij, 1962). Another discusses the processes of plant domestication and the problem of how agriculture originated—that is, the processes by which domesticated plants arise through cultivation, irrigation, and modern plant breeding (Darlington, 1963).

For evidence as to time and place of agricultural origins, we are indebted principally to archeologists and paleobotanists. Geographers and anthropologists are at work on the interpretation of the archeological evidence, trying to throw light on the questions of where and when agriculture originated.

THE LAKE IZABAL PROJECT

One of the best examples of interdisciplinary cooperation and crossfertilization in a specific area is to be found in the Tropical Development Project, directed by Dr. Hugh Popenoe, in the Lake Izabal Basin in Guatemala. Research is focused on man and his environment with an eye to learning how the high biological productivity of the tropical environment might be better utilized.

Headquarters for the project are located at Murcielago on Lake Izabal on the Caribbean Coast of Guatemala. Five thousand acres of land have been lent by Mr. Christopher Hempstead for research purposes. An airstrip has recently been completed on the land as well as housing facilities. Since Lake

Izabal is approximately 30 miles long and 15 miles wide and is connected to the ocean by a navigable river, a large area in the lake basin is accessible by boat for investigations in a humid tropical environment.

The works of archeologists, anthropologists, historians, political scientists, medical doctors, nutritionists, soils scientists, biologists, climatologists, ecologists, botanists, and entomologists (the list is not intended to be complete)—all are relevant to the geographer's task of *regional* analyses and interpretation.[1]

Studies are in progress on the processes of acculturation and the search for national identification on the part of the Indians living on the north shore of Lake Izabal.

Malaria is widespread in this area and may have been a major factor in discouraging resettlement and development. Public health measures would reduce the incidence of malaria and might be one of the factors that would bring about a marked increase in population, of children born in the area as well as those who immigrate. A study of the various developmental or settlement projects that have been attempted at Lake Izabal may reveal common denominators, both cultural and environmental, of the large number of failures. From archeological evidence it is known that this area once supported a much denser population than it does now. The historian might be able to throw some light on the *why* of this situation.

Climate, soils, and vegetation—all are being intensively investigated. A better understanding of general meteorological patterns and the energy relationships in ecosystems should be helpful in organizing improved ecological models for tropical land management.

It must not be assumed that dramatic environmental change is proof of a change of climate. Recent investigations all over the world suggest that far more weight than has been given in the past should be given to ecologic factors, to the disturbances brought about by forest clearance, by rapid run-off and erosion, by leaching of the exposed soil, by exposure to winds, and so on. The ecological approach should consider the interrelations of cultures and environments, allowing for the inheritance of traditions from earlier phases of adjustment.

PALYNOLOGY

Pollen analyses of six sediment cores from the bottom of Lake Izabal indicate that corn agriculture probably reached a peak about A.D. 200. It declined gradually until about A.D. 800, at which time it disappeared almost completely. Pine pollen, on the other hand, began increasing about A.D. 400 and reached a maximum around A.D. 800. The trend from then until the present is a gradual replacement of the pine forest with hardwoods (Tropical Rain Forest), the most common vegetation type today. Elsewhere in the

1. Much of the material that follows has appeared in unpublished reports of Dr. Popenoe, at present Director of the Center for Tropical Agriculture, University of Florida.

world, pine forests have been considered an early successional stage, but this possibility had been overlooked for the Maya area. Pine forest succession would indicate that the Maya shifting cultivation was much more intensive 1,000 years ago than it is today. Under the present system, abundant coppicing takes place from the roots of the felled forest trees to begin a new succession. Only a very intensive rotation of shifting cultivation or permanent agriculture would completely eliminate the hardwood forest trees and pave the way for invasion by pine.

Sediments from Lake Izabal that are 3,000 years old contain a few corn pollen and numerous carbonized leaf fragments, perhaps blown from agricultural clearings. Although agriculture has been prevalent around Lake Izabal for several thousand years, the actual time of its introduction has not yet been ascertained. One lake core which was collected should yield a record of the past 6,000 years when analyzed.

ARCHEOLOGY

Archeologists have mapped out house mound sites to determine density and duration of prehistoric human occupation around Lake Izabal. The prehistoric distribution of population and land-use patterns will eventually be correlated with the present-day picture. The archeological record indicates that the lake area was never heavily populated, though it was occupied throughout the Formative and Classical periods. So far, no large ceremonial structures have been found such as those farther north in the Peten, or farther south at Quirigua and Copan.

NUTRITION

A nutritionist spent two months at the Nutritional Institute of Central America and Panama compiling data collected by that organization in their nutritional surveys, and relating the data to environmental parameters. In addition, a third month was spent in detailed study of three villages in different bioclimatic zones.

The investigations so far indicate that cultural limitations are more important than environmental limitations in areas of malnutrition. Symptoms of malnutrition are principally found in populations that have moved from the highlands to the lowlands. The immigrants have tried to maintain traditional eating habits and traditional sources of food supply in a new environment. However, these foods may not be present in adequate amounts. Many new types of plant products are available but are not sufficiently utilized, since eating habits are difficult to change. Thus, stresses in diet are mainly caused by cultural resistance to change.

SOILS AND VEGETATION

Soil analyses are shedding light on the relationship of productivity and chemical composition of young second growth on different soil types. This work is designed to indicate the effect of soil nutrient content on regeneration of second growth after shifting cultivation. In addition, the efficiency of native vegetation will be compared with crop plants in the extraction of nutrients, which are in short supply, from the soil. The research may lead to a method of analyzing native vegetation rather than soils in new regions to evaluate soil fertility. The relation between soils and vegetation in the rehabilitation of shifting cultivation lands will also be better understood.

BIOLOGY

One problem in tropical biological work is the large number of species present. The interaction and competition between species to develop niches are little understood. Systematic trapping was undertaken of rodent populations in agricultural land and in secondary successions. As might be surmised, the rodent population builds up very rapidly in newly cleared land. Usually, the numbers decline drastically after the first weeding and as predators move into the area. The number of rodents which were trapped decreased as the rainy season progressed. Rodents were almost nonexistent in forested areas.

NITROGEN FIXATION

Problems of protein deficiency are quite common in areas of the low humid tropics. Many people suffer from *Kwashiorkor,* a protein-deficiency disease, but often this is caused by cultural problems, as previously mentioned, or by an imbalance in the uptake of various amino acids. However, in crop and pasture production, nitrogen deficiencies are quite severe, since nitrogen leaches rapidly under conditions of high temperature and rainfall. The use of legumes in tropical agriculture has an obvious place, but very few experiments have yielded positive results.

LAND MANAGEMENT

Investigations have been under way at Lake Izabal for three years on the evaluation of current land management practices and trials of new modifications. The investigations have been separated into two categories: (1) traditional practices requiring large labor and low capital inputs, and (2) intensive practices which require low inputs of labor but large industrial inputs.

Investigations of traditional agricultural systems have tested practices such as burning, weeding, and the use of fertilizer, crop rotation, legumes and pest control. Yields of fields farmed by shifting cultivation methods have been used for comparison. Soils in shifting cultivation lands have been sampled periodically to determine fluctuations in soil properties in relation to seasonal and agricultural effects.

Pests, so far, have been the main limiting factor and, even though weeds have been controlled and soil fertility maintained, yields inevitably decline on continuously farmed plots. Cultivation of the soil by hoe or plow helps to reduce crop losses. The pest problem is made doubly difficult because of the great number of different varieties; hence, chemical controls are extremely difficult. Usable management systems will probably involve tree crops or crop rotations which produce less modification of the local environment.

Plots that have been continuously exposed to burning are covered almost completely by grass. Unburned plots are covered about 75 per cent by legumes which have come in as volunteers. These native legumes could be quite useful in long-term rotations.

Investigations of mechanized agriculture are still under way. Forest land is being cleared by a Caterpillar tractor; clearing costs compare favorably with clearing by hand, even in this area where laborers receive 75 cents a day! Over one thousand acres have been cleared. Much is now planted with corn—the local staple crop—and with oil palm. A few experiments have been initiated with pangola grass pasture. After an area has been cleared for pasture by tractor, the annual clearing costs by machinery are much cheaper than they would be otherwise by hand.

So far, crop yields have been much higher on machine-cleared areas, but the subtle changes that may be taking place in the environment can be measured only by long-term studies.

CONCLUSIONS

I have referred to the great number of disciplines that have been enlisted to investigate the diverse physical and cultural facets of this geographic region to make it clear that, in order to understand a modern cultural landscape, the reconstruction of former cultural landscapes is indicated. This requires intimate familiarity with the terrain, and perception of the highly complex relations of human life to the web of plant and animal life sustaining it.

Again, a quotation from Professor Sauer is pertinent:

Knowledge of human processes is attainable only if the current situation is comprehended as a moving point, one moment in an action that has beginning and end. This does not constitute commitment as to the form of the line, as to whether it has cyclic qualities or shows no regularity; but it does guard against overemphasizing the importance of the current situation. The only certain advantage of studying the present scene is that it is most fully accessible to inspection. Yet out of the contemporary data in themselves it is not possible to find the means of selecting what is diagnostic of important processes and what is not. I am inclined to say that geographically the two most important events of my lifetime have been the settlement of the last of the prairie lands and the coming of the Model T Ford: one an end, the other a beginning of a series of cultural processes. Yet how well did we, whose business it was to do so, pick out these, critical processes at the time of their happening, or link them with the changes derived from them? And why did we miss them, if not because we were unaccustomed to thinking in terms of processes?

The reconstruction of past cultures is a slow task of detective work, as to the collecting of evidence and weaving it together. The narrative historian may accept anything out of the past as grist at his mill, but not so the culture historian; and I wish to reckon historical geography as a part of culture history. Our obligation is to glean classified data on economy and habitation so that a valid filling of gaps of area and of time can be made (1963, p. 361).

A PERSONAL NOTE

A number of years ago I was struck by the fact that the two great natural grasslands of South America, the Llanos of Venezuela and the Pampas of Argentina, had each produced a great political leader, or *caudillo*, Paez and Rosas. Both had ridden to national leadership from the great plains, at the head of a kind of half-disciplined rabble on horseback. Both held supreme power for a score of years or so. Since much had been written about Rosas, but almost nothing about Paez, I decided to write a paper about the latter, and presented it at a meeting of geographers. The only adverse criticism it received was to the effect that it was a subject in the field of political science, not geography. My reply was that since no political scientist had worked in the area or in the subject, or seemed about to, I had moved in to the vacuum, as it were. The article was published shortly afterward in the *Revista Geográfica Americana* of Buenos Aires. Now, to show you how my past caught up with me, 28 years later, Professor Hugh M. Hammill, Jr., was editing a volume on *Dictatorship in Spanish America* (New York, 1965) and wrote to ask me if I would give Knopf and Company permission to include my article, "Geography and Caudillismo: A Case Study." I was of course very happy to learn that after all those years people were still interested in the paper, and I gladly gave my consent to its inclusion in that book.

I vividly recalled words of Professor Sauer:

Particularly depressing has been the tendency to question, not the competence, originality, or significance of research that has been offered to us, but the admissibility of work because it may or may not satisfy a narrow definition of geography. *When a subject is ruled, not by inquisitiveness but by the definitions of its boundaries, it is likely to face extinction.* This way lies the death of learning. Such has been the lingering sickness of American academic geography that pedantry, which is logic combined with lack of curiosity, has tried to read out of the party workers who have not conformed to prevalent definitions. A healthy science is engaged in discovery, verification, comparison, and generalizations. Its subject matter will be determined by its competence in organization. Only if we reach that day when we shall gather to sit far into the night, comparing our findings and discussing all their meanings, shall we have recovered from the pernicious anemia of the "but-is-this-geography?" state (1963, pp. 354–55; italics added).

EPILOGUE

FIELD WORK, THE SINE QUA NON

It is in the field that the teacher—no matter what his age—as well as the student learn and exercise techniques of observation. It is in the field where they tread new paths together, and where they may take off in strange new directions, to come up with what might be unorthodox, but highly fruitful and productive, ideas. I have found it extremely valuable, both to the teacher and to the student, to accompany a doctoral candidate over his dissertation area—in Mexico, in Costa Rica, in Guatemala, along the Amazon, and so on. One of the most important desiderata is, in my opinion, to make it possible for students in geography, anthropology, ecology, history, political science, and sociology to carry out field investigations, accompanied for as long as possible by their professors. I feel that field work is basic. In Quaker phraseology: "I have a concern," and I am ever hopeful that, having the concern, "a way will be opened." And it is my fervent hope that the door to continued fruitful endeavor and crossfertilization (interdepartmental as well as international) will be made possible by foundations and government agencies in the form of field grants.

In his presidential address before the Association of American Geographers almost fifty years ago, Professor Fenneman made many observations that are pertinent today:

If we are concerned for our independent existence no amount of fortifying our border will take the place of developing our domain. What we need is more and better studies of regions in their entirety, their compositeness, their complexity, their inter-relations of physical, economic, racial, historic, and other factors. No other science can swallow that and live.

Animals have more than one way of evading the jaws of their competitors. The turtle is encased and puts up a good defense but is weak on the offensive. It is the same with the oyster. Others, like the squash bug, owe their safety to a peculiar flavor or odor. Still others specialize in modes of escape. But all such special provision belongs to the weak rather than to the strong. If geography will cultivate its own strength like the large mammals, it will not be necessary for it to encase itself like the oyster or cultivate the peculiar flavor of the squash bug to avoid being eaten.

Insofar as there are frontiers between the sciences, let us have them ungarrisoned and let us have free trade. Let there be among sciences the same struggle for existence and law of survival that Darwin found among species. Then every field of study that answers to an intellectual need will have due recognition (1919, pp. 173–74).

Speaking from my own experience, I can say that the single most important influence in making possible the carrying out of my own basic research was the continuing grant of the John Simon Guggenheim Memorial Foundation that has for almost three decades made possible my investigations in the field and in libraries, of human migration from the high, bleak, densely populated Andes into the hot country to the east, and, in Ecuador, to the west. This has enabled me to work and to write on diverse aspects of human incumbency in the Andes and tropical lowlands, running the gamut from the influence of tropical soils and climate on human ecology—and vice versa—to the aspects of geography in Latin American novels.

Herodotus believed that "everything could happen in the length of time" (Bowra, 1957, p. 191). He realized that the Greeks of the fifth century before Christ were increasingly capable of shaping nature to suit their own ends. The studies of geographers over the centuries have shown a profound belief in the special worth of all men, individually as well as collectively, from the isolated dweller of the tropical forest to the throngs living in urban agglomerations. Whether he practices fire agriculture or makes jet planes, whether he dots the landscape with bouquets of skyscrapers, or of cathedrals, or pockmarks it with the craters of hydrogen bombs, man is ever worthy of awe and wonder, an unprecedented creature; and his numbers are increasing at an appalling pace. May our field studies of the diverse relations of man to land and of man to man, and the sage conclusions to be drawn from them, be helpful in orienting his activities toward the end of living in peace for 'the length of time'; if this goal can be achieved we will be able to sing again with the chorus of Sophocles: There are many strange wonders, but nothing more wonderful than man (Bowra, 1957, p. 211).

REFERENCES

Bowra, C. M. 1957. *The Greek experience*. New York: World.

Darlington, C. D. 1963. *Chromosome botany and the origins of cultivated plants*. (2d ed.) New York and London: Hafner.

Fenneman, N. M. 1919. The circumference of geography. *Geographical Review*, March: 168–75.

Gourou, P. 1965. In W. L. Thomas, Jr. (Ed.), *Man's role in changing the face of the earth*. Chicago: University of Chicago Press.

Hammill, H. M., Jr. (Ed.). 1965. *Dictatorship in South America*. New York: Knopf.

Harris, D. R. 1967. New light on plant domestication and the origins of agriculture: a review. *Geographical Review*, January: 90–107.

Prothero, R. M. 1965. *Migrants and malaria*. London: Longmans.

Sauer, C. O. 1952. Agricultural origins and dispersals. *American Geographical Society Bowman Memorial Lectures*, Series 2, New York.

———. 1963. *Land and life*. Berkeley and Los Angeles: University of California Press.

———. 1965. The agency of man on the earth. In W. L. Thomas, Jr. (Ed.), *Man's role in changing the face of the earth*. Chicago: University of Chicago Press.

Thomas, W. L., Jr. (Ed.). 1965. *Man's role in changing the face of the earth*. Chicago: University of Chicago Press.

Zukovskij, P. M. 1962. *Cultivated plants and their wild relatives*. Abridged translation by P. S. Hudson. Commonwealth Agricultural Bureaux, Farnham Royal, Bucks.

14

LINGUISTICS AND THE SOCIAL SCIENCES

Francis P. Dinneen

In an interdisciplinary meeting such as this I am sure we all have found it difficult to decide upon the best approach. A topic must be selected which will be intelligible and related to a number of the participating disciplines, yet not be presented in so technical a fashion as to obscure its importance. Striving for this leads to a certain amount of oversimplification and the danger of giving the impressions that one is speaking *for*, say, linguistics, rather than *about* linguistics. What follows here concerns a problem that should be of general interest in the social sciences, but it must be stressed that there are very many differences of opinion among linguists with respect to the topic.

The topic I should like to deal with concerns semantic primitives. This kind of study is recent in modern linguistics, although the problem is quite an ancient one. I would like to show what makes the modern study peculiarly linguistic and therefore distinguishes it from former studies as well as from the related problems in other social sciences.

LINGUISTIC ENTITIES

Modern linguistics is primarily concerned with the study of language structures. These structures consist of linguistic units of various sizes and the relations among them. The relations discussed are primarily intralinguistic and this fact is part of the difference between linguistics and other disciplines which are more concerned with the relations of language and its parts to extralinguistic factors. It is possible to conceive of a hierarchy of entities and relations which would enable us to pass in an orderly fashion from linguistics to the other social sciences, and in an attempt to formulate such a hierarchy, the points of contact among the various disciplines concerned, as well as the legitimate abstractions each field makes, can emerge.

The entities and relations linguists deal with are ultimately social in the sense that they are connected with aspects of communal human cognition

261

and behavior. Elements such as words and grammatical constructions are social in the sense that they are shared conventions members of a community use to interact. It is also reasonable to assume that some aspects of linguistic structures reflect common physical, biological, or psychological capacities of human beings. The concern of the majority of linguists, however, has been the study of linguistic forms themselves, and not the activities or capacities with which they are connected. This latter sort of study is often referred to in semiotics (Morris, 1964) and from a linguistic point of view semiotics might be said to inquire about what factors restrict the occurrence of linguistic forms, or what factors cause linguistic forms to be uttered. In examining a sentence like "The farmer killed the duckling," the linguist would be interested first in the restrictions involved in the selection of the various parts of the sentence and in their proper construction. He would not usually consider it directly pertinent to his field to inquire into the environmental, social, or psychological factors which cause or prevent the occurrence of the linguistic elements. There are scholars equally proficient in the fields of psychology and linguistics who have inaugurated studies of this type in the field of psycholinguistics (Osgood and Sebeok, 1965) as well as those combining sociology and linguistics in the field of sociolinguistics (Bright, 1967). Linguistics, like any science, must set up its own scope, criteria, purposes, and methods, in order to be distinct and autonomous. There is as yet no clear agreement among all workers recognized as "linguists" concerning the ideal circumscription of the scope, criteria, methods and purposes of their field. There are, of course, large areas of agreement.

When the task of linguistics is taken to be predominantly to describe languages, there are general agreements about scientific procedure. The method is to be based on a reasonable hypothesis and to be exact, public, and produce replicable results. The degree of empiricism to be demanded varies. When the goal of linguistics is understood to include explanation in addition to structural description, the role of intuition in locating the entities to be dealt with and the relationships to be described is more explicitly acknowledged (Chomsky, 1965; Lamb, 1966).

CONVENTIONAL SIMPLIFICATION

In order to make the study of language "scientific," a pioneer in the field, Ferdinand De Saussure (1916) called for a "conventional simplification of the data." In De Saussure's understanding, the linguist was to abstract from the undeniable fact that languages change and to study the abstract, stable, self-defining system of restrictions behind utterances. This system was termed *la langue* and opposed to actual utterances which fluctuate, *la parole*. The study which abstracted from change was called synchronic linguistics and was opposed to the historical investigation of changing language, called diachronic linguistics. There are further conventional simplifications in linguistics that have become more explicit with passing time. These are "conventional" in the sense that workers in the field with a common interest agree to restrict themselves to those aspects of linguistic behavior suited to their particular talent and ability to observe without claiming to give a total explanation for the production of language in general or of a particular utterance. Such a "simplification," of course, must be motivated by more than the investigator's lack of competence. One of its motives is to obtain clarity; another is that the investigator already knows by experience that it will prove fruitful. This is well explained by Hjelmslev (1961) in discussing the arbitrariness and appropriateness of theories.

There is another conventional simplification widely employed in linguistics which will make clearer the connection between semantic primitives as studied in linguistics and as studied in other disciplines. This is the distinction of language functions into at least three basic ones, the *cognitive*, the *affective*, and the *effective*. Other, more exhaustive, classifications can be made (Lenneberg, 1964; Miller, 1964). By the cognitive use of language—or perhaps better, the cognitive *aspect* of an utterance—is meant that use of language that is intended to communicate from speaker to hearer a maximally objective message, devoid of information about the speaker's emotional state, his desires about the reaction he expects from the hearer, environmental influences, etc. By the affective aspect of language is meant that use of language whose prime purpose is to make the listener aware of the subjective state of the speaker, without particular regard to the objective content of the message or the desired response of the listener. By the effective aspect of language is meant that language use which is intended to produce a particular reaction in the listener, in contrast to the objective message or the speaker's emotional state. Obviously, human beings do not use language in such distinct functions. In at least one of the situations, it is dubious that the possibility exists. That is the purely effective use of language. It would appear at least here that the actual basic nature of cognitive language is shown. Cognitive information is needed to specify the desired effect. For example, we might intend to produce fear in another, but if it is the case that a person must fear something, it would seem that he would have to understand what was being said to have the proper reaction, and if he heard such an utterance in a foreign language, he would doubtless assume some particular cognitive message to have been intended. Other animals demonstrate the ability to signal their affective and effective messages—but Lassie cannot give a description of the bank robbers even though she can show her excitement and the need of doing something about it.

Within linguistic structures, there are familiar constructions whose frequent function it is to implement one of these three aspects of language. The declarative sentence is often seen as exemplifying the cognitive function of language; the exclamatory types exemplify the affective use, and a good candidate for the effective use are imperatives. Since the most ancient times of linguistic analysis through the medieval and modern period, the declarative sentence, and therefore the cognitive use of language, has been taken, as a matter of fact and of descriptive convenience, as the basic fact of language. As a consequence, both in the acquisition of a foreign language or in the description of one's native language, an effort can be made to account first for the basic types of simple, active, declarative sentences, and then to account for the rest of the language in terms of comparison with, deviation from or transformation of, these basic structures. Such a sentence is of the form investigated by logicians and philosophers, and therefore has a long history of study behind it.

LINGUISTIC HIERARCHY

In either an analytic or a synthetic approach to language, linguists assume that there are important hierarchic entities and relations. In an analytic approach, one can start with a text, analyze it into its constituent parts such as paragraphs, analyze these into sentences, and then analyze the sentences progressively into their minimal constituents, the morphs or morphemes. These in turn can then be analyzed into their phonological constituents, although on different criteria, yielding syllables and phonemes, which in turn are analyzable into distinctive features. This is the basic outlook in Hjelmslev's work (1961) and although other linguists would object to some aspects of the approach it is a reasonable starting point for our discussion.

In a synthetic approach, one could start first with the establishment of the distinctive features or phonemes, describe the phonotactics and then pass to the morphological constructions, syntactic constructions, and so on, to the largest constructions. In both approaches, the cognitive function of language could be kept in the forefront, and the other functions along with their proper phonological signals introduced in a controlled fashion. When factors are added which are strictly extralinguistic, that is, not part of the signaling processes required by the particular language being described, we would be said to be passing from linguistics to one of the other social sciences.

While this sounds fairly simple, in actuality the procedure would be much more complex. It would only be with an artificially controlled text that one could proceed on cognitive data alone in the analytic approach, and it would only be after a complete analysis that one could start a valid synthesis on cognitive data which was later to be related, say through transformational rules, to the exponents of the other types. For the purpose of suggesting a relationship between linguistics and other social sciences, however, the difficulties inherent to the linguistic analysis are not crucial. No one actually works on a purely analytic or synthetic approach in any science, to my knowledge. However, the results of the analysis can be presented in either fashion.

The basis of the tentative connection that is seen here between linguistics and the social sciences lies in the fact that linguists are now seeking methods of isolating semantic primitives which underlie the successful use of the cognitive function of language and are attempting, through an objective examination of linguistic structures and relations, to account for the ambiguities that are found in normal utterances. Just as it has been suggested that there are a finite set of distinctive oppositions in the sound systems of all languages (e.g., Jakobson and Halle, 1956) it can be investigated whether there are a finite set of semantic features mastered by the native speaker of a language at a reasonably young age, in terms of which he will be able to understand and produce endlessly novel utterances for the rest of his adult life.

It does not appear that this assumption has been explicitly discussed in earlier linguistic work, although it does appear to underlie a certain part of ancient work stemming from such semantic primitives as Aristotle's Categories and in the attempts of lexicographers to arrive at a uniform defining procedure. It also seems to be implicit in the structural linguist's assumption that a finite description of the grammatical patterns of a language provides us with the framework in which the lexical entries are instances of more basic patterns. It is clearly suggested in Hjelmslev (1961) that, just as distinctive features or phonemes can be called figurae and are said to be non-sign constituents of signs, so too, he felt, there should be on the content plane of language content figurae which are also in some sense non-sign constituents of signs. He illustrated this by analyzing "ram" and "ewe" or "stallion" and "mare" into 'horse,' 'sheep,' 'he,' and 'she,' suggesting by the single quotes that the content figurae are not exactly on the same plane as the other familiar signs they are said to constitute. A parallel between expression and content figurae is that both are to constitute a finite, limited inventory which can account for a larger inventory. In the case of expression figurae, e.g. phonemes, the larger inventory may be finite; in the case of the content figurae, however, the larger inventory must be infinite or indefinitely expandable if it is to account for the possible lexicon of a language. There are other difficulties with this view as well. Whether we call them "content figurae," "semantic features" or "semantic primitives," it is difficult to study them scientifically unless there is some structure into which they can fit. The ideal ordering would be hierarchic. Compared to the linear ordering of speech, there is no obvious temporal priority in which a set of semantic features must be considered. Secondly, the semantic features or primitives in the literature so far have been identified through other expressions present in the language which have a more generic reference than the terms of which they are supposed to be constituents. But terms like 'she,' 'he,' or 'horse' simply coexist in normal language for the mature speaker without any provable need for one sign being more primitive than another. Thirdly, since that part of a language in which we discuss the rest of a language is still part of the same language, the concept of "metalanguage" versus "object language" presents peculiar difficulties for natural languages.

The hierarchic order suggested as holding among semantic primitives in the language is essentially paradigmatic, and the genus and species analysis of Hjelmslev may be ultimately an a priori logical order superimposed by the investigator. Other types of order may derive more from the ordering of other linguistic levels than from the inherent relationships among lexical semantic primitives. The polysemy that is perhaps more characteristic of lexical than of grammatical items makes an inherent order difficult to establish. As a consequence we find it difficult to discover criteria for clearly settling questions of semantic acceptability or semantic deviations. One source of our difficulties may be the method of using essentially binary choices, as seen in the work of Fodor and Katz (1963), Weinreich (1966) and Hjelmslev (1961). The open-ended and inventive nature of lexical combinations—particularly if environmental factors are to be taken into account —also argues against an inherent, fixed ordering.

On the other hand, there have been types of semantic ordering in older works which are useful though limited. In the fourteenth century there was extended discussion of semantic primitives in the works of the so-called Modistae, such as Thomas of Erfurt. This study concerned modes or manners of meaning, not positive lists of obligatory semantic features. It also dealt with the meanings of the main form-classes of the language in their normal use in declarative sentences. In addition, the meanings of the "grammatical accidents" such as person, number, gender, tense, case were discussed. Their discussion was confined largely to the level of parts of speech in terms of modes, not semantic components required for the lexical level.

It seems that the "discovery procedure" used to isolate the semantic primitives in part accounts for the order, or lack of it, that a particular approach unveils. A genus-species-individual series such as "thing-animate-human-male-adult-man- John" is obtained on an essentially paradigmatic plane. The criterion of order is "decreasing generality of reference" and the procedure is not unlike the method of substitution discussed by Bloomfield (1933) for establishing form classes, although his criterion is grammatical equivalence and does not require referential information. Ogden's (1932) choice of 1650 expressions to constitute Basic English is of the same type, as is Roget's selection of 1000 categories on which he bases his *Thesaurus* (1946). Holger Steen Sørensen (1958) found Hjelmslev's concept of content figurae unacceptable and proposed another method for discovering the semantically primitive signs of an object language: those signs are primitive which can no longer be defined through other signs of the same language, since all the others have already been employed in defining the rest. All of these approaches are essentially paradigmatic.

Fodor and Katz (1963) and Weinreich (1966) made decisive progress because they employ syntactic as well as paradigmatic information in order to resolve the ambiguity of pairs of sentences that appear to be identical.

They point out that the usual dictionary would list the following meanings
for the word "bachelor":

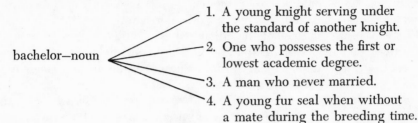

bachelor—noun

1. A young knight serving under
   the standard of another knight.
2. One who possesses the first or
   lowest academic degree.
3. A man who never married.
4. A young fur seal when without
   a mate during the breeding time.

In order to show the semantic features the various meanings have in common and those that distinguish the various meanings, they suggest a tree
diagram representation:

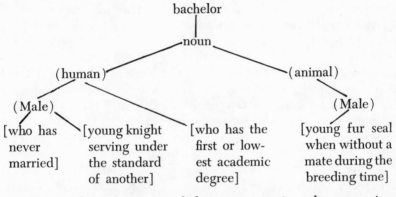

bachelor

noun

(human)   (animal)

(Male)   (Male)

[who has   [young knight   [who has the   [young fur seal
never   serving under   first or low-   when without a
married]   the standard   est academic   mate during the
                of another]   degree]   breeding time]

According to the conventions of this representation, the expressions in
parentheses, such as (animal) are semantic features of components common
to all the elements in the succeeding paths. The expressions in brackets such
as "[who has never married]" are to be semantic distinguishers, expressions
that appear only once in the dictionary and therefore assumed to be peculiar,
not common semantic features. In their discussion of this particular entry
Katz and Fodor then point out that further subdivisions, such as "young"
to distinguish the medieval bachelor and the seal, should be added to indicate further shared components. In his critique of Katz and Fodor's work,
Bolinger (1965) points out that the final entries in brackets, such as "[who
has never married]" are not, as the original proposal seemed to suggest,
unique semantic properties that might appear only once in the representation. Like other expressions, they are analyzable into further semantic features. In addition, inclusion of such extralinguistic features as "medieval
chivalry" seems required. Bolinger's conclusion is that semantic features
dealt with in this way may well be as indefinite in number as the expressions
they seek to clarify, so that the scientific control of such study seems uncer-

tain. Weinreich (1966) offered several ingenious suggestions to improve on the initial proposals of Katz and Fodor, and pointed out that there are still several sources of unpredictability we will have to cope with such as ellipsis, metaphor, and deliberate ambiguity. Although Lamb (1966) and Hockett (1966) make use of elements describable as semantic features or semantic primitives, they discuss no method by which the minimal, sufficient number of features can be discovered. It would appear that the method common to Katz and Fodor, Weinreich, Lamb, and Hockett is to take instances of sentences which are polysemous, such as, "We saw the bachelor today," and adduce as many semantic features as are needed to keep the intuitively or otherwise known possible meanings separate. This method does not seem to give promise of an orderly development in the search for the finite inventory of semantic primitives that can be provided by intralinguistic means to account for the cognitive meanings of the sentences producible in a language.

Although there are considerable disagreements among linguists of various methodological and theoretical persuasions, it hardly seems wise to tie the highly structured levels of analysis that have been evolved into a semantic component that is essentially unordered, since the whole could scarcely overcome the weakness of its final component. What is then to be done?

There is no obvious and convincing answer to the problem, but perhaps one more "conventional simplification" of the data might serve a useful purpose. On the assumption that we are unlikely to discover an internally motivated hierarchy among semantic primitives, an arbitrary, conventional, and, one would hope, appropriate source of control might be introduced which relies on the basic insights of all workers who have dealt with these problems. In this way it would be possible to specify the amount of information we could require linguistics to supply and indicate the point in the analysis where other social sciences would have to have their say. Weinreich's (1966) idea of a "semantic calculator" is of this type; Hjelmslev's (1961) concept of "degree of derivation," which is readily translatable into Chomsky's (1961) "degrees of grammaticalness" and Halliday's notion (1965) of "delicacy" have much in common.

Instead of starting from the lexical periphery of many sentences to collect the sufficient inventory of semantic primitives—a task which is surely beyond our powers at the present state of our knowledge—it seems more indicated that we should start from the core of the language and work out. According to this conventional simplification, one would take the simple, active, declarative sentences, and then attempt to assign the "meanings" first of the obligatory aspects of the language: the required syntactic functions, the meanings of the grammatical affixes, both inflectional and derivational, and then the optional modification structures, and the substitutional possibilities, etc. In these, one has at least a start on the overt, obligatory distinctions the language requires. The notions "subject," "object," "modifier," etc., are fairly well understood; Joos (1964) has done excellent work on English verbs, yet little has been done on derivational affixes. Beyond this point of "delicacy" or "degree of derivation," one could perhaps calculate with Weinreich the likelihood of combinations. It is when one passes from the overt to the covert restrictions that it would appear linguistics might call on other disciplines. For instance, there are familiar restrictions on the use of pronominal substitutes so that only masculines, feminines, or neuters are permitted and the form of the pronouns in the singular are overtly marked. But there are covert distinctions, such as those which would restrict us from saying something like, "He drank the steel." One way in which this is handled derives from the type of representation Katz and Fodor have pioneered. Instead of merely using the word "drink," one uses a complex symbol (Chomsky, 1964) which can list both the semantic features and selectional restrictions, including such features as

$$
\left[\begin{array}{l}
\mp \text{ animate subject} \\
\mp \text{ transitive} \\
- \text{ human object} \\
- \text{ solid object} \\
\cdots \cdots
\end{array}\right]
$$

The $+$ indicates required features, the $-$ those which are excluded, and the $\pm$ indicates alternatives, for example, "The soil drank in the water," where 'soil' is $-$ animate subject.

This approach rests on some quite traditional principles of analysis as well as on some modern insights into the difficulties experienced in establishing the borderline between grammar and lexicon. The problem seems to reduce to this: just as the grammar of a language can be stated in a gross, but usable, way, so too the meaning of any lexical item in the language can be explained by substituting for it a limited number of more familiar terms in the same language. In other words, we define the unfamiliar through the more familiar. If it is possible to abstract from the defining terms a set of semantic features which could account for our understanding of the most novel lexical terms, the hope would be that we have come across some sort of cultural, socially dictated, or biological, cognitive perceptual units.

At the present, linguists have offered no other way of stating these primitives except through the use of terms already a legitimate part of the language. Two other possibilities suggest themselves: it might be the case that the semantic primitives of a language are merely types of relationships whose most familiar exponents are the semantically primitive terms we have discovered, such as 'animate,' 'transitive,' 'count,' etc., but the expressions used are not themselves the primitives; secondly, the semantic primitives might be the acts or potentialities of human perception, cognition and experience, and the terms in which they are expressed, such as 'human,' 'transitive,' etc., are again not identical with the primitives, but their most intelligible examples. In either event, linguists at the present seem to have no other way of dealing with the problem except by using expressions of the object language plus the conventional agreement that 'human,' when it appears in a complex symbol, is not the same as *human* in the actual utterances of ordinary language. It is a metalinguistic expression.

HIERARCHY OF SOCIAL SCIENCES

It is not within my competence to establish a hierarchy among social sciences, but in the foregoing I have suggested a point of view according to which one could take linguistics as the basic social science since it deals ultimately with the semantic primitives of a language. It deals therefore with some kind of social entity of a highly abstract nature which has some biological as well as conventional origin. It deals with that aspect of human behavior which is peculiarly human—the use of cognitive language. Through a conventional simplification, linguistics can start from a basic form of human language, the simple declarative sentences, show the formal relationships and mechanisms of transformation by which all other types of constructions, no matter how complex, can be produced from the "kernel sentences" (*cf.* Chomsky, 1957), or related to them, and establish on overt, formally linguistic grounds, a certain number of meaning features in terms of which more specific expressions can be understood or produced. There comes a point, however, when the linguistic form itself does not supply all the clues necessary to understand an expression. Here, it would appear, is certainly a point where other social sciences seem to be required, and where linguistics could expect to receive some illumination for its own procedures and presuppositions.

Take, for instance, the assumptions about meaning that underlie Bloomfield's (1933) approach: for him the meaning of an utterance is to be sought in the recurrent, stable, partial aspects of the practical events which precede an utterance and in the practical events that follow it. From Hjelmslev's (1961) main point of view, this presupposes that the variable, speech, is being explained in terms of one constant, the cognitive meaning of the utterance and its parts. He shows that language so considered can be called a denotative semiotic, that is, a use of language which is satisfactorily explained by appeal only to the denotative (cognitive) function. But as we all know, language is seldom used in this way. Hjelmslev suggested another designation for the noncognitive aspect of language in his expression "connotative semiotic." In such use we have the interesting phenomenon of an apparently meaningful utterance being used as the signal of a different message the listener can understand from nonlinguistic clues. A simple example is the use of irony, as when a dominating wife might say to her husband, returning in the early morning hours, "I hope you had a good time, dear!"

Phenomena somewhat similar to this led in older times to the distinction of the grammatical versus the logical form of sentences, and more recent times, to Chomsky's (1965) distinction of surface vs. deep structure of utterances. In this latter system, a sentence like "The man who persuaded John to be examined by a specialist was fired" is said to be a "surface structure" which is understood in terms of certain transformations of the underlying deep structures. These are not readily statable in acceptable surface-structure expressions, but correspond roughly to surface sentences such as "The man persuaded John," "A specialist examined John," and "The man was fired." In developing the deep structures, elements which have the strange qualities of the cognitive semantic primitives we have been discussing occur, such as 'manner,' 'auxiliary,' 'determiner,' and 'passive.' At higher levels, there are categories such as 'noun phrase,' 'predicate phrase,' etc. One way of illustrating the deep structures is through tree diagrams which readily lend themselves to the expression of the "degree of derivation" or degree of "delicacy" previously discussed. For instance, the deep structure said to underlie part of the sentence mentioned could be expressed as "the-man-past-persuade-John-of-dummy element-Sentence" and illustrated as

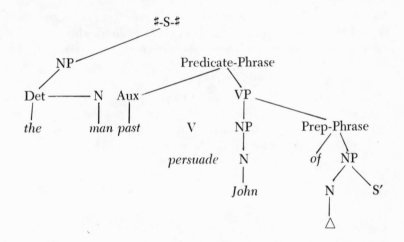

"Predicate-Phrase" in Hjelmslev's system would be a first degree derivate; counting down the number of categories through which one passes to characterize *John,* one finds that it is a fifth degree derivate, since the 0 degree is #S#, 2 = Predicate Phrase, 3 = VP, 4= N and 5 = *John. John* could be further specified by using a complex symbol of semantic features, as above. The "primitives" are therefore either relational or denotational, depending on the degree of derivation or delicacy. Further "delicacy" is obtained by employing, in addition to the paradigmatic type of information used here, syntactic information: *John* is not a count noun, since it does not take the article; since *he* can substitute for it, it is both animate and personal. Had the expression been other than a personal noun, further restrictions on its combinatory possibilities could be noted. Instead of an expression like *gentleman,* for instance, in such a sentence, one would be dealing with a complex symbol containing the selectional restrictions and the semantic features that serve to define the word.

On sheerly linguistic grounds, therefore, it would appear so far that ultimately the decision to choose some particular degree of derivation, delicacy, or grammaticalness is an esthetic one, requiring a conventional simplification. If the suggestion proposed here be accepted, that the linguist consider his task finished when he has accounted for the obligatory distinctions a language must make, there would appear a clear, motivated, but not a natural boundary line between linguistics and the other social sciences.

CONCLUSION

The current work in linguistics, seeking to isolate semantic primitives, suggests a conventional method by which the field of linguistics and the other social sciences may be related and distinguished. The entities dealt with are of interest to all the social sciences. The most obvious contribution linguistics makes to their study is to provide the linguistic signals by which they can be isolated within a given language. By including more and more syntactic information, a larger number of covert semantic restrictions and features can be discovered. It would appear that the proper concern of linguistics in discussing semantic primitives stops where the ordering is no longer intralinguistic, but due to extralinguistic factors. The extralinguistic factors, such as sociological factors and psychological states, etc., seem more properly the field of other social sciences from whose studies linguists can draw profit without losing the autonomy of their own approach.

REFERENCES

BLOOMFIELD, L. 1933. *Language.* New York: Holt.

BOLINGER, D. L. 1965. The atomization of meaning. *Language,* 41: 555–73.

BRIGHT, W. S. 1967. *Sociolinguistics.* The Hague: Mouton.

CHOMSKY, N. 1957. *Syntactic structures.* The Hague: Mouton.

———. 1961. Some methodological remarks on generative grammar. *Word,* 17: 219–39.

———. 1965. *Aspects of the theory of syntax.* Cambridge: MIT Press.

FODOR, J. A., and J. J. KATZ. 1963. The structure of a semantic theory. *Language,* 39: 170–210.

HALLIDAY, M. A. K., A. McINTOSH, and P. STEVENS. 1965. *The linguistic sciences and language teaching.* London: Longmans.

HJELMSLEV, L. 1961. *Prolegomena to a theory of language.* (Trans. by F. J. Whitfield.) Madison: University of Wisconsin Press.

HOCKETT, C. 1966. Language, mathematics and linguistics. In *Current trends in linguistics III: theoretical foundations.* The Hague: Mouton.

JAKOBSON, R., and M. HALLE. 1956. *Fundamentals of language.* The Hague: Mouton.

Joos, M. 1964. *The English verb, form and meanings.* Madison: University of Wisconsin Press.

LAMB, S. M. 1966. *Outline of stratification grammar.* Washington, D.C.: Georgetown University Press.

LENNEBERG, E. H. (Ed.). 1964. *New directions in the study of language.* Cambridge: MIT Press.

MILLER, G. A. 1964. Language and psychology. In E. H. Lenneberg (Ed.), *New directions in the study of language.* Cambridge: MIT Press.

MORRIS, C. W. 1964. *Signification and significance.* Cambridge: MIT Press.

OGDEN, C. K. 1932. *The A B C of basic English.* London: Kegan Paul.

OSGOOD, C. E., and T. SEBEOK. 1965. *Psycholinguistics.* Bloomington: Indiana University Press.

ROGET, P. 1946. *Roget's International Thesaurus.* New York: Crowell.

SAUSSURE, FERDINAND DE. 1916. *Cours de Linguistique Generale.* Paris: Payot. (Trans. by Wade Baskin as *Course in general linguistics* [New York: Philosophical Library, 1959].)

SØRENSEN, H. S. 1958. *Word-classes in modern English with special reference to proper names, with an introductory theory of grammar, meaning and reference.* Copenhagen: Gad.

THOMAS OF ERFURT (PSEUDO-SCOTUS). 1902. *Grammatica speculativa.* Ed. by O. Garcia, Guarrachi.

WEINREICH, U. 1966. Explorations in semantic theory. In T. Sebeok (Ed.), *Current trends in linguistics III: theoretical foundations.* The Hague: Mouton.

15

SOME RELATIONS BETWEEN PSYCHIATRY AND POLITICAL SCIENCE

Arnold A. Rogow

The relationship between psychiatry and political science reminds us of those long engagements that somehow never eventuate in marriage.[1] The two have known each other for a considerable period of time and like all tentative lovers they share an uneasy rapport compounded of affection, dislike, dependence, and suspicion. Cohabiting when mutually inclined, they occasionally produce offspring who are feeble and short-lived; if one of these products of timorous coupling survives into adolescence, it is then cast off by one or both parents, and dies. Despite or perhaps because of such vicissitudes, the engagement continues, with neither party able either to break off the relationship or to set a firm date for the wedding.

But the future is full of promise, since all the evidence suggests that our timid lovers are drawing closer together, indeed are moving rapidly toward fruitful collaboration. In psychiatry, the increasing concern with social psychiatry and community mental health programs indicates that the broader sociological context of disturbed behavior is becoming a major field of interest in the discipline. A small but growing number of political scientists have revived an inquiry, going back to Plato, into the psychological foundations of political stability and the role of personality variables and motivations as clues to the behavior of figures long since dead. Practitioners in both disciplines articulate a dissatisfaction with traditional research methodologies and canons of evidence, and insist on the need for a more scientific approach. Such trends, and others to be explored in due course, underline the possibilities for productive research within and between the disciplines that constitute the behavioral and social sciences.

The engagement, nevertheless, has been a long one, and its fructification,

1. This chapter is a shorter version of material included in J. Marmor (Ed.), *Modern Psychoanalysis* (New York: Basic Books, 1968) and is titled there "Psychiatry, History, and Political Science."

assuming that optimism on this score is not unwarranted, owes something to more than 2,000 years of speculation about the nature of man and the political institutions he could and should establish. Plato perhaps showed the first awareness of the debilitating effect on the individual of passions at war with each other, and he certainly was the first to posit a psychology of social classes when he developed his famous characterological distinctions between the rulers, warriors, and workers in the ideal city state.

Aristotle, who probably would have accorded psychoanalysis a welcome far warmer than Freud's medical colleagues, dealt with problems that psychiatrists of all persuasions continue to find challenging: the variety and meaning of dreams, the extent to which instincts (the id) can be integrated with other personality components, and the question whether frustrations of one sort or another can be sublimated. It was also Aristotle who thought of happiness as a harmonious and focused "energy of the soul," and he saw clearly that the health and stability of the polity depended on friendliness and affection among the citizenry.

Despite such early enterprise, it remains true that political science is the last of the social sciences to even tentatively embrace psychiatry and psychoanalysis.

Of the reasons that may be advanced for this failure, three in particular stand out. The first is the long and tenacious tradition within political science of conceiving of the discipline as consanguinely related to law, history, and philosophy rather than to behavioral science. Emphasizing the study of constitutions and enactments, approaching the state and other political entities descriptively rather than analytically, treating the history of normative political ideas as the sum and essence of political theory, political science for a very long period eschewed a dynamic interpretation of political life. The founding fathers of American political science, many of whom did graduate work in German and British universities, could not conceive of the personality dimension as relevant to political science; most of them, at the beginning of the present century, were unhappy with efforts to view the political process as a function of groups competing and bargaining for power, much less the outcome of individual and group interrelations influenced in part by unconscious motivations. Even today, it is worth noting, political science in Europe and elsewhere remains steeped in legalistic, historical, and philosophical exegesis, although there are exceptions and indubitably modernizing trends are under way.

A second cause of resistance to psychoanalysis is the challenge posed by Freudian principles to the heuristic rational and super-structural models which, for a very long time, constituted nuclear political science. Freud's belief that mental processes are essentially unconscious appeared to undermine the Enlightenment view, incorporated into political science, that man was a reasoning calculator of his own self-interest whose judgment of what would benefit himself and society would improve with increasing education and diffusion of knowledge. The conviction of Freud that culture itself was the result of a fragile tension between constructive and destructive tendencies in man, with the latter frequently in ascendancy, threatened the very root structure of the belief in progress and its corollary liberal doctrine of change and perfectability in human nature. Psychoanalysis, insofar as it was understood by political scientists, seemed to be saying, finally, that the entire political superstructure—conservative and radical parties, ideologies, voting, the state itself—could be "explained" in terms of childhood traumas, oedipus complexes, father figures, castration fears, libido diversion, and the like. Freud, it appeared, like Marx before him, was suggesting that political institutions were essentially a facade, a veneer, a gloss to mask the real interests and motivations of man, and much of the treatment accorded Freud was similar to that accorded Marx and other demolishers of the superstructure: disbelief, disdain, disinterest. There were also those in the political science profession, the moral views of which have always been closer to Calvin than to Casanova, who shared and still share the opinion of the Dean of the University of Toronto in 1910 that Freud was an advocate "of free love, removal of all restraints, and a relapse into savagery" (Jones, 1955)—in short, a *dirty old man.* After Freud, as (from another perspective) after Hitler and the national insanity of Naziism, it could no longer be maintained that man was cast in the image of God or, if not God, at least Thomas Jefferson or John Stuart Mill.

The third source of estrangement between psychiatry and political science, and one that constitutes a major threat to continuing possibilities for collaboration, has to do with methodological developments in both disciplines. Since World War II political scientists have been increasingly concerned with the discipline's methodological lag behind the other social and behavioral sciences. Doctoral candidates in political science, unlike those in economics and sociology, knew no mathematics or statistics; hence their models and paradigms were verbal constructs, and there was little agreement even within the profession about the words used, especially such words as *power, influence, consent, coalition, authority,* and so forth. Few political scientists were skilled in techniques of quantitative and qualitative measurement; therefore they were unable to process aggregate data such as that produced in sample surveys, or to undertake multivariate analysis. One major consequence of this technological lag was that certain research areas, notably research in public opinion formation and voting behavior, were transferred, as it were, from political science to sociology and psychology. Another result was that studies undertaken by political scientists—for example, studies of interest groups, or local governments, or decision-making processes—tended to be, however illuminating, subjective and frequently idiosyncratic. They were difficult, often impossible to replicate, were not susceptible to proof or disproof, and hence were of little utility in that slow and painful construction process by which a discipline transforms itself into a science.

While this is not the occasion to discuss all the motivations for change, it may be noted in passing that a professional inferiority complex, especially among younger practitioners, has played an important role, as have a number of foundations whose funds are seemingly available without limit for "hard" research. The impact of the Center for Advanced Study in the Behavioral Sciences, where political scientists and historians have been welcomed since operations began in 1954, should not be overlooked; shifts of emphasis within the Social Science Research Council and National Science Foundation have also been important.

The contributions of psychoanalysis and unfortunately, psychiatry to our understanding of politics are limited by the inordinate "softness" of much psychiatric research. While in psychiatry, too, there is growing dissatisfaction with traditional methods, what has been said about methodological lag in political science applies with even greater force to psychiatry. It may or may not be an overstatement to suggest that "psychology can be of use to the social sciences *only* if its use can be reduced to a technique which is verifiable, teachable, and can be corrected or changed in the face of new evidence" (Kardiner, 1945; italics added). Nevertheless, it is plausible to suggest that the limitations of much psychiatric research—for example, the lack of standardization in the concepts and measures employed by psychiatrists, the proneness to generalize findings that are based on a highly selective, nonrepresentative, middle-class population sample, the tendency to minimize the importance of variables found to be significant by political scientists, such as social class, income, education, and religious affiliation—constitute a severe restriction on its utility.

While it is evident that many psychiatrists are more interested than ever before in interdisciplinary methodologies and research efforts, it is far from clear, at least to an outsider, what the effects will be, on the one hand, of the increasing separation between clinicians and researchers, and, on the other hand, of the growing interest in biochemical and engineering approaches to mental illness. No doubt it is too early—it may be totally in error—to say that the most imaginative and competent psychiatrists are gradually abandoning clinical practice for research, instead of engaging in both, but the implications of such a development, especially implications for interdisciplinary training and research programs that include political scientists are not all of them happy ones. Similarly, it may be wrong or at least premature to conclude that the interest in biochemistry and psychophysiological research will draw psychiatry back toward medicine and the natural sciences, which is where Kenneth M. Colby (1960) and others feel it belongs, and further away from the social sciences. In psychiatry, as in all other branches of knowledge at the present time, there are conflicting trends; the only certain thing is the necessity of continuing discussion and analysis of trends.

But assuming, once again, that psychiatry and political science are drawing closer together rather than further apart, what does psychiatry have most to contribute to political science? What can political science offer psychiatry? Where are the interdisciplinary frontiers and "cutting-edge" areas, and the richest possibilities for innovative developments?

The contributions of psychiatry to political science can be roughly classified under the headings of method, emphasis, and insight. In terms of methodology, Freud's most significant achievement was undoubtedly the unstructured, free-associational interview. Depending as it does on observational techniques that require special interpretational skills on the part of the investigator, the free-association interview has not been fully exploited by political scientists interested in contemporary affairs and the recent past. Yet it would appear that the psychoanalytic-type interview is an indispensable tool for intensively exploring and theoretically charting areas of political behavior that are not amenable to other methods of inquiry.

For example, much research by political scientists into the etiology of right-wing extremism suggests that members of organizations like the John Birch Society are plagued by high levels of anxiety, low self-esteem, strong needs for inviolacy, and hostile and misanthropic orientations toward the social order. Many of them belong to the discontinued classes of society— that is, they are the older residents of burgeoning towns and cities, the proprietors of neighborhood stores and small businesses threatened by the huge chains and shopping centers, the elderly retired who are made apprehensive by small children, non-whites, noise, traffic, and tax increases—and these drop-out citizens are attracted to subcultures of despair such as the Birch Society. Unfortunately, they are much less likely to cooperate with social investigators using survey research and other "hard" instruments of research than individuals who are more sanguine in both personality and outlook. Hence, studies positing a relationship between, say, alienation and extremism are characterized by a high refusal rate for requested interviews and questionnaire returns, and consequent failure to demonstrate that the relationship holds at levels of statistical significance. In fact, we know very little altogether about those who consistently refuse to participate in survey studies whatever their nature. Surely here is a collaborative area that would benefit from a merger of the "soft" technique of the clinician with the "hard" techniques currently used in political science.

Even less developed than the free-association interview is the application of free-association to the analysis of documents, letters, diaries, and written records of all sorts. Although the political scientist and historian frequently deal with handwritten accounts, almost no effort has been made to analyze changes of handwriting, including sudden changes in the way one signs letters, that are known to occur under conditions of great internal as well as external stress. Hence we are uninformed about the relationship of such changes to life and career experiences. While handwriting, to a great and growing extent, has been replaced by the telephone, the typewriter, and the tape recorder, it is by no means impossible to search typewritten and spoken messages for clues to traumatic events. Much could be learned, for example, by approaching taped political interviews, speeches, press conferences, and so forth, in a fashion similar to that employed in the analysis of taped psychiatric interviews and group therapy.

Related to the free-association interview is Freud's emphasis on the "latent, unconscious, irrational, and archaic aspect" of behavior, and the stress he placed "on the formative influence of early childhood, of dreams and of phantasies" (Frenkel-Brunswik, 1952). Little of this emphasis has penetrated research in political science, although efforts are now under way to study the processes by which children become interested, involved, and partisan to politics (Easton and Hess, 1960, 1962; Greenstein, 1960, 1965). So far as is known, no attempt has been made to collect and interpret the dreams and fantasies of political figures. No doubt this is due in part to the fact that what we know of living individuals is by and large what they want us to know, and what we know of the dead is by and large what their families and their posterity permit us to discover. But it is also true that special skills are required for the analysis of inferred motivations as opposed to those that are manifest; lacking such skills, political scientists tend to confine themselves to that which is conscious, declared, and easily observable. Thus the latent, underlying motivations of both individuals and institutions, in the concealment or disguise of which all advanced societies excel, may be totally overlooked by the political behaviorist.

If this were not the case, we would know much more about the origins of deviant political and social behavior, and the role of such behavior in history. Most political scientists see the universe as conveniently dichotomized into political and apolitical strata. Focusing upon the extended middle range of attitudes and behavior, they find that about 10 per cent of the citizenry are activists, that is, people who vote regularly, join political organizations, contribute money, communicate their opinions to public officials, and even run for office. The activists are usually well informed about public affairs, and firmly committed to democratic rules of the game, for example, the protection of civil liberties (Stouffer, 1955).

The great mass of citizens, however, is found to be apathetic and indifferent to politics. Their commitment to democratic rules and procedures may be viewed as tenuous. The prevailing interpretation of such behavior is that these persons remain outside the political arena because they attach a low priority to political affairs relative to other forms of gratification, or because they believe that values allocated by the public sector will come to them even if they do not participate, or because they have a strong sense of political inefficacy or impotence. It is rarely observed that from time to time some of these apathetics venture into the political arena and convert their anger and frustrations into punitive acts directed at political actors and objects— hence the disaffected, lower-class Negroes who convert the community into a phobic sector through street riots and other forms of anomic behavior; the alienated, Caucasian, lumpen proletariat who form "patriotic" and paramilitary societies dedicated to overthrowing the democratic rules of the game, such as the Minutemen, American Nazi Party, and Hell's Angels motorcycle clubs; and those who endeavor to punish the powers-that-be by assassinating the President. The conditions under which these deviant types of behavior develop can hardly be specified if the political world is seen and studied as a crucible of moderate activism, the characteristic style of which is pragmatic, consensual, brokerage involvement. Because it is this world, not the deviant one, that elects Presidents, the deviant zones of society are generally ignored, although they are often decision-making zones at local levels (school boards, for instance) and generate much of the rhetoric that flows through the political mainstream. In effect, the truncated and culture-bound vision that dominates American political science is here joined by a "hard" approach that rejects Freud's emphasis as well as his method. As a consequence, it is rare to encounter in the discipline, even in investigations of deviance, that "deep and penetrating study of individuals [that] may often tell us more about the themes of a contemporary society than will a surface description of the existing institutions" (Frenkel-Brunswik, 1952).

The third insight component of Freud's contribution to political science and history is that large body of psychoanalytic and psychiatric literature that deals with politics and history. The term insight is used because such literature is designed to provide an analysis in depth, based on psychoanalytic and psychiatric theory, of phenomena that are only partly explored or understood by political scientists and historians. Most of this literature, for reasons already discussed, has originated with psychiatrists themselves, but an increasing amount is being published by psychoanalytically inclined social scientists not all of whom have cared to acknowledge their indebtedness to Freud and his progeny. Indeed, in certain areas, notably biography, it is customary *not* to acknowledge a debt to psychoanalysis, however large and conspicuous it may be.

Broadly speaking, the history of insight literature is, like other histories, a history of changing times, interests, and intellectual styles. Someone once remarked, in an effort to explain a Supreme Court decision, that the "Supreme Court reads the headlines." In a similar vein it may be observed that psychiatrists read the headlines and are affected by them, at least insofar as their insight writings are concerned. Thus, during the "long twilight" that glowed over Europe between the Franco-Prussian War and 1914, Freud and his colleagues wrote very little outside the area of primary concern, that is, the origins, symptoms, and treatment of neuroses and psychoses. While Freud early demonstrated an interest in literary and artistic themes, he did not turn his attention to problems of war and peace until 1915 when he published "Thoughts for the Times on War and Death." His preface, "Psychoanalysis and War Neuroses," appeared in 1919. During the relatively peaceful twenties, he wrote little on the subject, but in 1930 his *Civilization and Its Discontents* was perhaps more prophetic than anything else that year of the approaching end of tranquility or, in Harding's coined phrase, "normalcy." The Freud-Einstein exchange of letters, "Why War?" was published in 1933 (although the letters were written in 1932), on the eve of the long Nazi march.

The psychiatric interest in the conditions of war and peace, it need hardly be said, has had no cause to diminish since Freud observed in his letter to Einstein "that owing to the perfection of instruments of destruction a future war might involve the extermination of one or perhaps both of the antagonists. All this is true, and so incontestably true that one can only feel astonished that the waging of war has not yet been unanimously repudiated" (Freud, 1932, p. 285).

During and immediately after World War II the writings of Franz Alexander (1941, 1942, 1943), G. Brock Chisholm (1946), Trigant Burrow (1941), and others argued that war is not inevitable from a psychiatric point of view, although it does serve as a release for frustrations and conflicts of all sorts. Much of the literature of this period built less on Freud's conception of the place of Thanatos in human affairs than on the sequential "frustration and aggression" theme developed by John Dollard and his associates in 1939.

With the founding of the Group for the Advancement of Psychiatry in 1946 (usually referred to as GAP), the attention of psychiatrists was specifically drawn to the problem of war and related problems that beset the national and world communities. Since 1960, the writings of Jerome D. Frank (1960) and Judd Marmor (1964), some of which are addressed to lay audiences, have been influential, and in 1964 GAP itself published a widely read report titled *Psychiatric Aspects of the Prevention of Nuclear War.* Citing as difficulties in the way of nonviolent solutions such factors as psychological defense mechanisms, "primitivising effects of extreme fear or panic," increasing dehumanization, ethnocentric perceptual distortion and other factors that contribute to the psychological escalation of aggression, the GAP study nevertheless insisted that other ways could be found "of conducting conflict between groups of people, or between nations, that can serve these psychological needs more adaptively in our modern world." War, concluded the report, "is a social institution; it is not inevitably rooted in the nature of man."

A second area of interest between the two world wars and for some years after 1945, although perhaps an area rather more developed by psychoanalysts than psychiatrists, was the concept and dimensions of national character, especially the character of Germany. That Germany received focal attention is understandable in view of the fact that the disruptions attributable to German-provoked wars and, above all, to National Socialism, included the persecution and forced migration of a large number of psychoanalysts including, in addition to Freud himself, Rank, Adler, Stekel, Fromm, Fromm-Reichman, Alexander, Horney, Reich, Erikson, and Reik. Almost all of these prominent exiles from Nazi-occupied territory were of Jewish extraction, and paralleling the interest in the psychopathology of German national character was a deep concern, personal as well as professional, about the possible spread of virulent anti-Semitism.

To be sure, the Germans were not the only ones to receive attention. A survey of the relevant literature reveals numerous articles and a few books dealing with the American, British, Russian, Chinese, Japanese, and even Norwegian so-called national character. But in books such as Richard M. Brickner's *Is Germany Incurable?* (1943) and Wilhelm Reich's *The Mass Psychology of Fascism* (1946), in articles such as Erik H. Erikson's "Hitler's Imagery and German Youth" (1942) and Fritz Moellenhoff's "The Price of Individuality: Speculations about German National Characteristics" (1947), German national character and Naziism, its most virulent expression, were subjected to a psychoanalysis more searching than that accorded any other topic or theme in the social sciences. Much of this analysis was devoted to an explication of paranoid tendencies in German history and thought and the means by which these tendencies could be abolished or at least reduced after the war, but there were also efforts, as in the writings of Erich Fromm (1941), to gaze at Germany and the general problem of authoritarianism through spectacles, the right lens of which had been contributed by Freud, and the left donated by Marx.

Since 1950, interest in Nazi Germany has very largely been confined to historians, some of whom have attempted to apply psychoanalytic categories while the study of national character as such is now only a marginal interest in both psychiatry and the social sciences.

Ethnic group prejudice, on the other hand, is a continuing concern. There have been shifts of emphasis, however, reflecting changing problems and research needs. A vast literature dealing with anti-Semitism, to which psychoanalysts and psychiatrists have made influential contributions, has succeeded in exposing the roots of anti-Semitism, although precise boundaries are not fixed as between religious, historical, social, economic, and psychopathological causal explanations. Since publication of *The Authoritarian Personality* (Adorno *et al.*, 1950), the most significant effort made to link anti-Semitism to a variety of individual and social disorders, most work on anti-Semitism has been in the form of surveys that attempt to measure distribution of opinions in a given population.

After 1954, the year of the momentous school desegregation decision of the Supreme Court, interest conspicuously shifted to problems in white-Negro relations and related civil rights activities. Prior to the *Brown* v. *Board of Education* decision of a unanimous Court in 1954, American psychiatry, like American society itself, did not demonstrate much concern for Negroes apart from an occasional article dealing with race riots or with high incidence of mental illness in predominantly Negro communities. Perhaps this neglect owed something to the relatively small position that Negroes occupy in psychiatry either as doctors or as private patients. Whatever the explanation, not much was known about the psychiatric aspects of either segregation or desegregation prior to a 1956 roundtable on the subject sponsored by the American Orthopsychiatric Society. In 1957 a GAP publication, *Psychiatric Aspects of School Desegregation,* was an important contribution to the small body of literature on the subject, and since then race relations themes have been dealt with in a number of articles published by psychiatrists. It remains broadly true, however, that psychiatry, much less psychoanalysis, has not given to the civil rights area the attention it has given to other problems in the social psychiatry field, or the attention that civil rights problems deserve. Partly for this reason, there is as yet no published work as substantial as *The Authoritarian Personality;* indeed, the most significant book on race relations is still Gunnar Myrdal's *An American Dilemma* (1944), and Myrdal was neither an American nor a psychiatrist, nor yet a political scientist, but a combined economist-sociologist of Swedish nationality.

A fourth dimension of psychiatric insight literature, and one closely related to research on ethnic group relations, has been concerned with democratic and non-democratic modal personality types. Most psychiatrists who have written on social issues have had something to say about contrasting authoritarian and non-authoritarian character structures, although it is fair to comment that their work, like that of political scientists with similar interests, is given more to implication than explication, especially with regard to non-authoritarian character structure. Much of what has been published is also vulnerable to a criticism similar to that leveled at *The Authoritarian Personality,* namely, that the nuclear concept excludes left-wing behavior. While efforts have been made to study individual communists, the personality type occasionally referred to as the authoritarian liberal remains elusive, at least in research terms.

Insofar as authoritarian and nonauthoritarian modal types can be extrapolated from the diverse body of literature specifying certain essentials of democracy and dictatorship, it would appear that the authoritarian type, from a psychiatric point of view, is a coercive, anxious, suspicious, and id-rejecting individual who is oriented toward power and extremely limited in his capacity to give and receive affection. Demanding from others either dominance or submission, the authoritarian type tends to be the total leader in one kind of situation, and the total follower in another. "Intolerant of ambiguity," in Frenkel-Brunswik's phrase, his problem-solving methods are rigid, quick, and direct, and his preferred solution is always simplistic. He prefers his wife passive, his children submissive, his home life undemanding, his friends deferential, and his employees docile. He is frequently skilled in masking his basic hostility behind a facade of spurious warmth and friendliness and he is often a master in the art of dissimulation. Enjoying the delusion of rectitudinous grandeur, he may see himself as an honest man who has not been discovered by Diogenes, or as an unappreciated Nero who has every right to burn since Rome does nothing but fiddle. If he is conservative as well as authoritarian, phrases and words such as communist, socialist, Stevenson, one world, Medicare, and beatnik may engender spontaneous combustion. If he is liberal as well as authoritarian, the inflammable terms are capitalism, Wall Street, Hoover (both Herbert and J. Edgar), CIA, military-industrial complex, and Catholic hierarchy.

The democratic type, by contrast, is a persuasive, secure, trustful, and id-accepting individual for whom power is only one of a number of values. Able to give and receive affection, his relations with others are characterized, in Erikson's wording, by "mutuality." Lacking the desire to be either the absolute leader or absolute follower, the democrat as husband, father, and employer does not demand that others strip their own egos in order to clothe his own; his role may require that he be *primus inter pares* in decision-making situations, but he is supportive in such a role and he takes others into account. He can accept criticism, understand frailty in others as well as himself, and limit his hostile and aggressive impulses or discharge them harmlessly. Politically he may lean to either side, but whether a conservative or liberal he rejects devil theories of politics and controls his emotional reaction to manipulation of symbols irrespective of their plus or minus value in his belief system.

Clearly these characterological types should be of immense importance in the study of political behavior, and yet very little use has been made of them by political scientists. Some reasons for this have already been noted—the "hard"-approach infatuation of many political scientists, the reluctance to utilize either the method or the insights of psychoanalysis, and so forth—and in addition, many students of political behavior feel that the authoritarian and democratic personality models are too vague and imprecise to be of research utility. Some critics go so far as to suggest that such models are more imaginative than descriptive, arguing that the key concepts are not dichotomized terminals between which a given population distributes itself, but points on a personality continuum within individuals. The same person, they maintain, will be authoritarian in one situation, and democratic in another. They also express doubts that the authoritarian subculture, assuming one exists, plays a significant role in American life, or that it is increasing in size and importance.

These reservations and criticisms may or may not be legitimate; what is certain is that they will not be resolved unless "hard" and "soft" methods are joined in a collaboration between psychiatrists and political scientists. From psychiatry, for example, we need much more specificity with regard to the interpersonal (family, school, workplace) environments that nourish democratic and authoritarian personalities, and recommended measures for strengthening democratic as opposed to authoritarian tendencies in society. From social science and history we need more information about the economic, social, and political conditions which have given rise to authoritarian subcultures and paranoid pseudo-communities in democratic societies.

From political science we need to know more about the extent to which authoritarian tendencies in political life can be modified by role settings and expectations, by interaction between authoritarians and democrats, by enlightenment, and, finally by restriction and confinement in the larger social environment. These demands made upon the several disciplines hardly exhaust the research needs and opportunities with reference to possible linkages between personality types and political behavior.

Indeed, it is difficult to think of any insight area in social psychiatry, or any research in political behavior, that would not benefit from collaboration between these disciplines. The study of voting behavior, for example, a "hard" research field in social science if ever there was one, would become more exciting and significant if voting motivation and intention underwent psychological scrutiny in depth; adaptations of the psychiatric interview would add an important dimension to research into the behavior of bureaucrats, congressmen, state legislators, city councilmen, and the like. While psychiatrists have gradually become aware of correlations between socioeconomic variables and mental illness (and the treatment thereof), more research is needed on the national cultural aspects of mental health and illness. If political biographies are to serve as rich tapestries of entire lives and not merely pale sketches of names, dates and places, political scientists and others will have to acquire some skills from psychoanalysis in making inferences, reconstructions, and interpretations.

The frontier areas of these disciplines, however, require less an exchange of methods and insights than their merger into a comprehensive science of social behavior. In this development the psychiatrist is likely to find himself working in tandem not only with medical specialists but with social scientists and historians who share with him a common interest in man's fate. The merger of methods and insights in the future may even extend to practices, treatments, and therapies. It requires little imagination to foresee the time when there are psychiatry members of political science departments, and when political scientists are attached to hospital and clinic staffs.

The emergent science of social behavior will not lack for challenging research areas; indeed the problem will be to assess priorities among problems that demand attention. But by any test, one urgent problem is bound to be the problem of defining democracy in terms that are meaningful in a twentieth-century world of nuclear weapons, superpowers, gross inequalities of wealth, racial tensions, and, in the so-called advanced portions, giant organizations that transform men into pigmy automatons and ant-like robots. Put another way, the problem is how to make the world safe for democratic character development, and unsafe for those authoritarian and destructive tendencies that threaten an end of the human experience. In short, the most urgent question facing the emergent science is the question of man's survival itself.

A collaborative approach to the question of survival might initially focus on those institutions and behavioral patterns, national and international, that create or contribute to neurosis and psychosis. Reference here is not to the concept of "society as the patient," as useful in certain circumstances as that concept may be, but to the belief that a good deal of disturbed behavior, both social and individual, is rooted in societal conditions. While efforts have been made to identify these conditions and relate them to deviant behaviors, much remains to be known about the nature and treatment of such relationships.

It is fairly well established, for example, that the distribution of mental illnesses is inversely related to class and income, that, to take one case, proportionately more of the poor than the rich suffer from schizophrenia and other illnesses. There is also evidence that Americans in general worry more about financial insecurity than about any other problem in their lives. Clearly, the unhappiness of a great many, and the psychoses of some, Americans is to some extent a reflection of the economic and social environment in which they find themselves. It follows that the environment needs changing, and gradually—all too gradually—it is being changed, in some respects. But for the short run, at least, much could be accomplished if we could account for the fact that not everyone in a poverty culture becomes schizophrenic or otherwise mentally ill, and not all Americans are equally worried about financial insecurity. What factors, then, *in addition to environment,* determine whether one does or does not become ill or markedly insecure? Here, surely, is a collaborative area the exploration of which would save many more from crippling illnesses than are now saved by conventional treatment methods.

Another neglected area of research, and one of equal challenge, is the relationship between sexual and social behavior. While it is a truism, since Freud, to declare that psychosexual disturbances in the individual are a prime cause of neurosis, very little research has been done on the extent to which the sexual aspects of culture promote as well as reflect disturbed behavior in political and social arenas as well as individual lives. Many of those who work with young people are persuaded that they especially suffer from the strains and tensions that are built-in features of American sexual culture —although, again, we cannot discriminate with any precision among the factors that predispose some to suffer more than others. But it is not only the young people. There is evidence that adults also suffer from what Sullivan called the "lurid twilight" of sexuality in America, a "twilight" made up of unrestricted stimulation, on the one hand, and restricted response, on the other. No doubt Sullivan had in mind some sections of the mass media which, quite apart from their catering to voyeuristic tastes, parade before us a thousand inviting male and female images, although the mores make us do with one husband or wife at a time, inviting or otherwise. Despite sporadic protests, New York is now publishing books banned in almost all other Western countries, and Hollywood is making movies for popular consumption that were formerly reserved for stag evenings at American Legion halls. The unprecedented rise of *Playboy,* the only magazine in its price class ever to reach a 3,000,000 per month circulation, is a related phenomenon, as is the appearance of the bare-bosomed waitress.

If our sexual mores had changed *as much* as the books and magazines, there would be fewer problems arising from the supercharged erotic atmosphere. The mores, however, while they have undoubtedly changed, still do not endorse premarital or extramarital sexual intercourse, nor are they tolerant of deviant sexual practices. The frequent result of the visual *do's* and verbal *don'ts* is a psychic state inimical to either physical or mental health. Yet there have been few efforts to study the "lurid twilight" in terms of its relationship to political extremism, delinquency, violence, ethnic group tension, and other problems.

A third important and somewhat neglected research area is the relationship between personality and political leadership. The psychodynamics of political leadership is largely unexplored territory despite the efforts of some political scientists and historians to make limited and not always successful use of psychiatric insights in particular cases. For reasons not entirely clear, psychiatrists and psychoanalysts have written relatively little about political leaders; apparently they have preferred to deal with cultural and religious figures. As a consequence, we know relatively little about the role of personality factors in opinion formation and in the shaping of political career patterns. We are even less informed about the influence of physical and mental illness on decision-making processes, although the list of sick statesmen is a long one. It is also thoroughly international, and it may be significant for an understanding of certain key decisions that have had a decisive effect on world history (L'Etang, 1958, 1961; Rogow, 1966).

It is fascinating to think what might be accomplished by systematic research and discussion of the role of personality variables in the decisions to drop the Bomb on Hiroshima, or to intervene in Korea and Vietnam. Much could be accomplished if most of the 266 psychiatrists in the District of Columbia were willing to collaborate with political scientists in studying the consequences for decision-making of stress, tension, and illness. As it is, neither psychiatrists nor political scientists can say much about the factors that predispose particular individuals to successfully tolerate stress in decision-making situations. We simply do not know who breaks down, and why, and what the effect has been in policy terms. Practically nothing is known about the influence of tranquilizers and related drugs; for that matter, nothing reliable is known about the role of psychiatry itself in the nation's capital apart from the fact that Washington, D.C., is a leader in the ratio of psychiatrists to population. Here, again, collaboration between the disciplines could have only the most beneficial results in terms of both public welfare values and research frontiersmanship.

The stability of the democratic community may also be threatened by the impact of automation in areas that have always been characterized by warm, face-to-face interpersonal relations. In medicine the day is not far off when diagnosis and treatment will be carried out by computers, and in psychiatry there are those who believe that in the future many varieties of mental illness will be diagnosed and prescribed for by tape-fed machines rather sophisticated in processing somatic data. Within ten years or less the average patient, without leaving his hospital bed much less his room, will be able to feed and bathe himself, administer certain medications, take his temperature and have it recorded, and even undergo surgery. Clearly the need for confrontations with doctors, nurses, technicians, orderlies, nurses' aides, and other hospital personnel will be sharply reduced.

The automated university is hardly further away than the hospital. Much of the teaching now done by professors will be done by teaching machines, closed-circuit television, tape recorders, and other devices. Perhaps the day will come when the student, like the patient, need never leave his room to obtain the benefits he has paid for. Students already complain that they rarely see their professors; in the future, at a great many universities, they will *never* see their professors.

All this signifies that in medicine and education, not to mention the factory and office, there will be a marked decrease in interpersonal contacts and face-to-face relationships, in short, a decrease in opportunities for rewarding human relationships. What will be the consequences for mental health? Family life? Our economic and political institutions?

If these questions are to be answered in a positive and hopeful fashion, and before the full consequences of technology are upon us, collaboration between the social and behavioral sciences may have to go beyond research into the practice areas themselves. If it be assumed for example, that the technological revolution will be accompanied by a rising incidence of psychiatric disorders, notwithstanding the material benefits conferred by technological development, then it is clear that something more is needed than a collaborative research orientation and the conventional treatment methods now in effect in psychiatry. Perhaps what is required is collaboration in broadening and deepening the concept of the therapeutic community to make it apply, not to the mental hospital and psychiatric clinic (Jones, 1955), but to any subculture of society that directly or indirectly promotes mental health and democratic citizenship. In this sense, a therapeutic community is one that not only treats those who are ill; it seeks to prevent illness by establishing an environment that is supportive of health, rationality, and creativity. Oriented toward the whole man and not merely one of his roles or functions, a therapeutic community helps develop in everyone the potential for neurosis-free behavior in both the personal and social setting.

One such therapeutic community, in this sense, is the university, although it is rarely thought of that way. For four years or more in the lives of millions of persons, the university constitutes a distinct subculture of society providing not only education but moral instruction, social life and companionship, physical activity, and esthetic uplift. Education in terms of formal classroom instruction is perhaps the least important aspect of university life, at least as regards time. Each week the average student will spend between twelve and fifteen hours in class, and the average professor will devote between six and twelve hours to teaching. The remainder of the student's time is spent in the library, dorm or fraternity house, dining room, union, dating, and attending sports events. Professors devote much of their time to reading and writing, department meetings, committee work, advising students, answering mail, and so forth. Evenings and weekends are generally given over to the family, but on many campuses even family life is campus-related: the dinner party guests will be drawn mainly from the faculty, and the children's friends are likely to be the children of colleagues.

Clearly the structure and function of this subculture, the extent to which it satisfies basic needs, are important in considering such campus problems as suicides (second-ranking cause of death among college students), nervous breakdowns, drugs and alcoholism, theft, sexual promiscuity, failures, and dropouts. Needless to remark, the faculty, too, has its share of these problems, and it is a share that is increasing. Yet within the university these problems are rarely discussed as societal problems, that is, as problems generated by stresses, strains, and tensions in the academic community as such. And when they are discussed, it is comparatively rare for administrators to draw on the specialized knowledge of either behavioral or humanistic scientists. Psychiatrists and political scientists are usually less consulted than such other behavioral experts as electrical engineers, biochemists, and deans of business and law schools. The problems mentioned are invariably approached as administrative problems which, by definition, are problems that can be solved by a new rule or disciplinary action.

But the university is only one type of organization rarely thought of as a therapeutic community. While universities lag far behind corporations and law firms in developing the equivalent of executive health programs, the latter do not yet see themselves as therapeutic communities in which there is a central concern for mental as well as physical health. Existing health programs too often focus on the maximization of productivity, commonly defined in terms of output, job-performance, or some other crude measure of efficiency. It therefore is no surprise that many of these programs function at the expense of health, rationality, and creativity rather than in support of these values.

If the concept of the therapeutic community is to be successfully redefined, there will have to be significant changes in the training of behavioral scientists and in the role played by them in society. Since the supply of clinicians is extremely limited, clinical training must be provided for all those whose occupational positions require them to serve as teachers, counselors, advisers, and social planners—in short, for all those who occupy important posts in the therapeutic community. In the university, for example, the larger part of the guidance in function is performed by the professors with whom students are in frequent contact; in effect, the professors are called upon by students to act as clinicians, irrespective of whether they have any clinical training or vocation for clinical practice. Moreover, if the university is to be successfully transformed from a learning factory into a therapeutic community, those who plan and direct the transformation must be familiar with psychiatric methods and insights. Decisions about the curricula and degree requirements, the design of buildings and physical settings so as to provide the necessary amounts of privacy and collegiality, rules and regulations, student and faculty housing arrangements, and much more—these decisions require more than the part-time consultative services of a social psychiatrist or clinical psychologist. Ideally those who make these decisions will be generalists, not specialists, and as generalists they will be participant-observers in therapeutic processes that draw on the whole range of the behavioral and social sciences.

The challenge presented by and to the therapeutic community is a formidable one, to be sure. But if the challenge is very great, so, too, is the opportunity presented to increase the potential, individual and social, national and international, for health, rationality, and creativity. Insofar as these values of the therapeutic community are realizable only in a world that has abolished war, peace itself would not be least among the outcomes of a fruitful collaboration between psychiatrists and political scientists.

But it would be naive to imagine that collaboration will be either easy or immediately productive, considering that innovative, "break-through" thinking is not the foremost characteristic of either the clinic or the academy. At least twice in his life Freud observed that there were three "impossible" professions: educating, healing, and governing. He has not yet been proven wrong.

REFERENCES

ADORNO, T. W., et al. 1950. The authoritarian personality. New York: Harper.
ALEXANDER, F. 1941. The psychiatric aspects of war and peace. American Journal of Sociology, 46: 504–520.
———. 1942. Our age of unreason. Philadelphia: Lippincott.
———. 1943. The march of medicine. New York: Columbia University Press.
BRICKNER, R. M. 1943. Is Germany incurable? Philadelphia: Lippincott.
BURROW, T. 1941. Neurosis and war: a problem of human behavior. Journal of Psychology, 12: 235–49.
CHISHOLM, G. B. 1946. The psychiatry of enduring peace and social progress. Psychiatry, 9 (1): 3–20.
COLBY, K. M. 1960. An introduction to psychoanalytic research. New York: Basic Books.

DOLLARD, J., *et al.* 1939. *Frustration and aggression.* New Haven, Conn.: Yale University Press.

EASTON, D., and R. D. HESS. 1960. The child's changing image of the President. *Public Opinion Quarterly,* 24: 632–44.

————. 1962. The child's political world. *Midwest Journal of Political Science,* 6: 236–47.

ERIKSON, E. H. 1942. Hitler's imagery and German youth. *Psychiatry,* 5: 475–93.

FRANK, J. D. 1960. Breaking the thought barrier: psychological challenges of the nuclear age. *Psychiatry,* 23: 245–66.

FRENKEL-BRUNSWIK, E. 1952. Interaction of psychological and sociological factors in political behavior. *American Political Science Review,* 46: 44–65.

FREUD, S. 1915. Thoughts for the times on war and death. In *Collected Papers, IV.* London: Hogarth Press, 1949.

————. 1932. Why war? In *Collected Papers, V.* London: Hogarth Press, 1950.

FROMM, E. 1941. *Escape from freedom.* New York: Rinehart.

GREENSTEIN, F. 1960. The benevolent leader: children's images of political authority. *American Political Science Review,* 54: 934–43.

————. 1965. *Children and politics.* New Haven, Conn.: Yale University Press.

JONES, E. 1955. *The life and work of Sigmund Freud, Vol. 2.* New York: Basic Books.

KARDINER, A. 1945. *The psychological frontiers of society.* New York: Columbia University Press.

L'ETANG, H. 1958. The health of statesmen. *The Practitioner,* January.

————. 1961. Ill health in senior officers. *The Practitioner,* April.

MARMOR, J. 1964. War, violence and human nature. *Bulletin of Atomic Scientists,* March: 19–22.

MOELLENHOFF, F. 1947. The price of individuality: speculations about German national characteristics. *American Image,* 4: 33–60.

MYRDAL, G. 1944. *An American dilemma.* New York: Harper.

REICH, W. 1946. *The mass psychology of fascism.* New York: Orgone Institute Press.

ROGOW, A. A. 1966. Disability in high office. *Medical Opinion and Review,* 1: 16–19.

STOUFFER, S. A. 1955. Indices of psychological illness. In P. F. Lazarsfeld and M. Rosenberg (Eds.), *The language of social research.* Glencoe, Ill.: Free Press.

16

OBSTACLES TO A RAPPROCHEMENT BETWEEN HISTORY AND SOCIOLOGY: A SOCIOLOGIST'S VIEW

SIDNEY H. ARONSON

Historians and sociologists frequently complain about the puny results of their interdisciplinary efforts, but few ever do anything about it.[1] Every now and then, it looks as though a rapprochement is at hand. In 1954, the Committee on Historiography of the Social Science Research Council published a volume, *The Social Sciences in Historical Study,* the purpose of which was to familiarize historians with the sociological perspective. That work concluded: "The Committee believes that collaboration between historians and other social scientists should be cultivated as effectively as possible." And when that occasional study that bridges the two fields appears, some reviewer is guaranteed to say: "This book is a fruitful result of the cross-disciplinary approach to history which has been so long a-borning" (Douglass, 1964).

But the cross-disciplinary efforts of historians and sociologists continue to be long a-borning, and it may be that all that such statements illustrate is the value placed in the academic world on interdisciplinary research. For despite the rhetoric of collaboration, both disciplines remain aloof and few sociologists and even fewer historians are really convinced that a relationship between the two will be useful or productive. This can be seen, for example, in the role that history as a discipline plays in the training of future sociologists and in the role that sociology plays in the training of young historians.

The word "history" does not appear in the index of Elbridge Sibley's *The Education of Sociologists in the United States* (1963). In examining the

1. I would like to thank Professor Abraham S. Blumberg of John Jay College of the City University of New York and Professor Herbert Danzder of Herbert H. Lehman College of the City University of New York for their contributions to this paper.

requirements for doctoral candidates in sociology, Sibley did notice that there were pressures to take a minor in a field in some other department but that such pressures were characteristics of departments "with lesser resources of personnel and facilities" that "do not consider their own offerings sufficient to justify the award of a doctoral degree" (Sibley, 1963). It is notable that none of the most prestigious departments impose this requirement.

Although the word "sociology" is cited eight times in *The Education of Historians in the United States,* the authors of that work discovered that in recent years graduate departments of history require that their students take more courses in history than they had ten years earlier (Perkins and Snell, 1962). If these requirements still leave the students time for study in other departments, it is to political science rather than sociology (or psychology) that they are likely to turn. This can be partly understood in terms of the traditional emphasis in history on politics.

Nor do sociology or history departments themselves do much to teach about the other's discipline. The fields of concentration offered by graduate sociology departments only rarely include courses that apply the sociological perspective to history. Only one department, in the major graduate departments surveyed by Sibley in 1963, offered "historical sociology" as a field of emphasis. Of course, the historical dimension is dealt with in sociology courses on social change, in area studies, and in comparative institutions. This usually means that students who enroll for these courses read Weber and Marx and others who combined history and sociology, or they read conventional histories.

Graduate training in sociology seemed to be taking a major step toward a rapprochement with history in 1954 when the Department of Sociology in the Graduate Faculties at Columbia University appointed to its faculty a young man who had recently earned his doctorate in history and who thought of himself as a historian. It was hoped that his presence would encourage graduate students and faculty members, too, to use history. Columbia was then—as it is now—a hotbed of survey research, and the appointment of a historian to its department was truly revolutionary. The time of the appointment coincided with a period when "crude empiricism" was being criticized and was held to be responsible for the "foolishness of some sociological work" (Berger, 1963).

The Columbia department produced a few doctoral dissertations in historical sociology but the new specialty did not really catch on in sociology as a whole. As noted, only one major department offered historical sociology as a special field, and Columbia also probably remains alone in that it has a historian training sociologists—although he may no longer think of himself as a historian.

Somehow, it is unthinkable that any graduate department of history would give a full-time appointment to a sociologist to help prepare future historians.

The Columbia Sociology Department was a party to another attempt to bring the two disciplines together when their distinguished Paul Lazarsfeld offered—in an address to historians—to incorporate into the interview schedules administered by sociologists the questions to which future historians might want the answers. It has been said that the response was somewhat less than overwhelming (Lazarsfeld, 1950).

How does it happen that, despite the value given to interdisciplinary research, and despite the fact that the subject matter of history and sociology is of common interest to both disciplines, there is little rapport between the two? A sociologist's answer to that question does not mean that the historian will be the villain; they both must be doing something wrong. Basically, the problem boils down to the fact that most sociologists and historians have no clear understanding of what historical sociology really is. Furthermore, the sociologists must take the major blame for this state of affairs since they developed the field and they list the area as a specialty.

Perhaps the most brilliant example of historical sociology is in the work of Max Weber, the person who is frequently credited with establishing the field (Salomon, 1945). As is well known, Weber's treatise deals with the emergence of a new social structure, industrial capitalism. His thesis is that modern capitalism is the product of individual historical circumstances involving religious considerations and not the product of inescapable historical necessity (Weber, 1958). He was aware that according to scientific canons of logic and procedure it was not enough to document the "fact" that Calvinism preceded capitalism in order to support a hypothesized causal connection. It was also necessary to find other situations in history that, at a certain level of abstraction, were comparable to Europe at the advent of capitalism. Through extraordinary research, he carefully elaborated the magic, ritual, moral, and religious elements that prevented the rise of industrial capitalism in various civilizations despite the fact that political and economic conditions were favorable to establishing that form of economic organization (Salomon, 1945; Weber, 1920).

It is a mistake to dismiss Weber, as some historians do, because subsequent research has shown that he had some of his "facts" wrong. The genius of Weber was that he established a new approach to historical materials that included both the kinds of questions that were asked and a method by which these quesions could be answered. The central question was one that occupied the attention of many of the founding fathers of sociology: how did modern Western society develop? That question involved the nature and structure of preindustrial society; but it went beyond that to raise questions about the sources of new social structures, the shift in the primacy of social institutions, the role of ideas in social change, and the relationship between sociocultural conditions and individual personality. Thus, in brief, did its founder define the field of historical sociology.

The method to be employed in testing this kind of theory can be abstracted from Weber's approach to the study of capitalism. It utilized the scientific model of categorizing and contrasting comparable situations. No one denies that there are major difficulties in finding comparable situations in history; yet Weber's method for explaining social change is probably the most fruitful devised thus far.

There is evidence to suggest that sociologists and historians did not learn Weber's definition of historical sociology. Graduate training in sociology rarely includes any self-conscious attempts to give students the sophistication to ask questions about social change or the skills to answer them. If a survey were made of the contents of sociology graduate courses that attempt to teach students to use history, it would probably be discovered that those courses largely repeat what graduate students in history are taught in their "methodology" courses. Such courses try to teach sociologists how to do history, not how to do historical sociology. It is not surprising, therefore, that young sociologists do not specialize more in historical sociology: it was not their intention in registering for these courses to learn how to become historians, but rather how to use history to develop and test social theory.

Since courses in historical sociology are rare, graduate students in sociology are exposed to the importance of the historical dimension in other specialties. Perhaps the subfield which, more than any other, communicates to the student the importance of history is the field of social change. In these courses students are exposed to Weber and Marx and Toynbee and other historical sociologists and they read their works. But it is not enough to read Weber in order to learn how to deal with the emergence of modern society. Students must be taught how to *do* Weber, that is, to test theories of change according to his methods.

There are other reasons for the fact that sociologists neglect history. The training of young sociologists frequently requires an apprenticeship in a research institute which is appended to the department of sociology. Such bureaus are largely self-supporting and the research is done on contract. The survey research thus assumed is concerned mainly with the attitudes, opinions, or behavior of living people. Such research is not always concerned with broad theoretical issues in sociology. As a result of his socialization in such a bureau, the young sociologist is likely to feel that research in the field of his choice ordinarily starts out with an interview schedule or questionnaire and a sample of living people. And that, incidentally, is probably consistent with the image that most people have of sociologists. Little wonder the society in which sociology is most important and furthest advanced has yet to produce a Max Weber.

There is also the belief among sociologists that it is easier to study the present than the past (Feldmesser, 1963). When living people are studied there can be reasonable certainty that the sample is a cross-section of some population. Furthermore, one has greater control over the information that is collected. In dealing with the documents the dead leave behind, such as diaries, memoirs, confessions, autobiographies and the like, one can never be sure that the people studied are characteristic or that one will find the information required in order to answer the questions raised. This uncertainty has always been a source of difficulty for historians who are rarely sure—no matter how much digging they do—that the objects of study are representative and who have problems, therefore, with the validity of the findings.

There is also a widespread prejudice among sociologists against using data that have been collected by someone who is not a trained sociologist. We are especially wary about information reported in the newspapers because of the well-deserved reputation the papers have for inaccuracy and selective reporting. Sociologists are frequently amazed at the reliance historians place on the press.

These biases are not likely to push sociologists in the direction of history. Yet questions concerning new structures, new elites, new personality types cannot possibly be checked by reference to the present alone. Sociologists would be better off developing techniques for knowing what portions of historical documents such as newspapers can be relied upon, rather than in rejecting them as inferior substitutes for freshly gathered survey data (Danzger, 1968).

American sociology's indifference to historical documents is all the more puzzling because in the few instances that they were used, the rewards in terms of conceptual and theoretical advances were great. One such instance is the work of William I. Thomas and Florian Znaniecki whose five-volume *The Polish Peasant in Europe and America* appeared between 1918 and 1920. In this study of Polish life in Poland, Germany, and the United States, the authors utilized materials more characteristic of the historian than the sociologist: letters written by immigrants, newspaper archives, commemorative parish histories, unpublished autobiographies, and records of sodalities. Like Weber, Thomas and Znaniecki were interested in social change, specifically the forms of social disorganization and reorganization the peasant was experiencing in the Old World and the New. This is not the place to examine that vast and somewhat controversial work. Suffice it to say that at least two central concepts in sociology and social psychology have come from it: values and attitudes. The study of values and attitudes is so taken for granted as an important activity of social scientists that it is difficult to imagine how novel it must have appeared at the beginning of the century (Madge, 1962). And Muzafer Sherif who did so much to expand the usefulness of those concepts has credited *The Polish Peasant* as a source of his insights (Sherif, 1963).[2]

With the notable exception of Thomas and Znaniecki and a handful of

2. Two other approaches in sociology utilize history but handle the problem of social change in a narrower, more microscopic level and, therefore, do not as a rule fall under the definition of historical sociology presented here. These consist of longitudinal studies, such as trend and panel analyses, and demographic works (see Lazarsfeld and Rosenberg, 1955).

other sociologists, American sociology has failed to apply its perspective to historical materials. Why is it that historians have not capitalized upon this situation? The value of interdisciplinary research notwithstanding, many historians are repelled by the prospect of a more sociological history. Indeed, to some historians the word "sociology" is a term of opprobrium, and the sociologist is the village or, better, the campus "idiot." One of the reasons for that characterization is that the sociologist's disregard of the historical dimension is an offense of the historian's ideal of the civilized man (Berger, 1963). This image of the sociologist is illustrated in the delightful novel about academic life by Stringfellow Barr, a historian, whose sociologist is so obtuse he could not apply a major concept in sociological analysis to his own situation—taking the role of the other, that is, to see himself as others do.

Perhaps, another source of hostility is the fact that sociology is "in" in a way that history is not. We are living in the age of sociology. Its language is commonplace. Its research proposals have resulted in vast grants of money and the establishment of research institutes. On some campuses sociology professors command higher salaries than many of their colleagues in the humanities, and are often able to buy released time from teaching, to employ ant colonies of graduate students, and to do other things that may antagonize their less affluent associates.

Some historians, although certainly not all or even most of them, are prejudiced when it comes to sociology and sociologists—they respond to the label. Once they see the label they frequently impute to the sociologist a host of undesirable traits—jargon, methodology, statistics. Every sociologist has had experience in refuting these criticisms with students and with the public, but it does get tiresome to deal with strictures of such little substance, especially when they come from civilized academics. Besides, as has been suggested, the major failing of sociology when it comes to history is that it has not properly defined the area of fruitful collaboration. Yet this observation is rarely made.

It is necessary, however, to deal with the stereotype for it is a barrier to interdisciplinary cooperation. Historians accuse sociologists of writing and speaking what Peter Berger calls a "barbaric dialect." One often gets the feeling that to some historians the definition of jargon is prose which has been written by a sociologist. One historian reviewed a book in historical sociology done by a sociologist as follows: "It is one of those sociological tracts that force the reader to spend half his time mastering a jargon that is solemnly referred to as 'methodology'" (Rubenstein, 1964). One is justified, perhaps, in suspecting prejudice in this case by the fact that another, more distinguished, and clearly more intelligent historian wrote of the same book that its author, a sociologist, had produced a "clearly written text which is free of all unnecessary jargon" (Kurtz, 1964).

Any discipline must develop a terminology—in physics to deal with matters unknown to most people and for which no words exist. But terminology may be more important for the social sciences just because their subject matter is familiar and because words with many referents do exist to denote them. A word like "class," a central concept in sociology (and, incidentally, one which Marx said he obtained from historians), has many meanings. Yet the sociologist must have a precise, unambiguous definition of the concept if his work is to proceed with any degree of rigor and if it is going to be understood (Berger, 1963).

How barbaric is the writing of sociologists? Is it any more so, on the average, than that in other disciplines which do not specialize in literary expression? As Robert Bierstedt pointed out many years ago, many works in sociology provide the opportunity to read good prose—the writing of Peter Berger, Robert K. Merton, George Homans, and George Simpson are just a few examples. However, even if there were no fine writers among sociologists, the complaint is irrelevant. Sociology is not an art form, and sociologists need not be primarily concerned with writing good prose.

The term "methodology" is a horrible example of jargon, and it is a source of prejudice in its own right. But why is the term "historiography" less jargon and more literate than the term "methodology?" Both seem to have similar meanings.

Sociologists are self-conscious about the procedures they use in empirical research. This self-consciousness has produced an uneasiness on the part of historians about the preoccupation with the strategies employed in research and the development of technical skills at the expense of history and philosophy. Many American sociologists are committed to the scientific ethos, and this means that they are bound by certain canons of procedure: their statements must be arrived at through the observation of certain rules of evidence (Berger, 1963; Feldmesser, 1963). Wherever possible it means applying the classical experimental model or a variant of it.

Sociologists take methodology seriously because they are aware from horrible examples that the strategy of research employed and the underlying logic determine the results of the study. Yet it is this self-consciousness about methodology, including its explicit description in our studies, that is repugnant to some historians. For example, one of the reasons for the origins of the mythology about a radical change in the social composition of officeholders in Andrew Jackson's administration was carelessness about the logic and procedures of empirical research. The historians responsible, in part, for the misapprehension about a widespread democratization of the civil service in the Jackson era based their generalizations on a handful of cases (Aronson, 1964). Yet I was taken to task by a reviewer for criticizing James Parton and Hermann Von Holst for using such a tiny sampling of officeholders on the grounds that nineteenth-century historians could hardly be expected to be familiar with newfangled sociological notions about representativeness (Borden, 1964). The truth is that notions about representativeness predate sociology, and they predate the nineteenth century.

The use of statistics can be seen in the same light. In fact, most sociologists have little more than a cookbook knowledge of statistics. To quote Peter Berger once more, they "treat it with about the same mixture of awe, ignorance, and timid manipulation as a poor village priest would the mighty Latin cadences of Thomist theology." Statistical data by themselves are not sociology; they become sociology only when they are sociologically interpreted and put within a theoretical frame of reference that is sociological (Berger, 1963). When this is done, statistical information does provide understanding of social processes. A distinguished historian, Gaetano Salvemini, frequently said that in the analysis and understanding of critical events in history it was always a question of more or less. Statistical analysis makes it possible to know whether it is more or less.

It is likely that many sociologists shy away from history because they feel that historians are not properly self-conscious about their methods. Sociologists remember that the history they were exposed to in high school and in college rarely contained statements about the research strategies employed to produce it and few tables supporting the conclusions. One exception was the tables depicting population growth; but there was never a hint of the major difficulties involved in trying to enumerate a population or of the reliability of the figures (Feldmesser, 1963).

The absence of quantitative analysis in history is partly a result of the fact that it is hard—not impossible, but hard—to do that kind of study retrospectively. How can you find out how many and which colonists (sociologically speaking) supported the American Revolution, how the American family changed during the Industrial Revolution, what values were being taught in the common schools in the period preceding the Civil War, how much social mobility there has been in the history of American society? When the historian using traditional methods tries to answer questions of that sort, he immerses himself in whatever material he can find—he rarely determines in advance what information he must have in order to demonstrate a trend—and then tries to come to some assessment. There is, obviously, a major problem concerning the validity of the findings.

Sometimes one historian repeats the study of another; but since replication in history often means a reinterpretation of the same materials, the reader is faced with two opposing but plausible views. Occasionally, because of the historian's indifference to the methodological advances made in sociology, it happens that a sociologist using quantitative methods debunks these findings. More often, the conclusions of the historian must stand because no one has done the logical, rigorous, and systematic analysis necessary to validate or challenge them, or because data are not available for such an approach.

It sometimes seems as though historians believe that the difficulties they face in establishing the validity of their conclusions do not represent a liability but are actually advantageous. This position is expressed in the contentions that quantitative analysis has a dehumanizing effect on history and that it has difficulty dealing with significant human problems. Thus Arthur M. Schlesinger, Jr., argues that the historian's methods despite their limitations may "yield truths about both individual and social experience which quantitative social research by itself could never reach" (Schlesinger, 1962).

It goes without saying that quantitative analysis cannot and need not be applied in most research in history. Furthermore, it is easy to understand why historians are frequently unimpressed by the findings of empirical sociology. Historians, however, ignore quantitative social research where relevant and where feasible at the price of knowing significant truths about social experience. One historian who is aware of this is Stephan Thernstrom. Utilizing sociological methods and concepts and painstaking study and analysis of historical documents, Thernstrom (1964) made an important contribution to our knowledge of social mobility in nineteenth century America. He demonstrated that in the years 1850–80 in Newburyport, Massachusetts, the vast majority of manual laborers remained manual laborers, and children born into working-class families rarely achieved any marked improvement in their occupational status. Yet Thernstrom was chastized by a colleague on grounds that his careful counting and tracking of mobility patterns may have missed the whole point about social mobility and that Thernstrom was deficient in qualitative analysis (Berthoff, 1965).

Quantitative analysis far from depriving the individual who dominates history of his humanity can give greater insight into his personal qualities. One example familiar to this writer is the traditional approach of historians to Andrew Jackson's relationship to the Second Bank of the United States. Historians have tended to accept Jackson's statement: "Everyone that knows me does know, that I have been always opposed to the United States Bank, nay all Banks." Much history of the period deals with Jackson's reputed aversion to banks. Yet an examination of Jackson's top appointments to the civil service turned up the information that he filled twenty elite positions with people who were at one time directors of private banks and who, in a period when government officials did not have to worry about conflict of interests, probably did very well when the federal deposits were transferred to private banks (Aronson, 1964).

These two examples illustrate that significant variables in the "historical equation" are susceptible to quantification.

A major obstacle to interdisciplinary cooperation is the fact that historical sociology will require the historian who is oriented to traditional methods to drastically alter his approach. He will no longer be able to indulge his penchant for straight narrative. He can no longer be satisfied with reporting unrelated facts or sequences of unrelated facts. He will have to pay attention to explanation, to theory—a term almost as anathema as methodology. This is not to say that historians have not tried to deal with explanation. As Robert A. Feldmesser has pointed out, however, historical explanation tends to account for an event in terms of other events which preceded or accompanied them: what is lacking are "relationships, relevance, theory—structure —without which the facts make no sense" (Feldmesser, 1963).

According to the scientific framework within which historical sociology operates, the explanation of facts and their relationships must be established differently than by determining the sequences of events. In attempting to explain an event, science proceeds by sampling other events which are similar to it according to certain criteria. Then it determines what principle is common to all of the events. The common principle then serves as an explanation of all events of the same class. The implication is that science never fully explains *any* unique event (Feldmesser, 1963).

The scientific method of explaining events puts the historian in a predicament. He tries to account for events that *are* unique, if for no other reason than the fact that they happened at one time rather than another. To be scientific, the historian must place an event in its suitable categories and apply to it the relevant principles. But in order to do that, he must overlook for the moment that the event did occur at one time rather than another, and since it is that very fact which is the hallmark of history, he is therefore, in seeking explanation, no longer a historian. He is some kind of social scientist—an economist, a political scientist, a sociologist, depending of course on the nature of the problem being investigated (Feldmesser, 1963).

If the historian is "to be scientific" he must follow this approach. No one argues that all historians must be scientific or that even most should be. History is an art, a humanity and as such has its own methods of arriving at the truth. And as has frequently been pointed out, the concern with the unique in human experience—a central concern of the historian—is "an inevitable and precious part of civilization" (Feldmesser, 1963). Indeed, one reason for the anti-sociology bias is the sociologist's slight of uniqueness in favor of generalizations about classes of phenomena.

History can be a science—a social science. As such, it is capable of producing a kind of truth other than uniqueness and which is more akin to scientific truth. This scientific approach to history, which has here been referred to as historical sociology, gives the greatest hope for answering questions about social change and the forces producing modern society. Furthermore the sociological perspective is also indispensible to the historian who is not interested in historical sociology but who prefers to specialize in the development of a single nation. Jackson Turner Main demonstrated that the general categories developed in sociology for describing the structure of societies can be used to organize historical societies (Main, 1965). More important, sociological theory and sociological methods can suggest relationships among historical phenomena that were hitherto unperceived (Diamond, 1967).

Because few sociologists are attracted to history and few historians are drawn to sociology, theories of social change—so crucial to an understanding of the human experience—are, perhaps, the thinnest in sociology. The absence of rapport between the two disciplines is all the more disappointing since the issues separating them are not critical and the advantages of collaboration are obvious: sociologists do have the methodology, a conceptual apparatus, and some theory; historians tend to be broadly educated and, further, they know what records there are and where they are likely to be found.

What, then, can be done to stimulate interest among sociologists and historians in historical sociology? More sociologists might be persuaded to give up their bias against history if historians broadened the definition of historical documents—as many are already doing—to include previously neglected "objective" kinds of data that have a high degree of reliability and that at the same time satisfy the sociologist's requirements for representativeness. For example, if records of land ownership, tax payments, occupation and income patterns, family histories, budgets, and living styles, voting rolls, lists of school enrollments, census records, memberships in voluntary associations, and so on, were available for whole communities, the sociologist would be able to apply the methodology that so concerns him.

A very promising mechanism to stimulate such interest is the joint appointment. Apparently, interdisciplinary cooperation as a value is such that the college professor who qualifies for an appointment in two departments enjoys more prestige than his more specialized colleagues—all other things being equal. This situation should be capitalized upon in such a way so that many more historians and sociologists find themselves in the same department—for part of the time, at least. As is well known, there is a new breed of historians, scholars who may find certain kinds of sociology departments more congenial than history departments staffed with traditionalists. Similarly, some sociologists feel comfortable and stimulated by historians, especially since such interaction facilitates their inquiry into the process of social change.

Joint appointments may also promote rapid learning of one another's fields, although the historian in the sociology department will have some uncomfortable months until his colleagues realize that it is unreasonable to expect him to know everything that ever happened. On the other hand, the sociologist who spends some of his time in a history department will have some anxious moments when it is discovered that he knows nothing about mathematical models. Joint appointments may also be the best technique for getting historians and sociologists to give up their stereotypes of one another. Of course, there is always the danger that the person receiving the joint appointment will resemble the stereotype, with a resulting setback for collaboration. In recruiting an academician to fill an interdisciplinary position it is indispensable, therefore, to find one who is capable of taking the role of the other.

REFERENCES

ARONSON, S. H. 1964. *Status and kinship in the higher civil service: standards of selection in the administrations of John Adams, Thomas Jefferson, and Andrew Jackson.* Cambridge: Harvard University Press.

BARR, S. 1958. *Purely academic.* New York: Simon and Schuster.

BERGER, P. L. 1963. *Invitation to sociology: a humanistic perspective.* Garden City, N.Y.: Doubleday.

BERTHOFF, R. 1965. Review of Stephan Thernstrom, *Poverty and progress: social mobility in a nineteenth century city. American Historical Review,* 70: 900–901.

BORDEN, M. 1964. Review of Sidney H. Aronson, *Status and kinship in the higher civil service. William and Mary Quarterly,* 21: 625–27.

DANZGER, H. 1968. Civil rights conflict and community power structure. Unpublished Ph.D. dissertation, Columbia University.

DIAMOND, S. 1967. Review of Jackson Turner Main, *The social structure of revolutionary America. American Journal of Sociology,* 72: 418–19.

DOUGLASS, E. P. 1964. Review of Sidney H. Aronson, *Status and kinship in the higher civil service. American Historical Review,* 70: 190–91.

FELDMESSER, R. A. 1963. Social science, humanities, and the social studies. Paper presented to Educational Services, Inc., Cambridge, Mass. (Mimeo.)

KURTZ, S. G. 1964. Review of Sidney H. Aronson, *Status and kinship in the higher civil service. New England Quarterly,* 37: 537–39.

LAZARSFELD, P. F. 1950–51. The obligations of the 1950 pollster to the 1984 historian. *Public Opinion Quarterly,* 14: 617–38.

––––––, and M. ROSENBERG (Eds.). 1955. *The language of social research.* Glencoe, Ill.: Free Press.

MADGE, J. 1962. *The origins of scientific sociology.* New York: Free Press.

MAIN, J. T. 1965. *The social structure of revolutionary America.* Princeton, N.J.: Princeton University Press.

PERKINS, D., and J. L. SNELL. 1962. *The education of historians in the United States.* New York: McGraw-Hill.

RUBENSTEIN, J. S. 1964. Review of Sidney H. Aronson, *Status and kinship in the higher civil service. Fordham Law Review,* 33: 351–54.

SALOMON, A. 1945. German sociology. In G. Gurvitch and W. E. Moore (Eds.), *Twentieth century sociology.* New York: Philosophical Library.

SCHLESINGER, A. M., JR. 1962. The humanist looks at empirical social research. *American Sociological Review,* 27: 768–71.

SHERIF, M. 1963. Social psychology—interdisciplinary problems and trends. In S. Koch (Ed.), *Investigations of man as socius: their place in psychology and the social sciences.* Vol. 6, *Psychology: a study of a science.* New York: McGraw-Hill.

SIBLEY, E. 1963. *The education of sociologists in the United States.* New York: Russell Sage Foundation.

Social Science Research Council. 1954. *The social sciences in historical study.* Bulletin 64. New York: The Council.

THERNSTROM, S. 1964. *Poverty and progress: social mobility in a nineteenth century city.* Cambridge: Harvard University Press.

THOMAS, W. I., and F. ZNANIECKI. 1918–20. *The Polish peasant in Europe and America*. Boston: Gorham Press.

WEBER, M. 1920–21. *Gesammelte Aufsaetze zur Religionssoziologie*. Tübingen: J. C. B. Mohr.

———. 1951. *The religion of China*. Glencoe, Ill.: Free Press.

———. 1952. *Ancient Judaism*. Glencoe, Ill.: Free Press.

———. 1958a. *The Protestant ethic and the spirit of capitalism*. New York: Scribner's.

———. 1958b. *The religion of India*. Glencoe, Ill.: Free Press.

17

HISTORY AND THEORY: THE NEED FOR DECADENCE

Daniel Calhoun

Sociologists and historians have long listened to each other fretting about the relation between history and the social sciences. We have listened to methodological expositions and endorsed much of their logic. We have watched large expanses of theory being spread out, and have wondered just what to do with it. We have also noted what has happened in specific cases, when historians or theorists have worked at the juncture of their fields, and we have usually been unhappy about the results.

There are two forms, among others, that dissatisfaction has taken: a feeling that the right kind of theory has not been suggested for historical work, and a sense that the history-theory problem has served ulterior ends, both as an indulgence in ideology and as a preoccupation with the workings of academic institutions. Much talk about theory and interdisciplinary effort has had its institutional correlates in conferences and training programs. There have been far too few men with specific theories to test or concrete problems to solve.

For the institutional preoccupation, it is tempting to suggest institutional remedies: programs that would center on specific theories or concrete problems, not on method or theory in general. This can be put in terms of John Dewey's old attempt to resolve the conflict between *interest* and *effort* as educational modes. In one sense, we have been putting too much effort into trying to try. We need to cultivate the gardens that are our separate projects and problems. Or, if the historian is to work in the neighborhood of theory, he needs to find theories more interesting than most that sociologists have suggested to him, theories that will have enough intrinsic intellectual interest to distract the historian from his biases. It may be that the availability of such theories will do more to make academic institutions work than any institutional devices can do to encourage good work on theory. As in recent advances in high-school teaching, it is available knowledge that produces new curriculum, and not the other way around.

Instead of true virtue, which would consist in presenting a specific theory that might apply to concrete problems, I wish here to look at some examples of specific work, ask secondary questions about what kind of theory might meet the deficiencies in these examples, and then consider whether the intellectual climate in which we live is favorable to the emergence of such theory. The examples I shall consider are: the status-panic controversy, as it has centered on the work of David Donald and Richard Hofstadter; the attempt by Lee Benson to move from theory to empirical work on voting behavior; the notably successful recent work by American demographers; and the larger relevance of developmental and modernization approaches, especially that presented by Marion J. Levy, Jr. In my comments I shall pay less attention to problems of method or logic than to the nature of the discourse in which the history-theory relation has been pursued.

The relevance of style or discourse was indicated a few years ago in one (necessarily anonymous) byplay between history and theory. An American historian had presented a general account of a topic, in which relatively little work had been done, in the form of a "hypothetical" description. This description included many challenging ideas, some of which had implications for other fields. An anthropologist picked up certain categories in this "hypothetical" account, translated them into propositions that could be tested by crosscultural contingency tests, and carried out the tests. Not surprisingly, he did not find uniform confirmation for the historian's first ideas, but neither did he find uniform negation. The historian, when he saw the result published, was not the least dismayed by the outcome as such. But he professed surprise that his account had been taken literally as a testable hypothesis: he had only intended the word "hypothetical" as a manner of writing, as a metaphor for the tentative and undogmatic spirit in which he was presenting his generalizations.

Part of what the anthropologist did that seemed strange to the historian was precisely to construct an array of alternative outcomes, in terms of which contingency tables could be constructed. The historian's procedural reflex had been to test the accuracy of such observations as he had, then to move impressionistically (but with plain honesty about the tentative character of the move) to ideas that would have general significance. The anthropologist's procedural reflex was to move from general ideas to bodies of data for whose accuracy he depended more or less on the credentials of field workers, and then to carry out his own tests upon the ideas as such. Now the historian in question is often reported as encouraging his students to undertake genuine unsolved problems, not mere fishing expeditions. The distinction between the historical and anthropological reflexes did *not* turn on any personal distaste for open inquiry, but rather on the larger rhetoric or vocabulary in which the two disciplines operate. Even when the historian is disposed to open inquiry, his field as a medium of communication encourages him to take his conclusions *as if* they have persuasive function, not analytic function.

This bias toward persuasion works also in the writing of historians who are commonly identified with the attempt at theories of social change. One such theory, the status-panic idea, is easiest to examine in the form of David Donald's compact essay on the abolitionists (Donald, 1956, but *cf.* Hofstadter, 1955). This essay may seem to offer a simple case of an unfortunate methodological oversight. It turns out, though, that the kind of oversight that occurred was homologous to the kinds of role criteria that Donald attributed to some of his subjects. What was plausible for them (although presented with a certain irony or condescension) was plausible in Donald (although not noticed by him at the time he was writing). The abolitionists as he conceived them were men who had personal or family backgrounds in the old mercantile, landed, or clerical leadership groups of New England; with the coming of a more commercialized or industrialized society, they had lost influence to newer kinds of men, and had compensated by taking up roles as critics of a society even farther flung than the one in which they had lost status. Some of the specific evidence for this argument came from statistics on the background or careers of certain abolitionists: backgrounds that were variously or combinedly rural, orthodox-ministerial, New Englandish.

The most direct criticism of this argument, as presented by Robert Skotheim (1959), is similar to the counterarguments against other status-loss discussions: among other things, he points out that men who were not abolitionists had similar backgrounds to those who were. Donald had not provided a control group. This argument, which is probably the most familiar to scholars among all polemical disputes about social science methods in *American* history, has the feature—hardly a distinctive feature, though—that no one involved in any part of the dispute took the idea of status-compensation seriously *as a theory*. If Donald was so concerned with abolitionists, and Hofstadter with progressives, that neither man constructed a test applicable to the general idea, it is equally true that the critics of these men failed to present any test applicable to the general theory. Donald, for his part, used the status-compensation idea as a way of positing a degree of intellectual order in a phenomenon that to him must have seemed arbitrary and even bizarre. One of the ways that he supported his argument was to neglect those alternatives that might have constituted a control group. His subjects, as he described them, preserved a sense of order in their universe while neglecting to pick up certain alternative careers that were, in a purely objective sense, presented to them by changes going on in the economy. This homology between Donald and the abolitionists-as-he-presented-them may suggest certain broader homologies between the historian's role as historian and the historian's role as imperfect sociologist.

The points for which the Donald piece has been criticized are simple enough; but if they amounted to nothing more than that certain considerations were overlooked, or that the investigator wrote too briefly and enthusiastically, they would tell us little about the cognitive or expressive needs that are generated when history and theory interact. But in this case the investigator summed up his own attitude, methods, and conclusions, all in two brief sentences: "Viewed against the backgrounds and common ideas of its leaders, abolitionism appears to have been a double crusade. Seeking freedom of the Negro in the South, these reformers were also attempting a restoration of the traditional values of their class at home" (Donald, 1956, pp. 35–36). The crucial phrase is the first :"Viewed against the backgrounds and common ideas of its leaders." Partly through its quiet pun on two meanings of "backgrounds," this phrase asserts a definite standard of historical judgment. The thing to be explained is a particular but somewhat generally defined movement, "abolitionism." The things in terms of which it is to be explained are a set of particulars within itself, the "backgrounds" and "ideas" of leaders. In the first place, the concept of "background" has here been used in a way that is logically bizarre even though it may describe well enough the way that sane men see objects. Normally, men ignore most of those varied stimuli that are literally described by the word *background*, and instead concentrate on certain characteristics that experience has shown to be important. Among such characteristics in ordinary life are the "backgrounds" of the men whom we have to employ or to whom we grant degrees.

The Donald article is committed deeply, at the level of its own imagery and rhetoric, to a cognitive process that serves the ordinary prudent man quite well indeed. It omits two kinds of intellectual activity that the prudent man also omits—in the prudential case, because these other activities would either take too much time or would undermine decisiveness. It omits any attempt to scan "all" of some particular dimension by which the subject may be measured. And it omits any attempt to evaluate the subject against the "background" of things external to itself: other kinds of movement, similar movements in other countries, or the ideological activities of groups outside those the article takes into account.

To many of us, these approaches to scanning of background are somewhat threatening, because they have a perceptually regressive quality—they suggest the drunk man's tendency not to discriminate between levels of importance in the things that he perceives, or the infant's reputed indifference to the distinctions between perceived objects or even between *ego* and *alter*. Even more: to the extent that Binet's conception of initial intelligence as a process of projecting percepts that can only later be tested against reality has any validity, and is matched by the notion that adult intelligence consists partly in an acceptance of once-random images that proved efficient, then the kind of mental process that Donald's metaphor does not allow for is one that any prudent man might do well to reject. But it is clear that, in the case of his study, prudence does not produce satisfactory results.

There are two alternatives: either some substitute for scanning can be built up gradually through negative criticism and adversary proceedings, which is roughly what seems to have happened in a decade or so of argument about abolitionism; or some way of admitting that theoretical discourse does not need to be prudent in any ordinary sense, even when it proceeds to submit itself to rigorous empirical tests. Attempts to join history and sociology assume that theory has value; but if theory has value, then the prudence of the working intellectual may be cognitive folly.

A bald distaste for theory is not the only form that prudent folly takes within historical discourse. Men who proclaim the values of theory sometimes produce intellectual failures as resounding as those who only try to make discrete points. The most obvious example is the gap between Lee Benson's earlier theoretical arguments (1957) and his detailed arguments on the nature of New York politics. His general prescriptions on how to study voting behavior are sound, and include an elaborate version of the same standards by which men have criticized the various status-panic studies. He seems to advise historians to scan the possibilities within their areas of investigation in a way that should preclude careless oversight. But some of what he presents in *The Concept of Jacksonian Democracy* (1961) amounts to his own elaborate version of what Donald and Hofstadter did in their status arguments. Since at many points he states that he has actually done the kind of research that the thorough-scanning principle would suggest, then it becomes even plainer that the difficulty lies less in concept than in presentation—in the kind of discourse that historians assume is reasonable when they enter the realm of theory-testing.

One concrete example of procedural failure may serve to introduce the problem of how discourse affects procedure. Presenting his analysis of the relationship between economic prosperity and voting behavior in rural New York in the election of 1844, Benson (1961, pp. 147–50) displays the data on rank order of Democratic voting and of average dwelling values for the various towns of Delaware County. These, he says, show no relationship between the two series. He then cites the figures on exactly ten other *towns* throughout the whole state, without giving complete displays of the data for their respective counties. These ten towns do generally conform to his thesis. He adopts no standard way of summarizing central tendencies or relations between variances in the counties at large, measures that could have been presented in hardly greater space than he devotes to his ten examples. He states that he has in fact analyzed the rest of the data, and assumes that detail is unnecessary. In terms of the form of his discourse, the operative sentences are: "Three counties from different parts of the state can serve as representative examples of the general tendency," and: "Perhaps the most dramatic way to illustrate the inaccuracy of the traditional claim about voting behavior is to present the data for the two towns in the state that received the highest and lowest Democratic vote."

Aside from the fact that full data are *not* displayed for the "three counties," there remains a difficulty. For Delaware County, the figures he gives show a slight though statistically insignificant tendency for poorer towns to vote Democratic. If Delaware County was a stong example in his case, then his assertion that there was "no significant relationship" between wealth and voting in the state at large remains a suspect generalization. The critical phrases in all this are "representative examples" and "dramatic way to illustrate." But illustration and exemplification alone do not demonstrate anything. Full display or systematic statistical description *may* demonstrate. Benson's thesis that there was little direct relation between wealth and Democratic voting may turn out to be true enough, but his technique of presenting material in a selective manner, which is still advised to most young historians as both good style and professional prudence, is admirably suited for suppressing the kind of systematic validity that Benson sometimes claims.

Failure to work out and use adequate methods for displaying his data has also the result of glossing over the fact that Benson deals only briefly and impressionistically with the larger part of the variance in the voting behavior he describes—that in the voting of native Protestant groups, especially those of New England background (pp. 175–85, 198–207). He argues convincingly that voting by these groups was not polarized toward any one party, accepts his own conclusion that it was not accounted for by variations in economic condition of voters, and then argues persuasively that it was probably accounted for by differences in ethical attitude toward economic endeavor and social mobility. He may well be right in this suspicion, but if he is, then his elaborate attempt at quantitative and theoretical work omits any effort to measure one kind of variable that recent modernization theory might have suggested to be especially important: namely, the variable of traditionalism versus modernism in attitudes toward social structure.

It must be conceded, of course, that these lapses or incompletenesses in Benson violate his own precepts. In his earlier essay, "Research Problems in in American Political Historiography," he argues well for the systematic collection and display of data to test hypotheses about election behavior. In the theoretical sections of *The Concept of Jacksonian Democracy*, he presents some unusually challenging hypotheses about the relationship between different kinds of voting motivation. But in the process of discussing the nature of hypothesis, he uses one revealing term: the "potentially verifiable" hypothesis. By this he means, not what the positivist would, a statement in logical form such that it can be confirmed or disconfirmed, but a statement that in addition to such form has already been confirmed to some degree and is therefore worth pursuing further (1961, pp. 289–90). This approach injects serious confusion into the nature of theory by suggesting that genuine intellectual adventure is to be discouraged unless it can show in advance that it is altogether likely to achieve success. When he presents results that contain little significant confirmation for any positive theory, the prescription of "potentially verifiable" hypotheses emerges as simply another approach to writing prudential, impressionistic history. Such prudential sobriety, except where it leads to the rigorous, summary display of research results, is not likely to contribute much to interesting theory, and Benson is at his best when "potential verifiability" is not illustrated by mere illustration and example.

To summarize the difficulties in the examples thus far: what critics in day-to-day polemic have seized on as errors or oversights have two general characteristics as marks of discourse. In the first place, the vocabulary and rhetoric with which investigators have worked have included a persistent confusion between figure and ground or, in another metaphor, between numerator and denominator. This confusion or even reversal has directed historians' attention away from theory, toward detail as a cognitive substitute for general ideas. Such reversal of vision has rested in part on professional deformation: the reputability of historians as such seems threatened by any obligation to display "all" their evidence in conspicuous form.

In the second place, as with almost all defects in historical work, historians have been overcommitted to certain value positions. These value positions have been in part identified with professional reputability, and have thus inhibited historians from seeing or presenting "all" the necessary parts of their problems.

These defects imply two needs for the kind of discourse in which history and theory can be successfully joined: style should predispose the historian to some neutrality about the value or worthwhileness of what he observes, and it should predispose him to scan freely over any scale or dimension or assortment of things that he takes up. Free scanning, especially, is strongly discouraged by much of the way historians do talk, and by the way they run their profession: selectivity and point of view have survival value, and historians rely more on adversary proceedings than on personal impartiality to produce attention to "both sides of a question."

As it happens, sociology does offer to history a cognitive form that is highly favorable to free scanning of fields. This is the game of paradigm construction, as it has evolved out of the originally value-charged work of Maine and Tönnies, into the Joycean marginalia of Parsons. For present purposes, I would like to consider Marion Levy's variation on Parsons, partly because its richness provides a good example of what paradigm-play can produce, but partly because it reveals a value bias that may be inherent in any theory that has much interest for men in the latter part of the twentieth century.

Parsons had come to his own outlook by a route not unknown to humanistic scholarship. The old dichotomies between status and contract, or between Gemeinschaft and Gesellschaft, or between nature and artifice, had long been suggestive, but had carried a simplistic, doctrinal tone. Much like a Lovejoy prying apart the different meanings that "nature" or "romanticism" might have, Parsons pried "status" into many different if somehow related qualities, so that he finally emerged with his set of pattern variables, most of which still relate to values and attitudes rather than to objective social events. In general, what Levy has done in the work that is summarized or expanded in *Modernization and the Structure of Societies* is to insist on cer-

tain additional kinds of realism: on more attention to economic resources
and political power, on the distinction between ideal and actual in social
institutions, and on a more explicit attention to continuity in the measuring
of social variables. In a way, these departures have only extended the basic
Parsonian reflex of crossing alternative classifications against each other in
such a way as to subdivide and mark out the cognitive space against which
social reality might be mapped. Levy, along with his attention to large-scale
change, has retained a bent for proliferating categories of the kind that are
pictured in the margins and cells of the Parsons paradigms.

Levy's copiousness has a Victorian quality that might serve nicely certain
needs in the construction of theory for historians. His focus on modernization
takes abundant care of any need for explicit relevance to the interests of the
historian as citizen. His demand for continuity, as against dichotomy, can
only support the historian's need to be kept off ideological hooks—even
though polarized variables would probably be treated in practice as continua by any open-minded, responsible investigator. But on another point,
the manner in which Levy seems to provide for a prime need of history actually puts a solid block in the way of the support that investigators need. (It
may be noted, for those who care about such things, that this problem is
related to that of "historicism.") Levy has some general hypotheses about
the nature of modernization in history. Among them is the statement "that
endemic in relatively modernized societies, if they are at all stable, is a constant increase in the level of modernization (1966, p. 712). His hypotheses
amount to a sophisticated, somewhat detached statement of the idea of progress. In more precise terms, they say that technology and its related social
characteristics are monotonic nondecreasing functions of time. Because in
general they can move in only one direction, the only serious historical questions become those of slippage or friction: whether some attributes are
changing faster than others, or at most whether some are temporarily stalled.

From the working historian's point of view, Levy's general structure
offers perilously little more than the antiquated notion of "cultural lag." Of
course, the detail of Levy's view, like that of the people who have worked the
American-uniqueness field with their own hands, is a lot more complicated.
He recognizes that many diffuse, particularistic modes of social action not
only survive, but in some sense must survive during modernization. He recognizes that the force of modernization can produce in some persons or
structures strong reactions counter to it. But for such reactions he has a significant term: they are "fundamentalistic" (p. 799). Transformed into "populistic," this term becomes part of the attitudes of the American-uniqueness
school, attitudes on which Levy is not generally hung up. Aside from the fact
that such terms are inherently lacking in the neutral tone toward which good
theory-play should tend, they have some unfortunate implications. They suggest that any structure that moves in the direction of diffuseness or particu-
larism, or especially in the direction away from rationality, is pathological

and therefore beneath the serious concern of any intellectuals except those out on exterminating expeditions. Now it may be true (and morally most of us hope it is) that secular trends work in the directions that Levy states. But it is reasonably certain that short-run process may not.

More: it is reasonably certain that successful historical prediction develops not by relying on theories of monotonicity, but by working from the erratic character of detailed process. This is perhaps easiest to show from recent developments in demographic theory, an area whose formal implications have been neglected in the whole discussion of the history-theory intersection.

Up through the thirties, demographers generally accepted the idea that the rate of population growth would decline and even level off in any advanced or modernized country. They had of course certain disagreements about how to view this process in theory. Some wished to describe and extend this leveling-off by a kind of mathematical curve that gave a plausible fit to what was happening. Others, seeking a more nearly causal explanation, sought factors underlying the decline in fertility, and this search produced some tension in turn between those who wanted to emphasize moral or psychological factors, such as rationality, and those who wanted to subsume the process under strictly economic models. Especially during the years just after World War II, much of this discussion was transformed into a discussion about the usefulness of demographic "stages" in describing the application of the process to modernization. Through all this, demographers who wanted to be content with simple counting and extrapolation remained uncomfortable with the efforts of theorists to impose high-flown "ideas" on their field (Notestein, 1945, 1953; Pearl and Reed, 1920; Pearl, Reed, and Fish, 1940; Vance, 1959).

All of this received a gentle jolt from the upturn in fertility in Western countries, notably in the United States, after World War II ("gentle" because demographers became aware of the first signs of this change well before it made any impact on popular consciousness). This development facilitated massive support for the improvement of demographic work. Procedurally, the central feature of this improvement was a finely drawn, dispassionate extension of the nineteenth-century practice of distinguishing between the birthrates of different ethnic, economic, or geographic groups. The process of distinguishing was now applied thoroughly to the different orders of birth (first birth to a mother, second birth, and so forth), and to the concept of "cohort fertility" (that is, the different fertility experiences of women born in different chronological years). From the point of view of historical theory, it is worth noting that this process of minute subdivision is almost exactly the same as that prescribed by Benson, not in *The Concept of Jacksonian Democracy,* but in his earlier essay in the Komarovsky volume. It is also worth noting that extrapolation from these subdivided measures produced some of the first solid predictions of the renewed decline in the rate of population growth that appeared in the late fifties (Kiser, 1960;

Whelpton, 1928, 1947a, 1947b, 1954). *If* the Bensonesque prescription is executed in far greater detail than he himself used, it may well produce satisfactory results.

In the analysis of American population movements, good results were also produced by a method that used some of the same subdivided measurement, but in the service of definite theory. Richard Easterlin (1961), in a partial return to the attempt to explain fertility as a simple economic variable, produced a fairly elegant account of family-founding and child-production as responses to change in the labor market, in educational differentials, and in age structure. From his own point of view, and also from the point of view of the history-theory problem, the crucial step in his analysis was his turning away from the phenomenon of secular change to the detailed phenomena of "Kuznets cycles"—that is, to the short-range fluctuations of growth rates around any long-term trend. Once this narrowing of focus was undertaken, and once the bugaboo of secular trend was laid, it became then possible not only to do something by way of prediction, but also to offer some plausible implications about the most general kind of theoretical problem—in this case, the problem of whether the theorist should use psychological or economic variables in accounting for his phenomena. That he plumped for the economic should hardly be taken as much substantive discouragement to those more interested in exploring psychological variables. But it should be taken as serious discouragement to those who believe that historical problems and theoretical concerns cannot be combined to produce significant discourse.

At this point it becomes possible to return to the "background" metaphor used by David Donald (1956), to compare it with certain unintended metaphors used by Easterlin (1961), and thus to bring out potentialities that literal-minded criticism has tended to suppress. The Donald metaphor treated a general phenomenon as a foreground object, and took some of the constituent parts of that phenomenon as background. This inconsistency of cognitive optics made any general theory impossible in context. The comparable "metaphor" in Easterlin's work is simply the sequence of graphs in which he first presents his data on American population trends over the last few generations. His first graph plots absolute population levels against time, and gives the slightly uneven upward-moving curve that is familiar in most population discussion. His second graph presents annual rates of changes in the birth rate, plotted against time, and it presents a picture of superficially random fluctuation about a midline.

This *picture* provides a cue for feedback into Donald. In the first graph, the plot of Easterlin's variable moves in a roughly monotonic way. In the second, it moves back and forth over its range in a way that suggests no theoretical precommitments about what value it should take at any particular time. The one-dimensional continuum that the first graph projects into a two-dimensional continuum is not a genuinely open field: the variable moves once across the dimension of population size and then has no place to go. There is very little opportunity here for internal differentiation and empirical application. The one-dimensional continuum underlying the second graph is, on the other hand, repeatedly scanned and enfoliated by the variable; and it is this very enfoliation that permits the analyst to find many comparable individuals within what would otherwise be an unanalyzable population of one. To put it in the old familiar terms of economic time-series study: a raw series by itself may not be amenable to statistical analysis even when the fluctuations within that series are amenable.

The potentially fertile aspect of all the status-panic studies is that each dealt with at least one recoil or enfoliation on the continuum from the traditional to the modern. The particular value of Donald's study was that his irony brought him fairly close to treating the non-modern end of his dimension as intellectually plausible. The defect was that his reversal of figure and ground implicated him in failing to measure variation in the phenomenon that was analogous to the growth-rate variable in the Easterlin study—namely, the degree to which the attitudes of seeming political innovators varied along the continua from diffuse-particularistic to specific-universalistic standards. From a theoretical point of view, the indicated subject of study was not abolitionism; it was status-orientation itself. And the same is true of other status-panic studies. Their fault has not been that they were excessively sociological or theoretical, but that they were not enough so. In the one case, as noted, indulgence in mere irony was its own acknowledgment of the claims of the monotonic, its own deference to the ideological seriousness that is the bane of theory.

There are two general ways in which the ordinary historian who works mainly on one country may find theory interesting enough to distract him from the claims of morality and ideology. He may, on the one hand, operate as a worker in the collective enterprise that is crossnational or crosscultural comparison. But this role entails taking a relatively undifferentiated view of the internal history of whatever country is the historian's own subject, and it entails an overcharged faith in progress, such that any faltering in modernization depends on disaster. Or the working historian may concern himself with variations around any secular trends, so that his own empirical work may remain morally uncommitted and intellectually flexible. This does not mean that the theory-using historian must identify himself with the impersonal procedures of the economic cliometricians. It means, in fact, something even more neutral and open. For the cliometricians, by the nature of the way they conduct their discourse, are implicitly committed to a world that is rational, universalistic, modern. Their rhetoric, even more than any of their specific conclusions, condemns most past economic policy as populistic or mercantilistic—in other words, traditional.

The ordinary historian venturing into theory needs a breather during which he is under no commitment to give *ideological* support to the rational (or to the irrational, for that matter). Even if the world is moving in some direction that is sustaining the hypotheses of Henry Adams and Marion Levy at the same time, the historian needs to be exempt from worrying about the order of the ages except as that order establishes a baseline for his own measurements. As a citizen, the man who happens to be a historian interested in theory has concerns as serious as anybody else's. As a professional, he needs journals with better puzzle pages and more frivolous art work, fewer patriotic panoramas and fewer editorials—even when those editorials take the form of grand cross-cultural comparisons.

Whether we like it or not, there does exist a persistent homology between the problem of relating historians and sociologists as kinds of intellectual workers and the problem of attending to both the traditional and the modern ends of the dimension in which much theory about social change is stated. The epistemological problems will always serve as projections for psychological and vocational differences, if we let them. This homology is related to another: that between ideological and cognitive problems. Our attempts to work out the interplay between rational and nonrational aspects of phenomena are necessarily related to how we feel about modernization as a real thing happening to society.

The kinds of theory we need, if they are to interest historians as well as others, do need to deal with the traditional-modern continuum. Other kinds of theory might conceivably prove engaging, but they hardly seem available in the world as we know it.

Yet for cognitive safety and cognitive success, certain other characteristics are needed in the style of discourse within which theory is pursued or tested. First, methodical and statistical checks are always needed, not just because they weed out the untrue, but also because they establish anchor points against which paradigm-play can move without the danger of running destructively free. Second, as stated earlier, the investigator needs to be supported in attitudes of neutrality toward his results and in a disposition to explore, map, or scan freely "all" the parts of whatever space he is examining. Third, because neutrality and the scanning disposition conflict head-on with the ideological biases inherent in modernization conceived as an overwhelming or undirectional process, the historian needs some framework within which he can discern change moving in either direction, regardless of secular trend.

Historians, if they are to work well with theory, need to find in specific theories an appeal that outweighs compulsion or ideology. While such theories should have the marks that any methodological prescription would include, such as propositional character and "middle-level"–ness, these do not deal directly with the need for interest and appeal. This is partly a question of psychology, not logic, to use an old distinction. In up-to-date terms, it is a question of how theory feels as a medium of expression, and whether that feeling can work any appeal in the particular intellectual climate that prevails among historians in the latter part of the twentieth century. In advance of the fact, is it possible to predict the kind of theory that might work?

There not only *does* exist, there *needs* to exist some homology between the formal structure of theory and the larger impulses with which intellectuals feel in touch. Even a theory whose function is objectivity must resonate to some subjective needs if it is to enlist the energy of investigators. One such pervasive need is that of freedom to orient oneself alternately to "artificial" and then to "natural" environments. In part, this is a matter of ordinary recreation: work proceeds mostly in artificial situations which depend for their viability both on a substratum of natural motivation and on the ability of participants to withdraw into other kinds of activity. If either kind of environment becomes less accessible, the ability to participate is threatened. For this reason the Parsonian pattern variables, or some variant on them, are probably essential to any theory that can take hold. They "act out" the need for guaranteed access to contrasting kinds of activity. At the same time, they tap the need that some intellectuals have to move back and forth between modernized and less modernized parts of the world in any comparative study or policy work that they do.

There is at work on the fringes of the current esthetic world an impulse that has dubious artistic merit but somewhat greater theoretical relevance: the habit, displayed especially in the rash of neo-art–nouveau posters, of filling out all available small parts of a perceived space with articulated detail. The analogy to paradigm-construction is obvious. This habit of playing with cells and categories in order to exhaust the possibilities of a cognitive space is precisely one of the intellectual eccentricities that can make theory a means of checking on bias rather than a means for transmitting bias. That the esthetic mode in which such combinatorial play operates is frivolous is only to the good. It spins out the ad hoc epicycles that are required to salvage any goodness-of-fit between phenomena and currently accepted general notions. The lusher it becomes, the more excessive and decadent, the nearer may it bring the time when creative thought cannot do without the effort to create new, more elegant levels of theory. Yet its lushness can act as barrier against premature simplification.

Besides, whether or not the kind of theory that engages attention can in fact be translated into projects that call for computer use, the need for homology in the intellectual world suggests that theory might well develop a pace and tone of discourse similar to that of computer technology. The main quality in this tone is not its adaptability for quantitative, statistical study. It is rather its joining of objectivity with profusion, its usefulness for following out all the details of a decadent prescription. The strategic procedures in computer languages are those that call for the execution of *all* the operations of a certain type, regardless of how trivial and unpromising certain items may seem. Computers virtually require that their users adopt either a "scanning" or a "branching" mode of discourse: instructions that attempt to shortcut profusion usually fail as technically inadequate. Homology does not mean that an investigator cannot construct falsely complete paradigms, but it can expose the incomplete paradigm as a dangerous indulgence in intellectual seriousness.

Is the indicated kind of discourse, as a setting for theory, likely to develop within the intellectual temper that prevails now? Probably it is, although the clues to such optimism come from aspects of our culture that most serious intellectuals have been considering irresponsible or frightening. As in the case of hopefully decadent art forms, and also as in work on subatomic particles, thesis and abstraction have often broken down in the face of a preoccupied tendency to map or fill all the parts of the spaces with which investigators work. While this often reduces immediate communication, as it certainly does in the enfoliated posters, it also carries a copiousness and impartiality that the culture needs. The specific forms that frivolity and short-range thought take will surely go out of date. The need for such forms will not date.

REFERENCES

BENSON, L. 1957. Research problems in American political historiography. In M. Komarovsky (Ed.), *Common frontiers of the social sciences*. Glencoe, Ill.: Free Press.

———. 1961. *The concept of Jacksonian democracy*. Princeton, N.J.: Princeton University Press.

DONALD, D. 1956. *Lincoln reconsidered*. New York: Alfred A. Knopf.

EASTERLIN, R. A. 1961. The American baby boom in historical perspective. *American Economic Review*, 51: 869–911.

HOFSTADTER, R. 1955. *The age of reform*. New York: Alfred A. Knopf.

KISER, C. V. 1960. Differential fertility in the United States. In National Bureau of Economic Research, *Demographic and economic change in developed countries*. Princeton, N.J.: Princeton University Press.

LEVY, M. J., JR. 1966. *Modernization and the structure of societies*. Princeton, N.J.: Princeton University Press.

NOTESTEIN, F. W. 1945. Population: the long view. In T. W. Schultz (Ed.), *Food for the world*. Chicago: University of Chicago Press.

———. 1953. Economic problems of population change. In *Proceedings of the eighth international conference of agricultural economists*. London: Oxford University Press.

PEARL, R. and L. J. REED. 1920. On the rate of growth of the population of the United States since 1790 and its mathematical representation. *Proceedings of the National Academy of Sciences,* 6: 275–88.

PEARL, R., L. J. REED, and J. F. FISH. 1940. The logistic curve and the census count of 1940. *Science*, 92 (2395): 486–88.

SKOTHEIM, R. A. 1959. A note on historical method. *Journal of Southern History,* 25 (3): 355–65.

VANCE, R. B. 1959. The development and status of American demography. In P. M. Hauser and O. D. Duncan (Eds.), *The study of population: an inventory and appraisal.* Chicago: University of Chicago Press.

WHELPTON, P. K. 1928. Population of the United States, 1925–1975. *American Journal of Sociology,* 34 (2): 253–70.

———. 1947a. Is family size increasing? An analysis of order-of-birth statistics of native white mothers, United States, 1920–1946. *Vital Statistics—Special Reports,* 23 (16): 319–25.

———. 1947b. *Forecasts of the population of the United States, 1945–1975.* Washington, D. C.: Bureau of the Census.

———. 1954. *Cohort fertility.* Princeton, N.J.: Princeton University Press.

PART IV
Organizational Riddles

18

OBSERVATIONS ON INTERDISCIPLINARY WORK IN THE SOCIAL SCIENCES

KENNETH D. ROOSE

Professor Sherif has asked me to make some comments about the interdisciplinary approach which is so crucial in his own work in the social sciences and which I am persuaded must be strongly supported if our research and findings in the social sciences are to be truly relevant. Therefore, I am going to make some observations about interdisciplinary work in the social sciences less from the standpoint of an active researcher in the areas than from my vantage point in observing trends in the organization of the social sciences and in the accommodation of the newer developments.

My comments will be centered about three general concerns I have relating to interdisciplinary programs in the university. The *first* is the kinds of people who tend to spark interdisciplinary programs in the university; *second*, the problems faced in administering such programs; and *third*, the appropriate time for involving the undergraduate student in interdisciplinary concerns and programs.

THE PROPONENTS OF INTERDISCIPLINARY WORK

In my experience, those who support interdisciplinary work in the social sciences tend to break down into two groups. The first consists of some of the most effective, able, best-trained, and insightful persons that I know; persons who sense the converging of discipline interests as increasingly complex and interrelated problems in the social sciences are encountered. It seems to me that by and large this group contains the most creative and advanced thinkers in the disciplines who pose the cutting-edge questions which require an interfacing of knowledge and approaches for their solutions.

Why are thoughtful people insisting upon the interdisciplinary approach in their work? I believe that several factors propel them in this direction. For one, the sheer complexity of the forces bearing upon any social problem makes it highly unlikely that understanding of the contributions of any one discipline can be obtained without consideration of the insights to be gained on the same problem from various other discipline standpoints. The developments of such newer interdisciplinary areas as are represented by social-psychology or political sociology, to take two examples, reveal the inadequacy of relying upon a single discipline for the effective treatment of a vital social problem or issue. It may well be that the growing involvement in the interdisciplinary approach will have the effect of reawakening interest in some of the historical areas of interdisciplinary concern as, for example, political economics. In any event, a problem that evolves in the social context cannot escape the impacts which come from intermixture of the economic, psychological, political, and social factors.

In my judgment, a second factor motivating this interdisciplinary concern is the increasing need to demonstrate the relevances of the theoretical concept or structure to the vital interests and problems of the contemporary society. This means that the problem-solving approach which has come to dominate the thinking of modern social scientists requires meaningful research which contributes to an understanding of reality and provides guidelines for effective policy formulation. I suspect, therefore, that the movement of the social scientist from the ivory tower into the market place has heightened his concern that his research and findings be realistically developed by allowing for the influence that the variety of related disciplines has upon both the interpretation and solution of the problem.

Still other factors may be influencing these bright and creative people who are in the frontiers of their disciplines. It may be their ability to see interrelationships and to place perspective upon human problems that leads them in this direction. Perhaps the contemplation even of the generalizations that may be possible provides the excitement or stimulation that heightens their enthusiasm and enjoyment in their scholarly efforts.

I turn now to the second group which presses for interdisciplinary work in the social sciences and which I believe often regards general education as the appropriate outlet for their interdisciplinary concerns. I can generate much less enthusiasm for this group and perhaps I interpret their motives ungenerously. These are the people, who, in my experience, have tended to cast unfavorable reflections upon the fundamental value and contribution of the interdisciplinary approach to the advancement of knowledge and policy. I may be harsh in my observation that many have inadequate training and are much less focused and insightful in their approach to problems. From my viewpoint, however, it is because of this latter group that doubts are often raised about the quality of interdisciplinary programs. It is this group, too, that tends to press interdisciplinary courses upon beginning students under the rubric of general education, thus giving substance to the charge that such courses deal in dilettantism and have insufficient roots and underlying base. I point to this second group because the next issue that I want to discuss—the problems faced in administering interdisciplinary programs—is heavily influenced by the conflicts associated with their position.

UNIVERSITY ORGANIZATION OF INTERDISCIPLINARY PROGRAMS

In university academic organization this could well be described as the age of interdisciplinary programs. Even as the faculty emphasis has been placed more and more pointedly upon the development of the professional caste in the discipline, new program ventures of an interdisciplinary character have spawned apace. Beginning with area study programs in the early post-World War II years, there has been a proliferation of interdisciplinary programs. Programs have been added in medieval studies, linguistics, comparative literature, biochemistry, biophysics, to name only a few. Strains have intensified between department discipline leadership and these emerging studies that cross conventional boundaries. Debates between discipline spokesmen and the interdisciplinarians have been enlivening our administrative and faculty meetings. Each of these new program areas seeks to develop undergraduate curricula which are correlated with graduate study offerings. Too often it seems to me that the interdisciplinary program is confused with the general education program and its interests so that highly irrelevant arguments occur and bitterness ensues in the debate. I will have occasion below to make my own recommendation concerning the level at which interdisciplinary programs should be structured into the undergraduate curriculum.

I find, however, that the opponents of the interdisciplinary approach are sparked by discipline department spokesmen who are really concerned about the watering down of knowledge which they associate first with general education but also with programs that are interdisciplinary in character before the student has knowledge in depth of a given discipline. Regardless of how this controversy is resolved, the question of the administration of these new interdisciplinary programs continues to be a very vexatious one. How do we determine the priorities in the allocation of resources to the traditional discipline departments and to the crossdiscipline programs? How can a department member who sees an interrelationship between his interests and those of a faculty member in another department convince his department chairman that the interdisciplinary interests deserve additional support before support is given for an extension of a specialization within the department? Is the answer to set up a new department to provide an umbrella for this interrelated interest? I think not, because the individual still retains roots in the discipline department and the reconciliation of the financial issues must still be effected. Regardless of how we organize to accelerate these trends, some sticky issues will still remain.

Why do the discipline-area people evaluate the work of their colleagues by being so suspicious of the broader focus required by the interdisciplinary programs? Is the person with the interdisciplinary interests bound to be disadvantaged in his academic recognition compared to his more traditional colleague? I sometimes fear that the mushrooming of interdisciplinary programs will result in my establishing within the dean's office, administrative and budget support for what may eventually become a gigantic department with no internal consistency but larger than any of the existing departments in the College of the Liberal Arts at Pennsylvania State University. At the moment I hold back from establishing formal administrative arrangements and controls over interdisciplinary programs, hoping that gradually we may evolve more sympathetic understanding and response from the disciplines which will render more rigid administrative structures unnecessary. An important part of the task necessarily must fall upon the active developers of interdisciplinary programs who, I think, must make every effort to bring the discipline people along into a willingness to accept the legitimacy and rightful role of these newer programs.

I observe one other development that eventually is bound to make an imprint upon administrative relations in interdisciplinary programs. This is that the younger social behavioral scientists are turning their attention to new areas of research and scholarship that have not been characteristic of professionals in their fields in the past. Thus, from where I sit in the interviewing of faculty, I have noted how many are directing their attention for instance toward the emerging health services. A political scientist whom we interviewed and appointed is studying the political and administrative problems encountered in the establishment of state mental health services; an economist who turned us down was developing an econometric model for the programming of state health expenditures; still another interviewee, a sociologist, was intensely interested in the sociology of health professions. It seems to me that these alert and vital young faculty members who are looking at contemporary problems from the various discipline standpoints will force the traditionalists in our departments to provide more flexible arrangements for the cooperative advancement of learning, scholarship, and research.

The more effective the people become who are engaged in interdisciplinary work, and the greater their stature outside of the particular university community, the less effective can be the resistance of the more traditionally oriented members of the discipline departments. I might add also that the more secure and confident a discipline department the less will there be attempts to downgrade and undermine the interdisciplinary interests of its members.

INTERDISCIPLINARY COURSES IN THE SENIOR YEAR

Finally, I want to call attention to the third concern—the question of the appropriate time for involving the undergraduate student in interdisciplinary courses and programs. It is my opinion that proper development in this area can go a long way toward resolving or reconciling the conflicts between interdisciplinary-area spokesmen and their opponents. As I indicated in my comments about the second group of faculty with interdisciplinary interests, I think there tends to be a confusion between the interdisciplinary approach and general education. For this reason I am opposed to and skeptical about the early emphasis upon interdisciplinary work for the undergraduate. Rather, I am persuaded that interdisciplinary courses of a capstone nature pointed for the senior year can draw upon the best from both the discipline insight and the interdiscipline approach. Because of the problem orientation and interests which increasingly are motivating faculty in the social sciences, I would hope that by concentrating upon the broad problem areas and drawing upon the competencies that have been developed by students in discipline areas, an extremely effective program of interdisciplinary study could be carried out in the senior year.

An example of the sort of topic I have in mind would be say urban redevelopment. Students who are concentrators in political science, economics, sociology, engineering, architecture, education, and the like, should be asked to supply their insights into the complexities of such a problem. The instructors' role should be not to provide the expertise in each of these areas but to coordinate the contributions offered by the fledgling student specialists in the various areas. Numerous other topics could provide this kind of experience. The problems of poverty, race relations, and automation, for example, all would lend themselves to this type of treatment. These are also topics that concern the student activists on the campus so that the program I am urging might well be an effective academic response to their agitation.

SUMMARY

In summary, then, I have distinguished between those who advocate cooperative efforts among several social behavioral sciences largely for their general education role and those who stress the added insights that may be gained thereby into the critical interdisciplinary contemporary problems. I have lamented the conflicts that seem to arise over the financial support and administrative structure of interdisciplinary programs. Finally, I have called your attention to the important task of instruction that can be served by placing the undergraduate student in the interdisciplinary context *after* and not *before* he has some knowledge and depth in his area of concentration.

19

ETHNOCENTRISM OF DISCIPLINES AND THE FISH-SCALE MODEL OF OMNISCIENCE

Donald T. Campbell

This paper is a preliminary exercise in the sociology of science—an exploratory application of principles of groups and intergroup organization to group processes in the institutionalization of science. Our goal in this book is a comprehensive, integrated multiscience. The obstacle described in this paper is the "ethnocentrism of disciplines," i.e., the symptoms of tribalism or nationalism or ingroup partisanship in the internal and external relations of university departments, national scientific organizations, and academic disciplines. The "fish-scale model of omniscience" represents the solution advocated, a solution kept from spontaneous emergence by the ethnocentrism of disciplines. The slogan is collective comprehensiveness through overlapping patterns of unique narrownesses. Each narrow specialty is in this analogy a "fish-scale." Figure 1 illustrates the title. Our only hope of a comprehensive social science, or other multiscience, lies in a continuous texture of narrow specialties which overlap with other narrow specialties. Due to the ethnocentrism of disciplines, what we get instead is a redundant piling up of highly similar specialties, leaving interdisciplinary gaps. Rather than trying to fill these gaps by training scholars who have mastered two or more disciplines, we should be making those social-organizational inventions which will encourage narrow specialization in these interdisciplinary areas.

The diagram of Figure 1 is of course an oversimplification, an analogy in two dimensions of what should be n-dimensional. Particularly likely to be dyscommunicative are the exaggerated gaps between the disciplinary clusters. The real situation is perhaps more often one of unrecognized overlap. The disciplinary clusters may at their edges overlap other clusters, but as ships that pass in the night, they fail to make contact. The clusters, as it

1. The preparation of this paper has been facilitated by the Council for Intersocietal Studies, which operates under a grant from the Ford Foundation to Northwestern University.

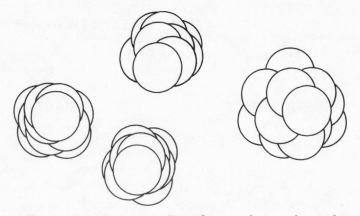

FIG. 1a—Present situation: Disciplines as clusters of specialties, leaving interdisciplinary gaps.

FIG. 1b—Ideal situation: Fish-scale model of omniscience.

were, may overlap but lie on independent planes. Such an alternate diagramming might be possible, and the reader is invited to substitute it in his mind's eye in what follows. The issue, too, is not one of total absence but of relative density of interdisciplinary specialties.

COMPREHENSIVE TRAINING AND THE LEONARDESQUE ASPIRATION

Too often in discussions of interdisciplinary training one hears calls for *breadth,* for *comprehensiveness.* Too often we attempt the production of multidisciplinary scholars, professionals who have mastered two or more disciplines, rather than interdisciplinary specialists. This orientation I will parody as the "Leonardesque aspiration": the goal of creating current-day

Leonardos who are competent in all of science. As a training program it is bound to fail in one of two directions. At its worst it produces a shallowness, a lowest-common-denominator breadth, an absence of that profound specialization which is essential for scientific productivity. At best it is evaded in the direction of the interdisciplinary narrowness here advocated.

The Burgeoning Literature and the Obligations of Interdisciplinarians

One of the several background facts that lies behind my emphasis is the enormous past and burgeoning present literature. Speaking for myself—any volume like this raises guilt feelings in that it acquaints me with the existence of scientific literatures of obvious relevance to my work which I have neglected. William McGuire's paper, for example, lies in an area of high relevance to my work, and yet I have not read or read-at even half of his citations, and was not at all aware of the existence of another sizeable proportion. But it is not only multidisciplinary conferences that have this effect. Unidisciplinary conferences remind me that I am failing to keep up in areas once central—and so does the arrival of one of the few journals I take (and read only 10 per cent of), or chance inspection of one of the many journals equally relevant to which I do not subscribe.

What seems to me essential is that moving into an interdisciplinary problem area not increase this obligation and guilt—that for every new literature we pick up we are excused from or drop some other literature, so that the interdisciplinarian be free to remain as narrow, as specialized, as any other scholar.

The Myth of Unidisciplinary Competence

Lying behind many models of interdisciplinary competence is an unrealistic notion of unidisciplinary competence—the image of scholars competent in one discipline. It will clarify the discussion of interdisciplinary competence to recognize at the outset that there are no such persons. What we have instead is a congeries of narrow specialties each one of which covers no more than one-tenth of the discipline with even a shallow competence. Yet individual disciplines do have some integrity, some comprehensiveness—at least in comparison with social science as a whole or with specific interdisciplinary areas. What must be recognized is that this integration and comprehensiveness is a collective product, not embodied within any one scholar. It is achieved through the fact that the multiple narrow specialties overlap, and that through this overlap a collective communication, a collective competence and breadth, is achieved. This approach is our only hope for a unified and complete behavioral science. The present social organization of science impedes it.

THE LOCUS OF SCIENTIFIC KNOWLEDGE IS SOCIAL

Philosophy of science and epistemology have not yet assimilated the fact that the problem of knowledge must, in the end, be stated at the social level —though Charles Sanders Peirce and James Mark Baldwin, for example, were making this point at the turn of the century. Moving the problem of knowledge from a solitary viewer's vision to language is a step, but the implicit model is still usually a single native speaker with perfect knowledge of a stable language. Sufficient attention is not yet given to the social and incomplete conditions of language learning, to the fundamental idiosyncracy and errorfulness of functional individual lexicons, to the very partial distribution of words that are still somehow "in" the language, to the effective redundancy which makes imperfect language as competent as it is. When these have been assimilated, the locus of "truth" and "knowledge" will have clearly shifted from individual "minds" to a collective social product only imperfectly represented in any one mind. Similarly in the philosophy of science, the competence, the discipline, the verification, the integration are all in the end social products, imperfectly and incompletely represented in the work of any one scientist. Michael Polanyi writes to this point in *The Tacit Dimension* (Doubleday, 1966) identifying the locus of scientific authority as the "Society of Explorers" itself:

. . . the *principle of mutual control.* It consists, in the present case, of the simple fact that scientists keep watch over each other. Each scientist is both subject to criticism by all others and encouraged by their appreciation of him. This is how *scientific opinion* is formed, which enforces scientific standards and regulates the distribution of professional opportunities. It is clear that only fellow scientists working in closely related fields are competent to exercise direct authority over each other; but their personal fields will form *chains of over-lapping neighborhoods* extending over the entire range of science. It is enough that the standards of plausibility and worthwhileness be equal around every single point to keep them equal over all the sciences. Even those in the most widely separated branches of science will then rely on each other's results and support each other against any laymen seriously challenging their authority (p. 72).

PRESENT DISCIPLINES AS ARBITRARY COMPOSITES

While it is probably not essential to the perspective, it is certainly relevant that the present organization of content into departments is highly arbitrary, a product in large part of historical accident.

Thus *anthropology* is a hodgepodge of all novelties that struck the scholarly tourist's eye when venturing into exotic lands—a hodgepodge of skin color, physical stature, agricultural practices, weapons, religious beliefs, kinship systems, language, history, archeology, and paleontology.

Thus *sociology* is a study of social man in European industrialized settings, a hodgepodge of studies of institutional data in which persons are anonymous—of individual persons in social settings, of aggregates of person data losing both personal and institutional identity, and of interactions which are neither persons nor groups.

Thus *psychology* is a hodgepodge of sensitive subjective biography, of brain operations, of school achievement testing, of factor analysis, of Markov process mathematics, of schizophrenic families, of laboratory experiments on group structure in which persons are anonymous, etc.

Thus *geograpy* is a hodgepodge of land-surface geology, of industrial development, of innovation diffusion, of social ecology, of political territoriality, of visual perception of areal photographs, of subjective phenomenology of mental maps.

Thus *political science* is a hodgepodge of political entities as actors and persons as actors, of humanistic description and scientific generalization, of history and of social psychology.

Thus *economics* is a hodgepodge of mathematics without data, of history of economic institutions without mathematics or theory, of an ideal model of psychological man.

There are no doubt many natural divisions within the domain of the social or behavioral sciences—but they are not employed in the allocation of content to disciplines. A hierarchy of levels of analysis exists in which the focus of differential description at one level becomes the assumed undifferentiated atoms of the next; this is the atom-molecule-cell-organ-organism-social group-etc. model. On this hierarchy, sociology, political science, geography, and anthropology are all mixed across the individual and group levels, and so is experimental social psychology. The experimental laboratory work of Sherif, Lewin, Lippitt, and Bavelas in many instances represents psychologists doing experimental sociology, experimenting with social structure, developing laws about social norms in which persons are treated as undifferentiated atoms, and in which the resulting laws relate social structural and group-product variables.

Another natural division is between the descriptive-humanistic, on the one hand, and the scientistic, on the other. On this dimension, too, our departments and disciplines are mixed, with all save history having both strong scientific and strong descriptive-humanistic factions.

There are ways of describing the internal logic and coherence of disciplines, but this cannot be done with singular principles and still capture both the reason for the content within one discipline and the reason for the same content's appearance or exclusion in others. And certainly the dimensions so used would be only a partial sample of potential classificatory criteria.

The specialties within disciplines are more coherent, and eventually such specialization takes over, each scientist allowing the congeries of irrelevancies within his own disciplinary knowledge to atrophy, journals to go unread, subscriptions to lapse, etc. The temporary disciplinary breadth transiently achieved in graduate school is of course not undesirable—the objection here is rather to the repetitious duplication of the same pattern of breadth to the exclusion of other breadths equally relevant but organizationally unsupported.

ETHNOCENTRISM OF DISCIPLINES

Effects of Organizing Specialties into Decision-making Units

Consider what would happen if we took a large domain of specialties and aggregated adjacent dozens into "departments," as collective-decision–making units. In this hypothetical example, let us suppose that the aggregation has been arbitrary except for the requirement of adjacency, that all specialties are equally well staffed to begin with, and that any specialty can belong to only one department. We are now interested in the effect of this second-level organizational structure, this superimposition of departmental boundaries upon the specialty boundaries. We are particularly interested in differential effects upon the future growth of the "central" specialties versus the peripheral or marginal specialties, this centrality or marginality being in this hypothetical case a purely arbitrary byproduct of where the administrative boundaries happened to fall. Figure 2a is an effort to portray this starting point. (In Fig. 2, A_p, B_p, C_p, are examples of peripheral specialties, D_c and E_c of central ones.)

Consider first purely internal decision-making. For most issues there are differences in priority and preferences which are associated with specialty points of view, and overlapping specialties are apt to have overlapping pref-

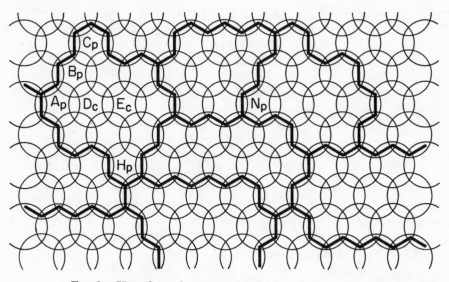

Fig. 2a—Hypothetical pattern of specialty overlap at the time of superimposition of arbitrary "departmental" boundaries (heavier lines).

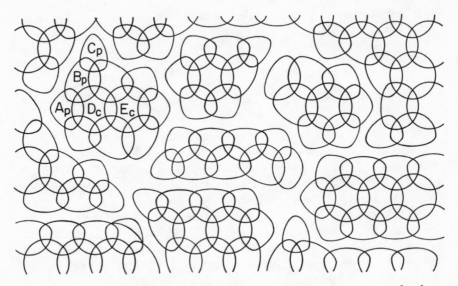

FIG. 2b—Resulting modification of specialty overlap as a result of organizing decision-making and communication along the arbitrary "departmental" lines. ("Departmental" boundaries omitted to facilitate inspection of specialty overlap pattern.)

erences. The situation will also be that collective decisions will be achieved only by a consensus of a plurality of specialties within the department. The accidentally central specialties have more natural allies within the department, and find it easier to achieve support for their concerns. The natural allies of the peripheral specialties lie in other of the arbitrary departments, and are organizationally prevented from effectively presenting their consensuses. The incidentally central specialties are also more frequently the compromise candidates, and when an ideology is needed to rationalize the historically arbitrary departmentalization it is the concerns of the central specialties that are chosen as epitomizing the true common denominator, as the essence of the initially arbitrary aggregate. Centrality becomes reinterpreted as common root, trunk, and fountain head when initially it meant only remoteness from the boundaries with other departments.

Here are some considerations which would illustrate these purely internal dynamics. The selection of a chairman in a peaceful department will follow these lines—only if a peripheral is a compromise between two strong factions each with some central specialties will he be a chairman. Deciding on a core curriculum to be required of all students, the minimum essential to their being sound, well-grounded X-ologists, will go in this direction. Pressure there will be to require one course from each specialty. Demands for time to meet the needs of specializing will preclude this in any but the smallest departments. The process of choosing a smaller set will involve the elimination of peripheral specialties because inherently in the arbitrary organizational structure there are fewer other specialists in the department who deem them important. This tautology may of course be expressed ideologically as "that's not really X-ology—it even comes close to being Y-ology." The setting of qualifying exams and dissertation committees will exercise a constant centralizing bias on the training of graduate students in peripheral specialties. Going across departmental lines in study programs is wasted effort as far as these important hurdles are concerned. The peripheral specialist himself will be anxious that his students show up well on the central core content, and will be willing to see equally or more relevant crossdepartment content be neglected, since no punishment is involved in its neglect, no institutional reward in its achievement. This is a minor problem if these departmental hurdles are low. But there is great pressure on departments to achieve excellence, and there is a perverse tendency to see this as implemented by high standards in the achievement of passive regurgitative mastery of past achievements in the literature. Under the institutional decision-making arrangements here described, the inevitable effect of higher standards in training is greater neglect of peripheral and crossdepartmental content. And this is without the byproduct of increasing the profundity of specialized training for any but the central specialties.

Deciding who in the department merits a raise or is ready for promotion, whose competing offer it is essential to meet and whose the department has not the funds to match, whose specialty needs additional staff and space, all show the effect of the arbitrary location of departmental boundaries on what becomes defined as central or peripheral. In my professional career at four universities I have repeatedly seen men who were of exceptional creativity and competence, and who were absolutely central as far as social science or behavioral science was concerned (occupying positions like those designated as H or N in Fig. 2a), be budgetarily neglected and eventually squeezed out because the departmental organization of specialties made them departmentally peripheral. That in some cases these were arrogant men does not explain the result, because their detractors were also arrogant men, but more centrally located. However, a selective feedback may well be at work, it may be that of all those who are initially attracted to peripheral, boundary-crossing specialties, only the arrogant persist in bucking the institutional pressures which would otherwise move them to more centrally defined specialties.

The dynamics just described are internal to our hypothetical departments. These arbitrary budgetary units compete with each other as budgetary entities, for budget increases, space increases, personnel increases. The specialties within the arbitrary departments thus come to share common fate, and become joint actors in competition with the other arbitrary aggregates of specialties. This common fate, though arbitrary in its initiation, is real enough in practice to provide the basis of an ingroup identification against competitive outgroups. There also develops implicit or explicit competition for the most talented students, and indoctrination procedures designed to maintain the loyalty of those who have tentatively joined. Characteristic of ingroup-outgroup relations in other settings, these indoctrination procedures not only emphasize ingroup virtues and ideology but also contrasting outgroup faults. Philosophy and sociology departments have frequently maintained internal solidarity by teaching about the wrongness of behavioristic psychology. Sidney Aronson in his paper for this volume has documented the manner in which historians build ingroup morale by deprecating sociologists. (It is even symptomatic of ethnocentrism that the first illustrations that come to his and my mind are ones in which our own departments are being wrongly disparaged by outgroups, rather than vice versa.)

If we add to our hypothetical example the feature that on most university campuses the arbitrary aggregations into departments be parallel as to which specialties are combined, further institutional pressures emerge. Departments' students must be prepared to appear adequate to centrally dominated hiring committees at other universities. The new faculty appointments to the department must be ones that inspire admiration on the part of the parallel departments of other universities.

Effect of Departmental Organization on Scientific Communication and Specialist Competence

In this topic we come to the most direct effect of departmental organization on scientific knowledge. Each scientist's competence, his participation in the collective activity of science, is based upon communication. The hypothetical departmental organization under consideration affects communication patterns in many ways. In our hypothetical example, suppose that those specialties aggregated into an arbitrary department be housed adjacently, but that departments be scattered at random. Incidental oral and paper-passing communication links thus become predominately intradepartmental, and the extradepartmental aspects of peripheral specialties suffer great relative neglect in comparison with their intradepartmental overlaps. Shop talk, reading of dissertations, reading of each other's preprints and reprints, looking at laboratory setups and research instruments, all illustrate primary modes of communication seriously warped. The bias extends also to books and journals read. One is rewarded socially for shared detailed reading of exciting new developments. No such reward occurs for unshared reading, and thus the literature in the crossdepartmental aspects of a specialty loses ground to the reinforced intradepartmental reading.

With a parallel arbitrary organization occurring at other universities and in national and international disciplinary organizations, still other boundary effects occur. Professional organizational membership and their journal discounts to members lead to stereotyped patterns of journal subscription with most members limiting themselves to journals within one field—these are invariably so voluminous that one excuses himself for not reading in other fields by noting that this would be foolish when he is not even able to keep up in "his own field." "Own field," needless to say, tends to become defined in terms of these arbitrary departments whenever it goes beyond the narrow specialty. Abstracting sources, annual reviews, handbooks, etc., further the redundant repetition of intradepartmental patterns of breadth at the expense of equally relevant crossdepartmental ones.

(The annual reviews and handbooks do another disservice from the fish-scale model. Even within departments, each scholar's coverage must be partial, collective competence being assured by different partialities for each. Annual reviews and handbooks become crutches leading large numbers of scholars to the *same* partiality, and the inevitable neglect of other partialities. The degree of this partialness is generally underestimated, impressed as we must be at the long bibliographies appended.)

The departmental grouping of communicators allows unstable language to drift into unintelligibility across departments. A basic law is that speakers of the same language, once isolated into separate communities, drift into local idiosyncrasies and eventually unintelligibility, once the discipline of common conversation is removed. This tendency produces departmental linguistic idiosyncrasy even for shared contents and referents. Furthermore, as Edmund Leach and others have noted, such idiosyncrasy may be exaggerated as an ingroup solidarity device. What is despised as jargon by the outgroup may be the shibboleth of adequate professional training by the ingroup.

Resulting Ethnocentrism of Disciplines

Figure 2b shows the results of these dynamics. A few isolated specialties have been lost and the peripheral specialties have allowed their crossdepartmental edges to atrophy, producing departmental discreteness and interdepartmental gaps.

What started out as a hypothetical case has occasionally in the previous paragraphs drifted into the description of current actualities, perhaps blurring the point being made: Even if the true nature and the historical starting point had been one of a homogeneous texture of overlapping specialties, the organizing of specialties into departments and disciplines for decision-making and communication purposes would have produced disciplinary discreteness, cohesiveness, and interdisciplinary gaps such as exist at present. These features therefore should not be judged to justify as natural the existing arrangements of specialties.

The historical origins of departments and disciplines are of course quite other than those of our hypothetical example. The actual histories add historical depth to the tribal myths of origin and no doubt provide a greater true commonality to departments than in our hypothetical instance. Yet no matter what the degree of valid core and discreteness, the dynamics described here would inevitably have the effect of artificially enhancing it.

In this volume, many have commented on features of interdepartmental collaboration and staffing which would be included here as symptoms of the ethnocentrism of disciplines. Mikesell, in the discussion at this conference, has referred to "disciplinary nationalism." Clark has given it important status as an obstacle to work on real problems. The theme is central to Aronson's paper. This has been particularly so for the conference presentations of the administrators, not all of which are reprinted here. Pennsylvania State University's Vice-President Elburt F. Osborn, in his welcome, described the role of departmental partisanship in hampering novel appointments, of the tendencies for existing departments to require of interdepartmental types that they qualify as central-departmental specialists too. He spoke of the "walls" between departments and between colleges. Kenneth D. Roose, Dean of the College of Liberal Arts, spoke of the rareness of intercollegiate collaboration at Pennsylvania State. He also noted the conflict between effective specialization and interdisciplinary programs, and illustrated what this paper has called the Leonardesque aspiration in the tendency of interdisciplinary programs to become dilute and shallow forms of general education. R. H. Heindel, Dean of Faculty at Pennsylvania's new Capitol Campus, has spoken in his address to us of the inhibiting role of interdepartmental loyalties and his hopes that group conflicts at Capitol Campus may at least fall along novel rather than the stereotyped lines.

INTERDEPARTMENTAL PROGRAMS

Past Efforts

Before commenting on past interdisciplinary programs in the light of the fish-scale model, a word needs to be said about such judgments in general. Just as we found an inexplicit false ideal of a complete interdisciplinary scholar was being used in setting interdisciplinary standards of competence, so too a false model of departmental educational success and intradepartmental collaboration arises in evaluating interdisciplinary research and training programs. For example, it was for a time fashionable to regard Yale's ca. 1935–55 Institute of Human Relations as a failure. A failure by what standards? Perhaps it achieved less than was promised in the proposals which originally funded it, but certainly its record of productivity and significant innovation exceeded any unidepartmental aggregate of similar size. In like manner, unproductive or unintegrated interdisciplinary ventures are often reported as though all unidisciplinary ventures were successful, when in fact for them, too, but a minority are.

The Yale Institute of Human Relations did not fail in any scholarly or achievement sense, it just disappeared in an institutional sense. In very considerable part this was erosion due to the persistent pressures of departmental organization such as we have been describing. The departments remained the dominant budgetary and promotional units. The truly interdisciplinary specialists, no matter what their productivity, were denied and delayed as to tenure and no doubt salary. The route to academic adequacy remained through disciplinary centrality, through achievements respected by X-ologists and Y-ologists at other universities. Even the strikingly successful early interdisciplinary contributors for the most part moved their careers to safety within traditional departmental bounds. So through career changes in some departments and personnel changes in others, the interdisciplinary specialists disappeared.

The Social Relations department at Harvard is a more recent example. The internal organizational revisions in recent years have been steadily in the direction of traditional departmental structure and more undisciplinary, less multidisciplinary content in graduate training requirements. In this instance, the Leonardesque aspiration must have been hard to avoid, for the new department included most of sociology, more than half of anthropology and more than half of psychology. In their training program they must have been tempted with the goal of competence across this broad field. Backing away from this unworkable goal, and under the pressure of the extra-university disciplinary organizations, the return to traditional patterns of narrowness was almost inevitable. While they turned out as students and recruited as faculty some outstanding interdisciplinary specialists with the novel narrowness here advocated, the goal of novel narrow interdisciplinary specialties was never formalized in training requirements, and the goal of breadth, of anti-narrowness, continued to receive lip service long after it had begun to be abandoned in practice.

These are, of course, the unstudied observations of an outsider. We need active sociology of science research on these and other instances, such as the Michigan and Columbia social psychology departments, the Chicago Committee on Human Development, etc., comparing them with analogous unidepartmental efforts. Such data abound. For example, Northwestern University is just abandoning some seventeen years of experimenting with several interdisciplinary freshman courses, one fusing anthropology, psychology, and sociology, another fusing economics, history, and political science, etc. Ethnocentrism of departments contributed in many ways. For example, it was not allowed that the content be shrunk to an integrated common core using a common vocabulary. Instead, the course had to serve as the prerequisite to advanced courses in each of the three departments, had to touch upon all of the hodgepodge of concerns typical of introductory courses in each of the departments, had to teach each of the overlapping-but-not-quite-translatable jargons, etc. In addition, there were no institutional rewards to the faculty for doing the job of integrating, preparing the common-language texts, etc. While incidentally the program turned out some interdisciplinary specialists such as Karl de Schweinitz who combined economics and political theory in this conference, to the students the course remained three elementary courses stirred together at random. A part of the failure was due to the Leonardesque aspiration, a part due to creating no budgetary-promotional-professional institutions to correspond.

Contained in a number of the papers presented in this volume are both comments on reasons for past failure and recommendations for optimal inter-disciplining which are in line with the fish-scale model. Note Dubin's insist-ence that interdisciplinary integration has to take place within single minds, rather than in teams without individual overlap. Note also his suggestion of "contiguous problem analysis," a suggestion to create appropriate fish-scales without attention to existing departmental boundaries. The Sherifs' approach through core problems (rather than through disciplinary focus) and through cross-level validation, point in the same direction. Clark in our conference described in detail how problem focus leads to need for problem special-ists overlapping (and thwarted by) existing disciplinary boundaries. De Schweinitz's chapter illustrates how disciplinary specialty-bounding has led economic advisors to developing countries to overlook political necessities behind economic decisions. In many of the others similar points are made.

CURRENT EFFORTS

A number of institutions are reacting to this situation by trying to elimi-nate departments as budgetary units, substituting either transient problem-oriented affiliations or more permanent divisions along novel lines.

Pennsylvania State's Capitol Campus, concentrating on upper division and graduate training, will start out with no budgetary departments within the division of social science. If they forego the temptation of turning out "well-rounded social scientists," and allow as narrow a specialization as any tra-ditional department, but with freedom for novel narrowness, the training program should be successful. As faculty size grows, an administrative need for budgetary subunits will arise, and the temptation will be to do this along standard departmental lines.

Under the leadership of Dean James March, the Social Science division of the University of California at Irvine initially substituted research teams of five or so persons for departments, with the notion that these research teams have finite duration. For a variety of reasons, some relevant to the problems here discussed, these have been replaced by more loosely bound "interest groups" or "programs" of limited size (25 faculty as a maximum). Both the original research teams and the current interest groups cut across traditional departmental lines. Interdisciplinary introductory courses are being taught around specific concepts recurrent in the social sciences, courses not broader than usual unidisciplinary courses, but with novel dimensions of selectivity —ideal "fish-scales" in the terms of this paper. If these novel and flexible groupings survive with the expansion to full California university size, they might provide the budgetary alternative to the department, particularly if teaching is allowed the same idiosyncratic patterning. This can easily be rationalized on the grounds that education is only partial anyway, and that the system of science as a whole would benefit from creating at Irvine novel patterns of incompleteness. The ethnocentrism of disciplines may cause panic at this point, however, and call for a stereotyped "adequate grounding" in traditional disciplines.

For the purposes of this paper, it is useful to point out a specific hazard in the earlier concept of "research team." From the idealized fish-scale model, there would be no reason at all for interdisciplinary research to be more frequently collaborative than unidisciplinary study—solitary interdisciplinary specialists would thrive as easily as solitary undisciplinary ones. Insofar as "research team" connoted detailed collaboration on joint projects, there might have emerged as unhappy a state as if unidisciplinary departments at other universities were forced into five-man collaborative research teams. But in the Irvine case, had the team approach proved to be unsatisfactory, there would have been a strong tendency to wrongly blame this on the interdisciplinary feature rather than the team feature.

The relative bureaucratic rationalization of salaries and promotions in the University of California system (the relative absence of the wide differences in pay scales from department to department that characterize other universities) should reduce much the budgetary salience of departmental membership. In such a setting as Irvine, a flexible utilization of the "interest group" mode of organization may be a permanent possibility, with a sociometric reassignment of all persons to groups every five years, these groups to be housed together, to control educational programs, to supervise dissertations, and to collaborate in research at an optional frequency such as is found in happy unidepartments. Flexibility of teaching arrangements must be emphasized. Theoretical integration still comes as much from the activities of teaching as from data collection.

At the new Cleveland State University, Vice-President and Dean of Faculties James G. Miller is experimenting with research institutes as the budgetary unit and primary group membership. Academic departments would then be assembled on an ad hoc or secondary basis to approve training programs and award degrees. While there might emerge locally as rigid a partisan loyalty and boundedness to the institutes as to ordinary departments, from the collective scholarship perspective there would be a fish-scale type gain from the fact that these rigid local institutes were organized around unusual aggregations. It is to be expected that, as exemplified in Michigan's Mental Health Research Institute under Miller's direction, the institutes will allow for individual as well as team research effort.

The new University of Sussex in England is another that is attempting to do without departments and to substitute problem-centered "schools." Again, they are still too small to have felt the full force of administrative needs for department-sized units. Again, the standardization of academic salaries in England should make the department more dispensable as a budgetary unit.

There are no doubt many other such experiments (the University of California at Santa Cruz is discussed below). They are worth more detailed analysis than here provided. Let us hope that each can create the freedom for novel specialization on the part of both students and faculty while evading the unworkable Leonardesque aspiration.

A MISCELLANY OF REFORMS

A New Ego Ideal for the Scholar as Student

At the present time the ego ideal of the scholar calls for competence, for complete knowledge of the field he claims as his. In his everyday interaction with fellow specialists, he tends to feel guilty when he finds that he has not read what they have read. While he inevitably learns to live with such guilt feelings, this ego ideal spells the direction of his guilt. If the scholar takes to heart the notion that scientific competence can never be embodied in single minds—that his guilty neglect is not his unique shame but the inevitable predicament of all, and that science is somehow achieved in spite of this, he may come to substitute a quite different ego-ideal, a quite different focus of guilt. Rather than praying, "May I be a competent and well-read X-ologist, may I keep up with the literature in my field," he will pray, "Make me a novel fish-scale. Let my pattern of inevitably incomplete competence cover areas neglected by others." Each scholar would then try to have a pattern of journal subscriptions unique to his department, university, or profession. Noting that he and a colleague were reading the same set of journals, he would feel guilty and vow to drop one of these in favor of some other. Recognizing that the interdisciplinary links in the collaborative web of knowledge are the weakest, he would give up some ingroup journal in favor of an outgroup one. He would feel guilty if he did not cut attendance at ingroup conventions to attend relevant outgroup ones, etc.

There is a secondary payoff in crossdisciplinary reading and conventioning. Scholarly reading for the true scholar is ideally recreational, something he enjoys doing and would choose to do reactionally even if he had some other profession. The social system of science, particularly in graduate school and in the first stages of a scientific career, associate such activities so strongly to the reward and punishment system of competitive evaluation that they cease to be relaxing or effectively recreational. In the current disciplinary organization, the scholar will often find that the journals and conventions of a neighboring discipline can still serve this recreational function—particularly if he accepts his role as smatterer and does not assume the obligation of "mastering" that literature. If our fish-scale model were to become the norm, such reading would of course tend to become more obligatory and run the risk of ceasing to be recreational.

(While on the themes of recreational reading and the duplication of fish scales, it seems appropriate to deplore the tendency of social scientists to feel that they all should read current newspapers, particularly the *New York Times*. Certainly the collective perspective would be better if most spent the equivalent time with newspapers of other epochs, or with historical, anthropological, archeological, or literary descriptions of quite other samples of social milieus. Rather than the ego-ideal of keeping up with the current worldwide social developments, the young scholar should hold the ideal of foregoing current informedness for some infrequently sampled descriptive recreational literature. Too often our ego-ideals call for uniform omniscience, knowledge of both past and present, of both here and there, and too often we settle for the same pattern of compromise all our colleagues are settling for. Compromise from the Leonardesque aspiration there must be, but even in leisure reading let us hold as ideal the achieving of unique compromises.)

AN EGO-IDEAL FOR THE SCHOLAR AS TEACHER

Under the ideology of disciplinary competence, a department feels that its staff should be able to provide competent guidance in the Ph.D. programs it offers, that students should bend their interests to the locally available specialties or go elsewhere, that to train a student properly the faculty should be more competent than the student in the student's area of study. Combining this with the organizational advantages of one-headed decision-making units in dissertation direction, etc., a strong tendency toward duplicating of identical fish scales within departments results.[2]

Under the fish-scale ideology, the professor would feel guilty when he turned out "chips off the old block," Ph.D.s who showed the same pattern of overlap as he. The goal instead would be to encourage each new Ph.D. to select such a novel specialty that he could indeed within his graduate training become one of science's leading experts, a fully contributing specialist. Note the difference between this approach to instant expertness and that of exhaustive mastery of an exceedingly narrow realm within one specialty. The latter asks the graduate student to be narrower than his mentor, to subspecialize within his mentor's range. The former asks him to achieve a novel range, not necessarily broader or narrower than the mentor's. One greatly needed implementation of this goal is to encourage the Ph.D. to give up some traditional intradisciplinary subfield in favor of mastery of a crossdisciplinary one of relevance. A common reason given for rejecting this is that for such a content we X-ologists would have no way of checking his competence—a typically ethnocentric reaction, illustrating again the way in which, given our present organization into departments, concern over evaluation of competence decreases the crossing of departmental bounds in specialization.

2. For total careers, there is, of course, considerable freedom to redefine personal specialties within disciplines. This, combined with the needs for autonomous personal identity within face-to-face departments, reestablishes the needed texture of overlap within disciplines.

Using the Advantages of Smallness and Bigness

Generally speaking, the larger the university, the wider the variety of specialists available and the more likely that the full range of possible specialties be represented by actual persons. This being so, one might expect the interdisciplinary gaps to be less and interdisciplinary collaboration to be more frequent. In actual practice, the contrary is more apt to be the case (though we need studies to verify this), and the laws of group organization and size applied to departmental organization explain this. The larger the department, the more obligatory relationships there are intradepartmentally, and the more the totality of obligatory and informal relationships is predominately intradepartmental. The larger the department, the more required courses there are for graduate students within the department (Aronson in this volume cites a study by Sibley to this effect), and the less opportunity and the greater jeopardy for crossdepartmental study. In the smaller department, the loyalty demands are less, informal communication and friendship links are more frequently crossdepartmental, collaboration across departmental lines is less apt to involve loss of intradepartmental esteem, and graduate students are more apt to feel sufficient mastery in their home departments to have time to explore outside. Northwestern University has had an exceptionally productive period of interdisciplinary collaboration in recent decades, at a time when most universities have been finding such relationships increasingly impracticable. The explanation lies in part in the chance accumulation of a few key leaders with this orientation, such as Richard Snyder in political science, but more significant, I believe, has been the smallness of its departments combined with low teaching loads and a full commitment to research and graduate training. Most places this small are focused on undergraduate training. Most places focused on research and graduate training combine this with largeness. In contrast stands the University of California at Berkeley where interdisciplinary contacts have steadily decreased as departments grew, and where once interdepartmental institutes have become annexes of single departments.

Many of Berkeley's problems stem from the overload of obligatory relationships which size produces. The fact that the students they recruit are eager participants in scholarship makes matters worse. On some campuses—even with large undergraduate enrollments—one can post and live up to generous office hours and be left in peaceful solitude during them. Not so at Berkeley. Students and fellow faculty with legitimate demands on one's time, with genuine shared interests, absorb to the fullest all the time any professor makes available. For previously productive and hence visible faculty, these pressures are particularly great. In the end, those who remain productive limit their accessibility to others so severely that the feeling of community is lost.

A suggested solution, focused on organizational limitation of obligatory relationships, is the complete fragmentation of existing departments into discrete budgetary and curricular units of 12 ± 2 faculty members, within which the undergraduates would major and the graduates would meet qualifying requirements. Even were such narrow-content departments to be carved out entirely within existing departmental lines, their complete separation from the rest of their present fields would free their extra-specialty contacts to go in directions now ruled out by larger departmental demands. Thus members of a small department of psychological social psychology would be more likely to develop contacts within a small department of sociological social psychology than these specialists have time for at present. Similarly for the comparative psychologists and the behavioral zoologists, the physiological psychologists and the neuroanatomists, the verbal learningists and the functional linguists, the industrial psychologists and the industrial economists, etc. And even within departmental lines, contacts of the social psychologists with the obviously relevant learning theorists could hardly be less than they are now.

Since the Santa Cruz campus of the University of California, under the direction of Chancellor Dean E. McHenry, represents a creative organizational innovation designed to curb Berkeley-like problems diagnosed much as reported here, it deserves special mention. Through organizing undergraduates and faculty into small residential colleges of 600 to 1,000 in enrollment, with faculties of 60 to 100, and with two or three members of any one discipline at most, the obligatory relationships between undergraduates and faculty are being kept down to a workable minimum, and repeated contacts of specific faculty member and specific student (as well as student-student) are frequent enough so that acquaintance is possible. The introductory courses are duplicated in each college with only the advanced courses in a major taken across college lines, using the resources of the entire university. If major advising, repetition of courses with the same professor, supervision of undergraduate independent study, and honors theses be restricted to within colleges, the advantages of small colleges will be achieved. Such restraints on student freedom of choice also preserve some of the limitations of the small college, but such restraints would seem essential to keep limited the obligatory relationships that swamped Berkeley.

Informal scholarly communication channels across disciplines within colleges will be furthered by the fact that each of the eventually twenty colleges will have some degree of unique scholarly emphasis, and that perhaps half of the faculty of each will have been selected with that in mind. Thus Cowell College has a particular type of humanistic emphasis, with an existential-phenomenological flavor to its historians, psychologists, philosophers, sociologists, English professors, and modern language professors. Stephenson College has a social science emphasis, Crown College a biological emphasis, another college an international relations emphasis, etc. Recognizing that each student at any level gets but a partial education anyway, they are in accord with the fish-scale epistemology in providing a wide variety of such partialities, each with its own unique effort at integrity. The deliberate effort to recruit faculty for congeniality and common interests across disciplinary lines within colleges makes these contacts more likely to generate the new fish scales along the interdisciplinary gaps. At the graduate level, quite novel Ph.D. programs are being established as well as conventional ones, and faculty will participate in both. From a sociology of organization point of view, the one dangerous feature is dual decision-group membership for each faculty person. Both the colleges and the graduate divisions with their traditional departments are budgetary units. Both are involved in hiring and promoting, etc. There should result a near doubling of the committee-work overhead, and of opportunities of mutual veto, features which are bad enough even in the more conventional branches of the University of California.

The examples of Northwestern and Santa Cruz, would lead to the expectation that the high-quality small colleges would generate good interdisciplinary scholarship. We have examples such as the collaboration of the psychologist Helson and the physicist Michels to confirm the expectation. By and large, however, institutional revisions would have to be made for this to be prevalent. Even the best small colleges have not yet made themselves attractive to the research-oriented scholar. Research scholars employed in colleges typically have their eye on university positions. The decision processes in the universities are such that only those doing research in central disciplinary areas will be agreed upon. Thus such small college researchers will wisely neglect the local interdepartmental opportunities in favor of "pure" disciplinary research. To have the small college advantages for creating interdisciplinary specialties utilized, they must be made attractive to research scholars as permanent careers. Reduction of teaching loads from twelve to six hours (as some are doing), relabeling "independent study" courses as "research apprenticeship," achieving publishable honors theses, offering limited numbers of M.A. and Ph.D. degrees based upon multidisciplinary combinations of faculty—all this without increasing size—might achieve such a result. The scholar's identification with the future scholars he trains, a one-time characteristic of the Ph.D. program, is being lost in many large Ph.D. programs, and is achieved to a remarkable extent at places like Oberlin (e.g., under Stetson in psychology two decades ago, under Ikeda and others in sociology today).

Reprise: bigness increases the isolation of departments, decreases the interdepartmental fish scales, unless organizational reforms are devised to prevent this.

AD HOC INTERDISCIPLINARY TRAINING PROGRAMS

Even at Northwestern, what crossing of disciplines we achieve is mostly at the faculty level. My own graduate students are as unidisciplinary as any and rarely do more than a required course or two outside of psychology.

Were I to push them to a real mastery of some relevant-to-them cross-disciplinary specialty—be it time-series analysis in economics, analysis of ideology in sociology, or child rearing customs in anthropology, I would be adding to an already inhibiting burden of requirements. But if I could at the same time relieve them of the need to master some physiological psychology, or the sensory discrimination literature, or the like, such programs would be possible. They are also much needed, not because they would be better than the present mix but because they individually might be as good and because the combination of some of these plus some of the standard would be collectively stronger than the present all-of-one-type.

At a place with relatively good (though minimal) interdepartmental contact like Northwestern, one should be able to train hybrid specialists such as these, with an ad hoc assembly of core courses, fields for prelims, and dissertation committees tailor-made for each student. The adviser and student would assemble an ad hoc training advisory faculty and schedule of courses. Perhaps a divisional review committee would have to check the program, to assure that it was as exacting and as coherently specialized as the standard programs required in the overlapping departments. Such a committee would also conduct written and oral qualifying exams, and guide the dissertation. If the possibility of use to evade difficult requirements emerged, the program might be restricted to only the top half of entrants. If perceived as a vehicle for inadequate professors, the prerogative of advising on such programs could be limited to an elite of proven unidisciplinary capability, etc. To coordinate with the labels of the disciplines nationally, the Ph.D. would be designated according to the department of his senior advisor. If departments objected to thus annointing an inadequately trained X-ologist, a dual labeling could be adopted, Ph.D. in X-ology (Divisional) for the new type, Ph.D. in X-ology (Departmental) for the old. In the present academic market, we should have no difficulty placing such Ph.D.s. Thus with no such drastic reorganizations as creating new rigid interdepartments, with no new budgetary units, no new staffs, a congeries of new specialties each as coherent and narrow as our present Ph.D. programs could be achieved.

Paralleling such ad hoc training programs for graduate students, ad hoc decision groups substituting for departments in deciding on raises, promotions, and tenure might well be established for interdepartmental faculty appointments, with some divisional funds allocated for such purposes separate from departmental budgets.

ORGANIZATIONAL ALTERNATIVES FOR JOURNALS AND CONVENTIONS

Our academic professional organizations publish journals and offer them to their members at reduced rates. There results a repetitious patterning in the several journals each scholar takes. If our associations would make these same rates available to the members of other disciplinary associations (as indeed some do), novel journal sets would become more frequent. In the creation of new journals, broad interdisciplinary scope should be eschewed for novel narrowness. The new *Journal of Verbal Learning and Verbal Behavior* sets an excellent example. It is much narrower than the *Journal of Experimental Psychology*, which it overlaps heavily, but it juxtaposes work by experimental psychologists and by linguists so as to eventually nurture some novel fish scales.

Our professional conventions are too large, have too many simultaneous meetings, cover too wide a range of specialties, and last too long. If our conventions instead were held at different times by each specialty (e.g., by divisions within the American Psychological Association), and if the scholar did his annual conventioning by attending several of these shorter ones, he would be much more likely to cross disciplinary lines.

SUMMARY

Interdisciplinary programs have been misled by goals of breadth and multi-disciplinary training. Even within disciplines, disciplinary competence is not achieved in individual minds, but as a collective achievement made possible by the overlap of narrow specialties. This fish-scale model of collective omniscience is impeded in interdisciplinary specialty areas by the ethnocentrism of disciplines, by the organization of specialties into departments for decision-making and communication. For an integrated and competent social science, we need to invent alternative social organizations which will permit the flourishing of narrow interdisciplinary specialties.

NAME INDEX

Abel, T., 88, 97, 99
Abelson, R. P., 44, 46, 49
Adams, H., 316
Adorno, T. W., 150, 153, 174, 282, 290
Alexander, F., 281, 290
Alker, H. R., 37, 38, 44, 46
Allbright, W. F., 94
Allee, W. C., 132, 135
Almond, G. A., 40, 49, 213, 215, 216, 218, 222
Alonso, W., 241, 243
Ando, A., 37, 46
Andrews, F. M., 38, 49
Annis, A. P., 40, 46
Apter, D. E., 213, 222
Ardrey, R., 145, 146, 174
Arensberg, C., 83, 97
Ariès, P., 41, 46
Aristotle, 78, 185, 265, 275
Aronson, E., 32, 46, 49, 176
Aronson, S., 292–304, 338, 344
Arrow, K. J., 215, 222
Asch, S. E., 22, 165, 174
Atkins, R. D., 58, 59, 63
Autret, M., 193, 195

Baldwin, J. M., 331
Bales, R. F., 43, 51, 71, 76
Baran, P. A., 210, 222
Barbichon, G., 168, 174
Barbu, Z., 159, 160, 161, 174
Barr, S., 297, 303
Barrows, H. H., 228, 242
Barth, F., 231, 242
Bartlett, F. C., 14, 19
Baskin, C. W., 273
Bauer, R. A., 39, 46, 221, 222
Bavelas, A., 332
Beaujeu-Garnier, J., 236, 242
Bechtel, R. B., 43, 46

Becker, H., 66, 75
Becker, H. S., 53
Becker, L. A., 32, 47
Beg, Mirza, Ashan, 127, 136
Bell, W., 18
Benary, W., 188, 195
Bendix, R., 63, 94, 97
Benedict, Ruth, 82
Bensman, J., 83, 99
Benson, L., 306, 309, 310, 313, 314, 318
Berelson, B., 43, 46, 246
Berg, I. A., 33, 46
Berger, P. L., 293, 297, 298, 299, 303
Berkowitz, L. B., 25, 46, 160, 161, 174
Bernstein, A., 44, 46
Berry, B. J. L., 232, 235, 242
Berthoff, R., 300, 303
Bettelheim, B., 89
Bhatt, V. V., 210, 222
Bierstedt, R., 298
Binder, L., 213, 222
Bisco, R. L., 39, 46, 48
Black, M., 68, 75
Black, P., 58, 59, 63
Blanksten, G. I., 209
Blaut, J., 238, 242
Blaylock, H. M., 37, 38, 47
Bliss, E. L., 136
Bloomfield, L., 266, 270, 272
Blumer, H., 58, 63, 79, 86, 97
Boas, F., 87, 99
Bolinger, D. L., 267, 272
Borden, M., 298, 303
Borgatta, E. F., 49
Boring, E. G., 3, 19, 189, 195
Boskoff, A., 97
Boudon, R., 37, 47
Bowdy, R. A., 43, 44, 49
Bowra, C. M., 260
Brayfield, A. H., 33, 47

349

SUBJECT INDEX